[illegible] or
[illegible] ve
[illegible] span
[illegible] and
[illegible] ever, we

[illegible] among the
[illegible] ms of
[illegible] grey in
[illegible] deal
[illegible] could
[illegible] was
[illegible] –based
[illegible] hidden
[illegible] Most of
[illegible] site
[illegible] our

Handbook of Environmental and Nature-Based Tourism

Handbook of Environmental and Nature-Based Tourism

Jitendra K. Sharma

KANISHKA PUBLISHERS, DISTRIBUTORS
NEW DELHI-110 002

KANISHKA PUBLISHERS, DISTRIBUTORS
4697/5-21A, Ansari Road, Daryaganj
New Delhi-110 002
Phones : 2327 0497, 2328 8285
Fax : 011-2328 8285
e-mail: kanishka_publishing@yahoo.co.in

First Published 2010

ISBN 978-81-8457-220-9

PRINTED IN INDIA

Published by Madan Sachdeva for Kanishka Publishers, Distributors, 4697/5-21A, Ansari Road, Daryaganj, New Delhi-110 002; Typeset by Manas Enterprises, Delhi, and Printed at Rajdhani Printers, Delhi.

Preface

This "Handbook of Environmental and Nature-Based Tourism" is a complete reference book on the subject. It introduces readers with the concepts of environmental tourism, nature tourism, ecotourism, agri-tourism, nature-based tourism and sustainable tourism. Selected national and international experiences have been discussed. Similarly, related model project proposals and status reports have been given as selected case studies. Special focus lies on the kinds of environmental tourism and ecotourism taking place in the Asia-Pacific region. The impact assessment of such tourism activities for Maldives are being described in detail. The relationship between forest resources and ecotourism are also being discussed in brief highlighting the aspects related to services, issues, trends, implications and options.

The case study of Asia-Pacific region in this regard is being made. An overview of selected country ecotourism notes has been included. Major issues and related matters/reviews/findings of nature-based tourism in Western Australia have been covered in an elaborate manner. This handbook also focuses on the economic aspects of nature-based tourism. Selected case studies from South-Asia and India have been presented to further elaborate upon this aspect. India's position in world tourism scenario has been presented. Insights into the tourism policies of Guyana and Indian state have been provided. This handbook also provides readers with reviews of tourism action plans of selected developed and developing countries, with focus on Canada, UK and Commonwealth. The code of ethics for tourism and that of tourists has been highlighted. Similarly, the charters and the principles dealing with sustainable tourism at global level have been presented. The focus also lies on management of tourism destinations and the local Agenda 21 approach in this regard. In addition, the processes and the guidelines related to tourism and biodiversity have been dealt in detail. The "CBD Guidelines on Biodiversity and Tourism Development" have been presented in brief illustrating all relevant aspects. Also, the CBD "Sustainable Tourism Development Guidelines for Vulnerable Ecosystems" has been outlined. The handbook also contains relevant appendices regarding "International Year of Ecotourism", "Antarctica Tour Operators", "Conservation Areas of India" and "Related Environmental Organizations". A detailed bibliography further makes this handbook user-friendly and research oriented.

Jitendra K. Sharma

Contents

1

Introduction to Environmental Tourism, Nature–Based Tourism, Ecotourism and Sustainable Tourism

ENVIRONMENTAL TOURISM, NATURE TOURISM, AND ECOTOURISM

Nature Tourism or Ecotourism

Environmental tourism, ecotourism, or nature tourism provides an opportunity to visit undisturbed natural areas, scenic vistas, and observe plants and wildlife. Washington state offers many opportunities for local governments to share their natural environments with visitors. While maximizing the economic, environmental and social benefits from ecotourism, the local environment must be protected. This chapter provides links to information on how to create and promote a nature tourism destination.

NATURE–BASED TOURISM: AN OVERVIEW

A segment of rural tourism is referred to as nature–based tourism, ecotourism or sometimes recreation–based tourism. Nature–based tourism attracts people interested in visiting natural areas of the United States for the purpose of enjoying the scenery, including plant and animal wildlife. Examples of nature–based tourism include hunting, fishing, photography, bird watching and visiting parks.

NATURE-BASED TOURISM: AN AUSTRALIAN EXPERIENCE

The nature-based tourism sector contributes $23 billion to the Australian economy each year and is a crucial aspect of Australia's reputation as a 'clean, green' tourism destination. Our natural assets give us a unique competitive advantage in the global market – but they must be appropriately protected, managed and developed. Tourism & Transport Forum (TTF) strongly supports the sustainable development of nature-based tourism through partnerships between the tourism industry, government and the conservation sector. In 2007, the Federal Minister for Tourism launched TTF's Natural Tourism Partnerships Action Plan, which sets a framework for public–private partnerships to enhance natural tourism and conservation in Australian Parks. The Natural Tourism Panel of TTF members includes Australia's leading national and marine park management agencies, owners and operators of nature-based resorts and attractions, tourism marketing organizations and conservation organizations.

SUSTAINABLE TOURISM: A SCOTTISH EXPERIENCE

'Sustainable tourism' is simply sustainable development achieved through tourism. Sustainable development is economic development that takes a long–term view. It balances the benefits of economic development against environmental and social costs. Just as sustainable development assumes continued economic growth, so sustainable tourism assumes continued tourism growth. Sustainable tourism is not a marketing idea to attract new markets – it is a strategic term to describe a specific approach to the development of tourism. Sustainable tourism aims to take all impacts, positive and negative, into account. All tourism has the potential to be more sustainable. As well as encouraging continued tourism growth, sustainable tourism will ensure that Scotland's two-key tourism assets, our natural heritage and our communities, will survive and thrive. Sustainable tourism has the following characteristics:

Economic Prosperity

- long-term competitive and prosperous tourism businesses
- quality employment opportunities, fair pay and conditions for all employees.

Social Equity and Cohesion

- tourism that improves the quality of life of local communities,
- community involvement in tourism planning and management,
- safe, satisfying and fulfilling visitor experiences.

Environmental and Cultural Protection

- reduced pollution and degradation of the global and local environment
- tourism that maintains and strengthens biodiversity
- tourism that maintains and enriches our unique and diverse culture

KEY CHALLENGES FOR SUSTAINABLE TOURISM

Following are the key challenges to the sustainability of Scottish tourism:

Challenge 1: Reducing the Seasonality of Demand

The concentration of tourism trips in certain periods of the year has a major effect on sustainability. Not only does it reduce the viability of enterprises to maximize capacity utilization and offer year-round employment, it can also place pressure on communities and natural resources at certain times while leaving surplus capacity at others.

Seasonality of demand makes it very difficult to plan and manage the provision of tourism facilities efficiently. A process of stimulating demand at less busy times of the year, taking up spare capacity, would enable revenue from tourism to grow while putting less pressure on the environment and community.

Appropriate action to strengthen the appeal of off–season visits includes:

- Adjusting target market selection towards less seasonal markets (e.g. business tourism, non–family segments and certain niche markets),
- Innovative product development, packaging, events and promotion in the off–season,
- Promoting price differentials and incentives,
- Joint working between service suppliers and operators to extend opening times and cooperate on marketing and promotional activity.

Challenge 2: Addressing the Impact of Tourism Transport

It is estimated that tourism transport (inbound and outbound) currently accounts for 8 per cent of CO_2 equivalent emissions in the EU. Daily revelations about the advance and impact of climate change and associations with transport emissions have made this a fundamental and high profile issue for tourism.

The tourism sector must respond actively and responsibly to this challenge. The approach should seek to increase total visitor spending and economic benefit (in line with the 50% growth target) while reducing emissions resulting from this activity:

- Promoting carbon–offsetting schemes to travellers, with the support of operators,
- Promoting alternative transport options (equally for the enjoyable experience they offer as well as for their low impact),
- Promoting Scotland to more local/domestic markets,
- Encouraging fewer, but longer, holidays while recognizing that this goes against recent market trends.

Challenge 3: Minimizing Resource Use and Waste

Tourism can be a significant and, at times, profligate user of environmental resources. Much of the action required to address this challenge rests with strengthening environmental management in tourism enterprises:

- Minimizing energy consumption and encouraging the use of renewable sources and improved technology,
- Promoting and facilitating the reduction, reuse and recycling of materials,
- Water quality, including the efficient treatment of sewerage, avoiding discharge into marine and river environments,
- Reducing and managing litter,
- Developing and using local supply chains, in particular to reduce food miles.

Challenge 4: Looking after our Natural and Cultural Heritage

The quality of the natural and cultural heritage is, in most areas, fundamentally important to the generation of economic prosperity through tourism, to the quality of life of local communities and to the visitor experience. All three can benefit from:

- Strengthening the relationship between protected areas, biodiversity and local tourism interests,
- Visitor management, information and interpretation, and monitoring,
- Increasing contributions to conservation and management from visitors and tourism businesses,
- Quality products and services.

Challenge 5: Enhancing Quality of Life for Scottish Communities through Tourism

Tourism has significant power to change the character and prosperity of the places where it occurs. Two types of change present particular challenges and opportunities for local communities at the moment; property development associated with tourism (e.g. the proposed Trump golf course or the building of houses to be used as self–catering or second homes) and the restructuring of local economies, resulting from a decline in traditional activities.

Careful destination planning and management is required to:

- Maximise the proportion of income that is retained locally and other benefits to local communities,

- Strengthen local supply chains and promote use of local produce and merchandise (e.g. craft goods), shops and other services by visitors.

Challenge 6: Improving the Quality of Tourism Jobs

One of the key impacts and benefits, that tourism has on Scotland is through the employment opportunities it offers. To make sure that tourism brings net benefits to those it employs we need to encourage:

- Exchange of good practice in tourism training and HR management,
- Integration of sustainability issues into mainstream tourism training and education,
- Active promotion of tourism as a career.

Challenge 7: Making Holidays available to all

Social inclusion and equity are important principles of sustainable development. It is estimated that around 40 per cent of European citizens do not take a holiday, often due to various forms of deprivation or disability.

This challenge has strategic implications for sustainable tourism. A policy of maximizing revenue from tourism without increasing volume could go against social inclusion. However, pursuing social tourism has also been shown to assist in reducing seasonality and supporting year–round employment, as many people who can be reached in this way, such as those on lower incomes, are well placed to travel outside the main season. Relevant action includes:

- Raising business awareness of the size of the market,
- Designing and adapting tourism facilities and sites to meet (not just legislative but market–driven) requirements for physical disability and sensory impairment,
- Improving information relevant to disabled people and under–privileged groups,
- Encouraging a broad price range in tourism facilities and experiences,

- Pursuing specific schemes to facilitate and encourage holiday taking by people on low incomes.

THE WORLD ECOTOURISM SUMMIT

The World Ecotourism Summit serves as a forum for a systematic and critical review of ecotourism as it stands at present and as a filter to identify priority issues and indicate general directions of action. The Summit (WES) conclusions and recommendations are meant to be reported to the World Summit on Sustainable Development (WSSD), to be held in Johannesburg, South Africa, 26 August–4 September 2002. The WES and the WSSD results will be brought to an IYE wrap up event at the end of 2002 in Australia.

The Canadian government offered to host the Summit in Quebec which will be the major landmark for the International Year of Ecotourism and bring together a wide array of practitioners, governments, industry representatives, and NGOs. As the WES is not an official UN meeting, ministerial attendance is not mandatory.

The Summit has been organized by UNEP and WTO/OMT, with the key support of the Government of Canada, and the Government of Quebec.

The WES Steering Committee is composed of UNEP, WTO/OMT, Tourism Quebec, and the Canadian Tourism Commission. Previous consultations were held with WWF, IFC, the Northern and Southern Co–chairs of the CSD NGO Tourism Caucus, Conservation International, Ecological Tourism in Europe.

The main objectives for the Summit are:

- Strengthen the capacity of governments and the private sector to effectively use ecotourism as a tool for sustainable development and conservation of natural and cultural resources;
- Systematic review and exchange of lessons learned in current ecotourism practices and contribution to sustainable development;
- Assess the effectiveness of regulatory mechanisms and voluntary schemes for monitoring and controlling the impacts of ecotourism.

Outcomes of the World Ecotourism Summit:

- The Quebec City Declaration (summary of main issues);
- A global status and trend report (based on Preparatory Conferences);
- Report on issues and recommendations on the four WES themes (from thematic sessions); and
- Recommendations for action (based on the Ministerial, Private Sector and Development Agency Fora).

A Common Framework: The Four Key Themes and their Subthemes UNEP and WTO, in consultation with other organizations and ecotourism stakeholders, have defined and adopted the following main discussion themes for the International Year of Ecotourism. Together these themes cover all of the major issues and concerns raised by ecotourism development.

Theme A: Ecotourism Policy and Planning: The Sustainability Challenge

Sustainable ecotourism plans, policies and programmes at international, national and local levels. Integration of ecotourism policies into sustainable development plans and frameworks, land use planning, use of natural parks and protected areas, balance between development and conservation objectives in policies, development agency programmes on ecotourism and their role in funding major pipeline investments related to ecotourism, plans for human resource development in ecotourism.

Theme B: Regulation of Ecotourism: Institutional Responsibilities and Frameworks

Legislation, norms and other regulations for ecotourism activities, voluntary schemes and self-regulation, certification, accreditation and ecolabels, international and inter–governmental guidelines, principles and codes, roles of different stakeholders in ensuring compliance with regulations or voluntary schemes.

Theme C: Product Development, Marketing and Promotion of Ecotourism: Fostering Sustainable Products and Consumers

Building sustainable ecotourism products, multistakeholder cooperation for product development especially in protected areas and biosphere reserves, market research, marketing techniques and marketing channels, promotional methods, information to tourists, ethical behaviour, environmental education for consumers, public–private sector relationships for marketing and promotion, co–operative marketing for small ecotourism operations.

Theme D: Monitoring Costs and Benefits of Ecotourism: Ensuring Equitable Distribution among all Stakeholders

Measuring economic, ecological and social costs and benefits of ecotourism, contribution to conservation, assessing potential and actual environmental and socio–cultural impacts of ecotourism, taking precautionary measures at local, national, regional and international levels, integrating monitoring and evaluation procedures. Research needs and adaptive management systems.

Cross–cutting Themes

Throughout the discussions on the four themes the focus will be on the two main cross–cutting issues:

- The sustainability of ecotourism from the environmental, economic and socio–cultural points of view;
- Involvement and empowerment of local communities and indigenous people in the ecotourism development process, in management and monitoring of ecotourism activities, and in the sharing of benefits resulting from it.

MODEL PROJECT PROPOSAL FOR NATURE-BASED AGRI–TOURISM: A CASE STUDY

Nature-Based Agri–Tourism is a segment of rural tourism sometimes referred to as ecotourism, for APUC purposes an eligible business is defined as one which seeks to attract visitors to a working farm or any agricultural, horticultural or agri-business operation to enjoy, be educated or be involved in activities.

Nature-Based Agri–Tourism enterprises are designed to bring people to rural ND to engage in a recreational, sport, educational or labour assisted sales (self-harvesting) activity. Eligible facilities must provide restroom facilities, fresh water for sanitation, and other appropriate accommodations. These activities MUST be fee based and provide primary or secondary sources of economic activity. APUC realizes that these activities may be sporadic, seasonal, or fairly small in scope.

Examples of Eligible Projects

Eligible projects under the Nature-Based Agri–Tourism grant include but are not limited to the following:

- Farm or ranch tours
- Hands–on chores
- Self-harvesting of produce
- Hunting operations
- Fishing operations (located on applicants' land)
- Bird watching
- Trail rides
- Corn mazes.

Examples of Non–eligible Projects

Non–eligible projects under the Nature-Based Agri–Tourism grant include but are not limited to the following:

- Overnight stays in a bed and breakfast
- Visiting city, state, or national parks
- Community festivals
- Non–profit organizations i.e. 4H clubs, Chamber of Commerce's, etc…

Parameters

Funding for Nature-Based Agri–Tourism is normally restricted to marketing and advertising dollars for individual or preferably groups of individuals or companies, who are currently engaged in an eligible tourism activity. Projects are encouraged to work together and apply for grant dollars to promote an entire region, thus, multiple businesses are given high priority. Grants will be awarded as follows: (applies for individuals or companies)

1. 1 Enterprise = up to $1,000
2. Two Enterprises = up to $2,500
3. Three to five Enterprises = up to $6,500
4. Six or more Enterprises = up to $10,000

The maximum grant award is $10,000 and individuals (companies) are only eligible for one grant a year.

Guidelines

1. APUC will not fund anything but marketing or advertising.
2. Applications will be considered on a quarterly basis with the deadline for application falling on January 1, April 1, July 1, and October 1.
3. Peer reviews from individuals in the Tourism Department will be obtained.
4. Generally grants are for one year.
5. Grants are limited to projects located in North Dakota.
6. The applicant(s) may be asked to make a presentation to the full commission.
7. Applicants must demonstrate a well thought out marketing plan and a working knowledge of the industry.

Each grant application will be considered on an individual basis and on its own merits.

The Commission reserves the right to accept, reject, or partially fund any grant application.

When you submit this application please include 3 copies.

APUC Commissioners will consider the first 15 applications received by the deadline. 1st time applicants will be given preference.

TOURISM AND ENVIRONMENT: AN OVERVIEW OF INDIA AND MALDIVES

Tourism plays an important role in the economies of both Goa and the Maldives. For the Maldives, it provides 17 per cent of the gross domestic product, over 25 per cent of government revenue and around 60 per cent of the foreign exchange earnings; and for Goa, it generates 13.7 per cent of the state's net domestic product, 7 per cent of employment, and 7 per cent of state tax revenues. Although both states capitalize on their comparative environmental advantages, that is beach and sunshine, Goa also capitalizes on its unique historical and cultural heritage while the Maldives on its unique archipelagic and coral reef marine environment. Their products and approaches to tourism development are very different: Goa promotes heterogeneous tourism development with upscale and inexpensive charter tourism to international and domestic audiences while the Maldives concentrates on upscale, international tourism. The experiences in tourism of Goa and the Maldives vary in terms of their environmental impacts, social issues and conflicts and institutional responses. There is much that Goa and the Maldives can learn from each other. Other states could also learn from the experiences of these two tourist spots in South Asia.

The preservation of the natural environment, the prudent use of natural resources, disposal of solid waste and sewage, and the depletion and deterioration of groundwater—attributable to tourist inflows—are, among others, issues which both governments face. In Goa, "the growth of coastal tourism has been rapid and uncontrolled," notes the paper by Sawkar *et al.* Tourism development has resulted in the loss of biodiversity, erosion of sand dunes, declining fish catches, accretion and siltation and depletion of groundwater. Although the environmental diversity and sensitivity of Goa has been widely known, a complex mixture of customary rights, land ownership, a variety of stakeholders with very differing interests, and ineffective institutional and political structures seem to have made it difficult for Goa to define a tourism strategy and to enforce its implementation. In the Maldives, the rapid increase, *albeit* government controlled, in the number of resorts over the last two decades has also taken its toll on the environment. The paper on the Maldives by Saeed, acknowledges environmental damage from beach erosion, an alteration of ocean currents, loss of biodiversity, water, soil and nutrient pollution and damage to its coral reefs most notably from mining for construction, anchoring of boats and diving. The government has played a key role in promoting tourism on unoccupied islands (or abandoned islands where customary usufruct rights were compensated) through certain traditionally powerful families and with certain funding arrangements to encourage foreign investments; the government has closely monitored the development of tourism. Tourism development has many social impacts. The Maldives has avoided much social conflict due to its relatively isolated geographical location and small, somewhat homogenous population and culture. The Maldives' strategy of separating foreign tourists from the local residents by developing tourist resorts on uninhabited islands is critical to minimizing social impacts. This strategy has managed thus far to avoid social conflicts, but with the leakage of information from tourist areas, and the separation of resort employees from their families, the sustainability of this strategy under existing institutional and political structures remains to be seen. In contrast, as Goa does not have land which is untitled or unowned or which is not of some historical significance, the needs of tourists and the local population in Goa come into frequent conflict over the use of local resources (e.g., water, beaches, and transport). The Goan social scene is further complicated by the state's porous borders with the rest of India. While Goa's geographical location improves domestic demand for tourism, it has also lead to a large influx of labour from adjoining states, further exasperating social impacts. Conflicts over resource use and institutional responses to them is another area in which the experiences of Goa and the Maldives differ. The situation in Goa is rather complex due largely to the number of stakeholders involved in tourism: luxury hotels, family–run guest houses, the needs of tourists, local residents, and other sectors of the economy. Mechanism for resolving conflicts among the various resource users do exist, such as the panchayats ("communidades") and the courts, but the long backlog of cases has delayed justice. The high number of conflicts among users suggests that an improved institutional response is necessary. Comparatively, the situation seems less complex in the Maldives. At this point, legislating and enforcing environmental quality controls for tourism appears to create fewer conflicts among residents because of the geographical separation of resorts, the small number of facilities and the limited number of stakeholders involved in tourism. As tourism expands in the Maldives, additional review of potential conflicts over resource use must be considered. Environmental legislation and regulatory mechanisms are in place in both states. The Maldives has developed its institutional capacity to address these problems and to facilitate unique solutions (e.g., encouraging European airlines to take back the trash to the points of origin of the tourists). Having carried out a "proper evaluation of tourism" in 1983 and a survey in 1995 to identify the major existing environmental problems facing the resorts, the Maldives seems further down the road in its development of tourism. But, while the Maldives has increased its regulation of tourism, it tends to focus on future environmental damage, viewing current damage as more aesthetic rather than a serious threat. The sustainability of such policy is questionable. In Goa, while a Master Tourism Plan is in place, the implementation of the laws and regulations appears to be somewhat tardy. Although the paper alludes to several government departments charged with varied aspects of tourism planning in Goa, institutional strengthening is a clear issue. Similarly, a systematic study of the environmental impacts of tourism and the implementation of a monitoring and management system would also aid Goa. Fortunately, some of these issues will be covered by the "India Environmental Management Capacity Building Technical Assistance Project," supported by the World Bank, in which Goa is included.

In sum, these two cases provide a brief introduction to the complexity of pursing tourism as an avenue to development. Much can be highlighted from the two. The Maldives has excelled in moving forward with strengthening its environmental regulatory and enforcement framework. Not only has it increasingly developed its institutional capacity to address environmental problems related to tourism, but it has also concentrated its efforts on the "polluter pays" principle. In Goa, although institutional responses and the development of a tourism strategy which integrates the needs of all stakeholders has lagged, the active lobby of its citizenry at all levels, which has intensively documented its environmental impacts and brought environmental concerns to the public agenda, should be highlighted. The active participation of all stakeholders in the planning process lends itself to greater sustainability of tourism in the long–run. Clearly the complexity of both cases requires that Goa and the Maldives carefully review the sustainability of their approaches and how to strike a balance between tourism development and protecting the natural and social environments. As in any other sector of an economy, tourism requires a sound, well–defined and executed approach in which the government, the various stakeholders and the public cooperate.

Table 1. Benefits and Costs of Heterogeneous Tourism in Goa (G) and Upscale Tourism in the Maldives (MV)

BENEFITS	*COSTS*
Economic	*Financial*
■ Foreign revenue earnings (G, MV)	■ Increased local cost of living (G)
■ Funds raised from taxes, etc. (G, MV)	■ Seasonality of income and employment (G, MV)
■ Attraction of external/ foreign investments for local infrastructure/ services (MV)	■ Unstable market (G, MV)
■ Diversification of local employment and income (G, MV)	■ Cost of enforcement/administration (G, MV)
■ Service sector employment opportunities (G, MV)	■ Cost of training guides, managers, etc. (G, MV)
■ Support employment opportunities: e.g., Agriculture, Fisheries, Handicrafts, Cottage industries (G, MV)	■ Liability of service providers (G, MV): – Polluter Pays Principle (MV)
■ Development of export markets for local products, foods, etc. (G, MV)	
Political	*Institutional*
■ Maintenance of population within political boundaries (G, MV)	■ Exposure to undesirable social problems, e.g., child labour, pedophiles (G)
■ Maintenance of future development options (G, MV)	■ Separation of local population from external public (MV)
■ Small number of stakeholders (MV)	■ Large number of stakeholders (G)
■ Environmentally active civil society (G)	■ All lands privately or publicly owned used for tourism (G)
■ Government–owned land resources leased to entrepreneurs (MV)	
■ Unoccupied or abandoned lands used for tourism with compensation for usufruct rights (MV)	
■ Tourism policy closely monitored by the government (MV)	
Cultural	*Social*
■ Exposure to new information, lifestyles (G, MV)	■ Disruption of culture (G, MV)
■ Maintenance of traditional knowledge/products (G, MV)	■ Enhanced local expectations due to exposure to affluent visitors (G, MV)

(contd.).

BENEFITS	COSTS
■ Historical and cultural heritage (G)	■ Labour influx (G)
■ Conflict resolution by panchayats or communidades (G)	■ Conflicts over local beach and water resources, and transportation (G)
■ Conflicts limited by allocating leases to certain traditional powerful families (MV)	
Environmental	*Conservation*
■ Incentives/funds for parks/resource management: e.g., waste removal (MV)	■ Beach degradation due to improper waste management by tourists (G)
■ Incentives/funds for resource management research (G)	■ Groundwater depletion due to increased local demands (G)
■ Improved environmental education (G, MV)	■ Water scarcity due to over–exploitation for tourism industry (G)
■ Unique coral reef/island resources (MV)	■ Groundwater pollution due to improper waste management (G)
■ Strong environmental regulatory and enforcement framework (MV)	■ Beach and coastal erosion due to unsuitable infrastructure development (G)
	■ Coral reef damage due to mining for construction, anchorage of boats and diving (MV)

Source: Emmanuel D'Silva, Jose Furtado and Sherry Russell are from the Economic Development Institute of the World Bank.

2

Environmental Tourism and Ecotourism: Impact Assessment in Asia–Pacific Region

ENVIRONMENTAL TOURISM AND ECOTOURISM IN ASIA–PACIFIC REGION

Visitors have long been travelling to natural areas under the guise of recreation and tourism. This has led some observers to question whether ecotourism is simply a new name for an old activity (Wall 1994). However, several changes apparently have occurred in the last decade. First, for reasons discussed in Illustration 3.3, there has been growth in visits to many natural areas, particularly in developing countries. Second, many economic development professionals increasingly have viewed natural area visitation as a tool for providing employment in regions that have experienced decline, or lack of development in other industries. Third, many conservation and resource management professionals increasingly have viewed natural area visitation as an avenue for enhancing natural area finance and providing conservation–related benefits, particularly to residents living near natural areas. Fourth, there has been increasing attention paid to improving the sustainability of all tourism activities, including those occurring in natural areas. Thus, although ecotourism may not represent an abrupt departure from historic recreation and tourism, it does represent a change in the level of visitation for many areas and a change in the goals that various stakeholders attach to this visitation.

The Australia case exemplifies the development of the ecotourism phenomenon (Lindberg and McKercher 1997). In the late 1980s, ecotourism was an unknown entity that was just beginning to emerge in the popular lexicon. Its growth was spurred by the ongoing debate over tourism and the environment and as a direct result of the enthusiasm for ecologically sustainable development (ESDWG 1991). At first, its potential market base was seen to be small although, as a new product, its growth potential was seen to be large.

However, this niche concept changed in the early 1990s. The term ecotourism struck a chord with the tourism industry, the travelling public, and with private and public sector agencies charged with the promotion of tourism products. Ecotourism became a buzzword. The explosion of interest in ecotourism led to the emergence of a lively debate among academics and industry leaders about the merits of the activity. Ecotourism conferences resulted in the formation of a national ecotourism association, the Ecotourism Association of Australia. In the space of four years, the Commonwealth government (Allcock *et al.* 1994), state governments (DCE 1992), and even regional associations (NPWS 1996) produced a variety of ecotourism policies designed to encourage the industry's development. This same period saw rapid expansion in the number of ecotourism operators and the emergence of specialist tour wholesalers and retail travel agents to market ecotourism products (Richardson 1996; Southern 1996).

By the mid 1990s, ecotourism, as a concept, began to enter a period of maturity. Many of the claims made in earlier years began to be disputed, and the legitimacy of many players to call themselves ecotourism products was challenged. The travelling public either has become more aware of what ecotourism encompasses or more critical about the idea to accept blindly the claims that mass tourism destinations are ecotourism destinations. Assumptions regarding the benefits of ecotourism have been challenged through empirical research (Lindberg, Enriquez, and Sproule 1996; Driml and Common 1995). As a result, a more realistic understanding of what the product entails and the benefits it can provide is emerging.

Ecotourism, Definitions, Concepts and Visitor Types

Much attention has been paid to the question of what constitutes ecotourism, and numerous concepts and definitions exist

(Ballantine and Eagles 1994; Blarney 1995; Bottrill and Pearce 1995; Buckley 1994). The Ecotourism Society, based in the US and the most international of the ecotourism organizations, defines ecotourism as responsible travel to natural areas that conserves the environment and improves the welfare of local people. The Australian National Ecotourism Strategy defines ecotourism as a nature–based tourism that involves education and interpretation of the natural environment and is managed to be ecologically sustainable. Numerous other definitions exist around the world.

The variability in conceptual definitions like these is further complicated by the difficulty of moving from a conceptual definition to an operational definition. For example, a conceptual definition may involve sustainability, but when one tries to measure whether someone is an ecotourist or some tourism activity is ecotourism, a more precise definition of sustainability is needed. What are the criteria one uses to determine whether the activity is sustainable and thus qualifies as ecotourism?

Most conceptual definitions of ecotourism can be reduced to the following: "ecotourism is tourism and recreation that is both nature–based and sustainable," and it is this definition[1] that is used here. Three features of this definition merit further discussion. First, the definition clarifies the descriptive and the prescriptive components of the ecotourism concept. The nature component is descriptive or positive in the sense that it simply *describes* the activity location and associated consumer motivations. The sustainable component is prescriptive or normative in the sense that it reflects what people *want* the activity to be. An important point is that, as used here, sustainability incorporates environmental, experiential, *socio-cultural,* and economic dimensions.

Second, this basic conceptual definition incorporates more complex definitions. For example, some definitions focus on

---

1 The rest of this illustration shows that there is significant diversity in definitions of ecotourism and in the characteristics of ecotourism experiences. Typically, and as used here, most tourism activities that occur in natural areas are loosely considered ecotourism. In practice, ecotourism is concerned with making all nature tourism activities more sustainable–with achieving the conceptual definition presented above.

minimizing negative environmental and cultural impacts while maximizing positive economic impacts. Such a focus is a means to the end of achieving sustainability. Likewise, the definitional focus on environmental education tends to reflect a desire to satisfy tourists or to use education to reduce negative environmental impacts. In the former case, it is a means to the end of achieving a sustainable experience. In the latter, it is also a means to the end of sustainability. Because most components of ecotourism definitions either focus on the goal of sustainability or on means to achieve that goal, it is practical to use the simple conceptual definition of ecotourism being sustainable nature–based tourism and recreation.

Third, and related to the second feature, by focusing on ends (the desired condition of sustainability), this definition forces critical evaluation of what constitutes ecotourism. For example, is sport hunting ecotourism? Many observers feel that hunting is not ecotourism, but under this definition it would be if it met the sustainability criterion. Though hunting will be inconsistent with concepts of sustainability in some natural areas (or may be rejected on other grounds), it may be appropriate in others. Similarly, a large commercial group of tourists paying an entry fee to visit a hardened visitor centre and associated rainforest boardwalk may qualify as ecotourists to the same degree as a small group of visitors following low–impact principles in a pristine wilderness.

Given the importance of sustainability within the ecotourism definition, a fundamental question is "What is sustainability?" In simplified terms, tourism sustainability is postulated to result from a positive overall balance in environmental, experiential, socio-cultural, and economic impacts ("experiential impact" is used to describe the effect of visitors on each other and "socio-cultural impact" is used to describe the effect of visitors on local residents). Thus, tourism activities that generate more positive net benefits would be more sustainable, in general, than tourism activities that generate fewer positive net benefits.

The focus on benefits also clarifies ecotourism–related objectives. Historically, many sites have sought to increase the number of tourists, but this objective slowly is giving way to increasing tourist expenditure (a positive benefit), which does not always require increasing the number of tourists. Hopefully, this objective will progress to one of increasing income generated in the region of question (again, which need not involve an increase in expenditure). Ultimately, the objective should be to increase net benefits, a measure of benefits less costs. This refinement of objectives to focus on net benefits enhances the likelihood that ecotourism will be sustainable.

With respect to visitor types and activities, a key consideration is the diversity within the ecotourism market. Ecotourists may differ greatly in several aspects, including:

- Distance travelled;
- Length of stay;
- Desired level of physical effort and comfort;
- Importance of nature in trip motivation;
- Level of learning desired;
- Amount of spending;
- Desired activities; and
- Personal demographics.

For example, ecotourism experiences can range from (1) a foreigner spending thousands of dollars coming to Australia on a commercial tour to visit the Great Barrier Reef and the Wet Tropics rainforests to (2) a local resident camping over the weekend at an adjacent national park. Ecotourists might engage in a wide range of activities, including trekking (hiking, bushwalking), climbing, camping, hunting, photography, sight–seeing, fishing, birdwatching, whale viewing, and general exploration of remote natural areas.

Of particular interest, visitor surveys (e.g., Eagles, Ballantine, and Fennell 1992) and anecdotal reports indicate that many ecotourists feel it important for their visit to contribute to conservation and local development. Though this is not important for all ecotourists, it does present additional motivation for businesses and government agencies to support conservation and development efforts.

Lindberg (1991) provides a typology of nature/ecotourism types, though many other typologies are possible:

- *Hard–core:* scientific researchers or members of tours specifically designed for education, environmental restoration, or similar purposes.

- *Dedicated:* people who take trips specifically to see protected areas and who want to understand local natural and cultural history.
- *Mainstream:* people who visit the Amazon, the Rwandan gorilla park, or other such destinations primarily to take an unusual trip.
- *Casual:* people who partake of nature incidentally, such as through a day trip during a broader vacation.

Actors in the Ecotourism "System"

Ecotourism often involves numerous actors, including:

- *Visitors;*
- *Natural areas and their managers,* including both public and private areas;
- *Communities;*
- *Businesses,* including various combinations of local businesses, in–bound operators, out-bound operators, hotel and other accommodation providers, restaurants and other food providers, and so on;
- *Government,* in addition to its role as a natural area manager; and
- *Non–governmental organizations,* such as environmental and rural development NGOs.

The relevant actors will vary across sites. For example, local communities may be present at some sites, but not others. Likewise, businesses may play a large role at some sites, but little or no role at others.

A common phenomenon is that ecotourism can generate both symbiosis and conflict between the actors. The potential for ecotourism to result in symbiosis between conservation (e.g., natural areas) and development (e.g., businesses) has been widely touted, but the potential for conflict should not be ignored. For example, natural area managers and ecotourism businesses have a shared interest in conserving the natural environment. However, there often is conflict regarding the point at which tourism activity jeopardizes this conservation.

Overview of Tourism and Ecotourism in the Asia–Pacific Region

This illustration provides quantitative and qualitative information regarding tourism and ecotourism in the Asia–Pacific region. The statistical data are based on World Tourism Organization (WTO) and World Travel and Tourism Council (WTTC) estimates. In addition, the WTO figures in particular generally are for international tourism and do not include domestic tourism, which often is quite substantial.

More importantly, readers should remember the inherent limitations of tourism and ecotourism statistics. There are a several problems associated with measuring tourist flows and resulting economic impacts (WTO 1997). One of these problems is the lack of a universal definition of tourism. *Thus, the data presented here should be treated with caution.*

Caution is even more important when one turns to ecotourism, as definitions of this activity are even less universal. There have been relatively few attempts to develop an operational definition of ecotourism, one that allows the number of ecotourists or their economic impacts to be measured. Therefore, there have been very few estimates of the importance of ecotourism, either in absolute terms or as a proportion of tourism generally. Moreover, for practical reasons, the estimates that have been made typically are based on definitions focused on the nature component, with little or no consideration of the sustainability component. Thus, estimates typically reflect nature tourism rather than ecotourism. *In short, currently it is all but impossible to estimate with any accuracy the importance of ecotourism in the Asia–Pacific region.*

Given these important caveats, the following information provides an indication of tourism and ecotourism in the region.

Tourism in the Region

As noted by the WTO (1996), the Asia–Pacific region has experienced rapid tourism growth during the past decade. The absolute and relative growth in arrivals and receipts is shown in Figures 1 and 2, respectively.

As illustrated by the figures, tourism in the East Asia and Pacific region has grown much faster than in the South Asia region, and somewhat faster than global tourism. WTO (1997) estimates that the East Asia and Pacific region had 87 million international arrivals in 1996, with South Asia having 4.5 million international arrivals in that period. These arrivals generated US$80.8 billion and US$4.0 billion in receipts, respectively[2]. The importance of tourism relative to other economic sectors is illustrated by the share of tourism receipts in services and merchandise exports (WTO 1997:18):

Region	*Share of tourism receipts in services*	*Ratio of tourism receipts to merchandise exports*
Northeast Asia	30.3%	3.6%
Southeast Asia	42.3%	8.8%
Australasia (AU + NZ)	46.7%	13.9%
Other Oceania	260.4%	63.5%

Though tourism plays a particularly important role in Oceania, these figures indicate its importance throughout the East Asia and Pacific region. WTTC (1997) estimates of travel and tourism's impact on regional output are (includes domestic tourism, amounts in US$ billions):

Northeast Asia	751
Southeast Asia	105
South Asia	46
Oceania	67

Within the East Asia and Pacific region, the top ten countries in terms of international tourism receipts, excluding transport, for 1996 are (WTO 1997:51, amounts in US$ billions):

Hong Kong	10.8
China	10.2
Australia	8.7
Thailand	8.5
Singapore	7.9
Indonesia	6.1

---

[2] The Asia–Pacific region thus accounted for about a sixth of world international arrivals and nearly a quarter of receipts in 1996 (editor).

Korea (Rep.)	5.4
Japan	4.1
Malaysia	3.9
Macau	3.5

The top ten East Asia and Pacific countries in terms of average annual growth rate for receipts, 1986–1996, are (WTO 1997:40, 43, 46):

Indonesia	26.3%
Australia	20.9%
China	20.9%
Vanuatu	20.9%
Macau	20.8%
Malaysia	19.9%
Thailand	19.6%
N. Mariana Is.	17.0%
Hong Kong	16.8%
Singapore	16.2%

Importantly, the region is not solely a recipient of visitors from outside the region. Indeed, the following figures for market share (% of total arrivals in East Asia and the Pacific coming from each source region, 1996) indicate that countries within the region generate most of the region's tourism arrivals (WTO 1997:54):

East Asia/Pacific	79.3%
Europe	11.4%
Americas	6.9%
South Asia	1.6%
Africa	0.5%
Middle East	0.4%

Using a different country grouping, the Pacific Asia Travel Association (1996) reports that 61 per cent of the international arrivals in the Pacific Asia region originated from Asia, up from only 45 per cent a decade ago.

The current importance of intra-regional travel is illustrated by the case of Malaysia. As of 1994, the ten largest markets for Malaysia were, in decreasing order (MCAT 1995):

Singapore (by far the largest)
Thailand
Japan
Taiwan
Indonesia
UK
Brunei
Hong Kong
Australia
China

The future importance of intra-regional travel is illustrated by efforts by national tourism organizations and the private sector to increase such travel. For example, Tourism Malaysia's bimonthly publication *Malaysia Tourism* summarizes efforts to attract the Japanese (March/April and September/October 1996 issues), Chinese (March/April and July/August 1996), Indonesian (September/October 1996), and Indian (July/August 1996) markets.

Future Growth in Tourism in the Region

As noted by the WTO (1997: 10, 34), the reasons for regional tourism growth include:

- rapidly growing income;
- freer intra-regional travel;
- increased leisure time;
- dynamic trade and investment;
- government promotion measures, such as launching "visit years"; and
- political stability in many of the region's countries.

Many of these factors are expected to continue, with the result being continued tourism growth into the future. Indeed, the East Asia and Pacific region is expected to surpass the Americas to become the world's number two tourism region by 2010, with 229 million international arrivals (WTO 1996). Of all the WTO regions, East Asia and Pacific is forecast to have the highest average annual growth rate (7.6%) between 1990 and 2010, with South Asia having the second highest rate, at 6.7 per cent (the world rate is forecast at 4.1%).

The growth in arrivals is expected to result from roughly equal growth in the various source markets, including East Asia and the Pacific countries. Intra-regional source market growth is particularly expected from the emerging economies of China, Korea, Malaysia, the Philippines, and Singapore (WTO 1997).

The WTTC (1997) estimates that regional tourism output will increase by the following percentages in the ten years from 1997 to 2007:

Northeast Asia	52%
Southeast Asia	103%
South Asia	119%
Oceania	44%

Ecotourism in the Region

There has been much discussion and debate regarding the size and growth of the ecotourism market. Although supporters of ecotourism, or any other phenomenon, like to provide large estimates, others question this growth in some contexts (Blamey 1995). Estimates of market size depend on the definition used to describe the market. As noted above, the lack of a widely–accepted operational definition of ecotourism hinders estimates of the ecotourism market and prevents effective comparisons across sites. Moreover, because the sustainability component of ecotourism definitions is particularly difficult to measure, most existing estimates are based solely on the nature–based component. Therefore, most estimates of ecotourism really are estimates of nature tourism.

Keeping in mind that estimates should be treated with caution, Ceballos–Lascurin (1993) reports a WTO estimate that nature tourism generates 7 per cent of all international travel expenditure (c.f., Lindberg 1994). Campbell (1994) reports that approximately 20 per cent of all foreign tourists to Thailand (in 1990) visited nature tourism sites. In some countries, such as Australia, the percentage is even higher (Blamey 1995). *Assuming that the Asia–Pacific region follows the global pattern, 7 per cent might be used as an extremely rough estimate of the region's international tourism that can be viewed as ecotourism, with several countries exhibiting higher proportions.*

Lew (1997) divides ecotourism in the region into three zones: (1) South and Southeast Asia, which together comprise the major international destination region, (2) Australia and New Zealand, which have substantial domestic ecotourism industries, as well as a secondary international market, and (3) the peripheral ecotourism areas, including China and Japan to the north, and the Pacific islands to the east.

A thorough evaluation of ecotourism offerings and experiences across the region's countries was not possible given limited project resources. However, one ecotourism operator with many years of experience in Southeast Asia ranks countries in the following decreasing order in terms of ecotourism experiences: Papua New Guinea, Malaysia, Indonesia, Thailand, and the Philippines. Several other countries are not ranked and do not play major ecotourism roles, including: Laos, Burma (Myanmar), Cambodia, and Vietnam.

Currently, most nature tourists at some sites and for some activities are foreigners, typically from North America, Europe, and Australia/New Zealand. For example, Chudintra (1993) reports that 90 per cent of Thailand's jungle tour clients are foreigners. However, domestic visitation predominates at many sites. For example, Campbell (1994) reports that about 90 per cent of visitors to Indonesia's national parks are domestic tourists, while Chudintra reports that the percentage of such visitors in Thailand increased from 58 per cent in 1986 to 85 per cent in 1990. Further information on adventure and ecotourism source markets is provided in Aderhold (1996) and Wight (1996a; 1996b).

The characteristics of ecotourists and ecotourism vary widely across sites in the region. Nonetheless, Taman Negara in Malaysia illustrates some of these characteristics (DWNP 1996a, 1996b; Stecker 1996). From 1984 to 1993, visitor numbers increased 360 per cent, from 8,200 to 30,000, respectively. Numbers have continued to increase, reaching 36,924 in 1994 and 43,491 in 1995 (at 18% growth rate from 1994 to 1995). Of the 1995 visitors, 48 per cent were Malaysian, 8 per cent Singaporean, 7 per cent British, and 7 per cent German.

The majority of the visitors were male (58%), young (89% under 40 years old), university educated (71%) and of high income. Motivations for visiting the park include:

- To see and experience rain forests (45% of respondents)
- For a holiday (16%)
- To get new experience (10%)
- For relaxation and sightseeing (8%)
- To see wildlife (8%)
- For recreation and adventure (6%) and
- To enjoy the camping life (3%).

Activities undertaken by visitors include (in decreasing order of frequency) jungle trekking, birdwatching, swimming, caving, visiting indigenous forest dwellers, botany, mountain climbing, and fishing. Somewhat more than a third of the visitors were on pre–arranged package tours from Kuala Lumpur, while somewhat less than two–thirds made their own travel arrangements.

Past and Future Ecotourism Growth in the Region

Though estimates of ecotourism's growth are rare, due to the definitional problem, most observers feel that ecotourism has grown faster than tourism generally during the past several years. Based on a survey of ecotourism operators in the region, Lew (1997) found that average annual growth rates have been steady at 10 per cent to 25 per cent over the past few years, and many are projecting higher growth in coming years.

There are various explanations for ecotourism's growth, including:

- Increasing environmental awareness and interest, including the desire to be perceived by others as environmentally sensitive;
- Increased media exposure to natural areas around the world;
- Related to the above two, a desire to see natural areas before they disappear;
- Increasing dissatisfaction with traditional tourism destinations and products, and a desire for more educative and challenging vacations;
- Desire to go to novel destinations, sometimes as a way to "outdo" others (e.g., to be the first person one knows who has been to Antarctica); and

- Easier access to remote ecotourism destinations through development of air routes, roads, and other infrastructure.

Insofar as the increased motivations to experience and preserve natural environments stem in part from more fundamental changes in societal values (Blamey 1995; Inglehart 1990), the continuation of these fundamental changes, particularly in developing countries, should lead to continued growth in demand for ecotourism. Many observers believe that the growth rate for ecotourism will be higher than for tourism generally. Thus, assuming an increase in the proportion of tourism represented by ecotourism from 7 per cent to 10 per cent and assuming that the WTO forecast of 229 million international arrivals by 2010 is accurate, *an extremely rough estimate of the region's international ecotourism arrivals for 2010 would be 22.9 million.* To this, one must add the substantial number of domestic visitors to natural areas.

The ecotourism market is expected to evolve over time. Much of the ecotourism growth probably will stem from intra-regional travel (Choegyal 1996; Shukla 1996; WTO 1996; Wylie 1994). As noted above, growth in intra-regional travel is expected for tourism generally as incomes rise and infrastructure improves. Moreover, intra-regional ecotourism in particular is expected to grow as regional population centres become increasingly crowded and polluted, and as increased wealth and education lead to greater knowledge of, and interest in, the natural environment.

As noted in Illustration 4, growth in Asian ecotourism source markets will affect the type of experience sought by visitors. In general, it is expected that Asian ecotourists will travel in larger groups and will demand a higher degree of comfort than is the case for western ecotourists. They also may be more interested in ecotourism day trips while lodging and dining in comfortable resorts. An example of this is the Juldis Khao Yai resort and golf course on the border of Khao Yai National Park in Thailand. Asian visitors (mostly Japanese) flock to see the park, play golf, and stay in luxury in the middle of jungle surroundings.

Evolution probably also will result from demographic changes occurring in society. For example, in source countries the "babyboomer" population is ageing, which will increase leisure time amongst this group. However, the group may require ecotourism experiences that are less physically demanding, more easily accessible, and with more comfortable facilities.

In addition, various factors affect the types of ecotourism experiences sought. For example, substantial media attention has been focused on the loss of tropical rainforests, and many tourists wish to visit them partly out of a concern that they may be lost entirely. Future interest in forest visitation may depend on continued media coverage and public concern about forest issues.

Other trends, such as the increased popularity of SCUBA diving, may affect forest–related ecotourism to varying degrees, depending on individual site characteristics. For example, forest areas near dive sites may benefit from add–on trips to the forest by divers. On the other hand, some forest areas may lose visitation as potential visitors choose diving–oriented trips rather than terrestrial–oriented trips. Unfortunately, it is extremely difficult to identify future trends of this sort.

Several other factors, many of them external, may affect demand at individual sites and countries (Brandon 1996; Laarman and Durst 1993; Lindberg and Huber 1993). For example, political or economic instability may cause strong decreases in visitation, an event that has at times affected tourism demand for many countries in the Asia–Pacific region.

In summary, historic data, trends, and expectations indicate that:

- Tourism makes a substantial contribution to the region's economy;
- Tourism has experienced rapid growth in the region (though less so in South Asia), and this growth is expected to continue;
- Ecotourism in the region and globally has grown faster than tourism generally, and this probably will continue over the next several years;
- Domestic and intra-regional visitors are an important component of the region's ecotourism, and this importance is expected to increase in the future; and
- Ecotourism demand will evolve over time, and the region's ecotourism sites will need to adapt to these changes.

The Dimensions of Ecotourism

In order to provide background for Illustration 4 (ecotourism trends and options), this illustration describes the dimensions of ecotourism.

Environmental Dimension

By definition, the descriptive component of ecotourism involves the natural environment as an attraction. Conversely, the prescriptive component involves the impacts of visitation on the natural environment. Although most discussions of this dimension focus on negative impacts, ecotourism also can generate positive environmental impacts. For example, some tours involve cleaning trails or undertaking rehabilitation work. Also, ecotourism indirectly can generate positive impacts by increasing political and economic support for natural area conservation and management (Lindberg, Enriquez, and Sproule 1996).

Some argue that ecotourists are motivated to preserve the environment, so one would expect them to generate little or no negative environmental impact. However, as Wall (1994) pointed out:

- Ecotourists often go to environmentally fragile areas, such as alpine and arid areas;
- Visitation may occur during sensitive periods, such as during breeding or hatching periods;
- Visitation by ecotourists eventually may lead to mass tourism at the site, such that the ultimate impact is much greater than the initial impact; and
- Visitation may cause off–site impacts, such as the consumption of airplane fuel.

Despite the centrality of the environment to ecotourism, there is relatively little accumulated knowledge regarding ecotourism's impacts on the environment and the effect of these impacts on the ecotourist experience. In part, this is due to the complexity of these impacts, the difficulty of evaluating them rigorously, and the comparative lack of research in this area. Most of the analysis that has been undertaken has focused on North America or Europe and has appeared within the recreation or natural science literatures. Although several recent publications deal with tourism's environmental impacts (Buckley and Pannell 1990; Hunter and Green 1995; Mieczkowski 1995), there also is relevant literature from the recreation field (Hammitt and Cole 1987; Knight and Gutzwiller 1995).

Ecotourism's impacts often are categorized using groups like "direct" (effect or the visitors themselves) and "indirect" (effect of the infrastructure or activities necessary to provide the visitor experience) or "on–site" and "off–site." Using the latter groups, some on–site impacts include:

- Soil erosion and compaction;
- Disturbance of wildlife;
- Trampling of vegetation;
- Removal of vegetation (e.g., collection of plants or firewood);
- Accidental introduction of exotic species;
- Increased frequency of fire; and
- Litter and vandalism.

Some off–site impacts include:

- Reclamation of land for infrastructure (e.g., clearing of forests for hotels);
- Generation of solid waste (e.g., rubbish/garbage);
- Water and air pollution (e.g., effluent in rivers and oceans); and
- Purchase of souvenirs utilizing threatened or endangered species (e.g., black coral).

Given that ecotourism can generate some negative environmental impacts, the critical questions become:

- What are the acceptable levels of these impacts?
- What is the relationship between use and level of impact?
- How is this relationship affected by management activities?

The question of acceptable levels is particularly thorny and has frustrated resource managers and other stakeholders for years.

The answer is political rather than technical, and different stakeholders provide different answers.

The relationship between use and level of environmental change (i.e., the impact of ecotourism) is difficult to evaluate, in part because few environmental parameters are amenable to the requirements of experimental design needed to establish causal relationships. As a result, many studies are correlative rather than causal. The reliance on monitoring as a replacement for experimental analysis is an example of this problem. Monitoring can provide useful information, but one should be careful when inferring causality from monitoring studies due to the potential presence of confounding factors.

The research that has been conducted indicates that use–impact relationships generally are non–linear and vary across parameters. For example, the relationship between use and soil compaction may be different than the relationship between use and wildlife disturbance. Commonly, the relationship is asymptotic curvilinear, with marginal impacts at high use levels being small or non–existent (Hammitt and Cole 1987). That is, a medium number of visitors may cause significant change, but additional visitors may not cause significant additional change. Studies of recovery from impacts indicate that recovery occurs more slowly than the initial impact. Given such relationships, the common strategy of dispersion may be misguided, and concentration may cause less overall impact.

To further complicate matters, several factors may affect use–impact relationships, including:

- Level of site hardening;
- Types of visitors and their activities;
- Characteristics of the organism impacted; and
- Timing and location of interaction.

As discussed in Illustration 4, managers can reduce ecotourism impacts by managing visitor numbers and these other factors.

Experiential Dimension

Most of the attention within ecotourism, and within sustainable tourism generally, has been on environmental sustainability.

However, tourism should be sustainable in other dimensions, including the experiential dimension. If the visitor experience is sufficiently degraded there will be a reduction in visitation that jeopardizes sustainability. Despite the relative inattention paid to experiential impacts within the ecotourism literature, they have been a focus within the recreation literature (Kearsley 1995; Manning 1986; Shelby and Heberlein 1986). For some sites, experiential impacts may be a greater limiting factor than environmental impacts (Worboys *et al.* 1995).

At the most basic level, managers should monitor the quality of the visitor experience to determine what can be done to address concerns and to improve experience quality. Often, experiential improvements focus on the addition (or removal) of specific infrastructure or programmes. However, the experience often depends on how visitors affect each other. Such experiential impacts can be grouped into three categories (Roggenbuck 1992:155):

- *Crowding,* in which the quality of the experience is reduced by visitor perceptions that they saw too many other people during their visit.
- *Conflict,* in which the quality of the experience is reduced by visitor perceptions of incompatibility or animosity with other visitors.
- *Environmental degradation,* in which the quality of the experience is reduced by visitor perceptions of environmental deterioration caused by other visitors.

These impacts, and the associated concept of satisfaction, often are complex, affected by a variety of factors, and can be difficult to measure accurately (Manning 1986; Ryan 1995). Satisfaction is particularly problematic because simplistic measurement of this concept is popular amongst natural area managers yet can provide misleading information. For example, high levels of reported satisfaction may lead managers to become complacent. However, current visitors may report satisfaction while nonetheless desiring improvement in facilities, activities, or conditions. In addition, previous visitors who were unsatisfied during their visit likely would not be represented in the sample of current visitors, as they would have stopped coming to the site, a process known as displacement in the recreation literature. Similarly, potential visitors may never have come to the site due to word–of–mouth or otherwise–obtained knowledge regarding the experience offered.

The concern over environmental degradation, resulting from tourism or other causes, and its effect on the visitor experience is widespread. It has been argued that environmental integrity must be preserved if the visitor experience is to be maintained, thereby providing an additional rationale for conservation. However, the extent to which visitor experiences are affected by environmental degradation has not been well researched, and the research that has been conducted suggests that visitors often do not notice tourism–related environmental degradation (Roggenbuck 1992; Shelby and Shindler 1992). This is an area that would particularly benefit from additional research.

Socio-cultural Dimension

As with the natural environment, the socio-cultural environment serves as both an ecotourism attraction and a recipient of ecotourism's impacts. If these impacts become, on the whole, too negative, the local sustainability of ecotourism can be jeopardized. In some areas local residents have been sufficiently unhappy with ecotourism development that they sabotaged the natural resource on which this development was based. Many ecotourism activities involve relatively intense interaction between greatly differing cultures, and these differences may exacerbate the negative socio-cultural impacts of ecotourism.

The impacts of tourism on host communities, and resulting resident attitudes toward tourism, have been popular research topics in the past several years (e.g., Lankford and Howard 1994; Lindberg and Johnson 1997; Mercer 1994; Smith 1989). In addition, many policy makers are now becoming aware of the need (1) to incorporate local communities into the tourism development and natural area management process and (2) to understand and address the negative impacts on communities.

Though the difference between cultural and social impacts is blurry, one grouping might include the following as cultural impacts (Brandon 1996:17):

- Commodification of culture, in which cultural symbols are treated as commodities to be bought and sold;
- Changes in group social structure, the way in which lives are ordered and patterned;
- Changes in cultural knowledge, the body of information possessed; and
- Changes in the way in which cultural property is used and viewed.

The following grouping is of common social and socio-physical impacts. Depending on how tourism is developed, these impacts might on balance be positive or negative, and this balance may affect resident attitudes toward tourism (Lindberg and Johnson 1997):

- *Economic*—tourism can generate a wide variety of economic benefits (such as jobs) and economic costs (such as inflation).
- *Disruption*—tourism can generate an increase in traffic congestion, crowding in stores and other areas, and crime.
- *Recreation facilities*—tourism can increase both the number of recreation facilities and the demand for such facilities (recreation is used broadly here to include outdoor recreation, urban entertainment, and related activities).
- *Aesthetic*—tourism can contribute to an aesthetically pleasing environment, for example, by catalyzing waterfront revitalization; however, it can also detract from an aesthetically pleasing environment by, for example, leading to construction that is deemed inappropriate or by increasing the amount of litter or vandalism.
- *Interaction with non–residents*—tourism can lead to satisfying relationships with non–residents, even if those relationships are brief.
- *Interaction with residents*—tourism can affect local social relationships among residents, such as by reducing the friendliness of local residents.
- *Community/culture*—because tourists often are motivated by the desire to experience the host community and its culture, tourism can affirm that culture and lead to

community pride; it also can disrupt local cultures, particularly when international tourists visit remote areas with little historic foreign contact.
- *Influence over community decisions*—studies have shown that residents are more supportive of tourism when they have been able to influence the tourism development process.

These impacts, and resulting attitudes, can strongly affect the viability of ecotourism. For example, commercial tourism activity in natural areas in Australia is undergoing a period of rapid expansion. In Victoria's Alpine National Park, the number of licenses granted to tourist operators has increased four–fold in the past five years to more than 110. This level of growth, and the perception that park policy now favours tourism interests over use by local residents, has resulted in antipathy toward tourism (McKercher 1996). This may lead to ecotourism becoming the next target for the national park movement, thereby jeopardizing access privileges to natural areas.

Economic Dimension

The final dimension is economic. There are various stakeholders in ecotourism, from operators to natural area managers to local communities. One thing they have in common is that they often seek economic benefits from ecotourism, whether it be sales and profits for operators, user fee revenues for natural area management, or jobs and income for local communities.

With respect to natural area finance, many public natural area systems around the world have encountered severe financial difficulties as the number of national parks and other areas has grown while funding has remained stable or declined (Eagles 1995; Reynolds 1995). As a result, many area managers and environmentalists have turned to ecotourism as a source of revenue, as a means to at least cover the ecotourism–related park costs that historically have been financed by governments.

There have been numerous studies of user fees in the ecotourism context (e.g., Laarman and Gregersen 1996; Lindberg and Enriquez 1994; Lindberg, Enriquez and Sproule 1996; Mak and Moncur 1995; Tisdell 1996). Though a full discussion of this issue is beyond the scope of this paper, several points are worth noting (additional discussion is provided in Illustration 4). First, the appropriate fee system will depend on the objectives for the area. If the objective is to generate revenue, fees should be relatively high. If the objective is to maximize the number of visitors to provide job opportunities for local businesses, then the fees should be low or non–existent.

Second, there are strong economic reasons for charging user fees, including that ecotourism generates costs that would otherwise need to be financed by non–users (Lindberg, Enriquez and Sproule 1996; Yong 1996). In the case of developed country visitors to developing country public natural areas, it is particularly inappropriate for relatively poor local non–users to subsidize the visits of relatively wealthy users (Lindberg 1991).

Third, most analyses conclude that current fee levels at most sites could be increased with little or no impact on the number of visitors. In cases where fee increases would reduce the number of visitors, such increases may remain appropriate as a means to maximize total revenue and/or reduce negative environmental, experiential, or social impacts.

Fourth, often, there are opportunities for increasing non–fee revenues, such as through donation programmes or through souvenir sales.

With respect to job creation, natural areas provide many benefits to society, but few are tangible. Ecotourism–related jobs are one of the most tangible benefits provided by these areas. In some cases, these jobs can provide direct alternatives to practices, such as poaching of forest products, that threaten natural area conservation. In other cases, the jobs will simply, but importantly, diversify local economies (Lindberg and Enriquez 1994). As ecotourism jobs increase, it is likely that support for the natural areas providing the jobs will increase (Han and Guo 1995; Lindberg, Enriquez and Sproule 1996). Conversely, if ecotourism is perceived to generate more costs (e.g., reduced access to the area and its resources) than benefits, it may reduce local support for natural areas.

The economic impacts of tourism, or any economic activity, can be grouped into three categories: direct, indirect, and induced. *Direct impacts* are those arising from the initial tourism spending, such as money spent at a restaurant. The restaurant buys goods and services (inputs) from other businesses, thereby generating *indirect impacts.* In addition, the restaurant employees spend part of their wages to buy various goods and services, thereby generating *induced impacts.* Of course, if the restaurant purchases the goods and services from outside the region, then the money provides no indirect impact to the region, it *leaks* away. Figure 3 illustrates some of these impacts and leakages.

Several studies have assessed the local employment benefits of ecotourism (Lindberg, Enriquez and Sproule 1996; Powell and Chalmers 1995; Shackley 1996). Not surprisingly, the level of benefits varies widely. In part, this is due to variations in the level of direct impact (tourist expenditure), which may depend on the quality of the attraction, access, and so on. In part, this is due to variations in the level of linkage (or, conversely, the level of leakage), which may depend on the size of the economy and other factors.[3] The following estimates provide indications of the percentage of tourism spending leaking away from host country economies:

- 70 per cent in Nepal
- 60 per cent in Thailand
- 55 per cent for the typical developing country

More than 90 per cent of tourism spending is thought to leak away from communities near most nature tourism sites (Lindberg, 1991; Brandon, 1996; see also Soemodinoto, Lubis, and Oktaviany 1996).

Though the high level of leakage should be considered and should be reduced where possible, one should remember that this leakage not only results from the nature of the tourism industry, which requires substantial expenditure before arrival on–site, but also from the nature of the remote communities where ecotourism occurs. Other economic activities in these communities probably

---

3 There is often wide variation in leakage estimates across sites. This is partly a result of the type of tourism development and the size of the economy being evaluated. Small–scale nature tourism tends to use more local goods than does large–scale traditional tourism. However, smaller economies may have more leakages because a lower diversity of goods is produced in small economies than in large economies. Variation in leakage estimates may also be due to definitions and methods used.

also will exhibit high levels of leakage simply because the local economies are small and not very diverse. Moreover, though the number of jobs created will be low, in rural economies even a few jobs can make a big difference. Still, ecotourism benefits should not be oversold, or there may be a backlash as reality fails to live up to expectations.

TOURISM INDUSTRY AND ENVIRONMENTAL IMPACT MANAGEMENT: A CASE STUDY OF MALDIVES

The Republic of Maldives is a small island, developing state consisting of 26 coral atolls dominated by the sea and is situated in the Indian Ocean, south–west of India. In total, these atolls contain about 1,190 very small islands of which only 200 are inhabited. The capital of the Maldives is Male', an island by itself, and the Male' International Airport also has an island (Hulhule) to itself. Tourism development in the Maldives is base on the principle of isolation of tourists from the bulk of the indigenous population and the physical configuration of tourism development is an unusual one. In the Maldives, the "tourism industry" is synonymous with "resort islands" and each resort occupies a separate island and is totally self–contained. This isolation is practical because of the availability of a large number of uninhabited islands that can be developed into tourist resort islands. According to a tourist opinion survey in 1991 conducted by the Ministry of Tourism, the main attractions in order of priority are white sandy beaches, opportunities for snorkeling and scuba diving among coral reefs and spectacular marine life, sunny weather, clear lagoons and scenic peaceful environments. The expectation is one of a "Robinson Crusoe" existence without any problems where the "Art of Doing Nothing" is practiced in a relaxing atmosphere.

History

Maldivian tourism entered the international scene only in the early 1970s. Tourism commenced with the opening of two resorts in 1972 and about 1,000 tourists visited the islands. Until then the Maldives was virtually unknown to the tourist travel trade. By the late 1970, tour operators, notably from West Germany and

Italy, started to feature the islands within their programmes and international tourism had become an important source of income for the Maldives. The first decade (1972–1982) in the development of the Maldives tourism industry evolved essentially in an unplanned *laissez faire* manner. Hulhule Airport was the basic and only gateway entry to the Maldives and the natural hub for tourism development. Thus the first two resorts to be developed were Kurumba and Bandos both on islands in close proximity to Hulhule Airport and Male'. In 1973, along with three other resorts, Club Med established itself on Farukolhufushi island, also only 20 minutes by boat from Hulhule Airport. Tourism in Maldives originated from excursions from Sri Lanka and because of the reputation of Maldives as a diving destination. Tour operators identified the ideal combination of packaging the culturally–orientated product of Sri Lanka with the unique island paradise holiday of the Maldives. During the 1972–1980 period the market changed from the more limited and specialized divers' market to the much bigger mainstream market for beach holidays. With the growing importance of the mainstream market for sand, sea and sun holidays, the tour operators found that the market base was sufficient for introducing the Maldives as a separate destination. With the completion of the runway at Hulhule's International Airport in 1981, direct charters from Europe, using wide bodied planes, flew in tourists. The expansion of air travel assisted by various promotional and other concessional fares on scheduled services, together with the rapid growth of charters, has helped the growth and development of the Maldives as a tourist destination. In the beginning the facilities provided for tourists were basic. The room was furnished with just a bed and the essential cooling fan. Food with no exotic flavours was served by local people with no formal training, and scuba diving and island hopping were the only recreation facilities besides sun bathing and swimming. At present, a diverse range of facilities are offered at different resorts. At the luxurious end of the spectrum, public spaces have expensively tiled finished floors, vast varnished and carved timber frame roofs, elaborate light fittings and plush furniture, impressive reception areas, international cuisine, swimming pools, fountains, piped music and a lush landscape incorporating many ornamental imported species.

Indicators

Two resorts with a bed capacity of 280 opened in North Male' atoll in 1972. By the end of the first decade (1972–1982), 44 resorts became operational and bed capacity rose to just under 4,000. With the spatial policy shift towards opening of Ari Atoll, together with consolidation and upgrading of existing resorts, the next decade (1982–1992) saw the addition of 36 new resorts with over a doubling of bed spaces to reach a total of almost 8,500. By 1995, there were 74 resorts in operation in the Maldives. During the year of inception of tourism in the Maldives, 1972, only 1097 tourists visited the Maldives. The number of annual tourist arrivals (reaching over 300,000 in 1995) now exceeds the total indigenous population of about 244,000. Europe is the leading generating market followed by the Asian market. Germany and Italy are the two main suppliers of tourists and in 1994, shared 40 per cent of the total tourist arrivals to the Maldives. In the late 1970s, international tourism became an important source of income for the Maldives. The readiness of the Maldives to develop its tourist sector can only be understood in terms of its very limited economic possibilities, especially the absence of local raw materials to diversify into exports of manufactures. At 17 per cent of gross domestic product, which provides over 25 per cent of the government revenue and contributes around 60 per cent of the country's foreign exchange earnings, tourism is the second largest contributor to the economy and it is increasing in importance yearly.

Tourism depends on environmental quality more than any other activity and a central precept that has been preached in tourism is not to kill the goose that lays the golden eggs. Yet, in general, it is characterized by rapid, short–term development which more often than not damages the very environment the tourists come to enjoy and simply moves off elsewhere. Without careful attention to the balance between the volume and type of tourist activity, and the sensitivity and carrying capacities of the resources being developed, tourism projects can be not only environmentally harmful but also economically self–defeating. Tourism in the Maldives exists solely due to the physical and geographic features of the coral islands. The beauty of the underwater world at the reefs, clean water in the lagoons, white and pristine sandy beaches, a rich island vegetation and ideal tropical climate which form a virtual paradise that attracts tourists from Europe and Australasia.

Assessing Environmental Impacts of Tourism

The first proper evaluation of tourism in the Maldives was carried out in 1983 after 10 years of tourism development. It was revealed that the pollution of the sea with garbage, piles of waste found in the resorts often close to the tourist cottages, the picking of corals, the use of spearguns were features present that did not fit into the tourists, image of the Maldives. In 1991, after almost two decades of tourism development in the Maldives, the perception of impacts has changed. According to the present perceptions, the islands offer uncommon visual beauty unspoiled by human settlement, virtually unsurpassed marine environment and the strongest of all, unspoiled, under populated tiny tropical islands replete with natural beauty and abundant sea life. The Environmental Protocol prepared in 1992 by the Ministry of Planning and Environment to determine the carrying capacity constraints in the tourism sector concluded that the natural resources of the Maldives are in a sufficiently pristine state, and of such high aesthetic quality, that a period exists in which environmental deterioration can occur without an adverse effect on tourism. However, concern was expressed that the duration of this period cannot be predicted and with increasing environmental pressures, rising environmental sensitivity, and without compensatory environmental management, adverse effects may be felt sooner than later. According to a survey carried out in August 1995 involving the management of 47 resorts, beach erosion was identified to be the major existing environmental problem facing the resorts. The highly dynamic Maldivian beaches erode and build in response to wave action associated with storms, the tidal cycle, and the monsoons. The results of a survey carried out in 1992 showed that 12.8 per cent of the total shoreline of 32 resorts surveyed consists of seawalls and groynes and is not sandy. The same survey also showed that 12 of the 32 resorts surveyed (38%) had offshore breakwaters to protect the beach. The maintenance of natural beach is of paramount importance to attract clients to the resorts and the construction of artificial structures designed to control and limit beach erosion are not only unsightly but also expensive. Rubbish on beach is the next environmental problem identified by the resort management. Rubbish on beach mainly results from waste dumped at sea irresponsibly by neighbouring resorts and inhabited islands that get washed ashore onto islands with the current and to some extent from the messy habits of certain tourists. The resort management is quite emotive on this issue as this is one issue that will reflect very badly on the image of the resort environment.

Solid Waste

Solid waste disposal is one of the most obvious impacts of tourist resort operation and one of the easiest environmental management problems to deal with and thus has been addressed in a number of reports on tourism development in the Maldives. The pollution of the sea with garbage and piles of waste found in the resorts often close to the tourist cottages were identified in 1983 among features that was not aesthetically pleasing. In 1985 the Department of Tourism reported that the disposal of non–biodegradable waste was then a serious problem and that there was need for education to increase environmental awareness, and for the use of recycling technology. In the new Tourism Master Plan solid waste is identified as a major issue for resort islands and it is stated that at current tourism levels, problems are probably more aesthetic than environmental. The plan also points out that while solid waste itself may not currently pose a serious environmental threat, its impact in conjunction (e.g., synergistically) with the effects of other human activities should be considered.

Sewage Disposal

In 1980 only two resorts were reported as discharging saltwater flushed toilets to the open sea. In a survey of methods of sewage disposal reported from 34 resorts in 1992, 23 resorts disposed sewage into the ground while 11 discharged sewage to the sea. A survey in 1993 revealed that at 67 per cent of tourist resorts sewage effluent is piped into septic tanks, and the untreated sludge is dealt with by natural processes and soil absorption. At 33 per cent of the resorts analyzed, septic tanks and sea outfalls were the reported practices. Measures to protect the environment in cases of direct sewage discharge include the siting of outfall pipes 100m from the island and 30m below mean sea level. Sewage disposal has both health implications and environmental consequences. Aquifer contamination by faecal coliform bacteria or the contamination of bathing waters could give rise to health problems. Since a very small percentage of resorts pump sewage into the sea and even so, these resorts have a very small population it might be concluded that the current levels of sewage emission into the coastal waters of the resorts do not pose very serious problems to human health. The capacity constraints survey carried out in 1992 showed that the sewage discharges from resorts are relatively small and the observed effects were limited. Even though the volume of waste matter disposed is quite small, nutrients from sewage could build up over time, especially if the process of discharge is not managed well. However, volumes of water and rates of water exchange are large and in view of the productive fisheries, the atolls are probably already subject to relatively high nutrient input from upwellings as oceanic currents hit them.

Groundwater

There is an increasing move away from using groundwater as a resource in tourist resorts. Drinking water in tourist resort comes from rainwater which is collected on roofs and stored in large tanks and is now supplemented by desalinated water and imported bottled mineral water. There has also been a move away from the system in which groundwater was used for showering and flushing toilets to one in which saltwater is used for flushing with the wastewater pumped out to sea and desalinated water used for showering. Groundwater quality deterioration could be caused through increasing abstraction of groundwater which depletes the already thin freshwater lends; salt water intrusion into the freshwater aquifer; and contamination of groundwater from sewage discharges. In addition to sewage, groundwater can also be contaminated through the use of contaminated soils; the excessive use of fertilizers; the use of pesticides; and inappropriate solid and liquid waste disposal. An analysis of groundwater quality and pollution in tourist resorts, based on the results of Maldives Water and Sanitation Authority Surveys and consultants' opinions showed that groundwater quality in the resorts is deteriorating.

However, the capacity constraints study in 1992 concluded that whilst there is some evidence that groundwater quality has deteriorated on some resorts through tourism, the deterioration is not significant and is unlikely to be irreversible. The study also suggested a number of factors mitigating any possible deterioration and they are:

1. The sources of pollution are relatively benign though more and more pesticides are being used and rubbish buried on islands.
2. High rainfall backed up by evidence that salinity varying widely on many of the islands between the wet and dry season indicates that flushing rates, and oxidation of contaminants are likely to be rapid.
3. Before upgrading, resorts traditionally used groundwater flushing for toilets and for showering, this minimizes the historic loss of groundwater.
4. The contaminant adsorption properties of coralline soils are generally extremely limited. One advantage of this is that any contaminants should be flushed out eventually. This is good for the state of the groundwater but not so good for adjacent lagoon waters.

Coral Reefs

On tourist resort islands reef damage has been caused by scuba divers, and by snorkelers and bathers walking out across the reef flat. The greatest threat at present almost certainly arises from snorkelers and bathers, from both inadvertent breakage and deliberate removal of coral and coral fauna for souvenirs. A study at Kurumba Village has assessed the effects of snorkelers on the reef flat/crest at depths up to about 1.5 m. Results indicate breakage of 18 per cent of all Arcopora corals/month. Hence most or all coral colonies of this genus stand to get broken each year, suggesting a significant effect from snorkelers. The present evidence on reef degradation from sewage in the Maldives is inconclusive. The Environment Protocol reported that none of the 32 resorts surveyed in 1992, and none of the 70 dive base operators on 41 resorts, identified sewage as a problem causing reef deterioration. Direct and indirect damage to reefs is also caused by divers and tourists' demands. However, the greatest impact to reefs in the Maldives has originated from coral mining for construction purposes.

Island Vegetation

The image of a palm fringed sandy beach and lush tropical vegetation is integral to the perception of, and satisfaction with, Maldives as a tourist designation. At present there is no requirement to survey and consider the vegetation of an island as part of the planning approval process prior to resort development. In the construction process trees and shrubs are cut down and coastal vegetation is removed. Exotic ornamental and fast growing species are imported to replace the vegetation removed and for new resort gardens. The introduction of exotic species not only reduces the ability of the island to recover to its natural state but also the exotic species may overcome local ones directly or through the introduction of pests. There is also the matter of maintaining the natural perception of the island for marketing purposes. Whilst the palm is the most important vegetation feature on an island, there are local plants that have historic and cultural importance and so have marketing value which imported exotics do not have. Soil and fertilizer have largely been imported to improve the growth prospects of exotic imports. These imports are very much on trial and error basis and there is little doubt that many soils and a variety of fertilizers have been tried. This process detracts from efforts to use local vegetation which is already adapted to local conditions, and so should not have to be sustained artificially. Imports may also introduce soil associated pests and diseases for which local plants have limited resistance.

Environmental Management

National Legislation

The Department of Tourism and Foreign Investment was organized in 1978 and made responsible for supervision, co–ordination and maintaining standards of tourist services in the country. To develop and regulate tourism, and simultaneously to strengthen the institutional framework for administering and monitoring the industry, this department was renamed the Department of Tourism in November 1982 and made solely responsible for tourism management. In 1984, the Tourism Advisory Board was established as a consultative body affiliated to the tourism authority. The tourism sector was given elevated status in 1988 with the establishment of the Ministry of Tourism, according to the designating law 3/68 J under 1/69 J as at 1993, to provide ways to develop the tourism industry in the Maldives, to plan methods of income generation through tourism, to provide guidelines, and to administer the industry. The Ministry of Planning and Environment was established in 1988. This Ministry is responsible for the formulation of policies on environment, environmental guidance to other development sectors, the implementation of environmental impact assessment and the designation of protected areas.

Policy and Planning

During the first decade of tourism development, there was no specifically planned development; rather, tourism took place according to individual private sector initiatives in locations that offered market advantages principally related to the access opportunities offered by Hulhule Airport. This essentially informal development managed to generate almost 3,500 bed spaces of international quality and the industry was achieving enviable occupancy rates of up to 80 per cent in the high season. The first formal initiative to plan, in an integrated way, the future development of the tourism industry in the Maldives, came when the Department of Tourism and Foreign Investment commissioned Dangroup International in November 1980 to carry out a Maldives Tourism Development Plan. This long–range (10 years), tourism development plan was prepared for the Maldives in May 1983 and some, but not all, of its recommendations were considered feasible for implementation. The tourism plan provided some ideas for development. However, to date, most of the tourism planning and management has resulted from government initiatives, based on its evaluation of the best forms and standards of development. Many of the government's present approaches and standards have evolved through the monitoring of the earlier phases of development to determine what is most suitable. Approaches and standards have been refined—and some abandoned—based on the experience gained from previous types of development. By government policy, the resorts are located on uninhabited islands, in order to reduce any possible socio–cultural impacts. Also most islands are too small to contain both resorts and traditional villages. These islands are owned by the government and it can allocate them for resort use as needed. The resort developer receives a long–term lease and pays an annual rent that is calculated individually for each island. The resorts must supply their own infrastructure of electric power, water supply, sewage and solid waste disposal, boat dock and recreation facilities. They must also provide housing and related facilities for the resort employees. The families of the resort employees remain on their home islands, often some distance away. The government policy has been to expand tourism for its economic benefits, but in a systematic manner of staged development. In the late 1980s, Kaafu Atoll was considered saturated with resort development. This decision was made within the framework of maintaining high environmental standards for the existing resorts, and retaining sufficient land for village and urban expansion and recreation parks. All new resort development was then programmed to take place in Alif Atoll, which is accessible by sea and air from the international airport. In parallel the government policy turned to encourage expansion and upgrading of existing resorts to higher standards, including meeting present environmental quality standards. This upgrading was considered necessary to maintain the viability and competitiveness of these resorts and to maintain all tourism development at a reasonably high level, catering to quality tourist markets. As an inducement to achieve these objectives, resort leases were extended from 10 to 21 years and much of this upgrading has been accomplished. The Third National Development Plan (1991–1993) recommended the development of a ten–year zoning plan (1991–2000). Under strategies and policies to achieve the main objectives of tourism development, the NDP (1991–1993) included a proposal to assess environmental impacts of resort developments and operations, and further strengthen measures taken to protect and conserve the environment and natural setting for tourism, and to adopt remedial measures on environmental degradation. The issues that are examined in the new Tourism Master Plan draft include new markets, priority markets, air travel and other transportation issues, tourism infrastructure development, legal aspects, human resource development, gender situation, socio–cultural aspects and environmental impacts.

Environmental Impact Assessment

The Environmental Protection and Preservation Act of Maldives (4/93) provided the basic framework for the Environmental Impact Assessment (EIA) process in the Maldives and under Article 5 (1) of the Act, an impact assessment study shall be submitted to the Ministry of Planning, Human Resources and Environment (MPHRE) before implementing any activity that may have an impact on the environment. According to the EIA guidelines issued by MPHRE all new resort developments require an EIA study before approval for development can be made.

Carrying Capacity Limits

As an important basis for deciding the number of rooms and extent of resort facility development allowed on each resort island, the government has established carrying capacity standards. These are based on several factors. The cutting of trees is controlled so that the natural appearance and facade of the island are maintained and no buildings are allowed to appear above the tree tops. The maximum area of the island to be occupied by buildings is 20 per cent, with two story buildings allowed to conserve land area if there is sufficient vegetation to conceal these buildings from the ocean view. To preserve the tourists' perceptions and image of beach orientation, all guest rooms should be facing the beach, with a minimum of 5 meters of linear beach available in front of each room. Only 68 per cent of the beach length can be allocated to guest rooms as 20 per cent has to be allocated to public use and 12 per cent left as open space. Construction on reef flat and lagoon is discouraged; however, as over water bungalows are very popular among tourists, they are permitted provided that equal open space is left on the land for each building developed on the lagoon.

Architectural and Design Controls

The design of resort buildings is controlled so that they are well integrated into the island environment, take advantage of the tropical climate and use local building materials to the extent possible, such as thatch roofs. Previously many buildings were constructed from coral mined from the reefs. However, the use of coral is now restricted and use of imported materials is now encouraged, although these are expensive by local standards. Coral and sand mining from resorts and their house reefs is strictly prohibited. Hard engineering solutions for dynamic coastlines are discouraged and construction of solid jetties and groynes is controlled. Design of boat piers and jetties should be in such a way that they do not obstruct the original flow of currents or disrupt the wave climate within the lagoon.

Biodiversity Conservation

To protect and preserve marine biodiversity a number of measures have been prescribed. Spear, poison and dynamite fishing are strictly prohibited. Net and trap fishing is controlled and confined to certain areas. Removal of shells, juvenile lobsters and lobsters ready to lay eggs are strictly prohibited. The catching of turtles is strictly prohibited and trade in all turtle products is banned. The commercial exploitation and export of a number of other species is also banned. Resort operators also voluntarily prohibit the catching of reef fish from the house reef or tourist resorts. Fifteen important dive sites have been declared as protected areas in 1994, where fishing, anchoring, removal of coral and other destructive activities are prohibited. The Ministry of Tourism recognizes the importance of vegetation in maintaining the natural beauty of the islands and there are a number of regulations which aim to secure this resource. These include a limit of 20 per cent of the islands for building, the requirement that no buildings be put up that disrupt the natural facade of the island, that there be a minimum setback limit of 5 meters from the vegetation line of the island, and that no buildings should appear above the tree tops.

Waste Disposal

According to the regulations issued by the Ministry of Tourism, garbage from tourist resorts should be disposed off in a manner that would not cause any damage to the environment. All garbage disposed into the sea should be done as far away into the sea as necessary in order to ensure that it does not get washed onto any islands with the current. Tourist resorts are required to have incinerators and compactors adequate in size to burn all flammable materials and crush all the cans respectively. Those who lack these facilities are not allowed to operate. Plastic or polythene bags should not be thrown into the sea and such material should be burnt. Those who contravene these regulations are subject to fines and penalties. Two airlines have joined in the effort to keep Maldives clean by arranging for waste to be carried back to Europe. Under this programme all tourists who fly in to the Maldives in these airlines are given a bag and asked to bring to the airport, all the waste they produce during their stay in the Maldives when they depart. The airlines carry the waste to the original destination for recycling free of charge. Under sewage and excreta disposal the tourism book of regulation specifies that the sewage system should be prepared such that pollution of water supplies, beaches and other areas is prevented; nuisance, ugly sights, and unpleasant odors do not occur, human wastes do not come into contact with people, animal and food; and breeding of flies and mosquitoes will be prevented.

In sum, tourism in the Maldives began in 1972 and it then evoked the image of a lost paradise. The tourism industry of the Maldives is dependent entirely on environmental quality and since it established itself in the tourism market it has maintained its strong position in a rapidly growing market. A few critics in the 1980s proclaimed that environmental pollution had begun to rear its ugly head in the Maldives. However, the natural resources of the Maldives are still in a sufficiently pristine state and of very high aesthetic quality and environmental concerns are few. Environmentally unsound practices in solid waste and sewage disposal pose the most serious threat from tourism to the delicately balanced coral reef ecosystem of the Maldives. Though solid waste is a cause of environmental concern, at current level it is more of an aesthetic problem. In the past the portion of waste and garbage which could not be burned was dumped into the sea. This practice is now prohibited by law and waste incinerators and crushers have to be used in all resorts. Sewage effluent is discharged into the sea by the resorts. However, their discharges from resorts are very small and the evidence on reef degradation from sewage discharges is inconclusive. Some of the resorts are turning to the latest technology in sewage treatment using UV radiation to produce virtually pure water. The Maldives has developed a very suitable form of tourism, appropriate for the small island environment. The present form of tourism development has not generated any serious environmental impacts. This has been accomplished through careful management. The government has developed appropriate policies, legislation and plans and instituted mechanisms to apply strict standards and regulations.

3

Forests and Ecotourism: Services, Issues, Trends, Implications and Options

FORESTS AND ECOTOURISM: A CASE STUDY OF ASIA–PACIFIC REGION

Forest resources are central to conservation and development in the Asia–Pacific region. Not only do forests provide a number of ecosystem services to both the region and the world, they also are resources for economic and social development. The region includes a number of forest "hotspots" of environmental importance, as well as several countries undergoing rapid economic development and continued population growth. These forces make it critical that sustainable uses of forest resources be facilitated.

One of the means of facilitating sustainable use of forest resources is ecotourism. There are numerous definitions of ecotourism, and definitional issues are described further in Illustration 3.1. Ecotourism is defined as "tourism and recreation that is both nature–based and sustainable."

Ecotourism has been embraced as a tool for generating economic benefits from forests and other natural resources while simultaneously conserving those resources. However, it is not a panacea for sustainable resource use, as benefits have not always been as great as desired while costs have sometimes been greater than expected (Laarman and Durst 1993; Lindberg 1991). The balance of benefits and costs will depend on a variety of factors, including destination appeal and accessibility. However, it also depends critically on how well ecotourism is planned and managed. This chapter provides an introduction to ecotourism and services of forests, together with an outlook and options for future management.

The products provided by forests are grouped into the following categories:

- Timber production;
- Special forest products or non–timber forest products, such as rattan and medicinal plants; and
- "Services of forests" which incorporates the varied non–physical forest products, as described in Illustration 2.

This chapter focuses on the third category, and on ecotourism in particular. It should be stressed that though services of forests are less tangible than timber or non–timber forest products, they make highly important contributions to social and economic development.

The chapter is part of the Asia–Pacific Forestry Outlook study, which involves an assessment of the status, trends, and outlook for the forestry sector to the year 2010. Illustration 2 provides background on services of forests generally, and Illustration 3 provides background on ecotourism. These background illustrations are followed by Illustration 4, which describes relevant trends and issues, their implications, and options that might be implemented to achieve policy objectives. Lastly, the Annex contains notes on selected countries that provide additional background and illustrate issues.

Naturally, there is substantial variation across countries with respect to services of forests, relevant issues, and future outlook. For example, the concepts and implementation of ecotourism vary across countries, particularly between more and less developed countries. Nonetheless, there are significant commonalties, with general issues and principles relevant in a variety of situations. This working paper provides a discussion of general issues and principles, while also providing some specifics.

The chapter is inherently limited by the lack of ecotourism statistics. This lack partly results from the nature of tourism flows, which are not as easily measured as timber flows. It also results from the lack of common and easily–applied definitions for tourism generally and, especially, for ecotourism in particular. Lastly, the limited project budget precluded site visits or the contracting of country or topic specialists. For these reasons, the chapter primarily provides an overview, though significant effort has gone into providing illustrative details and data wherever possible.

Throughout, the term "natural areas" is used instead of "forest areas." This usage recognizes that many forestry agencies in the region manage non–forested areas. In addition, the term is used instead of "protected areas" to reflect that not all relevant areas are in public ownership or have legal protection. Nonetheless, many of the sites used for ecotourism in the region are national parks or one of the other IUCN protected area designations.

ECOTOURISM RELATED AND OTHER SERVICES PROVIDED BY FORESTS

The Asia–Pacific region is marked by a wide range of geographic and biological diversity. It includes the world's highest mountain systems, the second largest rainforest complex, more than half the world's coral reefs, and a diversity of island systems. Additionally, the region includes segments of three biogeographic divisions. There is consequently a high level of species diversity and endemism (Braatz 1992). However, this diversity and endemism is coming under increasing threat. According to Braatz (1992:1), "unless immediate, decisive steps are taken to counter the effects of deforestation and other forms of natural resource destruction in the Asia–Pacific region, much of Asia's biodiversity will be irreversibly lost within this generation."

Biodiversity loss is occurring through a combination of factors such as poverty, population increases and models of economic development that incorporate nature as a resource for exploitation. In this region, conservationists face "the twin challenges of development and under–development.... The region's countries are grappling with difficult choices governed by geopolitical, economic and demographic forces" (IUCN Bulletin 1993:12).

This illustration provides an overview of the various services of forests available within the Asia–Pacific region. Its aim is to introduce this variety within the context of services of forests being contested. That is, services of forests, their use and their conservation, may mean different things to different groups across the region. An example of this is the question of protection from what and for what? For instance, when conflicts arise between uses, such as ecotourism and indigenous use, which should take priority?

Services provided by forests cover a wide range of ecological, political, economic, social and cultural considerations and processes. This diversity means that there are no easy management solutions, and management is not a technical, mechanical process but one that must necessarily incorporate a variety of competing interest groups and views.

Categories of Services

Broadly speaking, services of forests can be categorized according to a number of criteria that incorporate specific processes. It should be noted that these categories are not exhaustive, nor are they discrete.

Ecological Services

There are a number of components to the broad range of ecological services that forests provide. According to Sousson, Shrestha and Uprety (1995), these include (c.f., World Bank 1997):

- The regulation of water regimes by intercepting rainfall and regulating its flow through the hydrological system;
- The maintenance of soil quality and the provision of organic materials through leaf and branch fall;
- The limiting of erosion and protection of soil from the direct impact of rainfall;
- Modulating climate; and
- Being key components of biodiversity both in themselves and as a habitat for other species.

Whilst these services are important, this report is more concerned with those that have a more specifically human dimension: economic and socio-cultural services.

Economic Services

Clearly, forests form the basis of a variety of industries including timber, processed wood and paper, rubber, and fruits. However, they also contain products that are necessary to the viability of rural agricultural communities. These products include fuel and fodder, game, fruits, building materials, medicines and herbs (Sousson, Shrestha and Uprety 1995).

Additionally, grazing occurs within forests, and local woodlands are used to satisfy basic needs. Rural people also grow crops on temporary plots within the forest, often on a rotational basis. These forest products contribute to a diverse rural economy and security when times are difficult. Therefore, the loss of these resources undermines the viability of agricultural practices in the developing world (Sousson, Shrestha and Uprety 1995).

Socio-cultural Services

Knudston and Suzuki (1992) have explored the protective function of culture within a comparative perspective. Others note that, for millennia, humanity has had a social and cultural basis for protecting nature. Forests are home to millions of people world–wide, and many of these people are dependent on the forests for their survival (Sousson, Shrestha and Uprety 1995). In addition, many people have strong cultural and spiritual attachments to the forests. Therefore, forest destruction undermines the capacities of these people to survive economically, culturally and spiritually.

The issue of indigenous knowledge is also important. Many local people understand how to conserve and use forest resources. It has been argued that forests currently are being destroyed, in part, because of the non–forest dwellers' lack of knowledge about how best to exploit the vast diversity of medicines, foods, natural fertilizers and pesticides that forests contain (Posey 1993).

Spirituality is important as well. The Hindu viewpoint on nature, for example, is based on a recognition that nature and its orders of life (such as trees, forests and animals) are all bound to each other. Thus we can understand services of forests within the Hindu cosmology to include religious values. Other indigenous cosmologies involve a highly–important role for forests and other components of the natural world. Thus, indigenous belief systems have a major protective role in a culture's relationships with the natural world, and in nature's relationship with a culture.

Scenic and Landscape Services and Values

This more general set of services highlights ideas of aesthetics and beauty as components of services of forests. For example, the Himalayas provide a service within this context, and one within which ecotourism operates. From a tourist's perspective, these values may be high on their decision-making priorities, which would indicate protection of these services is important for ecotourism. Scenic and landscape values also may be important for residents.

Relative Importance of various Services

It is extremely difficult to compare the importance of the various services provided by forests. In part, this is due to the fact that there is no universally accepted common metric that can be used in such measurement. However, economists and others have tried to measure various services, economic and otherwise, using the metric of economic value. It should be stressed that non–economists often oppose the use of this metric and that the metric requires strong assumptions. Nonetheless, estimates of the economic value of various services of forests does provide one indication of their importance relative to each other and to timber production and non–timber forest products.

Recently, Costanza *et al.* (1997) estimated the economic value of various services of forests at the global level. *These values should be considered extremely rough estimates (1) because of the assumptions involved in their calculation and (2) because they are based on global, rather than regional, evaluations.* Their estimates of annual economic value for services of the forest are:

Service	Value (1994 US$ ha^{-1} yr^{-1})
Nutrient cycling	361
Climate regulation	141
Raw materials	138
Erosion control	96
Waste treatment	87

Recreation	66
Food production	43
Genetic resources	16
Soil formation	10
Water supply	3
Disturbance regulation	2
Water regulation	2
Biological control	2
Cultural	2
Total value ($ ha^{-1} yr^{-1})	**969**

Though these estimates should be treated with caution and represent value that partly accrues to people living outside the region, they indicate the significant importance of services of forests.

Relationship between Services of Forests and Forest Production

Conflicts arise between the relative importance of services compared to other factors, such as production values. In one respect, conflict can be seen as arising out of different values related to forests, some of which are subtle and relate to cross–cultural differences in interpreting protection or use. Issues surrounding rights of access by logging companies in countries, such as Papua New Guinea, with customary tenure systems provide examples of conflicts arising over competing values related to services of forests, the rights of indigenous people, and land tenure.

In the specific context of ecotourism, there have been some positive outcomes from forest production. For example, forestry roads enhance access to areas for ecotourists, and small clearcuts can enhance views and can be used as camping places. Moreover, harvest of selected trees within an area can enhance the experience for some visitors (further discussion of silvicultural effects on visitor experiences is provided by Brunson (1996) and Mattson and Li (1994)).

However, extensive clearcuts will reduce or eliminate demand for most types of ecotourism. Put simply, ecotourists are motivated to experience a natural environment that is perceived as intact and generally pristine. Though some level of environmental degradation may be overlooked or tolerated, noticeably degraded landscapes will be unappealing to most visitors. As Dark (1987) suggests, the overriding question is not whether ecotourism should be integrated with other resource uses, but where, when and how such integration can be achieved.

Institutional and Policy Environment

Across the region, national and state governments largely determine how forests can be used. This is an approach to management that often has been implemented at the expense of indigenous or local management and control. This often has meant a loss of control at the local level, either by indigenous groups themselves or by local people who live in the forests or use its services, thereby potentially creating a situation in which certain services of forests (such as spiritual or religious values) are ignored or not recognized within the forest policy context.

However, there have been policy initiatives that reflect a movement away from a centralized top–down approach to management and government intervention. Two of examples of these initiatives are (1) the strengthening of protected area management and (2) a movement towards social and community forestry. These initiatives are described in Illustration 4.1.

Issues in Maintenance of Services of Forests

The wide range in services of forests highlights the diversity of forest "uses," and reinforces the idea that, for many people, forests have more than economic value. Thus, we are sometimes left with the tension between diverse forest uses, which is intertwined with priorities and the way forests are valued.

The immediate value of forests for timber continues to dominate considerations of forest management by individuals, corporate owners and even governments that represent the public trust. The reasons are many, and include tax policies, ownership of land, tenure issues, economic exigencies, greed, and corruption.

Dwivedi (1992) argues that viewing forests as a "resource" leads to an excessive weight being applied to economic value, and that it is crucial to now search out a new concept of forest "resources." There are signs that this is occurring. It is possible to see that the concept of "ownership" of forests is changing, in recognition that forests are an important part of the global commons. The public consequently has an important interest in forests and their conservation, not only because of the dependence of life on forests but for other interests such as ecotourism (Woodwell 1993).

Some of the major issues related to services of forests are geopolitical. Though forests are physically located within nation states, issues surrounding their protection go well beyond borders (Maini and Ullsten 1993). This means global geopolitical relations play an important part in the policy context of forestry resource management in the Asia–Pacific region, whether through the calls for international treaties on the banning of hardwoods, green consumerism, or access to the genetic resources of forests by private companies. For Maini and Ullsten (1993), many geopolitical issues can be distilled into four contexts which set the scene for forest management and forest service maintenance:

- The industrialized countries, which are responsible for major deforestation, are advocating strong measures to conserve and protect the world's forests. Many developing countries are rightly concerned that the industrialized countries' preoccupation with tropical forest issues is inconsistent with the amount of attention being paid to global warming and forest decline in developed countries.
- Many developing countries view attempts to protect forests by locking up forest resources as an intrusion on sovereign rights.
- The capacity of developing countries to protect biodiversity is dependent on receiving additional funding and technologies from richer countries.
- Many developing countries have expressed concern at the desire of some industrialized countries to gain free access to genetic resources.

Many geopolitical issues are thus related to more general relationships between nation states. It is often suggested that the development of agricultural lands has been at the expense of forests. This process often involves privatizing communally owned forests and grasslands (Repetto 1993). Two major issues related to services of forests arise out of this. First, because the traditional land rights claims of indigenous and local communities frequently are ignored or not included, land at the frontier is often an open access resource. Because of this market failure, the private price of frontier land cannot and does not reflect the value of services performed by forests (Repetto 1993).

The second relates to the argument that one needs to clear–cut in order to open up agriculture. Because clear–cutting is associated with agriculture, and because in many countries of the Asia–Pacific there are high levels of rural poverty, it is relatively easy to suggest that poor people are the cause of some forest destruction. Just how much depends on the ways in which researchers interpret their information and the paradigms they use, the level of poverty and so on. But this approach, which has been highlighted in research in countries such as Nepal and India, often fails to look at the causes of poverty. Therefore, the emphasis on the relationship between agriculture and forest use may provide only a partial picture, and therefore a partial solution.

Social and cultural issues vary across regions and across cultures within regions. The Asia–Pacific region shares with other regions this diversity, only some of which can be addressed here:

- *Issue: inter–generational responsibilities and the rights of forest dwellers, indigenous people and communities living in and around forests and who are dependent on them.* There are a number of specific components under this issue, including relocation and resettlement of populations, perceptions by the state (that are reflected in policies) that local or indigenous people are "backward" because of their beliefs and/or level of socio–economic development, and the uses of indigenous knowledge and issues associated with the transfer of intellectual property rights.
- *Issue: the impact of forest destruction on norms and values of indigenous and local cultures as well as the impact of cultural change on forest use by these people.* In many cultures within the Asia–Pacific, shrines and initiation rite ceremonies, taboos and other cultural values have developed to protect trees, shrubs and the sacred places themselves. Whilst this protective function has religious or spiritual significance, it also acts as an important mechanism for the reinforcement of local cultural values and, often, as a mechanism for conflict resolution. The destruction of forests, the relocation and resettlement of forest dependent communities and broader processes of social change serve

to undermine these value systems and their broader community function.

Overall Issues related to Services provided by Forests

Dominant values of forests have come to be equated with economic resources in an extractive industry that has contributed to forest loss regionally. As part of this, the social, cultural and ecological components of services of forests have been largely unrecognized or ignored.

The search for economic development in the region is an important one, but pathways towards development have environmental and social costs in terms of the destruction of services of forests. In this context, one person or group's economic development can be another person's or group's loss of culture, religion or beliefs. Attempts at drawing some people into the economic mainstream may result in the marginalization of others.

What is needed is a mechanism whereby the diversity of services that forests provide can be protected, while forests can still provide economic benefit to local and indigenous people, countries and others within the region. Such an approach would need to recognize the diversity of services from forests, but would also need to recognize the socio-cultural basis for these services, especially as they relate to indigenous and local people's rights. It would need to broaden out the predominant concept of forests that emphasizes economic considerations to include broader functions as well as provide a means to replace, at least partially, the economic benefits that have to be foregone to maintain the broad range of services of forests. It would also need to ensure that economic and social development occurs within the region by emphasizing the rights of local people. Ecotourism can be one such mechanism.

ECOTOURISM OUTLOOK AND FORESTS: ISSUES, TRENDS, IMPLICATIONS AND OPTIONS

This illustration describes several issues and trends, and their implications, in the services of forests and ecotourism fields. For each of these, one or more options are presented for achieving objectives given the trends, with ecotourism objectives focusing on sustainability in the dimensions described in Illustration 3.4.

Issues and options relevant to tourism generally, such as infrastructure development and promotion, are not addressed in detail. Rather, this illustration focuses on issues and options that are particularly relevant to ecotourism and may be overlooked by traditional tourism planning and development. The issues tend to be interrelated, such that the grouping is somewhat arbitrary and is used as an organizational tool.

Many of the options will be familiar to readers. They are commonly–noted means for achieving the potential benefits of ecotourism. It is recognized that political and economic realities may hinder implementation of these options and thus achievement of ecotourism objectives. In short, ecotourism rhetoric does not always translate into ecotourism reality. Nonetheless, the options are presented here to offer a vision of future possibilities and to guide those actions that are feasible. Many of the issues relate to achieving a balance between private and public objectives, between providing economic and other benefits from natural areas and conserving those areas.

Preserving Services derived from Forest: Protected Area and Social Forestry Approaches

Protected Areas and their Management

Protected area systems can be seen as conservation mechanisms that incorporate social and cultural factors alongside legal, economic and political mechanisms and ecological insights. The movement towards a more inclusive policy context that integrates local people and their rights within protected area management frameworks is indicative of this.

In a report outlining the role of protected areas in the Asia–Pacific region, Braatz (1992) prioritized the need for integrated national strategies and investment focusing on programme development rather than species preservation. Braatz has identified three major objectives that will be crucial to the protection of biodiversity in the Asia–Pacific region:

- Modifying policies that adversely affect biodiversity;
- Reconciling local people's needs with protected area management; and

- Ensuring the sustainability of investments.

In relation to participation, Braatz suggests that there are three countries well suited to demonstrate the importance of participation:

- Indonesia because of its importance for biodiversity and its foreign assisted development programme;
- India because of its active NGOs and strong participatory process; and
- Papua New Guinea because some 97 per cent of land there is under customary tenure.

Finally, in relation to sustainability of investments, Braatz suggests ecotourism and forest development as priority components.

Movements towards a Community/Social Forestry Approach

Many government agencies and non–governmental organizations in the region (for example, several in Nepal and India) are assessing the usefulness of community and social forestry approaches. In the specific context of policies and policy directions, these represent, at least potentially, an acknowledgement of the rights of local populations and the movement towards a policy context that incorporates a more inclusive range of interests and values.

Social forestry is seen as an important option for forest protection and the maintenance of services of forests (World Bank 1997). At least potentially, it exemplifies the characteristics of community involvement, participation, and development of some degree of self–reliance. In addition, it provides opportunities for reforestation and the maintenance or even enhancement of biodiversity with benefits accruing at the local level. It can also enhance the possibility for tourism and ecotourism. Social forestry programmes are those which are designed as to:

- Motivate large numbers of people to plant trees;
- Promote the kind of tree growing that best supplies firewood, small timber, grasses and income; and

- Provide increased benefits to the poorer strata in society.

These programmes are especially aimed at involving farmers and the landless. Social forestry can incorporate a wide variety of activities, including farmers growing wood to sell or use for firewood, and individuals earning income from the gathering, processing and sale of minor forest products such as fruits nuts, mushrooms, herbs, basketry materials, honey, and vines. It can also include government and other groups planting trees on public lands to meet local village needs.

Unlike in conventional production forestry, where the focus is on the wood that trees produce, a social forestry approach focuses on people, on community involvement and on the trees that provide direct and indirect benefits locally. The approach therefore is used to create immediate economic and social benefits to local people or communities from their immediate locality.

According to Gregersen, Draper and Elz (1989), social forestry is important for the following reasons:

- *Environmental protection connection:* Deforestation causes decline in agricultural land quality, soil degradation, flooding downstream results in loss of crops, and so on.
- *Agricultural productivity:* Social forestry can contribute to the livelihood of the poor by improving soil, providing food supplements, and providing wood for construction, fencing, fibre, shade, and fodder. Social forestry also can provide income for farmers and rural communities and can help raise people from mere subsistence. In many parts of the world, agroforestry, or the integration of tree growing into farming systems, is a main tool in social forestry programmes involving farmers. Agroforestry is a collective name for all land use systems and practices in which woody perennials are deliberately grown on the same land management unit as crops and/or animals.
- *Fuelwood:* Fuelwood is the primary source of energy for poorer urban households and for the vast majority of rural households in developing countries.
- *Employment:* Whilst social forestry cannot solve the problem, it can contribute to increasing locally available jobs and income.

However, social forestry is not a panacea. The assumption that local knowledge and management is preferable to western scientific knowledge and centralized management does not always hold true. Likewise, the role of women within social forestry does not always take into account the reality of family and class power relationships.

In summary, social forestry is an important option for resource management approaches incorporating a local development framework. At least potentially, it exemplifies important characteristics such as community involvement, participation, and building some degree of self–reliance. In addition, it provides opportunities for reforestation and the maintenance or even enhancement of biodiversity with benefits accruing at the local level. In this context, it also can enhance the possibility for tourism and ecotourism.

It is probable that protected area establishment and social forestry programmes will expand in the future. However, as noted in Illustration 4.4, a critical issue will be the level of financial and political support for both approaches, and thus the wealthier countries of the region probably will achieve the most progress in this regard. Protected area and social forestry programmes are not the sole options for preserving services of forests, but they can make important contributions toward this goal. If they are not effectively implemented, alternate approaches must be sought if this goal is to be achieved.

Need for increased Research and Utilization of Results

Insofar as research provides valuable information in decision–making processes, the conduct of research and use of results will enhance a site's ability to benefit from ecotourism while reducing its negative impacts.

Continued Funding Difficulties in Natural Areas

Collection and retention of fees not only increases available funding, but may also increase support for ecotourism amongst natural area managers. Many agencies responsible for natural areas have had strong conservation ethics of "resource protection" at all costs (see Illustration 4.3). Managers often are ambivalent and even hostile to the idea of tourism. This is made worse by tourist revenue being transferred to the central treasury. It is also reinforced by low budgets, few staff, and "all the tourist problems." Thus, retention of fees at the local level probably would increase managerial support for ecotourism.

At the most basic level, ecotourism can help address natural area funding difficulties only when fees are charged and when they benefit the area financially, usually through retention of fee revenue directly by the area. A recent survey of protected areas around the world indicates that only about half of the areas responding to the survey collected fees at that time (Figure 4) (Giongo, Bosco–Nizeye, and Wallace 1994).

Though there has been a trend toward implementation of fees over the past several years, many areas still charge little or no fee. Moreover, it is common for revenues from fees that are charged to be directed back to the general government treasury, thereby providing no direct benefit to the natural area.

An example of a site that charges fees but receives little direct benefit is the Dinghushan Biosphere Reserve (DBR) in China. DBR received an estimated 13.5 million yuan (approx. US$1.7 million) in entrance and related fees in 1995. However, this revenue has made little contribution to reserve management, as only 5 per cent is allocated to the management agency (most of the money goes to the local government tourism bureau). Thus, substantial revenue is generated, but the revenue primarily has contributed to infrastructure development by local government rather than to environmental interpretation, visitor management, or general reserve management.

It is worth noting that results of a visitor survey at DBR (Lindberg *et al.* 1997) indicate visitor support for a greater portion of entrance fee revenues to be dedicated toward reserve management, as opposed to local government. When asked how revenues from entrance fees should be distributed, 18 per cent selected the "100 per cent to conservation, research, and education" option while 43 per cent selected the "75 per cent to conservation... and 25 per cent to construction for tourism" option. Both options would represent a substantial change to the current distribution.

A similar distribution situation was found in study of tourism at Tangkoko Duasudara Nature Reserve in Indonesia. Kinnaird and O'Brien (1996 cited in Brandon 1996) found that the Department of Forestry, which manages the reserve, receives only

2 per cent of ecotourism revenues, and the reserve itself receives only a fraction of that.

Mt. Everest in Nepal, where the climbing fee is US$50,000, provides an excellent example of capturing potential fee revenue (Gurung 1996). Though few sites are able to charge such high fees, the distribution of revenue from this fee to conservation programmes serves as an example for other sites. In addition, a portion of the US$700 per person fee for ten days of trekking in the Mustang region of Nepal goes to conservation and development programmes, while the 1993 amendment to Nepal's Wildlife Conservation Act provides for the distribution of 30 per cent to 50 per cent of protected area revenue to surrounding communities (Brandon 1996).

If it is determined that fees should be charged, there are various ways they might be applied, including:

- *Entrance fee:* collected when tourists enter the site.
- *Admission fee:* charged for admission to a specific facility, such as a visitor centre.
- *Use fee:* charged for use of a specific object, such as rented equipment, or opportunity, such as a camping place.
- *License or permit:* like a use fee, this includes fees such as hunting or fishing permits.
- *Sales and concessions:* includes (1) profits from natural area sales of souvenirs, lodging and other goods or services, (2) license fees from concessions to sell these goods and services on site, and (3) revenues from licensing area logos and trademarks.

Experience in various countries suggests that:

- Fee systems will be most efficient if, within overall objectives, flexibility is provided for each site to implement the fee structure most appropriate to local conditions (that is, a single fee structure for the whole system may not be efficient).
- Earmarking at least a portion of fee revenues directly to the area collecting them (as opposed to the general government treasury) encourages efficient collection and enhancement of visitor experience quality.

- When fees are earmarked, this portion of the site's income becomes dependent on cyclical variations in visitation, such that an endowment should be considered as a means to even out income over such variations.
- Multi–tier fee systems, in which some groups pay more than others, can be used to reduce concerns about equity; for example, foreigners might pay more than nationals, or pensioners might pay reduced fees.
- In areas with low visitation and/or multiple entry points, it simply may not be practical to collect entrance fees, though alternative systems (e.g., annual passes) can be used.
- The responsiveness of demand to fees may be reduced by "hiding" fees in larger expenditure items (such as by incorporating fees as part of the price of a whole tour) or by explaining the importance of fee revenue for maintaining the natural attraction.
- Often, there are opportunities for increasing non–fee revenues, such as through donation programmes or through souvenir sales.

Depending on how they are implemented (as well as on site characteristics and other factors), fees have the potential to significantly supplement traditional natural area funding sources. If they are not implemented, ecotourism may make natural areas worse off because of the costs imposed by this activity.

Ecotourism Management: Low Level of Funding and Reliance on Simplistic Strategies like Carrying Capacity

Next, a commitment to planning at various geographic levels may be made (e.g., at the individual natural area, national, and even international levels). In particular, effective planning requires explicit statements of ecotourism–related objectives and ongoing monitoring to determine whether those objectives are being achieved (Chudintra 1993; Lindberg, McCool and Stankey 1997; Yong 1996). UN FAO (1988), Inskeep (1991), MacKinnon *et al.* (1986), and WTO and UNEP (1992) are examples of resources available to guide and facilitate planning efforts.

Of particular concern is the popularity of the carrying capacity concept. Though this concept is appealing in its simplicity and helps draw attention to the possibility of "overdeveloping" ecotourism, it simply is not adequate to deal with the complexity found within the ecotourism context. Therefore, it is proposed that this concept be avoided in favour of alternate frameworks that focus on identifying and maintaining desired conditions (these conditions might be environmental, experiential, social, and/or economic; for further discussion, see Harroun and Boo 1996; Lindberg, McCool and Stankey 1996). Alternative frameworks not only are more appropriate, but also may be more accepted by the tourism industry, as the focus on conditions rather than numbers encourages management actions that reduce negative impacts per visitor rather than the number of visitors.

Moreover, planning processes, such as the Limits of Acceptable Change system (LAC), that involve standards can be used to avoid the tendency, through multiple small developments, for tourism to undergo an undesirable amount of succession. For example, a wilderness site may slowly become more developed as the site is hardened, more and different types of people come, and hardening and infrastructure development continues. By setting standards reflecting wilderness qualities at an early stage (e.g., a low level of encounters with other visitors), management has a guide and rationale for implementing actions consistent with the standard (e.g., restricting the number of visitors to the site) or rejecting actions that are inconsistent with the standard. Succession, and thus the value of good planning, is also relevant at the community scale. Pattaya (Thailand) has been used as an example of tourism that gradually developed well beyond its small village origin (Chudintra 1993).

The recognition of ecotourism's complexity and the devotion of sufficient funding and support to its management will greatly enhance the likelihood of achieving ecotourism objectives in the long run.

Growth in International and Domestic Visitation

Much has been written about the management of tourists, particularly in natural areas (Cole, Petersen, and Lucas 1987; Hammitt and Cole 1987; Harroun and Boo 1996; Knight and Gutzwiller 1995; WTO and UNEP 1992). On–site management options include:

- *Site hardening,* such as building boardwalks.
- *Selective marketing and restrictions on activities,* such as marketing non–motorized uses (e.g., trekking/hiking/ bushwalking rather than Four–Wheel Drive use) and restricting motorized use.
- *Managing behaviour,* such as through education and persuasive communication (including use of visitor guidelines) – everything from keeping appropriate distances from animals to carrying out rubbish.
- *Overall limitations on use,* such as a maximum number of visitors per period (e.g., day or year) for the site.
- *Selective limitations on use,* including:
  - Refuge zoning, such as permanently prohibiting visitation in certain geographic areas.
  - Buffer zones, such as prohibiting visitation within X meters of active bird nests or within Y meters of whales while whale watching.
  - Temporal limitation, such as limiting visitation by season or time of day.

Of course, a combination of these strategies might be used. For example, visitors might be allowed within 50 m of bird groups during non–nesting periods, but only within 150 m during nesting periods. In addition, management of behaviour and spatial limitations can be achieved passively through trail/track and infrastructure design and layout rather than solely through more intrusive visitor guidelines. Though user fees typically are promoted as a way to generate revenue, they are also a potential management tool insofar as they can be used to limit use overall or distribute use spatially or temporally (e.g., high fees during peak visitation seasons).

Much attention recently has been directed at low impact design, construction, and management of visitor–related infrastructure in natural areas (CDOT 1995; Hawkins, Wood and Bittman 1995; US NPS 1993). Significant potential exists for the indirect environmental impacts of tourism to be reduced through utilization of alternate energy sources, the implementation of recycling programmes, and so on. The substitution of kerosene for firewood in Nepal is a widely–cited example of reducing such indirect impacts.

For both experiential and social reasons, it is recommended that buildings be designed in harmony with the local architecture and use traditional construction materials. Unfortunately, in many ecotourism areas, such as in Namche Bazaar in the Everest region of Nepal, lodges have been constructed of cement, which is unattractive to many western visitors.

Governments can play important roles in managing the environmental impacts of tourism infrastructure and operations through regulation and incentives. For example, in Malaysia the government has granted various incentives, such as pioneer status and income-tax exemptions, to promote tourism investment. These incentives could be used to encourage environmentally sensitive practices, such as energy and waste minimization.

Strategies for managing environmental impacts also can be used to manage experiential impacts. For example, conflict often is caused by visitor behaviour, in which case there may be opportunities to manage conflict by managing behaviour through visitor education and guidelines. At the most general level, crowding can be managed by limiting the number of visitors.

A site might disperse and spatially limit certain activities to reduce crowding or conflict. For example, motorized activities might be allowed in some areas, but only non–motorized activities in other areas. If the area is of limited size, managers may need to determine the most appropriate or desirable activity, and then market and manage for that activity. The strategy of dispersal illustrates the potential for conflict between strategies to manage environmental versus experiential impacts. It may be sensible to *concentrate* use to minimize the real extent of environmental impacts, but it may be sensible to *disperse* use to minimize experiential impacts.

With respect to increasing positive economic impacts, the issue of user fees and natural area finance is discussed in Illustration 4.4. With respect to increasing jobs and other economic benefits, the traditional approach is to increase the number of visitors. Given that negative impacts (environmental, experiential, socio-cultural, and economic) correspond, to varying degrees, to visitor numbers, generally it will be preferable to increase local benefits by:

- Increasing spending per visitor;

- Increasing backward linkages (reducing leakages); or
- Increasing local participation in the industry.

Spending per visitor can be increased through, for example, provision of handicrafts where such provision does not currently exist (Healy 1994). Backward linkages can be increased through greater use of local agricultural and other products (Lindberg and Enriquez 1994; Telfer and Wall 1996).

Though visitor management traditionally focuses on environmental and experiential impacts and, to a lesser degree, economic impacts, social impacts on local communities may have at least as great an effect on sustainability as do these other impacts. As one ecotourism operator put it, "ecotourism cannot be achieved if development is opposed by the community" (Jarvie 1993:55).

Probably the best way to minimize negative social impacts and enhance local economic benefits is to ensure local involvement in, and control over, tourism development (Brandon 1993, 1996; Brohman 1996). There are obstacles to local involvement, including local factionalism and a tendency toward centralized government planning. Moreover, this involvement may make tourism development slower and more expensive. However, it also probably makes it more sustainable. As noted by Brandon (1996), local residents can (and should) decide what level of tourism they want, what cultural practices they wish to share, and where tourists will be allowed to go. Several different levels of community involvement are possible, from full local development of facilities to partnerships or joint ventures with industry, to delegation of rights in exchange for fees. The Annapurna Conservation Area Project (ACAP) in Nepal is a commonly–cited example of effective local development of ecotourism.

The local involvement process should include education about probable tourism impacts so that residents can make an informed decision regarding the desirability of tourism. Lastly, development should keep in mind the impacts listed in Illustration 3.4/ Socio-cultural Dimension and should pursue opportunities for minimizing costs and maximizing benefits. For example, reduced access to resident recreational areas (e.g., beaches) is a commonly–cited cost of tourism, so continued resident access to these areas should be preserved.

Future increases in visitation can bring important economic and other benefits. However, it also can generate increased negative impacts. If effective visitor management is implemented, the benefits can be enhanced while the negative impacts are minimized. Indeed, in some cases it may be possible, through effective management, to reduce negative impacts from current levels despite an increase in visitation. On the other hand, if visitor management is not strengthened, increased visitation may severely jeopardize resource management and other objectives.

Change in Visitor Market

One of the primary changes will be in the balance of western and Asian visitors (with Asian visitors being both domestic and intra-regional). Though growth is expected for western ecotourists, faster growth is expected for Asian ecotourists, such that the latter will comprise a larger proportion of all visitors. In general, Asian visitors are more likely to prefer larger group sizes, relative comfort, and easy site accessibility. They may seek forest–oriented experiences, but are more likely to do so in the context of trips taken for other purposes, such as golfing or diving.

Moreover, there often is divergence between the on–site experiences sought by Asians and westerners, and this will compound the need for effective management. The issue of divergent experiences is illustrated by the case of Dinghushan Biosphere Reserve (DBR) in China (Lindberg *et al.* 1996). Visitor survey results suggest that many DBR visitors (almost all of whom are domestic) are motivated by the opportunity to view scenery in the reserve, as well as to learn about nature. These motivations lead to support for restricting activities, including infrastructure development, that might threaten natural features. Nonetheless, observation of visitor behaviour in DBR suggests that these responses should be interpreted cautiously and with due regard to the cultural context. For example, there is a much higher tolerance for littering in the reserve than would be the case in many western reserves.

Moreover, cross–cultural evaluations of human relationships with the natural environment suggest that, relative to western cultures, eastern cultures tend to favour human manipulation of nature in order to enhance its appeal, in contrast to preservation of nature in a pristine state (Kellert 1996). Thus, DBR visitors may be more tolerant of human changes to the nature reserve than would be true of visitors in many western reserves (this tolerance extends to the acceptance of, and possibly preference for, buildings with modern material like concrete rather than more natural materials like wood).

Though little empirical research has been conducted on cross–cultural motivations and desired experiences in ecotourism settings, observation and discussion with researchers and reserve managers in many countries suggest that substantial cross–cultural differences exist. The example of litter suggests that perceptions of depreciation and environmental degradation caused by other visitors varies across cultures. Similarly, perceptions of crowding may vary across cultures. Of the 242 respondents (in the DBR visitor survey) who reported that they saw at least 200 other people during their visit, fewer than 25 per cent selected the number 5 or higher on a scale of 1 to 9, with 1 being "not at all crowded" to 9 being "extremely crowded." The reserve is located within two hours of a city of six million people, and it is unlikely that visitors expect a wilderness experience. Nonetheless, the level of crowding in the reserve probably is much more tolerable to Chinese visitors than to western visitors.

Of course, there is variability within cultures, with certain individuals and groups in Chinese society being more sensitive than others to environmental degradation and crowding. For example, Xing (1993) notes the high levels of visitation at Wuyishan, Changbaishan, and Huangshan reserves (with the latter having more than 10,000 visitors per day during peak periods) and observes that such visitation levels, and associated infrastructure, may devalue the natural beauty of the reserves.

Other trends also will cause changes in the visitor market. For example, the population in many source countries is ageing. Though older visitors may still seek ecotourism experiences, they are more likely to desire more comfort and greater site accessibility than their younger counterparts.

Ecotourism is a business and, therefore, the ecotourism product needs to adapt to changes in the marketplace (or choose to accept static or declining visitation if adaptation will lead to changes that are unacceptable with respect to other management objectives). Thus, if natural areas are to take full advantage of ecotourism, they will need to evaluate the market most suited to the ecotourism product offered, as well as tailor the product to the desired market as far as practical and desirable. It may be difficult to simultaneously satisfy markets with disparate desires and tolerances, such that a variety of spatially or temporally separated ecotourism experiences may need to be offered within or across natural areas.

Continued or Increased Competition, particularly for International Visitors

Though regional ecotourism visitation levels are expected to increase, competition for these visitors also is expected to increase as new destinations are developed and as visitors become more sophisticated and discriminating in their choice of destinations. On the supply side, various countries in the region, such as Mongolia, have begun developing their ecotourism potential. On the demand side, many visitors are seeking more than a generic visit to a rainforest. They may search for specialized itineraries, trips involving significant contact with local communities, and high–quality interpretive programmes (discussed in Illustration 4.9) (Wood 1997). Increased sophistication and expectations have been noted for westerners, but also will be increasingly true for Asian visitors in the future.

Thus, sites not only have to attract visitors in the face of increased supply, but they also have to provide a high quality experience once the visitors arrive, thereby helping to attract future visitors through word–of–mouth referrals.

One innovative option for reaching potential visitors in a competitive marketplace is the World–Wide Web (WWW). Though the Web offers small ecotourism companies the opportunity to reach visitors around the world, Web marketing must be done well to be effective and should not be viewed as a panacea for attracting visitors (Johnson 1996). Numerous ecotourism operators and government agencies already are on the Web. For example, Samoan ecotour operators can be found at http://public www.pi.se/~orbit/samoa/eco–oper.html while the Tasmania (Australia) Parks and Wildlife Service is at http://www.parks.tas.gov.au/. National parks and hill resorts are contained in the Malaysia Tourism Promotion Board site at: http://tourism.gov.my/. Marketing efforts generally, and Web marketing in particular, provide excellent opportunities for public–private partnerships.

In addition, destinations can maintain and enhance the quality of the visitor experience and offer the visitor something different than other sites and/or what the same site offered previously. Some sites have a natural advantage with respect to offering unique experiences. For example, only China can offer giant pandas in their native habitat. However, other sites can develop competitive advantages through, for example, enhancing access or predictability, enhancing trip quality through improved interpretation, developing or linking with complementary attractions, and so on.

Increased competition, increased expectations on the part of visitors, and the apparent trend for ecotourists to be less likely than sun and sand tourists to make repeat visits presents substantial challenges to natural areas. A flexible, business-oriented approach to marketing and trip quality can help ensure continued visitation and visitor satisfaction. If sufficient action is not taken, traditional ecotourism destinations in the region may lose their market share to new destinations as they are developed. For example, Choegyal (1996) states that Nepal has lost market share to regional competitors.

Importance of Interpretation

Development of interpretive centres and other interpretive material has occurred at many sites within the region. For example, the Malaysia Department of Wildlife and National Parks recently constructed interpretive centres at Bota Kanan and Sungkai (DWNP 1996a). However, interpretation has been largely neglected at many sites in the region (Lindberg *et al.* 1997; Campbell 1994). For this reason, and due to its importance in ecotourism, it is discussed in some detail here (further discussions are available in Ham (1992) and other interpretation resources). Though the focus here is on using interpretation to manage visitors and enhance the visitor experience, it also serves to develop a keener awareness of an area or issue and to promote public understanding of the natural area management agency and its policies.

Put simply, interpretation seeks to help people understand and appreciate the environment through various communication processes. Interpretation is more than just providing information or explaining the environment (Wylie 1994). Tilden (1977) defines interpretation as "an educational activity which aims to reveal meaning and relationships through the use of original objects, by first-hand experience and by illustrative media, rather than communicate factual information." The concept of interpretation is illustrated by the saying, "through interpretation understanding, through understanding appreciation, through appreciation protection."

The following are some of the considerations for effective interpretation (expanded from Allcock *et al.* 1994):

- The level and type of education will depend on the interests and expectations of the tourist and will include a broad range of educational opportunities through interpretation, interactive and participative approaches, and the use of various media;
- The interpretive component may acknowledge the natural and cultural values of a destination and also can address issues such as resource management and the role and attitude of the host community;
- Content can include information and orientation, rules and regulations, activities, local flora and fauna, ecological processes, management issues and the cultural history and prehistory of the area (in short, topics can be broad and varied, and are only limited by the imagination of the interpreters); and
- Interpretive material should be easily accessible, accurate and stimulating to encourage responsible behaviour and an ongoing interest in the environment and conservation after the visit.

The "art" of interpretation has been well–developed in many countries, but planning has been slower to progress. It has frequently been omitted, *ad hoc* (Upitis 1991) or in many cases reinvented. However, planning for interpretation can help managers:

- Decide what they want to achieve, by identifying what opportunities are offered to raise public awareness, and what management issues can be addressed through interpretation; and
- Work out the most effective and efficient way to achieve goals.

Proper planning is required for effective evaluation, and thus effective strategic planning. Upitis (1991) summarizes the questions that should be asked when planning interpretation:

- Why communicate?
- What is the objective?
- What is the message?
- Who is the audience?
- How/when/where is the best way to communicate with the audience?
- What have we achieved?

Interpretation can be included as part of the management planning process of the site, rather than being considered as an after-thought. Interpretive considerations can have a major influence on the placement of facilities, such as trails/tracks and campsites.

The range and type of interpretation will vary considerably from country to country as well as site to site. In Asia and the Pacific, interpretive services have traditionally been fairly basic, and often have been designed for a limited domestic market. Interpretation is one area in which consideration must be given to the differences between domestic and international visitors. This is not just a challenge in terms of language, but also in terms of the type of media, style of presentation, and the content. Often, there will need to be provision for multilingual interpretation, whether in the written media or guides.

Interpretation also can be a valuable tool to increase the awareness and understanding of local people who may live adjacent to the natural area. Interpretation can illustrate how they can contribute to the protection and sustainability of the area's natural resources upon which they may depend for subsistence or income. Indeed Ceballos–Lascurin (1996) suggests that there is increasing evidence to indicate that on–site interpretive programmes in developing countries have an important strategic environmental education function.

Ceballos–Lascurin (1996) goes on to describe the case study of the Kanah National Park interpretive centre in India. The interpretive centre was created entirely by local staff and utilized local resources. The development of this highly successful interpretive centre has resulted in a number of spin–offs. It has demonstrated the abilities of the Indian staff and has encouraged other park managers to develop their own interpretive services. It has given interpretation a higher profile within the Indian parks system and has allowed the continued development of expertise in planning, design and development of other interpretive facilities. It is also significant that this project was developed as a partnership between the managers and the local people who had been relocated from the park when it was designated.

The effective implementation of interpretive programmes can greatly enhance the visitor experience, thereby making the site more competitive. In addition, interpretation can be used to manage visitors in a non–intrusive manner, thereby reducing negative impacts and increasing positive impacts. Moreover, it can be used to raise the general awareness and level of support for resource management policies and agencies.

Importance of Partnerships among Ecotourism Actors

Almost every ecotourism observed notes the importance of forming partnerships among ecotourism actors. Such partnerships not only promote the setting of balanced objectives, but also promote achievement of these objectives through utilization of the varied skills and contributions each actor can make. For example, government clearly has an important role in ecotourism, but the private sector and NGOs offer skills, flexibility, and political independence that government agencies and local communities may lack. Moreover, the private sector and NGOs may be more efficient in achieving objectives, even in such traditional public sector activities as conveying the importance of conservation to surrounding communities.

Despite significant barriers to forming and maintaining such partnerships, the fact that they can provide substantial benefits but currently are relatively rare leads many observers to expect a future increase in partnerships. The public sector role in ecotourism typically is to:

- Provide environmental protection (the natural area itself);
- Provide infrastructure, such as roads and airports;
- Provide security and enforcement;
- Monitor and control impacts;
- Allocate access;
- Provide information, such as through interpretive programmes; and
- Resolve conflicts.

The private sector role in ecotourism typically is to:

- Provide accommodation and food;
- Provide transportation, such as busses and airlines;
- Provide information, such as guides and brochures;
- Promote sites to potential visitors; and
- Provide consumer products, such as souvenirs.

Various types of partnerships might be pursued, with national or regional ecotourism councils as one option. A specific example of public–private partnership is the formation of the Nepal Tourism Board, with representation from both the private and public sectors (Gurung 1996). An example of inter–agency cooperation is the Joint Committee on Nature Attraction Utilization in Indonesia, with representation by the Directorate General of Tourism and the Directorate General of Forest Protection and Nature Conservation (Nababan and Aliadi 1993). Joint marketing between natural areas, regional/national tourism agencies, and ecotourism businesses is another example of opportunities for partnerships to achieve mutual objectives in a cost–effective manner.

More extensive partnership opportunities also exist and likely will expand in the future. These include co–management of natural areas (e.g., government–NGO and government–local communities) and joint ventures between the private sector and local communities (Christ Forthcoming; Pfister and Jubenville Forthcoming).

Depending on the type and effectiveness of the partnership, it can be an important means for achieving ecotourism and natural area management objectives more efficiently or in ways that individual actors alone simply cannot do.

Greater Private Sector Roles in Management of Natural Areas

In simplified terms, natural area managers face three options with respect to pressure for increased private sector roles. First, the natural area can resist this pressure and retain the *status quo*, which limits negative impacts and loss of control, but also limits ecotourism–related benefits (e.g., additional revenue). Second, the natural area can follow a traditional concessionaire model, which may generate some additional revenue and may obviate the need for the natural area management agency to be involved in tourism itself. However, the revenue benefits may be less than their potential, and control may be lost. Third, more creative relationships may be explored, such as the hotel model noted above. Though such an option would require some natural area agency involvement in tourism, this commitment likely would be repaid in terms of retention of control and greater financial benefits.

Pressure to use Natural Areas for Activities that are not Nature–Dependent

Related to the previous issue/trend, there is pressure to use natural areas for activities that are not nature–dependent. For example, golf courses have been proposed, and in some cases developed, in several national parks and other protected areas in the region. At the same time, the supply of natural areas with little or no environmental degradation continues to decline. Therefore, it should be questioned whether it is either environmentally desirable or economically efficient to locate non-nature–dependent activities in natural areas preserved for conservation or nature tourism purposes.

In simplified terms, two options are to allow or to not allow non-nature–dependent infrastructure and activities in national parks and similarly–designated natural areas. If they are allowed, the natural areas may gain concession fees and/or political support, but negative environmental and experiential impacts may outweigh these benefits. Insofar as the infrastructure and associated activities are less dependent on intact ecosystems than in the case for ecotourism activities like birdwatching, it may be better to locate them outside protected areas for both economic efficiency and conservation reasons.

Professionalization of Operators and Desire to exclude those not meeting Professional Criteria

The following illustration describes some ecotourism operator difficulties and needs, using the Australian context as an example (Lindberg and McKercher 1997). Though there is variability across countries, similar difficulties exist elsewhere (Yong 1996), and several observers stress the importance of enhancing professionalism amongst ecotourism operators (e.g., Chudintra 1993).

Best estimates suggest that about 600 businesses are involved in the Australian ecotourism sector (Cotterill 1996). Dozens of new operators are entering the industry monthly and a similar number likely are deciding to leave the sector. Cotterill's profile of the industry suggests that (in Australia):

- The industry is comprised of small operators with most having four or fewer staff;
- The average life of enterprises is 10 years; and
- Each operator primarily provides either day tours or extended tours to one to three natural areas.

The industry faces many operational issues that will affect the long-term viability of many businesses. Given a goal of sustainability, the industry as a whole, if not individual operators, must remain viable. A major issue for the sector is the lack of business expertise on the part of new entrants (Cotterill 1996). Most new entrants have little practical business or business planning background, and many also are woefully under–capitalized. Business planning emerged as one of the three most critical issues identified by Australian tour operators in a survey of new eco and adventure businesses conducted by the Victorian Tourism Operators Association (VTOA 1995). Information needs include basic business planning, business development, marketing issues, accounting and book keeping, accessing finance, pricing, booking and reservations procedures, taxation issues, cost control and new business development. Indeed, the issues identified by the ecotourism sector are similar to those identified by the small business in general (Meredith 1993; Reynolds, Savage and Williams 1994).

The lack of business expertise affects all aspects of the ecotourism operation including such fundamental issues as product development. Cotterill's (1996) research identified the need to package products better, coordinate itineraries, and improve product quality and presentation. The ecotourism sector is unique in that it serves small numbers of clients, often has a limited number of trips, and often is constrained by seasonality issues. As a result, gross revenues often are low and the industry as a whole faces seasonal cash flow crises.

Marketing often emerges as a key issue for ecotourism businesses. Traditionally, ecotourism products have not been marketed effectively through the travel trade (Wild 1996). Many operators do not understand how the travel trade works. Moreover, many have not developed their pricing structure to accommodate up to 30 per cent commission demanded by wholesalers and inbound operators. On the other hand, the travel trade largely has been uninterested in selling ecotourism products. The inbound, wholesale, and retail travel system is geared to selling mass tourism experiences in which large numbers of people purchase carefully packaged and standardized products. Until recently, few travel agencies have been interested in selling specialist tourism products (Richardson 1996; Southern 1996).

Practical operational problems that affect the profitability of some ecotourism operations also were identified. Cotterill (1996) cited the need to ensure product consistency. He notes that in some locations the accommodation is substandard for the quality and price of the experience offered. The end result is deficient product quality, which threatens to reduce consumer satisfaction. Although many ecotourists are prepared to trough it, the facilities and services must be at suitable standards. A more strategic approach to planning the tour and a better understanding of satisfying client needs would address this weakness.

In a similar manner, the effective hiring, management, training, and rewarding of staff emerged as a significant issue in the Cotterill

(1996) study. The first imperative is to determine the appropriate staffing level. Some larger businesses have a client to staff ratio as high as 20:1. For specialist products, the client–staff ratio can be as little as 2:1. The second imperative is to find enough suitably skilled staff to perform the necessary duties. Sourcing suitable staff in rural areas can be a problem, and training staff is costly. The third imperative is efficient employment in the face of seasonality. Like most tourism businesses, ecotourism operators experience peak periods in which large numbers of staff may be needed. During the rest of the operating season, a few key staff people may be suitable for operating the business. In the off-season, an organization may have no need for any salaried staff.

Finally, Cotterill's (1996) research identified a number of personal issues as important factors that limit the commercial profitability and, in some cases, viability of ecotourism operations. The greatest personal challenge facing all small business operators is the risk of burnout. This risk is especially strong with ecotourism operators who may face the gruelling combination of a heavy work load, a lack of support systems, and a lack of financial resources to hire additional staff. Many ecotourism businesses offer their trips on weekends, yet they also must work a full Monday to Friday schedule to operate the office, prepare for trips, and be available to answer customer inquiries. As a result, operators may find themselves working seven day weeks for the entire operating season.

To some degree, these weaknesses and difficulties can be overcome by appropriate assistance through government agencies, industry associations, and vocational and/or university training programmes.

Accreditation has been pursued in part as a means to exclude businesses that do not follow ecotourism principles. The term "ecotourism" has become a positioning statement and a politically correct form of mass tourism. As such, virtually any type of tourism activity has claimed to offer an ecotourism experience. In Australia, bus tours that once were sold as day sightseeing trips from Sydney or Melbourne now are being marketed as ecotourism experiences because the tours stopped at wildlife parks. Yet there was no change in the tour itinerary nor the qualifications of interpretive staff. Locations outside Australia have followed similar paths (Wight 1993). Golf resorts in Hawaii became ecotourism resorts (Remington 1994). Singapore, possibly the most urban of all nations, promoted itself as an ecotourism destination because of its renowned zoo (STPB 1993). The Desaru resort being developed in Johor, Malaysia will have 12 hotels with 5,000 rooms and three golf courses, yet will "promote ecotourism" by setting aside 242 of the 1,600 hectares as a natural reserve (Manam 1996). South Pacific island nations like Fiji and Western Samoa began to promote themselves as ecotourism destinations, though three years earlier they had been positioned as mass tourism resort destinations.

The danger of abusing the ecotourism label comes not so much from large resorts using the term, because consumers presumably will be able to easily determine the type of experience they are purchasing. Rather, the confusion occurs when operators working in natural areas use the term while not complying with ecotourism principles. Such operators may be able to underprice those complying with the principles and may provide inferior experiences that, through negative word of mouth, can jeopardize demand for site and thus the viability of other businesses.

Accreditation is an option that enables consumers to identify those operators that comply with ecotourism principles. Australia is in the process of implementing such an accreditation programme, and more information can be found at http://lorenz.mur.csu.edu.au/ecotour/neap.html. The pluses and minuses of accreditation programmes, and the different types of such programmes, have been widely debated (for example, see Basiuk 1996 and Kumar 1996), and the experience of implementation in Australia and elsewhere can be used to guide future accreditation efforts.

Tendency for Dominance by larger Operators and those located in Regional or National Centres

Often, larger operators play important roles as intermediaries between consumers and small local operators. However, the dominance of larger operators can work against the goal of providing local economic benefits. Moreover, there is a common perception that large and out–of–region operators are less environmentally and socio-culturally sensitive than smaller and/ or local operators.

Options include

- *Local involvement in planning and management.*

- *Local training.* This training would cover a range of topics, including general overviews of the ecotourism industry, hospitality management (including hygiene), relevant language skills, interpretive material, cross–cultural considerations, and so on. Training can be based on existing tourism programmes, such as those conducted by the Malaysian Tourism Promotion Board, but should be supplemented with material specifically for ecotourism (Yong 1996). This training also is relevant to guides and businesses from outside local areas.
- *Provision of local capital through microcredit and other programmes.*
- *Facilitation of outreach to visitors and to other sectors of the ecotourism industry, such as inbound operators.* One of the key needs for local businesses is to reach potential visitors directly or through inbound operators. For many ecotourism sites, it is important to identify appropriate marketing outlets. For example, getting information into "backpacker" guidebooks may be more important than putting glossy brochures in tourist centres.
- *Natural area requirements that local guides be used.*

Opportunities for greater local benefits from ecotourism exist not only within the ecotourism industry itself (such as guides or operators), but also within related industries. For example, training and capital might be targeted at developing the type, quality, and reliability of agricultural products used by local restaurants and lodges. Various resources relating to business development, community ecotourism development, and guide training are available, including Bushnell (1994), Pedersen (1995), and Pond (1993).

Finally, innovative strategies for small operator marketing can be pursued. One strategy, that of utilizing the World–Wide Web, was noted in Illustration 4.8. This is an important potential strategy, but its usefulness should not be overstated, as it may become more and more difficult for small operators to become noticed on the Web as the number of sites proliferates. Indeed, it is possible that the Web ultimately will favour larger operators that are able to establish and maintain a higher Web profile. Again, partnerships may play a critical role here. Groups of operators, possibly in conjunction with natural area management agencies, can pool resources for combined sites that may be more attractive and useful to consumers than would be sites for individual operators.

Overall Issues, Trends, Implications and Options

Various demographic, tourism, and other trends will present challenges and opportunities for the region's natural area managers into the future. To some degree, these trends will put pressure on managers to maintain and improve their present activities. However, they also will put pressure on managers to take on new and different responsibilities and perspectives. For example, effective resource management will require increasingly greater social and political skills.

An overarching issue is the need for ecotourism to be dealt with in a business–like approach in terms of reacting to changes in the marketplace and satisfying ecotourists as customers. There are two general options for doing so: either natural area management agencies can take on this responsibility themselves or they can invite the private sector to do so in a partnership mode.

It should be stressed that this does not mean that important resource management objectives should be sacrificed to the desires of tourists or the tourism industry. Indeed, it may be critical for natural area managers to cultivate additional political support for such objectives in order to resist desires that are inconsistent with the objectives. Rather, it means that a more flexible, business–like approach can be taken within the constraint of achieving these objectives. Such an approach will enhance the probability that ecotourism objectives will be achieved into the future.

SELECT COUNTRY ECOTOURISM NOTES: AN OVERVIEW

This illustration contains a variety of country reports, arranged alphabetically. Due to the difficulty of obtaining current and/or detailed information without site visits (which were not possible for this project), the amount of information inevitably is limited. In addition, the statistical limitations discussed in Illustration 3.3 make it impossible to provide meaningful quantitative trends in ecotourism. Some country–level trends in general tourism are provided for 1994 to 1996 in WTO (1997).[1]

Many of the countries exhibit the trends and qualities discussed above, such as non–existent or under–funded interpretive programmes. Because they were incorporated into previous illustration, and detailed country–level information was largely unavailable, these trends and qualities will not be presented in detail for individual countries. The country reports are not comprehensive, but are included to further illustrate concepts and provide basic background information regarding ecotourism in each of the countries.

Country Note: Australia

Services of forests are sometimes a subject of controversy and contested in a number of arenas in Australia:

- Cultural attachments to place and sacred sites;
- Sustainable hunting and gathering by indigenous groups;
- Moral and ethical positions on the rights of nature; and
- Aesthetics and landscape values.

In addition, and often in direct conflict to those advocating the above positions, there is a well-organized forest industries alliance that seeks to use forests for production purposes, and a labour-based movement that is concerned about timber–related job losses.

The National Forest Policy Statement (NFPS 1992) quotes the Ecologically Sustainable Development Working Group on Forest Use as specifying three main requirements for forest use:

- Maintaining the ecological processes within forests;
- Maintaining the biodiversity of forests; and
- Optimizing the benefits to the community from all uses of forests within ecological constraints.

The fact that protection of native forests in Australia is such a contested issue is indicative of the difficulties in operationalizing such aims as "community benefit," especially within a context where "community" is so contested.

---

[1] Country–level tourism estimates in this illustration generally are from national tourism offices and may differ somewhat from WTO estimates in Illustration 3.3 due to differing years, differing definitions, and other factors.

This represents a good example of the ways in which different interest groups have acted upon competing values related to forests and services of forests, and is indicative of the ways in which these competing interest groups frame their arguments to be heard on the public agenda in Australia. Forests and their services are at the centre of a considerable amount of public debate and controversy over management, activities and actions.

The Office of National Tourism (1997) reports tourism generated export earnings of AU$13.1 billion (US$10 billion) in 1995, representing an increase of 17.2 per cent in 1994. This figure is projected to increase to AU$21 billion by the year 2000. The industry accounts for some 500,000 jobs, or around 6.6 per cent of Australia's workforce. In 1995, there were over 3.7 million international arrivals, with an expected increase to 6.3 million by the year 2000. Still, domestic tourism accounts for about 75 per cent of total tourism expenditure.

Japan, Southeast Asia and New Zealand currently are Australia's three largest tourism markets. Though Japan is expected to remain the single largest market, tourism from other Asian countries is becoming increasingly important. Tourists from Asian countries other than Japan accounted for 26.3 per cent of all visitors in 1994.

As noted by King and McVey (1994:5), "Australia's appeal in the international marketplace has been based on its unique flora, fauna and landscape," and images of nature figure prominently in Australia's promotional material. However, the country has gone beyond simply marketing ecotourism and has made a significant commitment to research, government policy, and industry development.

Numerous studies of ecotourism visitors (e.g., Blamey 1995) and, increasingly, ecotourism impacts (Buckley and Pannell 1990; Powell and Chalmers 1995) have been conducted. The Commonwealth Department of Tourism (now the Office of National Tourism) developed a National Ecotourism Strategy (Allcock *et al.* 1994) and allocated funding for ecotourism infrastructure development, environmental management, and other projects through the Forest Ecotourism Programme and the National Ecotourism Programme. In addition, various tourism and land management agencies within state governments have undertaken ecotourism evaluations and/or developed ecotourism strategies (e.g. Chapman 1996).

The national Ecotourism Association of Australia (EAA) was formed and includes members from the industry, government agencies, universities and other groups. Several ecotourism conferences and workshops are held each year at different geographic levels. In addition, a WWW site has been developed for ecotourism professionals, both in Australia and internationally, at: http://lorenz.mur.csu.edu.au/ecotour/EcoTrHme.html.

Though the national government in many respects led the way in ecotourism, this is changing as the Labour government was replaced by the Liberal/National government in early 1996. The new government continues to support ecotourism, but at a lower level than was the case for the Labour government. Thus, the EAA and industry groups like the Australian Tourism Operators Association (ATOA) will need to take leadership roles. This is happening, as illustrated by their collaboration, with support from the Commonwealth, on the National Ecotourism Accreditation Programme (NEAP). This programme, which is industry-based rather than government regulation, currently is being implemented and may serve as an important precedent for other countries.

Despite widespread interest and support for ecotourism in Australia, there remain significant points of controversy (Figgis 1996). Government funding for natural area management, though higher than for many countries in the region, remains inadequate, and indications are that it will generally decrease rather than increase. As a result, there is a trend towards user pays and greater roles for the private sector. The state of Victoria (most natural areas are managed by the states rather than the national government) recently has corporatized its service delivery functions, while the state of Queensland is pursuing private sector management of park visitation.

Though there are benefits to both user pays and private sector roles, there also are concerns. For example, user pays is contrary to the traditional goal of free access to all. Moreover, it may increase pressure to satisfy interest groups. Figgis (1996) cites the case of the Four Wheel Drive registration levy in Victoria. This helps to fund track (road) maintenance, but it may also increase pressure to accommodate the Four Wheel Drive lobby in its desire to keep tracks open when they otherwise would be closed. Likewise, there is concern that when managing infrastructure and activities, the private sector will be less attentive than public agencies to conservation objectives.

Country Note: China

Forests have long been cleared for agriculture to feed China's population, and recently loggers have moved in to clear–cut for timber products (Taylor 1994). The implications for conservation can be gauged with particular reference to panda protection. Many of the reserves that protect pandas were proclaimed in the 1960s and 1970s, after clear–cutting had occurred. Unfortunately, pandas -will not re–establish in recent clear-cuts because of reduced bamboo supply, so clear–cutting needs to be stopped in panda habitat (Taylor 1994). This is a concrete example of conflict between production and services of forests. However, evidence suggests that it is possible for loggers and pandas to co-exist, as forests of fir, hemlock, spruce and birch that were selectively cut have a thick carpet of arrow bamboo that pandas can use. Selective cutting may not harm panda habitat, particularly when tree planting is done where slopes are gentle, as that is where pandas prefer to eat (Taylor 1994).

Many forestry issues have resulted from China's opening up of the economy to global market forces and from the movement towards a form of private property. China's economy continues to grow, averaging 13 per cent since the late 1980s, and its forest resources are coming under increasing threat (FAS Online). Production is shifting from the northeast's state–owned forests to collective owned farms in the south (FAS Online). Whilst the depletion of forest resources has aggravated erosion, desertification and stream sedimentation, the planting of the "four arounds" (around houses and villages, alongside roads and waterways) has provided a concrete example, at least in some areas, that reforestation has been possible.

In the more general sense of cultural dimensions to forest service maintenance, forest dwellers are seen as minority nationalities. These people have come under a state whose attitude was to develop "backward" peoples. Hence, it would appear that there are concerns related to the maintenance of services of forests that are founded in indigenous people's value systems.

In recent years, China has experienced rapid expansion in tourism development and strong increases in domestic and international visitation (Bailey 1995; Xing 1993). In part, this growth has resulted from the political and economic environment encouraging a more market driven industry (Zhang 1995). Though visitation may plateau in certain international source markets, tourism overall is expected to continue its growth. In order to encourage future growth, the China National Tourism Administration will pursue tourism themes that will change each year (UPI 1997). These will begin in 1998 with the "China Urban and Rural Tour" promotion and will continue in 1999 with "Ecotourism."

China is expecting a record 52 million tourists each year during the promotion, with expected earnings of more than US$30 billion. This growth presents a number of challenges, including the need to more widely distribute tourism (Yongwei 1995). With 90 per cent of China's tourism receipts being earned in cities and an overwhelming concentration of tourism destinations in coastal regions, the partial focus on ecotourism could help decentralize the tourism industry by dispersing tourism to rural areas (Wen and Tisdell 1996). However, as in other countries, the expected growth in ecotourism will put additional pressure on natural areas in China, as discussed in Illustration 4.6.

China has been rated highly in ecotourism value (Herath 1996). Almost 7 per cent of China's total land area is legally protected, with many of the nature reserves located in non-coastal areas. Amongst the first "conservationists" in China were the early Taoist and Buddhist religious orders, many of which sought isolated, mountainous areas to practice principles of harmony with the environment. These traditions meant that areas surrounding religious sites were conserved while other areas in China were cleared for agriculture or other economic activities. This has led to the presence of religious and cultural sites within many of the country's reserves. In more recent times, the growth in reservation of natural areas has been steady, with the number of nature reserves expanding from 34 in 1983 to 763 in 1993 (Han and Guo 1995). Of these, ten have been included in UNESCO's international biosphere reserve network.

Lindberg, *et al.* (1997) provide an overview of ecotourism in China. Ecotourism issues there include:

- Adoption of the biosphere reserve as the dominant protected area model. This model is consistent with China's level of population and priority on economic growth. It provides for local involvement and local economic benefits, two objectives consistent with ecotourism.

- Difficulties of coordination amongst agencies involved in nature reserves. Most reserves are under the management of the Ministry of Forestry, but several other agencies also manage reserves. Moreover, additional agencies play important supporting roles.
- Control over tourism development within reserves often rests with local government, and ultimately the communist party, rather than with the *de jure* management agency. This complicates efficient management and, as in the case of Dinghushan Biosphere Reserve, reduces allocation of ecotourism revenues toward conservation, environmental education, and visitor management.
- There appears to be widespread support for tourism by local communities. Residents value the benefits of job creation and the development of tourism–related infrastructure (e.g., roads and airports). Conversely, there appear to be relatively few negative impacts, perhaps because tourism has been developed only recently and because most tourism remains domestic, such that impacts resulting from pronounced cultural differences being hosts and guests have not been great. However, in some areas tourism development has led to reduced resident access to resources, which can lead to negative feelings toward tourism.

Several other issues were raised in other illustrations of the paper. For example, there is a general lack of interpretation and it may be difficult for sites to cater to both domestic and western visitors.

Country Note: India

Forests form an integral component of Indian culture, religion and folklore. As Raja (n.d.:1) suggests:

> Indian epics are strongly based on episodes in forests, portrayed wildlife as holy creatures, and saints led their whole life in huts called "ashrams" made of wood and leaves. Indians

worshipped trees, and their sages meditated under them. Ayurvedic medicine, developed through centuries of knowledge on the medicinal effects of plants, depends on forest trees and herbs to find cures for ailments. Ancient scholars educated and trained their younger generation at their homes situated inside forests, on the basis of which Rabindranath Tagore founded the open air university at Shantiniketan in more recent times.

Raja (1996) argues that India is approaching stability in forest cover by successfully protecting what is left. He suggests that this is a result of approaching the problem in a variety of different ways, including:

- Legal measures, such as the Indian Forest Policy;
- Improved forestry research and education, with the development, for example, of the Indian Council of Forestry Research and Education (ICFRE);
- Technological advancement in forest management, especially in increased capacity for inventory;
- Participatory management, including programmes such as Joint Forest Management (JFM), village woodlot programmes and the like (Furze, De Lacy and Birckhead 1996); and
- Environmental awareness and NGO activity that has occurred as a general result of environmental concerns being placed on the public agenda.

In the context of partnerships being formed with local people, JFM has been suggested as a successful approach to forest management and the maintenance of a broad range of services of forests. According to Sarin (1993), JFM has seen the development of a number of different local institutions that are concerned with the protection and management of forest areas, including:

- Groups emerging out of local initiatives (autonomous village institutions);
- Groups promoted and mostly regulated by forest departments under JFM programmes; and

- Government or NGO sponsored development groups that have assumed the additional responsibility for forest protection and management.

JFM represents a policy and local development context for the establishment of forest management and protection mechanisms.

Country Note: Indonesia

Indonesia is comprised of 13,667 islands and extends a distance of 6,000 km from the westernmost tip of Sumatra to the eastern border of Irian Jaya. Though the climate is equatorial, it can be cold in the mountains, with permanent glaciers existing in the highest peaks of Irian Jaya. Two–thirds of the country is classified as forest land, and the country contains tremendous biodiversity, with up to 17 per cent of the earth's species. The country contains some 1,600 species of birds, including the Bird of Paradise, Cockatoos, Hornbills, and Kingfishers, 500 species of mammals, 10 per cent of the world's flowering plant species, and 663 of the world's endemic or rare species (Nababan and Aliadi 1993 and other sources).

According to official statistics from the Directorate General of Tourism, international visitor arrivals in Indonesia have increased by more than 400 per cent over the decade 1985 to 1994, with total arrivals in the latter year being just over 4 million (for historic data, see Nababan and Aliadi 1993). Tourism receipts were US$5.2 billion in 1995, and continued growth in both arrivals and receipts is expected. The government hopes that tourism will be the country's largest foreign exchange earner by 2005, with a projected 11 million international arrivals spending at least US$15 billion (for further information on economic aspects, see Soemodinoto, Lubis, and Oktaviany 1996).

Tourism remains primarily focused on beach and culture, with Bali by far the most popular destination. The most popular packages combine Bali, Central Java, North Sumatra, and South Sulawesi, though there are government plans to expand visitation on the islands of Lombok, Bintan, and Biak. Singapore is the largest tourism source country, while approximately one–third of international visitors come from the U.S., Canada, and Europe combined. However, visitor surveys indicate that most nature/eco tourists come from Europe, followed by North America and Australia (Nababan and Aliadi 1993).

Tourism policies for the current 5–year plan (Pelita VI, 1994–1999 [MTPT 1993]) call for:

- Tourism to support quality of life improvements;
- Internationalization;
- Enhanced use of technology in the tourism product component;
- Encouraging development in remote areas; and
- Promoting the preservation of natural resources as well as culture.

National parks and nature reserves in Indonesia fall under the authority of the Directorate General Forest Protection and Nature Conservation (PHPA) (see Sekartjakrariri 1993 for additional background on Indonesian parks). As in some other regional countries, the protected area concept in Indonesia is said to differ from that in western countries, with less focus on wildness (Hitchcock, King, and Parwell 1993:319). Indeed, the Indonesian term for national park (Taman Nasional) can be translated as national garden. PHPA goals for nature tourism are (Nababan and Aliadi 1993):

- To encourage conservation efforts at nature–oriented tourist sites and the surrounding environment in order to ensure the sustainability of site attractions;
- To optimally use the typical and unique potential of each site as tourism attractions;
- To promote employment in addition to business opportunities; and
- To advance national cultural values in the international community and to counter current negative impressions about tropical forest management in Indonesia.

The 1990s have seen increased development of national parks for tourism, with almost all parks now providing at least basic tourist facilities, and with substantial investment in some parks, including Gunung Leuser, Way Kambas, Ujung Kulon, Baluran, Meru Betiri, Komodo, and Wasur. At present, tourists pay between

Rp. 1,000 and Rp. 2,000 (US$0.45 to US$0.90) to enter national parks. Thirty per cent of resulting revenues go to nature conservation in the province as a whole, while none is earmarked directly to the park being visited to support management or facility development. As noted in Illustration 4.4, there are prospects for increasing this fee and channelling a greater percentage to local conservation and development.

Despite recent development in Indonesian natural areas, attention appears focused on traditional concepts of tourism, rather than ecotourism. As Cochrane (1996) notes, "the potential for an alternative model remains largely unexplored, with insufficient understanding of the requirements of ecotourists and few concrete examples of ways in which this sector can contribute to the preservation and management of Indonesia's natural heritage." Nonetheless, some businesses and other groups within the country have embraced ecotourism principles. For example, Kalpataru Adventures allocates 30 per cent to 70 per cent of its tour revenues from foreign tourists to purchase of local community accommodation and transportation (A. Soemodinoto 1996 personal communication).

Attention to ecotourism has been increasing recently. The first national community–based ecotourism workshop, "Community–Based Ecotourism: Opportunity or Illusion?" was held in Bogor in April, 1995. It was organized by PACT Indonesia in collaboration with the Indonesia Environmental Forum (WALHI). The workshop drew 65 participants from different sectors, including NGOs, communities, policy makers, tour operators, and ecotourism specialists, and has laid the foundation for increased communication amongst ecotourism actors in the country. It also led to the second workshop, held in Bali in July, 1996, which resulted in the "Bali Declaration for Ecotourism," an agreement to form the Indonesian Ecotourism Society in order to:

- Increase awareness to conserve the natural tourism resources in Indonesia;
- Develop environmental education material for tourists that visit ecotourism destinations; and
- Stress the need for local community benefits.

In addition, the non–profit Indonesian Ecotourism Network (INDECON) was initiated by the Institute for Indonesian Tourism

Studies, Conservation International–Indonesia Programme, and Bina Swadaya Tours. INDECON was organized to facilitate networking between ecotourism actors interested in promoting effective and appropriate ecotourism in Indonesia. INDECON defines ecotourism as "responsible travel to protected natural areas as well as unprotected natural areas, which conserves the environment (natural and cultural), and improves the welfare of local people."

Country Note: Malaysia

According to Hurst (1990), it is difficult to provide a discussion of "Malaysian" forest policy or use because of the diversity of policy contexts that exist, especially given the relative autonomy of the subnational level of government. Though the factors that have impacted on deforestation have included poverty, economic institutions, and public policy, their specific roles are much more debated.

However, it is clear that wood production is a major focus of forestry in this country, which generates wood–products exports in excess of RM 13 billion (US$5.2 billion) (Nair 1996). Overlogging of up to 300 per cent of set quotas has been recognized and blamed on state government needs for timber sale royalties. Impacts of this type of logging on indigenous people have also been recognized (for example, Hurst 1990).

On 1 November 1996, Sabah partially lifted its ban on log exports because state timber revenue has continued to dwindle from a high of 65 per cent of total revenue (Nair 1996). Despite the obvious economic motivation for logging, there also has been increased attention given to ecotourism in forest, as well as marine, areas.

In 1995, there were 7.5 million tourist arrivals in Malaysia, with over half of these coming from neighbouring Singapore (Tourism Malaysia fact sheet and Tourism Malaysia (1997)). Tourism receipts totalled RM9.2 billion (US$3.7 billion). Tourist arrivals grew 50 per cent during the Sixth Malaysia Plan (1991–1995). Continued growth is expected, with Seventh Malaysia Plan (1996–2000) forecasts that arrivals and receipts will total 12.5 million and RM15.7 billion, respectively, by the year 2000.

Future growth is expected to focus on increased visitor volumes and return visits, as well as targeting of higher spending and longer staying tourists. Some of the strategies for the Seventh Plan include:

- Diversification of product and services, including ecotourism, agro–tourism, and rural homestays;
- Effective promotion and marketing;
- Greater private sector investment and participation in innovative tourism products;
- Increased involvement of local populations;
- Improved access to and within the country;
- Provision of infrastructure and amenities at designated sites; and
- Enhanced skills training.

As in Indonesia, Malaysia's tourism products and services are still aimed at mass tourists. However, products and services for ecotourism are increasing, awareness of ecotourism principles and potential is increasing, and the government has emphasized ecotourism through development of the National Ecotourism Policy.

The national Ministry of Culture, Arts and Tourism (MOCAT) and the state governments are responsible for developing and promoting tourism generally. Natural areas are managed by a variety of agencies, including the Wildlife and National Parks Department, Sabah Parks, and the National Parks and Wildlife Office of the Forest Department (Sarawak).

Though there have been annual variations, visitation levels at selected natural areas like Kinabalu Park, Taman Negara, and Telok Bahang Recreation Forest have generally shown increases, often substantial, during the 1975 to 1991 period (Mohd Nor and Wayakone n.d.). Visitation data for Taman Negara were presented in Illustration 3.3. Other parks receive much higher levels, with Kinabalu recording 301,924 visits and Sepilok Forest Reserve (known for its orangutan rehabilitation centre) recording 71,549 visitors in 1992 (actual visitation is thought to be even higher; Empau and Ayim 1994).

Mohd Nor and Wayakone (n.d.) estimate that 7 per cent of all Malaysian visitors can be viewed as ecotourists, with a higher percentage in Sabah and Sarawak. They note that "tropical rainforests are the country's greatest ecotourism assets due to their unique and special biodiversity and the great concern of the world community of the disappearance of these forests." Many forests are easily accessible, with, for example, tourists able to visit the rainforests of the Forest Research Institute of Malaysia (FRIM) within an hour's drive of Kuala Lumpur. At FRIM, visitors are able to walk in the forest canopy along one of three canopy walkways in the country.

Country Note: Nepal

Whilst the extent and causes of forest loss in Nepal may be debated, there is little argument that it is an ongoing issue. The conventional wisdom of deforestation in Nepal relates to the impact of subsistence families. The realization that a majority of households rely on biomass products led many observers to conclude that firewood consumption by subsistence farmers was the cause of rapid deforestation and desertification observed both in semi–arid and mountainous regions.

Critics have questioned the fundamental assumption that environmental degradation is caused by subsistence farming families. Three significant alternative causes of the environmental difficulties in Nepal often are overlooked: the geological characteristics of the region, illegal timber harvesting, and rapid modernization stimulated by the development process itself.

Recently, calls for the integration of indigenous knowledge into agro-forestry projects have become more common. This is at least partially caused by the need to better target research, ethical concerns about participation and power, and the recognition that indigenous knowledge systems are a potentially important source of understanding as complement to scientific knowledge. Incorporating this knowledge into development may be achieved through farmer participation in research planning and implementation, external survey of local needs as a basis for planning, and an active synthesis of indigenous and scientific knowledge (Walker, Sinclair and Thapa 1995).

Stevens (1993) provides an important view on services of forests and forest management within Sherpa culture. In the past twenty years there has been increasing international concern about environmental change in the Sagamartha (Everest) region, including that tourism and changing Sherpa lifestyles and land use have resulted in a deforestation crisis. These conclusions have enormous implications for local resource policy and for Sherpa life. Yet, according to Stevens, major deforestation has not taken place recently, and old deforestation has been mistaken for recent change. Therefore, the assumptions about the traditional Sherpa lifestyles and forest management have had to be revised.

In the Terai, issues are different. Land-ownership patterns with resultant levels of landlessness and near landlessness (L/NL) continue to exert pressure on forests. Change may be occurring with the movement towards Department of National Parks and Wildlife incorporating buffer zone management strategies and assessing the potential for this as a mechanism for forest preservation through community forestry. However, the problems remain related to funding of forest initiatives (in particular the national park systems) coupled with in–migration and entrenched landlessness, so there are no easy solutions.

Since the 1950s, there has been a tremendous growth in mountaineering and trekking tourism in Nepal. In 1988, 266,000 foreign tourists arrived in Nepal, with Indians comprising the largest group (27%) (Parker 1993). While Indians visit for pilgrimages, luxury holidays, and buying sprees, non–Indians primarily visit for culture, sightseeing, natural history and a variety of sporting activities. Using the latter two categories to represent nature tourism, Parker (1993) reports that 77,539 nature tourists, 31 per cent of all tourists, visited Nepal in 1987. However, this figure probably underestimates the number of nature tourists.

In 1988, tourism was the country's leading foreign exchange earner, and about 11,000 people were directly employed in the tourism sector (Wells 1993). Wells estimates that US$26.8 million in tourist expenditure (1988) is attributable to the country's protected area network. Fees are collected by various government agencies for activities such as trekking, rafting, and mountaineering, as well as for visiting national parks. However, for many years, the Annapurna Conservation Area fee was the only one specifically utilized for environmental and development purposes. Implementation of the 1993 amendment to Nepal's Wildlife Conservation Act, as described in Illustration 4.4, should lead to a greater distribution of ecotourism–related revenue toward community development.

The Annapurna Conservation Area Project (ACAP) represents a widely–cited innovative approach to community participation in natural resource management (e.g., Brandon 1996). Established in 1986, it was the first attempt to develop a central management plan to strike a balance between the needs of local people, tourism development, and nature conservation. The management of the area has been delegated to the King Mahendra Trust for Nature Conservation, a non–government organization. ACAP has encouraged local participation in natural resource management, in contrast to the top–down approach of regulations by outsiders, mainly the Nepal Army in Chitwan and Sagamartha.

Through the ACAP, local people benefit from fixed prices for food and lodging. ACAP also has introduced lodge management courses to improve service quality and energy–efficient applied technologies, such as backboiler water heaters. The area has been established as a multiple use area (hunting and collection of forest products are permitted) and involves delegation of management authority to the village level. The aim of the project has been to reduce the environmental impacts of visitation while simultaneously increasing the economic benefits from tourism.

A similar programme has been developed in Makalu–Barun. The priority is on increasing and diversifying incomes to reduce pressure on the core area. Activities include supporting ecotourism, promoting weaving and papermaking from indigenous natural resources, production and marketing of handicrafts, and improved agricultural production (Odell 1996). Handicraft and production activities are estimated to generate local revenues of some Rs. 500,000 to 1,000,000 (US$10,000 to US$20,000) or between Rs. 1,000 and 2,000 per family involved (approximately 10 per cent of average per capita income). The trekking programme is estimated to generate approximately Rs. 4 to 5 million. While the national park collects a US$12 fee from all entering trekkers, these visitors spend an average of US$10 per day in the local communities for supplies, porters, lodging, food, and handicrafts.

Odell (1996) goes on to note that the programme has led to increasing local environment awareness and improved local management of community forests, grazing lands, and natural resource conservation. Resident support for conservation is illustrated by (1) the local arrest of a poacher who was turned in to authorities, (2) the confiscation and reporting by local people of illegally harvested lokta bark used in manufacture of handmade Nepali paper, and (3) a petition by communities formerly opposed to the establishment of the park to be included within the project area.

There are several governmental and non–governmental agencies involved in ecotourism in Nepal, including the Department of National Parks and Wildlife Conservation, Department of Forestry, Nepal Army, Trekking Agents Association of Nepal and the Department of Tourism. In 1990 there were 82 registered trekking and mountaineering agencies (Parker 1993), yet a survey indicated that few were incorporating environmental awareness in their programmes.

Problems identified by trekking agencies include the need for education of personnel in the tourist industry on environmental issues, fuel depots, litter control, medical assistance and demand for agricultural produce on major trekking routes. Congestion on main trekking routes is also perceived to be a problem especially in the three main areas of Annapurna, Sagamartha National Park, and Langtang National Park.

Tour guides are required to be licensed and registered with the Tourist Guide Association of Nepal. They are required to complete a nine week training course through the Department of Tourism, though this has been reported as inadequate (Parker 1993). There is a need for additional specialized training, such as naturalists and refresher courses (see Illustration 4.14).

The negative environmental impacts increase when the movement and behaviour of tourists are not well-managed. This is especially problematic in Nepal with independent trekkers. There is considerable debate in the Nepal industry over the advantages and disadvantages of independent trekkers and group trekking. Some argue that groups are less damaging as they burn kerosene (though many do not provide it for their staff and porters) and have licensed guides. Groups have less cultural impact on the villages because they are self-contained. However, many groups do not contribute to the local economy, as they bring their food supplies and porters from Kathmandu. In comparison, independent trekkers contribute to the local rural economy because they stay and eat in locally run lodges, but they are more difficult to manage and monitor than group trekkers.

Tour guides are the key to educating tourists regarding environmental and cultural impacts. There needs to be training of "environmental guides" who can accompany trekking groups and particularly those to environmentally fragile areas. Currently, many of the guides accompanying trekking groups originate from Kathmandu and have limited knowledge of the specific areas. The use of guides from the area where the trekking is undertaken can improve this deficiency and is particularly important in the newly opened trekking areas which have not yet experienced significant impacts from tourism.

Country Note: Pohnpei

As noted by Van't Slot (1996:1), "sustainable tourism development is even more critical in the Pacific islands than in the continental regions of the world because the impact of any development is greatly magnified on islands." He goes on to note that Pohnpei (located in the Federated States of Micronesia) is showing signs of impact from a spectrum of development threats. This impact is expected to increase as US development funds from the Compact of Free Association will expire in 2001, thereby putting greater economic pressure on natural resources.

The tourism industry in Pohnpei is small, but has increased in the 1990s as Micronesia has become more popular as a dive destination.[1] Though tourism is seen as one option for replacing lost compact funding, there is concern that most of the benefits from tourism in the region have gone to Kolonia Town, rather than local communities (Van't Slot 1996). Still, ecotourism is seen as an important option and is being pursued on various levels. The College of Micronesia has held ecotourism workshops and training programmes focused on interpretive guiding.

Pohnpei has fewer sandy beaches than other Pacific islands, so forest ecotourism offers an alternative to beach tourism (Dominica provides a parallel example in the Caribbean). However, as is true for some other Asia–Pacific destinations, the forests of Micronesian islands, such as Pohnpei, will rarely be the primary attraction for visitors, but have great potential to complement dive sites and other primary attractions (Wylie 1994).

---

[1] Though not a focus of this working paper, dive tourism in the region illustrates the importance of forests not just for forest ecotourism, but also for marine and other forms of tourism, as well as for non–tourism industries (e.g. Hodgson and Dixon 1988).

Pacific islands must overcome distance from markets, difficulties of devoting sufficient marketing resources by small destinations (which illustrates the value of cooperative marketing on the regional level), and competition with existing regional and extra–regional attractions if they are to successfully develop ecotourism, or tourism generally. Thus, while several locations offer ecotourism potential, it is important not to become too optimistic (Wylie 1994; Valentine and Wylie 1993; Van't Slot 1995).

Agro-forestry also has the potential to serve as a tourism attraction, as well as to serve as a means for generating local inputs for the restaurant illustration (see Section 4.6). For example, visitor in Rota pay US$35 (as of 1993) for a fruit–tasting agro-forestry tour there (Valentine and Wylie 1993). In addition, there is potential to combine marine and forest resources, such as using sea kayaking tours that emphasize forest and cultural issues, including traditional construction of outrigger canoes.

Country Note: Thailand

According to Lohman (1993), forest cover in Thailand has declined rapidly since the 1950s, with particularly severe declines in the central and north–east regions. The causes of this decline include logging, development projects, and conversion to agriculture. State policy towards forests, commercial logging, and geo-political threats have been suggested as underpinning this decline (Lohman 1993). However, pressures for new approaches to land and forest rights are continuing to grow. According to Lohman (1993), these are the result of grassroot attempts at changing the nature of forest management and use. Some of the most visible of these has been with the securing of local control over community forests.

There appears to be a strong need for systems of land management in Thailand to be more collaborative and bottom up, sensitive to the variety of local needs that forests serve. But this is not straightforward, as there are a variety of local levels, each with different needs and wants, and different levels of forest service reliance (Lohman 1993). The task is to provide a mechanism that continues the tradition of grassroot activism.

Tourism Authority of Thailand (1997) statistics indicate 7 million international arrivals, the majority from East Asia, with 1995 total revenue of Bt190 billion (US$7.7 billion). Tourism is the country's largest foreign exchange earner, and continued growth is expected despite concerns that tourism is marketed better than it is managed (Muqbil 1995). Chudintra (1993) conservatively estimates that approximately 20 per cent of foreign visitors in 1990 participated in nature tourism activities, though this includes small–scale beach tourism. Most of the "nature tourists" are from the US, Europe, Australia and New Zealand, while tourists from East Asia and the Pacific tend to prefer city activities.

Perhaps Thailand's most famous ecotourism activity is jungle trekking in the northern mountainous area. Trips are led by a guide, often include rafting or elephant rides, and last three to five days on average (Chudintra 1993). Visits to national parks are also popular. National parks are managed by the Forestry Department, and Chudintra reports the following figures:

Year	Number of National Parks	Visitors (millions)
1986	58	4.4
1987	64	5.9
1988	69	6.8
1989	73	8.1
1990	85	9.5

As noted in Illustration 3.3, the domestic proportion of national park visitors has been increasing and stood at 85 per cent in 1990 (most of these are students travelling in large groups during summer vacation or long holidays) (Chudintra 1993).

Chudintra (1993) notes that tourism has generated many positive impacts, including new jobs and stronger awareness of nature conservation. However, it has also generated negative impacts, including inflation (land and general goods) and changes in social values. For example, younger generations in hilltribe areas have been influenced by tourism profits and have become more commercial and materialist–minded than prior generations.

The development of mass tourism within national parks has been a contentious issue in Thailand and exemplifies the difficulty of finding an appropriate balance between conservation and development. It is worth noting that an Institute of Ecotourism has been established at Srinakharinwirot University and that international ecotourism conferences have been held, with the second being in July 1996. That conference involved 150 delegates from 20 countries, as well as 80 Thai students.

4

Nature–Based Tourism: Issues, Matters and Reviews in Western Australia

Nature-Based Tourism: An Australian Perspective

Figure – A new Model for Nature-Based Tourism (Tourism WA 2004)

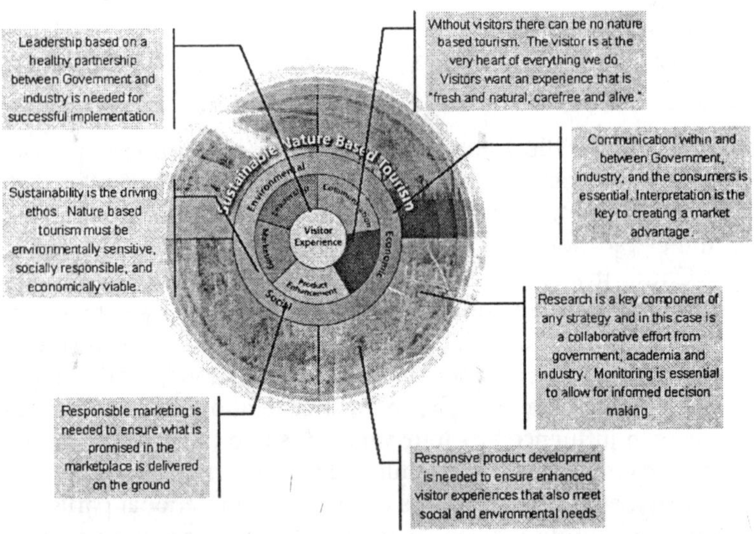

The development of nature-based tourism in a sustainable manner is guided by the need to enhance the visitor experience.

In 2004, Tourism WA released the strategy *"Keeping it Real – A Nature Based Tourism Strategy for Western Australia"*, thus adopting recommendations by the NBTAC.

The vision for this strategy is:

That nature-based experiences offered to visitors are real and sustainable.

Much of Western Australia's nature-based tourism product is based on experiences in protected areas (national parks, State forests, marine parks and other reserves) and interaction with the State's unique wildlife. There has been a dramatic growth in nature based tourism over the past two decades, with the number of operators licensed to undertake commercial activities in protected areas increasing from around 50 in 1994 to around 400 in 2006.

As a consequence of this growth and the increasing complexities associated with managing nature-based tourism activities, the Department of Environment and Conservation (DEC) and Tourism WA have been charged to undertake a "Review of Nature-Based Tourism."

The initiative was jointly announced by the Minister for the Environment and the Minister for Tourism on July 17, 2006 (a copy of the press release is included as Appendix A).

Tourism Co–ordinates was appointed to undertake this review, to be conducted in accordance with the following brief:

REVIEW OF NATURE-BASED TOURISM IN WESTERN AUSTRALIA: ISSUES AND OTHER RELEVANT MATTERS

The methodology applied for the review of Nature-Based Tourism (NBT) has been detailed earlier in this report and is strongly based on one–to–one interviews and a small number of written submissions.

During the past 15 years, NBT has been the subject of many studies and reports under a range of titles relating to eco–tourism, adventure tourism, wildlife tourism, tourism in protected areas, etc.

The growing relationship between protected areas and tourism during this time has prompted these reports, the majority of which generally seek to identify and address conflicts, real or perceived, that either have occurred, or may occur, from what many see as conflicting use requirements.

Rather than to duplicate important work already undertaken on NBT, this review has drawn on some of these reports, the views and findings of which are considered as relevant today as when compiled. In particular, the reports:

2003 CALM Licenced Tour Operator Survey Results
Prepared by Curtin Sustainable Tourism Centre

and

Licensing Nature Tourism Operators in Western Australia: A Review of Business Impediments and Recommendations for Reform

Prepared by Sabrina Genter, Jo Ann Beckwith and David Annandale

have been used as a source of information for this review.

While the brief for this review is specific and has been addressed item by item later in this report, it was considered that the most productive manner to achieve the outcomes desired was to first identify the issues considered by a range of stakeholders to be important for the future of NBT.

The following main section of the review is, therefore, a report on those issues, although the observations and recommendations are not necessarily supported by all stakeholders.

There is one unwavering principle in all aspects of this review report – that the sustainability of the protected areas is the number one priority at all times.

It is important, therefore, that the role and responsibilities of DEC be recognized and understood as a precursor to examining the issues.

DEC manages more than 25 million hectares of conservation and forest estate on behalf of the Western Australian public and the statutory bodies in which the land and water is vested.

These areas contain some of the State's most outstanding natural and cultural landscapes and wildlife, including tourist sites such as the Ningaloo Reef, the Purnululu massif, Mt. Augustus, the tall karri forests and wildlife, including whale sharks and dolphins.

Western Australia's wildlife and national parks are the foundation of the State's nature-based tourism industry. Without access to these areas and the opportunity to interact with wildlife, there would be no, or certainly a very limited, NBT industry.

NBT provides important economic and social benefits to the community. It is estimated that the value of the industry to the economy is in the billions of dollars. The economic impact of the Ningaloo Reef and Cape Range National Park to the Gascoyne community alone is estimated at around $140m per annum.

However, there is a need to manage these resources for both their intrinsic and instrumental values. The tourism industry has a vested interest in ensuring that the very values that it depends on to create its products and generate revenue are not degraded.

While the tension between use and conservation has eased over the years, differences in use philosophies will persist and so the key to achieving sustainable futures for both the tourism industry and the protected area system is good management.

DEC has a statutory responsibility to ensure that these natural and cultural values are protected in perpetuity for all Western Australians and for the full range of purposes and interests for which these reserves are provided. While being a highly important and influential sector, the tourism industry is only one of many stakeholders with an interest in protected areas.

The Conservation and Land Management Act 1984, provided the statutory basis for the management of land vested in DEC. The primary functions of the Chief Executive Officer (CEO) of DEC include:

- To manage land to which the Act applies (i.e. national parks, marine parks, State forests, etc.);
- To be responsible for the conservation and protection of flora and fauna throughout the State; and
- To promote and facilitate public recreation, in accordance with the Act.

In the case of national parks, marine parks and conservation parks, the CALM Act requires that these areas be managed in accordance with a management plan. The objectives of these plans are to:

> "fulfill so much of the demand for recreation by members of the public as is consistent with the proper maintenance and restoration of the natural environment, the protection of indigenous flora and fauna and the preservation of any features of archaeological, historic or scientific interest."

This provision provides a clear statement in regard to the constraints on the level and type of recreation and tourism activities that can occur in protected areas.

These statutory responsibilities are given further meaning in DEC's Corporate Plan 2002–2005, which identifies "creating sustainable community benefits" as one of four key strategic directions for the department.

Environmental sustainability is one of the primary objectives of DEC. In order to progress sustainability objectives in respect to NBT, DEC has instituted a system of licensing for any commercial activity that occurs on land and water it manages.

Licences are issued under the Conservation and Land Management Regulations 2002 by the CEO of DEC following consultation with relevant vested bodies (Conservation Commission of Western Australia or the Marine Parks and Reserves Authority) and with the approval of the Minister for the Environment.

The purpose of licences is to set conditions for the appropriate use of land and water to ensure that conservation and environmental sustainability objectives can be met. As such, licensing is a tool used to meet the statutory obligations placed on DEC under the CALM Act.

In a similar vein, DEC issues leases for persons and businesses to operate tourism ventures on land within national parks and State forests. Leases are issued by the CEO, following the same approvals and consultation process as for licences.

Issues

Licence/Lease Tenure

During the course of the review, the issue that raised the most comment from the tourism sector was that of the process of granting licences/leases for commercial operations within protected areas, and the terms and conditions under which they are approved to operate.

Whether marine or land-based, many commercial tour operators have concerns with the licensing/lease process, the tenure of leases and their general ability as tourism operators (TOs) to plan long term for business development.

Generally, TOs understand the role that licensing/leasing plays in managing protected areas. However, some believe the system is not fair and equitable.

These sentiments were echoed in the 2003 CALM Licensed Tour Operator Survey conducted by the Curtin Sustainable Tourism Centre. Twenty–three 'E' class TOs and 67 'T' class TOs were surveyed – only 36 per cent agreed with the statement that "Overall CALM licensing is fair and equitable for commercial operators."

While the principle of licences/leases is accepted, it is the processes, conditions and, in some cases, the cost that generates the most criticism from TOs – criticism that often is taken up on their behalf by Tourism WA and Tourism Council WA (TCWA).

DEC uses a two–class licence system – 'T' Class licences and 'E' Class licences.

The 'T' Class licence is a general use licence and, at the time of this review, 327 'T' Class licences were valid.

'T' Class Licence

General licensing information provided by DEC lists examples of 'T' Class licences as including safari tours, guided walks and general snorkel/dive charters. A 'T' Class licence is classified as unrestricted, with no current limitation on the number of licences available by application.

A 'T' Class licence must be renewed annually, unless specified levels of accreditation are achieved, so allowing an extension of the renewal period by either three or five years. 'T' Class licences are not transferable – a business purchaser simply applies for a new licence.

Special licensing provision is made for out–of–state operators who may seek to access protected areas in Western Australia once or twice a year. A two–month short season licence is available at a cost of $100 plus $50 application fee, compared with $300 plus $50 application fee for 12 months.

The initial 12–month licence period for a 'T' Class licence is regarded by some TOs as too short, with businesses having to meet additional administrative requirements and costs that apply when renewing on an annual basis. It also means that these licensees have to manage their businesses with little more vision than 12 months allows.

A five–year licence is available if the appropriate level of accreditation is achieved, recognizing the reduced management risk factor to DEC from an operator who has undergone the accreditation process.

However, it is a fact that some 'T' Class licence holders who are accredited, and therefore, have the right to extend their licence period to three or five years, have chosen not to.

From both a tourism and conservation point of view, it is important for all operators to successfully complete the accreditation process.

Without accreditation, the ability of the licensee to perform at the required level is considerably less certain because many start–up operators have limited basic knowledge of business operational needs and, in some cases, little understanding of the responsibilities that go with operating in a protected area.

Unfortunately, it is a fact of life that many start–up operators are chasing a lifestyle "dream" without any real understanding of the demands and responsibilities that come with a tourism operation, let alone one venturing into protected areas.

New entrants to the nature-based tourism industry (those seeking a licence from DEC, DPI, Fisheries and other agencies) should be fully informed of the requirements that will be placed on them before they enter the industry.

Ideally, 'T' Class licences should be issued to only accredited businesses, i.e. accreditation becomes compulsory, albeit that there is a danger that this approach might stifle innovation and not allow new operators and new products to emerge.

The opportunity and encouragement should always be there for new entrants, particularly in remote regional areas where it is often difficult to develop new product.

Nonetheless, it is time for tourism operators, and particularly those accessing protected areas, to lift the minimum standards of their business operations and to improve their understanding of the tourism industry and the requirements of operating within a protected area.

Accordingly, it is desirable that it be a prerequisite to achieve accreditation before being issued any form of operator licence requiring access to a protected area – DEC only licenses for protected areas. It is recognized that this may not always be practical given the requirements of some of the certification programmes, therefore some alternative type of process to qualify TOs before they are licensed may be required.

Tourism WA and TCWA have important roles to play in nurturing start–up operators through the accreditation process. It is not the role of DEC to train 'T' Class licence TOs, but simply to certify that they are competent to be licensed by virtue of their accreditation endorsement or pre–qualifications.

Start–up indigenous TOs, particularly in remote areas, may require the support services of Tourism WA/TCWA in fulfilling the licensing/accreditation requirements and clear procedures need to be put into place to accommodate this need.

It is recommended:

(1) That 'T' Class licences remain available on an unrestricted basis, for a 12–month period, subject to appropriate accreditation being achieved within six months of issue.
(2) That without operator accreditation, allowing tourism certification within six months, the licence is rescinded.
(3) That the maximum period for annual renewal of a 'T' Class licence is five years, with the current options of one and three years renewal periods to remain.
(4) That the two–month short season licence remains available where deemed appropriate by DEC.
(5) That Tourism WA and TCWA confirm responsibility for, and establish clear processes to providing assistance to, start–up tourism operators (TOs) requiring accreditation as a prerequisite to applying for a 'T' Class licence. Tourism WA/TCWA to assist DEC develop its On–line Training Programme (see recommendation 21 below) as a mechanism as part of the prequalification of TOs prior to a licence application.

There is also a need for government, as part of a whole of government approach, to take the requirements for TOs accreditation more seriously and to provide total support to the objective of lifting the standards in the delivery of tourism services.

The following process model is put forward as an example to be applied for a 'T' Class operator licence application:

Figure 1

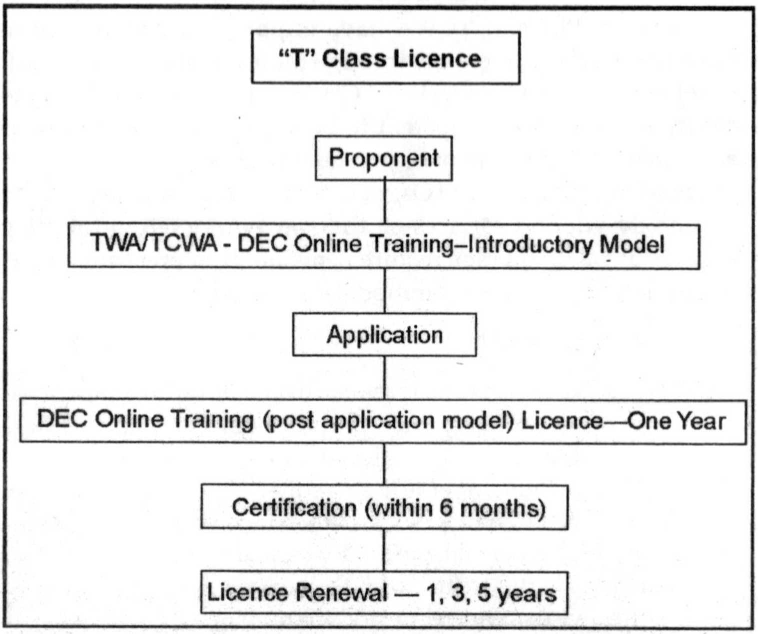

The current fee for a 'T' Class licence is $300 per annum (plus $50 application fee) and $100 (plus $50 application fee) for a short-term (two–month) licence.

Most TOs agree with the need for licensing and the application of a fee – 62 per cent of the respondents to the 2003 CALM Licensed Tour Operator Survey agreed that licence fees should cover the cost of administering and monitoring the system. This view was further supported in the Tourism WA 2006 survey "A Review of Nature-Based Tourism Operator and Investor Consultation."

The level of that fee will always be debatable. However, the present level of $300 per annum could not be regarded as being excessive. Where business operators become critical of costs is when there are multiple fees, e.g. Fisheries licence, Transport licences, plus the cost of accreditation.

DEC could offer incentives by having the one–year fee at cost recovery (estimated to be $500 [Fisheries fee is $600]) but have staged discounting of the three and five–year fee to encourage more operators to take up these options.

However, all of these are legitimate agency fees and simply must be accepted by businesses wanting to operate in a protected area. There may be scope to reduce some fees as an incentive for improved performance and/or longer licence periods, reducing administration costs.

DEC should monitor the fees level and look for such initiatives as a demonstration of its partnership arrangement with TOs. There may also be scope to introduce reduced cost "packaging" arrangements with other agencies like the Fisheries Department and the Department for Planning and Infrastructure, where multi licences are required by TOs.

"E" Class Licence

The 'E' Class licence is generally required when there are environmental and/or management reasons why licence numbers are required to be limited. Examples of 'E' Class licences include whale shark tours and boat tours in confined areas.

An 'E' Class licence is granted by an Expression of Interest (EOI) process and is currently issued for an initial five–year period and may be renewed for an additional five years. At the end of the 10–year maximum period, the licence is again open to a competitive EOI process.

'E' Class licences are not transferable. However, a buyer of a business can apply to DEC for a replacement 'E' Class licence. A replacement licence expires on the expiry date of the original licence.

At the time of this review, 48 'E' Class licences were valid.

Accreditation is compulsory for the issue of an 'E' Class licence.

While the maximum 10–year period works to provide the opportunity for new operators to enter the market, particularly in areas where the number of operators are limited for environmental reasons, there is a downside to this approach in that it does not encourage planning or investment beyond a 10–year timeframe.

Generally it takes many years for new tourism operators to develop marketing links and distribution networks and this effort can be lost if a licence is not renewed after 10 years.

From a tourism marketing point of view any change in business operation can be a major disruption to both product and destination awareness and could take a number of years to rectify as the new 'E' Class licence operator establishes a position in the marketplace.

There is also the potential for the business to be allowed to run down in the latter years, as uncertainty of renewal can result in operators cutting back on equipment and service upkeep costs.

The principal issue with the 'E' Class licence is the need to return to the competitive EOI process after 10 years.

The Tourism WA 2006 survey "A Review of Nature-Based Tourism Operator and Investor Consultation" further confirmed the very high levels of emotional and financial stress that TOs experience in relation to the renewal of licences.

Having spent 10 years developing a business, often as a family concern, the pressures of having to resubmit to an EOI process and the uncertainty that it brings, can be very telling on all concerned.

As a consequence, 'E' Class licence operators often have the approach that DEC is negative about NBT development, rather than a partner in helping their businesses grow.

The Tourism WA survey reports operators suggesting that:

> "'E' licences operate for a longer period (ideally indefinitely provided there are no significant breaches) so that there is an enhanced opportunity for the business to clear debts and invest in service improvements/ the provision of additional tourist experience."

This review supports such a view. However, consideration needs to be given to the implications of not having an expiry date on the licence.

The current 10 years maximum term allows DEC to review the progress of the business and to make environment impact assessments prior to re–applying the EOI process. A major concern for both DEC and Tourism WA is that without a specified maximum period for the licence, there is a risk that an under-performing operator would not be able to be removed/ replaced. Such a situation would have an adverse impact on the development of NBT.

It can also be expected that the lower the professional level of business operation, the greater the chance of adverse outcomes to the environment.

There is also concern that without a specified period for a licence there is a high risk that a proprietary value might result, with future compensatory cost implications for government, should a licence be rescinded.

Therefore, it is a matter of trying to find an approach to 'E' Class licensing that provides security and encouragement to the operator, while at the same time allowing DEC and Tourism WA to have flexibility in ensuring a high standard of tourist product and service delivery. At the same time, it will be critical to not allow a situation to develop that generates a proprietary value to the licence itself.

"E" Class licences should:

- Protect and enhance the visitor experience.
- Protect the environment.
- Drive product improvement.
- Protect government from exposure to compensation and liability (as happened in the taxi industry).
- Improve business security.

It is also noted that on a number of occasions those looking to invest and develop high–quality bush camp type infrastructure developments have had to make do with a "E" Class licence instead of a standard lease. It is difficult to attract nationally and internationally branded operators to invest under these conditions because they do not face similar tenure conditions when dealing with competitor destinations.

It is recommended:

(6) That 'E' Class licences continue to be issued through the EOI process and that the initial period be extended to up to 10 years, with annual audits against predetermined Key Performance Indicators (KPIs) and with a renewal period of up to 5 years, giving a total licence of up to 15 years.

(7) That the licence be subject to ongoing conformity with the issue conditions and KPIs applied by DEC, which will vary, and can be varied, from time to time, based on the

circumstances of specific protected areas. A significant breach of those conditions or KPI performance failure, to empower DEC to rescind the licence.

(8) That at the end of the maximum 15 years licence period, DEC has the option to reallocate the licence through a competitive EOI process. To reward best practice, part of the criteria for assessment should place high weighting on TOs who perform well in the annual audits and to take into consideration what is in "the public interest" when considering the options. EOIs should commence at least two years out from the expiry of a licence.

(9) That in adopting these recommendations, legal advice be first sought in relation to potential implications relating to proprietary value and possible government exposure to future compensation in the advent of a licence not being renewed.

(10) That all 'E' Class licences have a caveat applied that will allow DEC to rescind the licence in circumstances where it is deemed that the continued operation of that licence poses a threat, or threats, to the environment.

(11) The DEC has the ability to offer those licensed operators who have a proven track record, the option of converting the licence to a lease, where appropriate.

These recommendations seek to remove the most criticized aspect of 'E' Class licences – the requirement for TOs to have to return to a competitive EOI process, regardless of how successful their business operations are and how well they have met their licence conditions and KPIs.

On the other hand, DEC and Tourism WA need to ensure that the best level of operation is in place and can be upgraded through the competitive EOI process where standards of operation are not considered to be at a sufficiently high level.

It is believed both aims can be achieved through the adoption of the above recommendations, provided that the question of proprietary value can be addressed.

To have a policy requiring a mandatory competitive EOI process after 15 years, even where the previous licence holder is a highly regarded and even the preferred operator, not only puts fair pressure on that operator, but creates a situation that may see other applicants commit considerable resources for what, to all intents and purposes, is a forgone conclusion.

The following process model is put forward as an example to be applied for a 'E' Class operator licence application:

Figure 2

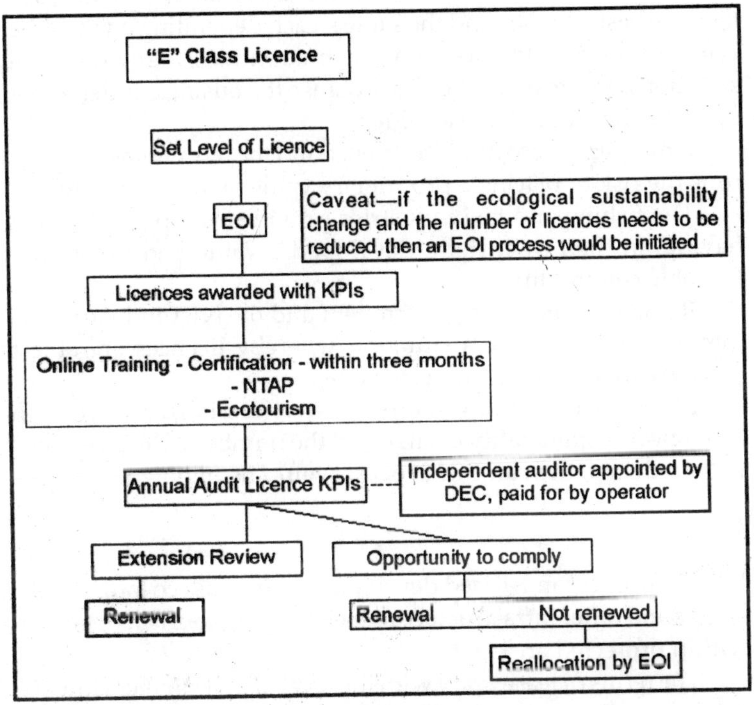

Where there is a fully issued limited number of 'E' Class licences in a particular area, this will mean that the only way a new operator can enter the marketplace within a 15–year period of the initial licence issue, is to buy out an existing business (subject to approving a replacement licence), or where the operator's licence has been revoked for failing to meet licence conditions or designated KPIs, through the re–applied EOI process.

If there is only one licence in a particular area, there will need to be checks and balances in place to enable DEC to ensure that the business operates in an appropriate manner, in what would be a monopoly situation.

The effect of this approach will be to give business owners confidence in their future, which in turn will encourage further investment and commitment to product development. Marketing initiatives and distribution channels will also remain intact, protecting the business, destination and the customer from the disruptions that flow from a change in business operation.

The fact that the business and licence are currently regarded as separate entities is still somewhat of an issue as, in some cases, they are basically one and the same – each depending on the other. With the business and licence as separate entities, the owner equity situation becomes complicated, because the business is dependent upon the licence to have a value.

However, to recognize the licence and the business as one entity runs the risk of placing a proprietary value on the licence itself.

The fishing and taxi industries provide examples of licences having, in their own right, developed a value and becoming a tradable commodity.

It will be in both the government and the NBT industry's best interests to not create a situation whereby licences are able to generate their own proprietary value.

A caveat over the issue of all licences is that should the ecological sustainability change and the number of licences needs to be reduced, then an EOI process would be initiated.

Leases

Leases apply to land–based developments such as eco lodges, safari camps and other infrastructure associated with tourism operations within protected areas.

The terms of leases vary with the level of investment. However, it is generally accepted that the maximum period would be 21 years, with a 21–year option – considered to be an adequate period for most investment amortization.

Leases are subject to an EOI process and are assignable subject to DEC/Ministerial approval.

While a 21 by 21 years lease may be appropriate for the majority of investments and is the maximum period currently available under the DEC Act, there needs to be provision to consider longer periods if significant developments are to be attracted to support nature-based tourism within protected areas.

There needs to be flexibility and a judgment of "each case on its own merits" if appropriate lease arrangements are to be put into place.

Before an EOI is called, DEC needs to clearly identify the land use area and identify/address matters that might have a commercial impact on any development, e.g. native title, no–go areas, water sourcing, access roads, etc.

The EOI process should also include input from Tourism WA and other relevant agencies, such as DPI and Fisheries, where marine licences are involved and require land–base facilities.

It is recommended:

(12) That DEC maintains the EOI process for issuing leases and applies an "each case on its own merits" approach in assessing the period of the lease. The lease period to be determined by such factors as environmental impacts, level of investment, the anticipated level of return on that investment, KPI compliance and conformity with protected area management plans. Lease terms to be set at the discretion of the Director General.

(13) That a legislative provision be made to remove the current maximum lease period of 21 years, with a 21 years option.

This recommendation addresses the most criticized aspect of being a lease operator within a protected area. Throughout the review, there was strong representation for a change in lease tenure to enable operators to see, and plan for, a future for their businesses.

A number of lease holders have large investments in both land–based facilities and transport vehicles. Despite the generally accepted position that DEC is unlikely to not renew a lease without there being a major breach of conditions or KPI performance, there is always a feeling of uncertainty.

The uncertainty can lead to lower levels of investment, reduced support from the banking sector and a lessened commitment to business development, particularly as the lease expiry date gets closer.

Regardless of the period of lease, the issue conditions and/or KPIs will be critical to the management process.

While there will be core KPIs in all agreements, each case will require specific provisions relevant to the site of operation.

A "one size fits all" approach will not work, with each set of KPIs needing to be specifically designed to meet the circumstances which will change with location, investment level, style of operation, etc.

The tourism accreditation programme should be linked to the KPIs to add to the quality of management and to provide consistency in the delivery of services and facilities. The accreditation programme is examined in greater detail later in this review.

KPIs should be reviewed annually and DEC needs to have the capacity to take immediate remedial action in circumstances where KPIs are not met. The ultimate action should be the termination of the lease where breaches are significant and clearly threaten the integrity of the protected area.

There should be facility to change KPIs at DEC's discretion in circumstances where ecological conditions change and this should be undertaken in consultation with the lessee. In these instances, there needs to be recognition of the lead time for the tourism industry to effect changes that have an impact in the marketplace.

Business Sustainability

An issue raised by operators is the matter of considering business sustainability and competitive forces. There is a perception that DEC does not generally consider sustainability factors in evaluating an application for a licence or lease, leaving it to "market forces" to determine the outcome of an individual business enterprise, or for that matter, the business sector itself.

This approach is consistent with the direction that the State Government has taken in all tourism operator licensing areas over the past 20 years, particularly in the transport sector, e.g. coach, ferry, charter boat, etc. where business viability is a matter to be determined by the proponent.

There are three main scenarios that apply to this issue:

- DEC consideration of business sustainability issues when setting the level of licences for an area of activity;
- DEC consideration of the business sustainability impact of decisions (viability issues) on operators when changing the number of 'E' Class licences (usually increasing competition) for a particular area or activity, and

- DEC consideration of the business sustainability impact of other management decisions that may have viability implications on tourism operators.

The tourism industry overall can be adversely effected through the impact of a business performing badly, with a resultant outcome of bad customer relations, a reluctance of the wholesale sector to deal with like products and a potential to effect the viability of other operators.

As an example, the market may currently sustain two operators providing similar programmes in the same location. These operators may have committed considerable time and resources to developing their product and distribution linkages to the point that their businesses have now begun to provide an acceptable return.

The entry of a third operator at this point can be devastating to the business success of all three unless the market is able to be expanded and so often this is not the case, with the new entrant basing business success on taking a share of the existing market rather than developing a new one.

Under this scenario all lose – the operators, the destination, the customer, the tourism industry and local communities that gain flow on benefits from visitors to their areas.

While it can be philosophically accepted as a "market force" outcome, these circumstances are very damaging to the tourism industry and the overall image of tourism in Western Australia. These effects are felt even stronger in regional areas where it is often difficult to encourage operators and where seasonality brings its own additional challenges.

An example of where "market forces" can have an adverse effect where seasonality is an issue is where other non–tourism businesses turn to tourism for a short–term gain at the expense of the long–term tourism operator. This could be a wet line fishing vessel that turns to tourism operator during the time the fishing industry is in recess or a school bus operator who becomes a tour bus operator during the school holiday periods.

As tourism is an adjunct to the core business of these short–term operators, they have the ability to operate at a lower price level and can undercut legitimate tourism operators who have invested in equipment and services that are generally at a far higher level.

It is a dilemma because governments do not want to be seen as trying to influence market forces, yet, on the other hand, want to see business develop successfully, want to encourage new businesses to start up and to generally foster development of tourism state wide.

The extent to which Government becomes involved in business sustainability factors will always be a balance, however, in the case of businesses operating in protected areas, DEC has a responsibility to ensure that outcomes have the greatest chance of success because the alternative can have an adverse effect on the protected areas themselves.

There are, however, implications in regard to the National Competition Policy and these will need to be addressed.

It is recommended:

(14) That DEC takes into consideration the business sustainability factors associated with issuing a licence or lease to the extent that there may be an adverse impact on other tourism operators and/or the tourism industry, arising from such management actions and decisions.

(15) That DEC draws on outside expertise, such as Tourism WA and/or business analysts, in taking economic factors into consideration before making a decision on an application for a licence or lease.

(16) That the implications of the National Competition Policy in regard to Recommendations 14 and 15 be examined.

Transferability of 'E' Class Licences

There is no issue with the transferability of 'T' Class licences because these licences are readily available upon application, subject to the applicant meeting the necessary entry requirements.

'E' Class licences restrict competition on the basis of maintaining the ecological sustainability of the site or activity allowed by the licence. This is the only public interest criteria applicable in the National Competition Policy that actually allows a restriction of competition in a protected area.

It follows that the principal consideration of an 'E' Class licence is the protection of the environment. This is why applicants for 'E' Class licences have to demonstrate to DEC a high level of experience and qualifications (including an ongoing commitment to accreditation) when conducting businesses in sensitive areas and should expect a correspondingly higher level of monitoring and management in relation to these activities.

'E' Class licences are not transferable, and because of the limited competitive market in which they are obtained and subsequently operate, confers a certain value on the licence. The licence and the business are in effect separate entities, reducing the security of the business and as a result, can have the affect of taking away the incentive for further investment in and improvement and development of the business.

The 'E' Class licence currently requires an EOI process every 10 years and only allows for the purchaser of a business to be issued with a new licence for the unexpired period remaining at the time the business changed hands.

Other studies have identified this situation as a major issue for operators who believe that transferability of licences will generate greater investment in the industry and make it easier to secure funding from lending institutions.

These are valid claims and the issue is linked to Recommendation 8 of this review for the option to extend licences beyond the initial 15 years period to allow for business continuity.

If the tourism industry is to develop in a strong and meaningful manner, the business structures to be applied to operators in protected areas should be the same as elsewhere and certainly not incorporate disincentives for growth.

While DEC allows licences to be replaced, the absence of an unfettered licence transferability policy is perceived to reduce the capital value of the business.

From DEC's stand point, the non–transferability policy maintains a level of control over the quality and experience of operators entering the elite (often environmentally sensitive) end of the protected area spectrum of tourism opportunities and ensures that expensive Government payouts are not required if licences need to be absorbed for environmental or other reasons.

It is also seen as protecting the integrity of the EOI process whereby unsuccessful applicants not able to demonstrate an ability to meet sustainability criteria can then enter the system via a replacement licence.

Current policy is that DEC licences should not be allowed to gain a proprietary (ownership) value so to remove the compensation risk to Government if, for appropriate reasons (such as the recent decision at Monkey Mia to reduce the number of licences), it were necessary to cancel or refuse to renew a licence Section.

It is recognized that proprietary value would be gained through an expectation, subject to compliance with conditions, that the licence will be renewed. Currently, DEC ensures no such value attaches by having conditions that ensure the licence holder is aware that at the end of the renewal (second) period of the licence, it ceases to exist and is reallocated through a competitive process.

The model proposed in this chapter (see Figure 2) proposes to extend the maximum period for an 'E' Class licence to 15 years before, at the discretion of the CEO of DEC, it is either renewed, or reallocated by an EOI process. The potential to reactivate the competitive EOI process should protect against the risk of the licence gaining a proprietary value, with the annual audits providing existing operators a method of demonstrating their standard of operation.

The option for the reallocation of licences after 15 years by an EOI will not open the Government to the risk of compensation if a licence is cancelled or not renewed because of reasons other than non-compliance with conditions.

The CALM Act as it stands [Sections 97A (7) and 101(2)] gives absolute discretion to the Director General (CEO), which means that there are limits to those proprietary rights. This is consistent with the DEC position that it should retain the right to ensure that an operator conducting activities in sensitive areas is suitably experienced and qualified.

The current replacement licence process for E Class licences is consistent with the requirement of the Act and provides a process similar to a lease assignment, where the new licence holder assumes the same terms and conditions of the original licence.

The same requirements should apply to replacement licences as to lease assignments in that DEC should not unreasonably refuse a replacement subject to the applicant demonstrating that they meet the specified criteria.

Section 101(3) allows the CEO of DEC to transfer the rights of a licence at his/her discretion. Using the term "Transfer" may convey the concept more clearly than the current term "Replacement", as long as it is understood that DEC can refuse a transfer at its discretion.

It is recommended:

(17) That the current replacement licence process for 'E' Class licences remains, but to use the term "Transfer" in accord with Section 101(3) of the CALM Act.

(18) That DEC maintains the right to not allow a transfer of an 'E' Class licence.

(19) That DEC, in adopting recommendations 17 and 18, first seek legal advice in relation to possible implications for Government in respect to conferring proprietary value on DEC commercial operations licences and the potential for claims of compensation in the event of licence withdrawal for reasons other than non–compliance with licence conditions.

Commercial versus Non–commercial

During the course of the review, a number of comments were received about perceived inconsistencies in the approach to commercial 'T' Class operators accessing protected areas, compared with non–commercial.

Commercial operators must have a licence, which is issued annually (or every three or five years), where non–commercial operators must apply for a permit for every entry into a protected area. Some non–commercial operators who use a protected area on a number of occasions in a year feel that this is an unnecessary administrative burden.

DEC is working with Outdoors WA to develop a permit system for non–commercial groups where it is appropriate.

School groups do not require a licence, even if the schools require a payment for participation. While "commercial" is defined in the regulations, the school group situation raises the question as to what is commercial and what is not.

It is recognized that if a school group engages a commercial operator to deliver the programme, that operator still needs to be licensed even though the school group may be entitled to a waiver of entry fees where they apply.

These arguments lead to the view that, whether commercial or non–commercial, the same use is being made of protected areas. Therefore, the same conditions of access should apply.

DEC's position is that all users need to comply with the regulations.

There is a need to more closely align the use requirements and procedures for access to protected areas by users, be they commercial, non–commercial or free independent travellers.

It is recommended:

(20) That non–commercial groups be given the option of a 12–month permit, where appropriate, for access to protected areas where their activities are conducted on a regular basis.

Licence/Lease Planning/Approval Process

All commercial users of protected areas are looking for the "one–stop shop" for the planning/approval processes that apply for licences and leases.

In many cases, a number of government agencies are required to issue a licence to enable a single operator to commence business. The principal agencies are DEC, Fisheries and DPI, each with different requirements and each with a different process of administration.

Most start–up operators are small businesses, with some owners that find it difficult to understand the systems, points of contact and the fact that at every point there is usually a cost.

It becomes even more difficult for potential operators based in regional areas where the levels of advice and support may be harder to secure.

Many new operators are not business people in the true sense, but rather are people who have a passion for being in the tourism industry as an adjunct to their affinity with nature, further compounding the problems of dealing with the necessary administrative and regulatory requirements.

This can particularly apply to the start–up of indigenous tourism ventures.

Be that as it may, a number of these low level start–ups have, over the years, proven to be very successful for both the individual and the tourism industry and the administrative systems need to be in place to encourage more participants, not to frustrate them.

While a "one–stop shop" might be the ideal, this will be very difficult to achieve because of the different regulatory requirements of each agency, the objectives of which are sometimes in conflict with the other.

What is more achievable is a streamlining of the process, particularly through the application of information technology, e.g. use of the internet.

Through this medium, the planning and approval process can be designed to incorporate the needs of all authorities in an endeavour to as close as possible, create a "one–stop shop."

The Queensland Government is moving down this path with the creation of a website (www.smartservice.qld.gov.au) that will co–ordinate applications through various agencies. The site is under development, but already it offers a booking service for national parks – refer to the later Bookings Section of this review.

A website that provided the information required by each relevant agency and then enabled an online application to be distributed to each of them for processing, would go a long way towards achieving the illusive "one–stop shop."

While DEC has a responsibility for the licensing process to allow commercial access to protected areas, the agency arguable does not have a role in training for good business management or in providing education on the tourism industry. While these qualities are an influence in, if not a prerequisite to, obtaining a licence/lease, the delivery of this knowledge is more the responsibility of others.

DEC's current "Online Tour Operator Training" programme has been well received by the industry and is currently mandatory for all licence holders within three months of obtaining the licence. The current format serves to demonstrate that tour operators have a general understanding of the basic requirements for operating within the DEC estate. This online training was always intended as an introduction to the concept of online training.

The ultimate goal would be to develop a state–wide training package for tour operators and their staff which accredits them with a Certificate III in Nature-Based Tourism. The package could be modelled on the National Training Information Service (NTIS) Tourism Training Package or draw together competency units to form a new package specifically for national and marine park tours.

The package would be required to address key issues associated with the management of commercial tourism operators, their staff and visitors and could deliver modules such as:

- *General knowledge* – licence requirements, safety, best environmental practice, managing social experience, etc.
- *Activity knowledge* – specifically deals with the management of particular activities in a general sense
- *Park knowledge* – specifically deals with individual park knowledge for parks which make up the tour, including interpreting the landscape, environment, species and cultural heritage.

Potential operators and staff would be required to nominate each park they intended to visit within the tour, allowing the training package to draw the nominated park units to make up the tailored package serving two purposes:

- The operator gets a tailored package specific to their requirements; and
- Adding parks would make the modules larger, therefore discouraging application to all parks and ultimately reducing the latent capacity associated with 'broad scale' applications.

In order to meet the requirements of accredited assessment, the online tool would need to include at least three different assessment components, such as:

(a) Online test (written, multiple choice and short answer);
(b) A case study scenario,
(c) Delivery of DEC/Park information to park visitors (face to face or via video tape).

In order to engage participants, the package would need to be multi–sensory.

The training package development would need to be driven by a project officer responsible for coordinating a consultant to build the software and DEC staff to input into the material.

The training package would then need to be delivered by a large Registered Training Organization, such as TAFE or a university, because DEC would not like to become involved in the administration associated with accredited teaching. If outsourcing delivery, a fee would need to be levied.

Two examples of where similar styles of package have been achieved include the Online Tour Operator Training for Kakadu Operators, as well as the Great Barrier Reef Marine Park Authority's "Onboard" Tourism Operators Handbook for the Great Barrier Reef.

The development of this programme would need to be resourced and could act as an entry qualification into NBT and would need to be phased in.

In particular, Tourism WA and TCWA have roles in this regard and should play a part in the licence/lease application process.

This can be facilitated through an internet application process that can be designed to draw on the advice and training programmes provided by TCWA through the accreditation programme, and guidelines for tourism developers available through Tourism WA.

It is recommended:

(21) That DEC/Tourism WA initiates the development of a tourism-based website information and licence application facility, for both land and marine-based tourism operators. The application system to have links with other relevant agencies (e.g. Department of Planning and Infrastructure and Department of Fisheries), with the DEC licence application models proposed earlier in this review being applied.

(22) That the online training component of the process be resourced and developed by Tourism WA and TCWA, as manager of the National Tourism Accreditation Programme.

(23) That a specific turn around time for processing applications be set by agreement of all agencies involved.

Booking System

The lack of a booking system for camping within protected areas and available to the general public is seen by many users as a management deficiency.

Aside from not allowing DEC to more efficiently monitor park usage, those looking for a unique nature-based experience are often disappointed when it transpires that one or more groups are at the same location at the same time. This can apply at sites such as camping areas, abseiling sites and rock climbing walls.

The nature-based experience is somewhat diminished when visitors to the site (at the same time) get beyond a certain number – the actual number depends on the attraction/experience expectation.

A booking system would allow flexibility in planning for visits to protected areas, particularly by groups who have a larger impact on the ambience of a site.

A booking system must be internet based and could incorporate a number of support services, such as education material for individual areas, park pass issuing and payment, DEC Alert bulletins, links to other sites, etc.

The Queensland Government currently operates an internet booking system for its national parks – www.qld.gov.au/camping. This is an example of the approach that could be taken in WA.

It is recommended:

(24) That DEC makes available an internet-based booking system for camping and other specific activities such as abseiling, climbing and caving, where appropriate.

(25) That such a booking system be integrated with the tourism distribution networks and be developed as part of the Tourism E–marketplace that other organizations, such as Visitor Centres, can access.

Introduction of a booking system is also relevant to the issue of threshold management examined later in this review.

The Role of DEC as a Tourism Operator

The review process encountered a number of philosophical arguments against DEC being a tourism operator where private sector management could be attracted, e.g. The Tree Top Walk.

Most of these arguments are based on the grounds that DEC's core business is conservation and land management (as indicated by the department's previous name – Conservation & Land Management) and environmental protection and that the agency's expertise in tourism marketing is very limited and under– resourced.

That tourism is also not a major focus of DEC is also seen as a restriction on the further development of a major attraction like the Tree Top Walk, which could benefit from the addition of additional facilities such as a coffee shop/café.

The fact that DEC is a government department is also seen to place it under political pressure when the agency is perceived to be engaging in commercial activities that compete with neighbouring businesses and communities.

Technically, the National Competition Policy guidelines should nullify any advantages Government might have in running a business that may compete (or is perceived to compete) with private businesses. Nonetheless, the perception of unfair competition will always persist.

While there is some basis to these arguments, tourism industry operators interviewed during the review were generally most supportive of DEC's management of protected areas and the facilities within them.

As DEC is responsible for the control and management of some 70 per cent of Western Australia's nature-based product, there is no question that the agency has an important role in tourism.

During the last 15 years, this role has become more accepted within the agency, which has undergone a significant change in culture in the recognition of tourism as a legitimate management tool and source of revenue to be applied to greater protection of the resource.

The question is: to what extent does DEC become involved in day–to–day tourism activities? Does it restrict its activities to land/ marine management, adding tourist attraction management and operation where the private sector is reluctant to participate? Or does it become a front line tourism operator as is the current situation with the Tree Top Walk?

From DEC's perspective, its operations that have a commercial element are not currently considered to be commercial operations. Rather, they are regarded as a platform for building awareness and delivering an understanding and appreciation of the natural and cultural world through professional education, interpretation programmes and activities.

These sites are seen as providing a rare opportunity for the agency to sell its conservation and management messages to a significant number of people in a captured situation. The commercial returns that accrue from some of these facilities help to offset the costs of facility management, maintenance and conservation activities across the region.

DEC's approach to tourism is understandable and reflects a "means to an end" philosophy based on the agency's core role of environmental management. DEC has not, to this point, adopted a role as a front line tourism operator.

The relatively low level of resources applied to its tourism area is a further reflection of DEC's current commitment to not being fully in the tourism industry.

However, the fact is that the gradual evolution of DEC's involvement in the tourism industry has reached a point where it is no longer appropriate or practical to treat tourism as an adjunct to the agency's previous core land/marine management activities.

By virtue of the magnitude of the tourist attractions under its control, DEC needs to take the final evolutionary step and recognize that it has a role as a front line tourism operator.

Where DEC designs, constructs and operates tourism infrastructure, facilities or amenities, then the agency should operate similar to a tour operator. DEC should in this case be able to participate in tourism distribution systems where it is a good business decision to do so.

In doing so, it must be accepted that the role and resourcing of DEC's tourism unit must be significantly expanded and also supported by an overall internal cultural change. The cultural change must recognize that protected areas are tourism products and that tourism is a desired and legitimate industry in which the agency is to be a major player.

This expanded tourism role will incorporate trade and consumer marketing, participation at trade and consumer shows, co–operative involvement with regional tourism organizations, brochure production, advertising, etc. and a revision of the Memorandum of Understanding (MOU) with Tourism WA.

At this point, no attempt has been made to quantify the resources that will be required for DEC to meet these new tourism obligations.

It is recommended:

(26) That when DEC directly operates tourism products it does so in line with established tourism business principles.

(27) That a review be taken of the role of DEC's Tourism Unit and that the Unit be restructured and resourced at a level to enable it to carry out that role.

(28) That DEC initiates a programme of internal change that has all areas of the agency understanding and supporting DEC's important role in tourism. Also, Tourism WA to implement an internal programme to ensure that its staff recognize and understand DEC's environmental and management requirements.

Accreditation

Two main tourism accreditation programmes operate in Western Australia.

The tourism business accreditation scheme – National Tourism Accreditation Programme (NTAP) –developed by Tourism WA and managed under licence by TCWA. This programme has subsequently been adopted by Victoria, Tasmania, Northern Territory, ACT and South Australia.

NTAP has developed a nature-based tourism module that attaches to the programme and applies to businesses operating in protected areas and other natural areas.

The Ecotourism Association of Australia (Ecotourism Australia or EA) operates a national ecotourism and nature-based accreditation scheme, called Eco–certification. This is highly relevant to protected areas and provides three levels of increasing compliance. Eco–certification also includes a business module similar to NTAP.

However, the development of a national tourism accreditation programme has not been without its difficulties.

In 1999, the Commonwealth Government's White Paper on Tourism highlighted the need to establish a genuine industry–led national, voluntary tourism certification system within an established, and more comprehensive national framework.

In 2003 a National Tourism Accreditation Working Group was established with $2m in funding. Australian park agencies were included as key stakeholders, with the Department of Industry, Tourism and Resources (DITR) recognizing that tourism certification programmes have not adequately met the needs of protected area managers.

The 1999 model was dissolved and Tourism Accreditation Australia Limited (TAAL) created. TAAL is an Incorporated Association with Board membership reflecting the sectorial and geographic interests of the Australian tourism industry.

DITR also produced, in cooperation with state and territory park agencies, a draft Standard for Commercial Tour Operator Certification in Protected Areas. The Standard details the essential requirements to be included in any tourism certification programme operating in a protected area.

The new National Tourism Certification approval body (TAAL) was to have ensured that these guidelines were addressed when approving applications for certification programmes that operate in protected areas.

In 2004, the Federal Government withdrew funding for the implementation of the plan and in mid–2005, the Federal Minister for Tourism announced that the $2m allocated in the Tourism White Paper for tourism accreditation would be reallocated to Decipher Technologies Pty Ltd (a business arm of the Sustainable Tourism Cooperative Research Centre) to develop a tourism business and accreditation portal.

The proposed website is meant to "assist industry to develop and market tourism accreditation and relevant products." As a consequence of this change in policy by the Federal Government, the draft Standard for Commercial Tour Operator Certification in Protected Areas has not been adopted.

The lack of a standard national accreditation scheme is most unfortunate and creates a range of problems, particularly in relation to operators who cross state borders.

Be that as it may, the TAAL managed NTAP scheme remains an effective model, albeit that there are a number of areas applying to Western Australia that require further enhancement.

The recognition of the accreditation scheme by DEC is undoubtedly the strongest endorsement given by any part of the tourism industry. The fact that DEC links its licensing processes with accreditation not only improves the quality of operator standards, but gives credibility to the scheme itself.

The biggest argument against accreditation by operators is that it is difficult to quantify the value of accreditation in a market sense when non–accredited operators are still generating business—"why should I go through all of the trouble and costs of accreditation when my competitor has not and accreditation is unlikely to make any difference to his or my business?"

For an accreditation scheme to work, it must have value to both the customer and the operator. Whether this outcome is currently being achieved is still debatable within the industry.

To date, the "carrot" rather than the "big stick" approach has been applied to attracting operators to the scheme, using incentives such as additional marketing opportunities with Tourism WA, reduced insurance premiums and, in the case of DEC, extended period for licence renewal.

These incentives have had almost no impact. The 330 'T' Class operators have had the opportunity since 2002 to obtain three– to five–year licences after achieving certification from one or more of the tourism certification programmes. The number of 'T' Class operators with NTAP accreditation in Western Australian protected areas in 2004/05 was 95. This represents less than a third of 'T' Class businesses operating in the State's protected area system.

As at 30 June 2005, only 36 of the 95 'T' Class operators eligible to take out longer–term licences had chosen to take advantage of the privilege, suggesting that either security of licence is not a concern to operators or the costs associated with certification outweigh other benefits including the incentives offered by DEC.

Ideally, both types of accreditation should be compulsory and DEC is in a strong position to play a leadership role in this regard because of the sensitive nature of operating within a protected area.

However, a whole–of–industry approach is required. It is not appropriate for DEC to lead the further uptake of accreditation through policy of compulsory uptake, unless this is supported by complementary action by Tourism WA, such as conditional access to marketing and promotion channels and financial support for marketing of both accreditation programmes and the improvements to auditing systems.

In the section of this review relating to 'T' Class licences, it has been recommended that accreditation becomes compulsory within six months of the issue of a 'T' Class licence, or that licence is rescinded.

Responsibility for assisting potential TOs to achieve the required training and accreditation rests with Tourism WA and TCWA. Tourism WA has a role in assisting operators in obtaining accreditation utilizing such resources as the Better Business Blitz programme.

It is recognized, however, that until NTAP, through TCWA, is able to deliver an accreditation programme that meets DEC's requirements, which will require separate programmes, or "bolt–ons", for such diverse tourism operations as eco–tours, safari tours, marine tours, guided bush walking, abseiling, etc., there will be administration difficulties.

It is recommended:

(29) That Tourism WA and DEC, in association with TCWA and Ecotourism Australia (EA), finalize accreditation programmes applicable to meeting the accreditation needs of protected area management and that those programmes become compulsory for 'T' Class licences (after 6 months from issue).

Once this has been achieved it would then be feasible to implement the 'T' Class model outlined in Figure 1. Following this, Tourism WA and DEC should initiate a system (phased implementation) to combine into a single process the auditing of the certification requirements and KPI functions as outlined in the model.

A tightening of the accreditation scheme and a regular and efficient audit of operators will be a critical component of the licence/lease tenure recommendations included in this review.

Rather than using the licence/lease procedures as a main means to control activities within protected areas, a combination of accreditation and KPI standard setting and auditing can be applied for the same effect.

DEC Communications

DEC has an extensive stakeholder network that requires well defined and relevant communication mechanisms.

In some cases, the frequency of communication is required on a daily basis, in others simply at regular intervals, such as quarterly meetings.

One of the key issues arising from the 2003 CALM Licensed Tour Operator Survey was that the DEC Tourism Unit did not communicate well with its licensed operators.

In the time following that survey, DEC has developed a sophisticated system of communication with licensed operators and other tourism industry stakeholders. These include:

- Regular news flashes (Tour Operator Alerts) regarding daily items of importance, such as road closures, fire control issues, weather alerts, etc;
- Regional forums with operators in conjunction with TCWA;
- A new on–line Touring WA Newsletter;
- Updated and improved website information;
- Online Tour Operator training course;
- Improvements to Tour Operator Handbooks; and
- Reduced approvals timeframe for most 'T' Class licences.

Communication does not appear to be as big an issue as it was at the time of the 2003 survey.

However, there are regular circumstances where different stakeholders have conflicting needs, making it even more important that DEC has the right processes in place that allow effective communication.

Following are comments on communication and relationships as they apply to different key stakeholders:

Tourism WA

Tourism WA, as the State Government agency responsible for tourism marketing and development, has a major investment in the DEC estate, which represents some 70 per cent of Western Australia's nature-based tourism product.

The fact that Tourism WA has no direct powers in relation to this estate, has, for many years, been a source of frustration for that agency and to some extent for the tourism industry in general.

For many years, there was a total standoff – conservation versus tourism – with the day–to–day management of the estate being based to a large extent on restricting access. This approach was totally opposed by tourism interests, which wanted better access to sites like the Pinnacles (Nambung National Park), Hamersley Ranges (Karijini) and the Bungle Bungles (Purnululu).

Over time and with increasing tourism numbers, there became a gradual recognition of the fact that the two interests were in fact compatible and one could support the needs of the other.

In more recent times, a number of mechanisms have been put into place to improve communications and the working relationship between DEC and Tourism WA, including:

- The entering into a MOU between both parties;
- The setting up of a tourism unit within DEC (formerly CALM);
- The establishing of a Tourism Industry Reference Group (TIRG) by DEC (CALM);
- The development of closer day–to–day contact between officers of both agencies;
- The involvement of Tourism WA in the EOI process for licences/leases; and
- DEC and Tourism WA jointly undertaking the Landbank proposal to identify and develop major attractions within protected areas.

As well, DEC (CALM) has:

- Taken the initiative in developing a major attraction like the Tree Top Walk;
- Participated in trade and consumer marketing activities;

- Developed its own trade show to promote nature-based tourism;
- Joined tourism industry bodies such as TCWA and Forum Advocating Cultural & Eco Tourism (FACET); and
- Conducted regional workshops with TCWA to industry and DEC staff.

All in all, the link between DEC and Tourism WA has never been stronger, albeit that until the time of this review there were some philosophical differences in relation to attraction operation and marketing.

It is recommended:

(30) That the DEC and Tourism WA continue to examine opportunities to strengthen their communication links and working relationship, including the possibility of applying a short-term (six–months) staff exchange system.

(31) That the Memorandum of Understanding (MOU) that is in place with Tourism WA be revised to reflect the outcomes of DEC's important and expanding role in tourism.

It is also important that Tourism WA take, within its structure, a better appreciation of the diverse role that DEC plays in conservation, management and tourism. An agency that has 70 per cent of its product under the control of another agency should seek to bring that agency closer to its own operations.

In this regard, forums such as the Nature-Based Tourism Advisory Committee (NBTAC) have an important role to play.

Throughout the review process, it was apparent that the NBTAC role is highly regarded, with a general desire to see this forum continue and so allow communication with a wide range of NBT stakeholders and to provide a "clearing house" for issues.

There is also scope to create another forum more directly associated with the day–to–day activities of both DEC and Tourism WA.

During the review process, examples were given of conflict between both agencies as a result of a different understanding of circumstances relating to issues that generated media coverage.

It was generally conceded that improved communication processes between DEC and Tourism WA could have avoided these conflicts and provided a clear "whole of government" position rather than the fragmented approach that resulted.

The creation of a Senior Officers Group by DEC and Tourism WA would greatly facilitate improved communications and understanding of each other's objectives.

Such a group might only need to formally meet three or four times a year. However, its prime value would be to formalize a procedure of communication to be applied on a day–to–day basis to address issues as they arise.

It is recommended:

(32) That the Nature-Based Tourism Advisory Committee continue to be operated by Tourism WA as a means of facilitating effective communication and providing a clearing house for issues, for the wide range of stakeholders in NBT.

(33) That DEC and Tourism WA establish a Senior Officers Group to improve communication between both agencies and to provide a mechanism to efficiently address day–to–day issues relating to NBT.

There is also a need for a whole of government approach in the recognition and support of NBT, which should incorporate the following:

- A Government statement on its expectations for leadership and cooperation between Tourism WA and DEC in relation to NBT;
- Government to reconfirm the NBT strategy that for sustainability and visitor experience, sets out the key objectives that both agencies should be striving for;
- The need for both agencies to sign a revised MOU as a matter of urgency;
- The importance of each agency having respect for each other's roles and responsibilities; and
- The importance of both agencies presenting a common and consistent face/message to the industry.

Tourism Council WA

As the industry body, TCWA provides an important link with operators and, even more significantly, is responsible for the National Tourism Accreditation Programme.

As identified earlier, the Accreditation Scheme has an important role in the future management of nature-based tourism within protected areas and needs to be further developed to give it strength and credibility.

TCWA has always had a representative on DEC's TIRG and often invites DEC officers to address its Board or participate in other communication functions with industry. DEC and TCWA conduct joint industry and DEC staff workshops throughout the regions.

The day–to–day contact between TCWA and DEC is strong and productive, but needs to be strengthened in relation to the Tourism Accreditation Scheme and its application to operators accessing protected areas.

Conservation Commission of Western Australia

The Conservation Commission of Western Australia plays an important role in the approvals process for the issuing of tour operator licences and leases.

Both the Commission and DEC endorse the current communication mechanisms in place, with a DEC representative attending Commission meetings.

The Commission accepts the rationale of the proposed changes to the 'E' Class licence period (Recommendations 6 to 10), however, would like to be consulted prior to a licence extension beyond the initial 15 years.

The Commission also believes that to assist in the management of protected areas, consideration should be given to appointing licensed operators as honorary rangers and given encouragement to report people who infringe – both operators and the public.

Marine Parks and Reserves Authority

The Marine Parks and Reserves Authority (MPRA) is a body established under Section 26A of the Conservation and Land Management Act 1984.

The MPRA's main functions are to control, manage and develop policies for marine reserves and relevant land vested in the Authority and to provide advice to the Minister on related matters.

The MPRA responsibilities in relation to the adoption and application of management plans for protected areas means that the Authority has a strong interest in the licence/lease process for tourism operations within the marine reserves and relevant land areas vested in the Authority.

The current process for approving new licence/lease applications requires that any application outside of those activities stipulated in the Operators Handbook, or not consistent with a protected area Management Plan, are to be submitted to the MPRA for consultation, prior to approval – the MPRA only seeks to be involved in non–standard licence/lease applications.

Communication with DEC in these instances is primarily by means of a DEC officer attending Authority meetings and providing advice in relation to the matters being put forward for endorsement. A Tourism WA representative is also invited to attend Authority meetings.

During the Review consultations it became apparent that there is some uncertainty by all parties as to their respective roles in the licence/lease application approval processes under circumstances where MPRA endorsement is sought.

This uncertainty appears to be being created by real or perceived communication shortfalls in relation to specific details and lead times of licence/lease applications submitted for consultation with MPRA.

To streamline the process and to ensure the availability of an appropriate level of information to enable the MPRA to make informed decisions in relation to the application's consistency with the management plan, there is a need to examine the current communication procedures between DEC and the MPRA.

It is recommended:

(34) That DEC and the MPRA jointly examine their current roles and relationship in the licence/lease consultation process and establish clear lines of communication to facilitate the ongoing decision-making responsibilities of both agencies.

As one of the stakeholders interviewed later in the Review process the MPRA was able to be advised of the issues that had been raised and the probable recommendation outcomes. No major concerns were raised in this regard.

Tourism Industry Reference Group (TIRG)

For some years, TIRG has performed an important communications role between DEC and the tourism sector, i.e. Tourism WA, TCWA and operator representatives.

Meeting quarterly, TIRG has provided DEC with an understanding of current issues and trends within the tourism industry, as well as allowing the tourism sector to bring forward matters relevant to operating in protected areas.

Over time, the representation on TIRG has been broadened to include other interests such as recreational users and commercial operators catering for activities such as education and corporate programmes.

To this end, it would seem that the TIRG role could be even further expanded to include representation from other stakeholders such as local government, fisheries and transport, all of which also have a role in tourism and a working association with DEC.

Some of these representatives may find it productive to only attend meetings identified as having a specific interest for them. However, regular attendance will aid the overall communications needs and increase the understanding of the cross interests of different parties.

It is recommended:

(35) That the role of the Tourism Industry Reference Group (TIRG) be expanded to incorporate wider interests, albeit that the tourism focus remains the main charter of the group. As a consequence, consideration should be given to renaming the TIRG as the Tourism & Recreation Industry Advisory Group (TRIAG).

From a government agency point of view it will be important that representation on TRIAG be at senior management level and the ability to appoint a deputy should be either removed or at least restricted, e.g. a deputy can only attend two in five meetings.

Local Government

With some 130 local authorities in Western Australia, there is a major challenge in maintaining communication links that are effective in liaising with this sector.

While the Western Australian Local Government Association (WALGA) provides a collective voice for local government, it is often difficult to gain consensus and that process itself is cumbersome – it can take a 12–week turnaround to gain a response on an issue.

More often than not, the local government position is directly relevant to local area issues, rather than being representative of an overall local government position.

Local politics can play a strong role, generally requiring DEC to have to deal on a one–to–one basis with local authorities, rather than a central representative like WALGA.

Individual local government authorities strongly defend their right to make their own decisions, making it difficult to use WALGA as the central communication point. Because of local circumstances, the same nature-based land use proposal in two separate local government areas may receive an opposite response.

This lack of a consistent position by local authorities on key issues such as the management of health issues in remote camps is a significant frustration for DEC.

While protected areas are generally outside of the jurisdiction of local government, matters such as health regulations and emergency services remain with local government and elements of these can be applied to change or delay the processes of developments within the DEC estate.

The reasons for such action by local government vary, but often are based on concern for competition on local town businesses from proposed commercial facilities within adjacent protected areas.

DEC cannot administer its own health regulations, but rather seeks to develop a working relationship with local government that recognizes the role that protected areas and tourism plays in the overall economy of regional areas. Usually where developments occur, local government processes building licence applications to ensure that buildings meet Australian standards. This has worked well in the Kimberley.

The development needs within a protected area, by virtue of the location and the experience expectation of visitors, are often outside of the requirements of regulations that apply in town centres and this needs to be taken into consideration when establishing bush camps, eco–lodges, etc.

While it would be ideal if communications with local government could be focused through a single source like WALGA, it would be unrealistic to expect that individual local authorities will not want to be directly involved in the decision making relevant to protected areas in their region.

Therefore, communications with local government needs to be on two fronts – to and through WALGA and direct to individual local authorities on specific issues relevant to those local authorities.

Communications with individual local authorities can be enhanced through regional DEC personnel structuring meetings/ forums that allow for a cross–flow of information with local government.

Undoubtedly there are already existing opportunities for such communications through established meetings, not necessarily convened by DEC, but by other agencies such as Development Commissions.

Each regional office of DEC needs to determine the most appropriate means of communication with local government and if necessary, take the initiative to establish appropriate communication mechanisms where they do not currently exist.

It is recommended:

(36) That DEC invites a WA Local Government Association representative to become a member of TIRG (TRIAG) and also to establish a clear point of day–to–day contact within that association.

(37) That regional offices of DEC be required to establish and report on communication strategies and procedures applicable to their own local needs.

Operators

In 2003, the Curtin Sustainable Tourism Centre undertook a survey of CALM licences tour operators – at that time around 340 in number.

A target sample of 100 was set and 12 opinion statements were set. The responses showed that the priority improvement that operators were looking for from CALM was that it should "listen, communicate and build relationships with local businesses."

Since that time, DEC has introduced an electronic "Tour Operator Alert" bulletin, which is distributed on a needs basis depending on the day–to–day advice required on conditions within protected areas, plus other general information.

While this initiative has addressed one area of communications with operators, the survey response was more associated with the licensing process and embraced such issues as initial contact point, length of licence, perceived bureaucracy, cost structures, etc. relating to obtaining a licence.

These are examined in detail in other sections of the review and recommendations have been made to improve the processes of licensing.

Public

Communication with the public is usually to provide information, or to a lesser extent, can be categorized as marketing. However, DEC's responsibility to provide interpretation of the values of parks is sometimes confused as marketing.

Information is important to educate the public as to the "dos and don'ts" within protected areas and to provide interpretation to enhance the visitor experience.

With regard to education, there is ample evidence that many "mistakes" made by visitors to protected areas are simply a lack of understanding of what is required when entering these sensitive environments.

With increasing visitor numbers to protected areas, the need for educative material has become stronger, as has the need for there to be an effective distribution system to enable visitor to have this information well before arrival at the destination.

Marketing information by commercial operators and/or tourism bodies can be misleading to visitors who build up expectations which, when not be realized, creates disappointment. This can generate negative publicity for the attraction.

An example is the publicity generated for Monkey Mia, where, in many instances, the message given has visitors believing that everyone will get to go in the water and feed the dolphins. When this expectation is not realized, there is disappointment.

While it is important to promote the State's natural attractions, it is equally important that there is true representation of the product on offer and where there are limitations or restrictions, these should be made clear. DEC has the best opportunity to provide assistance to operators in ensuring that marketing material is accurate.

DEC has also implemented a review system of its tourism related brochures to ensure that its interpretive responsibilities are understood by people who visit parks as well as providing basic promotional material for distribution through local visitor centres and the like.

While DEC has had limited participation in consumer marketing (Caravan and Camping/4WD Show), there is huge potential to participate with Tourism WA in positioning the State as a premier nature-based tourism destination.

DEC produces a number of high quality and expensive interpretive publications but does not resource publications that would have broader tourism functions.

There is scope to combine the interpretive and marketing messages and so broaden the focus of many existing DEC publications.

The acceptance of an earlier recommendation relating to DEC's tourism role and structure will rectify this situation.

It is recommended:

(38) That DEC, in partnership with Tourism WA and in line with recommendation 27 relating to DEC's tourism role and structure:

- Reviews all its publications to assess the effectiveness of tourism messages and consider reallocating resources to meet the needs of a broader market.
- Corporately resources the production of publications that serve the needs of the tourism market and complement nature-based tourism marketing.
- Undertakes an audit of its information/education material and marketing collateral made available to the general public and ensures that mechanisms are in place for the distribution of appropriate material

throughout the neighbouring regions of the relevant protected area (e.g. accommodation houses, caravan parks, visitor information centres, local government offices, etc.).

- Monitors the marketing publications of commercial operators and tourism bodies and initiates corrective action where the information provided is not consistent with the visitor experience that can be expected.

Interaction with Wildlife

While there is an important requirement to maintain stringent policies relating to interaction with wildlife, there is also a need to recognize that one of the main Western Australian tourism drawcards is the appeal of having a wildlife interaction experience.

Whether land or marine-based, it is the wildlife interaction experience that attracts many visitors who might otherwise seek to travel to other destinations.

This is a very complex area of NBT management – often a balance between science, policy, public risk and the requirements and expectations of the tourism industry.

Science provides information about the protection of the wildlife, as well as the human visitor – the tourism industry is seeking to offer unique experiences that are especially Western Australian.

The potential for litigation is also an influencing factor in the setting of wildlife interaction policies by DEC – examined in more detail later in the "DEC Risk Management" section of the review.

The Charter Boat Owners Association has a particular grievance with DEC's policy in regard to people swimming with sea lions and this presents a good example of the issues involved.

DEC policy is set by the Wildlife Conservation Act 1950 under the Wildlife Conservation (Close Season for Marine Mammals) Notice 1998 under subclause 8, which states:

Swimming with Marine Mammals

(1) Subject to subclause (2) and the Shark Bay dolphin notice, a person who is in the water may approach –

(a) a whale, dolphin or dugong to a distance of 30m but no closer or

(b) any other marine mammal to a distance of 10m but no closer.

(2) If a marine mammal approaches a person who is in the water so as to put the person in breach of subclause (1), the person must move away from the mammal until the person is no longer in breach of that subclause.

Understandably, the visitor experience is substantially enhanced through in–water interaction with sea lions. However, this introduces an increased risk factor for the swimmers who could be attacked by the sea lions themselves, or their predators.

Known instances of sea lions attacking people in Western Australia total 17 since 1978, the majority unprovoked and some resulting in very serious injury. The ratio of people being attacked in the water as against on the land is 50/50.

DEC is opposed to changing this policy position on the basis of this danger, which in turn exposes it to potential litigation, as any resultant injury or death could be linked to DEC's responsibilities for managing protected areas.

To protect against this situation, charter operators required their patrons to sign a waiver of responsibility, before they enter the water. This is for their own protection against litigation and also, they believe, to protect DEC.

The operators' argument is that if a client wants to take on activities that may present a danger to themselves, then that should be their right, provided they have all the data to enable them to make an informed decision. Some people deliberately seek risk activities such as parachuting, hang gliding, cave diving, bungee jumping, etc. for the thrills and experiences they provide.

It is claimed that to not allow these activities, provided there is no threat to the environment, is to overgovern, i.e. to create a "Nanny State."

The tourism industry claims that "wildlife interaction is a must."

The only area in Australia where it is permissible to swim with sea lions is one location in South Australia. While the species of sea lions is the same as those on the coast of Western Australia, they are regarded as being more placid. Western Australian marine tour operators use the South Australian situation as an argument for a change in local policy.

While in principle the Civil Liability Act 2002 may provide the required protection from litigation that DEC is seeking, it has not been tested, making DEC reluctant to review its policy on swimming with sea lions.

In the meantime, the Charter Boat Owners Association has advised that new insurance coverage has been arranged to give further protection to operators and to provide compensation in the case of any incident.

Despite the ideal situation of allowing people to swim unfettered with sea lions, it is difficult to move away from the science which clearly identifies the dangers that exist.

It is recommended:

(39) That the current policy Section 8 of the Wildlife Conservation (Close Season for Marine Mammals) Notice 1998 Act continues to be enforced and that DEC obtains legal advice in relation to the Civil Liability Act 2002 and the Occupiers Liability Act 1985 and the application of these Acts to any circumstance that might arise from people being attacked by wildlife (e.g. a sea lion) in a protected area.

(40) That the science associated with sea lions continues to be monitored and that marine tour operators be required to report all instances and circumstances under which sea lions have sought to interact with people.

Threshold Management

Because of Western Australia's isolation and the relatively low intensity of its tourism industry, the need for threshold management within protected areas has not been a prominent issue.

This will change over time and it is important to record that the tourism industry supports threshold management where there is any indication of a threat to the attraction, i.e. the environment.

In many cases, the threshold threats in Western Australia are not through total numbers of visitors, but through the compressed times that they arrive at a protected area. For example, most visitors arrive at Nambung National Park in the middle of the day, while at Monkey Mia, they arrive for the morning feed of the dolphins.

Unfortunately, this concentrated visitation can take away from the experience which is often most enjoyed when visitor numbers in attendance are small.

These situations can have a long-term effect on the appeal of the attraction to the detriment of both the State's tourism industry and the value of the protected area.

It is recommended:

(41) That DEC and Tourism WA closely monitor threshold situations and where concentrated visitation is impacting on the environment and experience, seek to encourage the tourism industry to respond with new programmes that contribute to a spread of the visitor load.

(42) That Tourism WA undertakes research into iconic tourism sites and the potential to use marketing to shift visitor loading to non–iconic sites.

New Sites – Landbank

The announcement by the State Government to establish a Landbank programme to identify and develop key tourist attractions including within protected areas, has been welcomed by the tourism industry.

With the Tree Top Walk showing what can be achieved with vision and creativity, other opportunities certainly exist to emulate this approach to tourist attraction development within protected areas.

Tourism WA leads this process and has an opportunity to pursue this Government initiative and create circumstances in which the private sector may be encouraged to invest and operate new attractions and facilities that are of a world–class nature.

Potential sites have been identified and include:

- Francois Peron
- Purnululu
- Northern Burrup
- Kalbarri National Park

- Shannon
- D'Entrecasteaux
- Cape Arid
- Cape Le Grand
- Windjana
- Bell Gorge
- Millstream National Park

There are concerns within DEC, Tourism WA and the tourism industry in general that Landbank's progress is being hampered through a lack of resources.

While site identification can be achieved relatively easily, it is the planning processes that require a dedicated effort, as many other agencies and stakeholders take their positions in regard to the specific sites.

It is recommended:

(43) That Tourism WA and DEC develop a structure and seek the resources needed to implement the Landbank initiative (as it applies to protected areas) as proposed by Government policy.

Other Matters

DEC Parks Pricing System

The national park fees pricing system maintained by DEC requires that any increase be approved under regulations by Parliament.

Because of the procedures associated with this requirement, it can be a lengthy process, the outcome of which may have an impact on commercial relationships which require lengthy lead times for the pricing and packaging of tour products.

There is also the risk that political considerations will inhibit developments that are based on commercial principles requiring a park fee structure that is appropriate to the level of investment.

It is recommended:

(44) That DEC seeks to have the setting of park fees and charges removed from the Parliamentary process and made subject to approval of the Minister for the Environment.

Social Research

At present, DEC does not have a coordinated or comprehensive approach to undertaking social research in relation to tourism, visitors and their relationship with host communities adjacent to parks with a strong tourism focus.

Research is required to better understand the needs, perceptions and attitudes of park users and potential users and their use and impacts on the natural environment and wildlife. DEC undertakes only limited social research in relation to visitor use of protected areas.

There is a growing demand by management, research institutions and industry for detailed data on visitors. Data on visitor impacts, level of expectation and satisfaction, means of transport, length of stay, etc is simply not available, other than in small samples where commercial operators or tourism bodies have undertaken surveys.

As a major participant in the tourism industry, DEC needs to have a good understanding of its client base and the resource in order to determine threshold levels of visitation, monitor use or develop policies and frameworks necessary to manage visitor use and impacts.

Importantly, the collection of such data need not be a sole DEC effort, as there are other parties that have resources, capacity and an interest in researching these matters, e.g. it is likely that synergies exist with universities, the private sector and other research institutions that could produce cost effective, co operative partnerships to undertake tourism and park-related research.

DEC will, however, also need to find the resources to fund and develop its own capacity to facilitate and coordinate the research effort and to undertake research in its own right.

It is recommended:

(45) That Government fund DEC in the development of a social research programme (including cooperative arrangements) that will provide a range of data on park visitors and visitor use of protected areas.

Two Approaches within DEC

From a tourism industry point of view, DEC is a single agency responsible for managing Western Australia's national parks and protected areas.

While DEC's Parks and Visitor Services Tourism and Marketing Unit has become the main point of industry contact, there are other divisions like the Nature Conservation Division that play a role in licensing commercial activities within protected areas.

Where there is interaction with wildlife, approval must be obtained from the Wildlife Licensing Section, as well as the Tourism and Marketing Unit, which has.responsibility for issuing commercial operations licences/leases.

The very nature of each area of operation means that from time to time there are disagreements relating to licence/lease applications that involve wildlife interaction.

While this in itself is not inappropriate within DEC, there is current confusion outside the agency, with tourism operators, or potential operators, claiming that they are getting two messages. This situation is creating confusion and generating a negative view of DEC's involvement in tourism.

This image of confused decision making can be removed by internal administrative arrangements that give the responsibility to the Tourism and Marketing Unit to facilitate direct discussions about wildlife licensing issues with operators. Where this happens regionally, the Parks and Visitor Services leaders in consultation with the Tourism and Marketing Unit would facilitate this. This will ensure a consistent approach across the State.

Such a structure would not remove any of the current responsibilities and powers of the Nature Conservation Division, but rather confine any divergent views between divisions within the agency.

It is recommended:

(46) That the Tourism and Marketing Unit of DEC be responsible for tourism licence/lease facilitating in consultation with other divisions of the agency that are

placed to provide scientific advice in relation to wildlife interaction and the overall use of protected areas. Where any issue cannot be resolved by the divisions, the matter to be adjudicated by the CEO of DEC.

(47) That DEC establish and distribute to the tourism industry, a clear process for tourism industry contact within the Department.

Penalties for Breach of Licence/Lease Conditions

The current structure for applying penalties for breaches of licence/ lease conditions has generally resulted in judicial outcomes that have not been considered to reflect the severity of offences. Penalties are prescribed more in general terms than in relation to specific events.

While this review has strongly recommended lifting the level of competence of TOs through licence conditions and KPIs, the fact remains that there will always be a few operators who are prepared to "chance it" by conducting their activities in a way that is detrimental to the interests of NBT.

There is a stark difference to the penalties prescribed for breaches of the Fisheries Act compared to the Wildlife Conservation Act and the Conservation and Land Management Act. The Fisheries Act is very specific on the level of fines that applies to different fish species. Under the Fisheries Act, there is a Head Power that allow the setting of minimum penalties.

There is a need to review the penalties that apply to breaches of conditions relating to licences/leases for commercial operations within protected areas, with the aim of establishing a fixed schedule of fines relevant to the indiscretion, but a set fine amount that should reflect the seriousness of the breach.

It is recommended:

(48) That DEC undertakes a review of its powers in applying penalties for breaches of licence/lease conditions and establishes a specific schedule of fines that reflects the nature and seriousness of the breach, including minimum amounts for fines and where appropriate, restoration costs.

DEC Risk Management

DEC's responsibilities in managing protected areas bring with them an inherent risk of litigation or adverse findings if there is an incident causing injury or death.

Despite comprehensive insurance coverage, both by TOs and DEC, there is concern that, as the owner of the protected area estate, DEC will always be exposed to litigation regardless of fault, or the fact that those affected may have signed an agreement absolving DEC of responsibility.

NBT, by its name, implies an element of risk – being close to nature takes people into uncertain, and in many cases unfamiliar, areas – with excitement and even danger being part of the visitor expectation.

Obviously the levels of that excitement and danger vary to a great degree from a passive walk in a national park to activities like abseiling, cave diving or scuba diving.

Managing these risks is a challenge for DEC, which seeks to find a balance between approved uses of protected areas and the exposure to liability should an incident occur through those uses.

Earlier in this review, reference was made to the Civil Liability Act 2002 and the Occupiers Liability Act 1985, both specifying the extent of DEC's exposure to litigation. However, there has yet to be a test case in court.

While it is a natural tendency to err on the side of caution when administering risk circumstances, the fact remains that the very attraction to protected areas for some people is the risk factor itself. To not allow risks to be taken where that experience is being sought can have a negative impact on some market segments of the tourism industry.

This is a very complex and potentially highly litigious area although at the same time, a critical one for the tourism industry that is seeking to offer unique NBT experiences, many involving challenging landscapes and wildlife interaction.

It is recommended:

(49) That, as prescribed in Recommendation 39, DEC seek legal advice to assist in reviewing the risk management policies to be applied to the full range of NBT activities.

REVIEWS AND FINDINGS ABOUT NATURE-BASED TOURISM IN WESTERN AUSTRALIA

Review Brief

The review of Nature-Based Tourism is to examine and provide comments/recommendations in relation to the statutory, regulatory and administrative framework applying to nature-based tourism, with a particular focus on:

- The statutory coverage of existing leasing and licensing framework;
- The impact of terms and conditions of leases and licences on nature-based tourism's economic and environmental sustainability;
- The management of risks to tourists and to the 'image' of Western Australia as a tourism destination;
- The role and impact of local government on nature-based tourism;
- The roles and relationships of DEC, Tourism WA, tourism operators, the Conservation Commission and the MPRA in developing, promoting and managing nature-based tourism and nature-based tourism facilities or attractions;
- The roles and relationships of DEC, Tourism WA, tourism operators in the provision of visitor information in regard to protected areas;
- The communication and representation mechanisms between DEC (including the Tourism Industry Reference Group), Tourism WA (including the Nature-Based Tourism Advisory Committee), tourism operators, the Conservation Commission and the MRPA regarding nature-based tourism; and
- The opportunities to improve and accelerate the integration of 'whole of government' delivery of opportunities for nature-based tourism (including specific initiatives such as "Landbank").

Methodology

The review has been undertaken with reference to numerous

existing reports and reviews that cover a range of matters relating to Nature-Based Tourism (NBT).

In particular, internal report documents of DEC have provided historical and technical information relating to commercial operator licensing/leasing and the processes that apply for application and approval.

Interviews were conducted with a wide range of stakeholders (refer to list in Appendix B). They included tourism industry representatives, operators and conservation groups, as well as relevant staff in the agencies involved.

Written submissions were invited through Tourism WA newsletters and notices posted on relevant websites. Eight written submissions were received (refer to list in Appendix C).

A number of meetings were held with representatives of DEC and Tourism WA to formulate a draft document for presentation to the Steering Committee to be finalized as the review report.

During the course of the review, Tourism WA commissioned a survey, "A Review of Nature-Based Tourism Operator and Investor Consultation." The survey's objectives were to:

- Determine how DEC and other bodies impact current tourism operators and potential developers/investors;
- Ascertain current views regarding existing DEC licensing and leasing policies and procedures;
- Determine the impact of lease and licence terms, costs and conditions on operators;
- Suggest changes or improvements that could be made to current lease and licence system;
- Investigate the effectiveness of current forms of communication with operators regarding nature-based tourism;
- Ascertain ways to develop, promote and manage nature-based tourism, including the role of DEC and Tourism WA;
- Explore potential opportunities for delivery of nature-based tourism products, including the need for additional infrastructure and services; and
- Understand how local government procedures and policies affect operators.

The survey findings were made available to the NBT review process and are incorporated in this report. Generally, the survey objectives and the responses are consistent with the independent findings of the review, as reflected in this report.

The approach to the review has been to identify and find solutions to a range of issues that have been put forward by those having an involvement or interest in NBT. Where appropriate, recommendations based on maintaining close co–operation and harmony between the needs of conservation and the needs of the tourism industry, are included.

While each sector provides important and valuable complementary benefits to the other, it is also important that there are rewards to operators who demonstrate not just compliance, but a genuine move towards continual improvement and best practice.

The relationship between protected areas and tourism is a very important one, requiring a whole of government approach that confirms a commitment to protect Western Australia's natural heritage for the education and enjoyment of those who seek to visit.

All observations and recommendations in this review are based on the first priority being extended to the protection and sustainable management of the resource – the DEC estate.

Steering Group

This review was conducted under the guidance of a Steering Committee comprising:

- Representative of the Minister for the Environment (Chair);
- Representative of the Minister for Tourism;
- Senior officer from DEC; and
- Senior officer from Tourism WA.

The Steering Committee met on three occasions.

Review Recommendations

Following is a summary of the recommendations contained in this NBT Review Report.

The background to, and basis of, the recommendations is provided within the Issues Section of the report, with the recommendation and page numbers provided for easy reference.

The adoption of these recommendations will require a commitment by government to ensure that DEC and Tourism WA are appropriately resourced to meet the obligations that flow from this review.

There are outcome linkages between many, if not all, of the recommendations. Therefore, this review, if accepted, should be seen in its entirety, not in individual recommendations.

NBT is a key component of Western Australia's tourism industry and the objective of this review is to provide the directions that will see an integrated and complementary balance between the protection of our natural environment and the ability of the State to attract people to visit and enjoy the many unique experiences on offer.

It is recommended:

Licence/Lease Tenure – 'T' Class Licences

(1) That 'T' Class licences remain available on an unrestricted basis, for a 12–month period, subject to appropriate accreditation being achieved within six months of issue.
(2) That without operator accreditation, allowing tourism certification within six months, the licence is rescinded.
(3) That the maximum period for annual renewal of a 'T' Class licence is five years, with the current options of one and three years renewal periods to remain.
(4) That the two–month short season licence remains available where deemed appropriate by DEC.
(5) That Tourism WA and TCWA confirm responsibility for, and establish clear processes to providing assistance to, start–up tourism operators (TOs) requiring accreditation as a prerequisite to applying for a 'T' Class licence. Tourism WA/TCWA to assist DEC develop its On Line Training Programme (see recommendation 21) as a mechanism as part of the prequalification of TOs prior to a licence application.

Licence/Lease Tenure – 'E' Class Licences

(6) That 'E' Class licences continue to be issued through the EOI process and that the initial period be extended to up

to 10 years, with annual audits against predetermined Key Performance Indicators (KPIs) and with a renewal period of up to 5 years, giving a total licence of up to 15 years.

(7) That the licence be subject to ongoing conformity with the issue conditions and KPIs applied by DEC, which will vary, and can be varied, from time to time, based on the circumstances of specific protected areas. A significant breach of those conditions or KPI performance failure, to empower DEC to rescind the licence.

(8) That at the end of the maximum 15 years licence period, DEC has the option to reallocate the licence through a competitive EOI process. To reward best practice, part of the criteria for assessment should place high weighting on TOs who perform well in the annual audits and to take into consideration what is in "the public interest" when considering the options. EOIs should commence at least two years out from the expiry of a licence.

(9) That in adopting these recommendations, legal advice first be sought in relation to potential implications relating to proprietary value and possible government exposure to future compensation in the advent of a licence not being renewed.

(10) That all 'E' Class licences have a caveat applied that will allow DEC to rescind the licence in circumstances where it is deemed that the continued operation of that licence poses a threat, or threats, to the environment.

(11) That DEC has the ability to offer those licensed operators who have a proven track record, the option of converting the licence to a lease, where appropriate.

Licence/Lease Tenure – Leases

(12) That DEC maintains the EOI process for issuing leases and applies an "each case on its own merits" approach in assessing the period of the lease. The lease period to be determined by such factors as environmental impacts, level of investment, the anticipated level of return on that investment, KPI compliance and conformity with protected area management plans. Lease terms to be set at the discretion of the Director General.

(13) That a legislative provision be made to remove the current maximum lease period of 21 years, with a 21 years option.

Business Sustainability

(14) That DEC takes into consideration the business sustainability factors associated with issuing a licence or lease to the extent that there may be an adverse impact on other tourism operators and/or the tourism industry, arising from such management actions and decisions.
(15) That DEC draws on outside expertise, such as Tourism WA and/or business analysts, in taking economic factors into consideration before making a decision on an application for a licence or lease.
(16) That the implications of the National Competition Policy in regard to Recommendations 14 and 15 be examined.

Transferability of 'E' Class Licences

(17) That the current replacement licence process for 'E' Class licences remains, but to use the term "Transfer" in accord with Section 101(3) of the CALM Act.
(18) That DEC maintains the right to not allow a transfer of an 'E' Class licence.
(19) That DEC, in adopting Recommendations 17 and 18, first seek legal advice in relation to possible implications for Government in respect to conferring proprietary value on DEC commercial operations licences and the potential for claims of compensation in the event of licence withdrawal for reasons other than non–compliance with licence conditions.

Commercial versus Non–commercial

(20) That non–commercial groups be given the option of a 12–month permit, where appropriate, for access to protected areas where their activities are conducted on a regular basis.

Licence/Lease Planning/Approval Process

(21) That DEC/Tourism WA initiates the development of a tourism-based website information and licence application facility, for both land and marine-based tourism operators. The application system to have links with other relevant agencies (e.g. Department of Planning and Infrastructure and Department of Fisheries), with the DEC licence application models proposed earlier in this review being applied.

(22) That the online training component of the process be resourced and developed by Tourism WA and TCWA, as manager of the National Tourism Accreditation Programme.

(23) That a specific turn around time for processing applications be set by agreement of all agencies involved.

Booking System

(24) That DEC makes available an internet-based booking system for camping and other specific activities such as abseiling, climbing and caving, where appropriate.

(25) That such a booking system be integrated with the tourism distribution networks and be developed as part of the Tourism Emarketplace that other organizations, such as Visitor Centres, can access.

The Role of DEC as a Tourism Operator

(26) That when DEC directly operates tourism products it does so in line with established tourism business principles.

(27) That a review be taken of the role of DEC's Tourism Unit and that the Unit be restructured and resourced at a level to enable it to carry out that role.

(28) That DEC initiates a programme of internal change that has all areas of the agency understanding and supporting DEC's important role in tourism. Also, Tourism WA to implement an internal programme to ensure that its staff recognize and understand DEC's environmental and management requirements.

Accreditation

(29) That Tourism WA and DEC, in association with TCWA and Ecotourism Australia (EA), finalize accreditation programmes applicable to meeting the accreditation needs of protected area management and that those programmes become compulsory for 'T' Class licences (after 6 months from issue).

DEC Communications – Tourism WA

(30) That the DEC and Tourism WA continue to examine opportunities to strengthen their communication links and working relationship, including the possibility of applying a short–term (six–months) staff exchange system.
(31) That the Memorandum of Understanding (MOU) that is in place with Tourism WA be revised to reflect the outcomes of DEC's important and expanding role in tourism.
(32) That the Nature-Based Tourism Advisory Committee continues to be operated by Tourism WA as a means of facilitating effective communication and providing a clearing house for issues, for the wide range of stakeholders in NBT.
(33) That DEC and Tourism WA establish a Senior Officers Group to improve communication between both agencies and to provide a mechanism to efficiently address day–to–day issues relating to NBT.

DEC Communications – Marine Parks and Reserves Authority

(34) That DEC and the MPRA jointly examine their current roles and relationship in the licence/lease consultation process and establish clear lines of communication to facilitate the ongoing decision-making responsibilities of both agencies.

DEC Communications – TIRG

(35) That the role of the Tourism Industry Reference Group (TIRG) be expanded to incorporate wider interests, albeit

that the tourism focus remains the main charter of the group. As a consequence, consideration should be given to renaming the TIRG as the Tourism & Recreation Industry Advisory Group (TRIAG).

DEC Communications – Local Government

(36) That DEC invites a WA Local Government Association representative to become a member of TIRG (TRIAG) and also to establish a clear point of day–to–day contact within that association.

(37) That regional offices of DEC be required to establish and report on communication strategies and procedures applicable to their own local needs.

DEC Communications – Public

(38) That DEC, in partnership with Tourism WA and in line with recommendation 27 relating to DEC's tourism role and structure:

- Reviews all its publications to assess the effectiveness of tourism messages and consider reallocating resources to meet the needs of a broader market.
- Corporately resources the production of publications that serve the needs of the tourism market and complement nature-based tourism marketing.
- Undertakes an audit of its information/education material and marketing collateral made available to the general public and ensures that mechanisms are in place for the distribution of appropriate material throughout the neighbouring regions of the relevant protected area (e.g. accommodation houses, caravan parks, visitor information centres, local government offices, etc.).
- Monitors the marketing publications of commercial operators and tourism bodies and initiates corrective action where the information provided is not consistent with the visitor experience that can be expected.

Interaction with Wildlife

(39) That the current policy Section 8 of the Wildlife Conservation (Close Season for Marine Mammals) Notice 1998 Act continue to be enforced and that DEC obtains legal advice in relation to the Civil Liability Act 2002 and the Occupiers Liability Act 1985 and the application of these Acts to any circumstance that might arise from people being attacked by wildlife (e.g. a sea lion) in a protected area.

(40) That the science associated with sea lions continues to be monitored and that marine tour operators be required to report all instances and circumstances under which sea lions have sought to interact with people.

Threshold Management

(41) That DEC and Tourism WA closely monitor threshold situations and where concentrated visitation is impacting on the environment and experience, seek to encourage the tourism industry to respond with new programmes that contribute to a spread of the visitor load.

(42) That Tourism WA undertakes research into iconic tourism sites and the potential to use marketing to shift visitor loading to non–iconic sites.

New Sites – Landbank

(43) That Tourism WA and DEC develop a structure and seek the resources needed to implement the Landbank initiative (as it applies to protected areas) as proposed by Government policy.

DEC Parks Pricing System

(44) That DEC seeks to have the setting of park fees and charges removed from the Parliamentary process and made subject to approval of the Minister for the Environment.

Social Research

(45) That Government fund DEC in the development of a social research programme (including cooperative arrangements) that will provide a range of data on park visitors and visitor use of protected areas.

Two Approaches within DEC

(46) That the Tourism and Marketing Unit of DEC be responsible for tourism licence/lease facilitating in consultation with other divisions of the agency that are best placed to provide scientific advice in relation to wildlife interaction and the overall use of protected areas. Where any issue cannot be resolved by the divisions, the matter to be adjudicated by the CEO of DEC.

(47) That DEC establish and distribute to the tourism industry, a clear process for tourism industry contact within the Department.

Penalties for Breach of Licence/Lease Conditions

(48) That DEC undertakes a review of its powers to set penalties for breaches of licence/lease conditions and establishes a specific schedule of fines that reflects the nature and seriousness of the breach, including minimum amounts for fines and where appropriate, restoration costs.

DEC Risk Management

(49) That, as prescribed in Recommendation 39, DEC seeks legal advice to assist in reviewing the risk management policies to be applied to the full range of NBT activities.

Addressing the Brief

The prime approach taken throughout the review has been to focus on identifying and finding solutions for issues confronting NBT. These issues have been identified by a wide range of NBT stakeholders and where consistent and relevant to the roles and responsibilities of DEC and Tourism WA, have been addressed by this review.

As most of these issues relate to one or more of the Brief items, it is considered that the most effective way of presenting the findings is by way of the Issues section of the report, with this section providing the linkage with the Brief.

The linkages are as follows:

The statutory coverage of existing leasing and licensing framework;

Statutory coverage for NBT rests with DEC under the Conservation and Land Management Act 1984, the Conservation and Land Management Regulations 2002 and the Wildlife Conservation Act 1950.

Tourism WA has no statutory powers relating to NBT.

With respect to the recommendations of this review the following statutory changes would need to be effected:

The recommendations:

(6) That 'E' Class licences continue to be issued through the EOI process and that the initial period be extended to up to 10 years, with annual audits against predetermined Key Performance Indicators (KPIs) and with a renewal period of up to 5 years, giving a total licence of 15 years.

(8) That at the end of the maximum 15 years licence period, DEC has the option to reallocate the licence through a competitive EOI process. To reward best practice, part of the criteria for assessment should place high weighting on TOs who perform well in the annual audits. EOIs should commence at least two years out from the expiry of a licence.

would require a change to the CALM Regulations 2002 as follows:

- Reg 96 to increase to 10 years.
- Reg 97 does not need to be changed as it already allows for 5 years.

- There may be a need for a new regulation providing the power to DEC to renew an 'E' Class licences after 15 years, without a competitive EOI process.

The recommendations 6 and 8 above and

(13) That a legislative provision be made to remove the current maximum lease period of 21 years, with a 21 years option.

require an amendment to the CALM Act 1984 in Sections 97 (1) and (2) for leases in State forests, and Section 100 (1) & (2) for other tenures (i.e. National Parks etc.).

The National Competition Policy will have an influence on recommendation 8 above as well.

(14) That DEC takes into consideration the business sustainability factors associated with issuing a licence or lease to the extent that there may be an adverse impact on other tourism operators and/or the tourism industry, arising from such management actions and decisions.

The Civil Liabilities Act 2002 and the Occupiers Liability Act 1985 will apply to recommendations:

(39) That the current policy Section 8 of the Wildlife Conservation (Close Season for Marine Mammals) Notice 1998 Act continue to be enforced and that DEC obtains legal advice in relation to the Civil Liability Act 2002 and the Occupiers Liability Act 1985 and the application of these Acts to any circumstance that might arise from people being attacked by wildlife (a sea lion) in a protected area.

(49) That, as prescribed in Recommendation 39, DEC seek legal advice to assist in reviewing the risk management policies to be applied to the full range of NBT activities.

The following recommendation relating to the removal of the pricing system from the Parliamentary process will also require a regulation change:

(44) That DEC seeks to have the parks pricing system removed from the Parliamentary process and made subject to approval of the Minister for the Environment.

All other recommendations can be implemented with administrative or policy changes by DEC and Tourism WA.

The impact of terms and conditions of leases and licences on nature-based tourism's economic and environmental sustainability;

This item has been the subject of considerable examination throughout the review and relates to the most contentious aspect of NBT.

The review provides a number of recommendations in relation to licensing/leases that are aimed at effecting improvements to both the economic and environmental sustainability of NBT.

As has been recorded on a number of occasions, environmental sustainability is the first priority and the terms and conditions of licences should be such as to make the maximum contribution to this outcome.

It can be argued that the stronger the economic situation in relation to TOs, the greater the encouragement to protect the natural asset.

The key components of this review that address this Brief item are:

- Compulsory tourism accreditation for 'T' Class licence holders – Recs. 1 & 2;
- Extension of licence period for 'E' Class licences to 10 years with 5 year option – Recs. 6 to 10;
- Consideration of business sustainability factors in issuing licences/leases – Recs. 14 to 16; and
- An upgrade of the tourism accreditation programme – Rec. 29.

Ongoing monitoring and the introduction of a social research programme to assess usage of protected areas –Recs. 40 and 45.

The management of risks to tourists and to the 'image' of Western Australia as a tourism destination;

Recommendations 39 and 49 relate to this item and refer to DEC's responsibilities under the Civil Liabilities Act 2002 and the Occupiers Liability Act 1985.

Managing risk factors requires a balance between the protection of visitors and providing a unique NBT experience.

The ability for people to interact with wildlife is a particular area where there are challenges between this protection (for both visitors and the wildlife) and the desires of visitors to enjoy that "get close to nature" experience.

An incident resulting in the injury or death of a visitor can have an adverse impact on the image of Western Australia as a tourism destination, or conversely can be perceived over–zealous restrictions on activities within protected areas.

It is again a matter of balance.

Western Australia's tourism image can also be adversely affected by the activities of unprofessional TOs or the failure of TO operations, which can have impacts on the total business sector as the support tourism industry loses confidence.

This is addressed in recommendations relating to accreditation (recs. 1 & 2) and business sustainability factors (rec. 14).

The role and impact of local government on nature-based tourism;

Generally, local government does not have a direct role in NBT, although it can have an influence on activities within protected areas through the application of health regulations and emergency service provisions.

Recommendations 36 and 37 relate to the relationships between local government, DEC and Tourism WA and seek to provide better day–to–day communication and management mechanisms for all parties.

The roles and relationships of DCE, Tourism WA, tourism operators, the Conservation Commission and the MRPA

in developing, promoting and managing nature-based tourism and nature-based tourism facilities or attractions;

While the roles and responsibilities of each of these stakeholders in NBT are different, the outcomes they seek to achieve are consistent and easily integrated.

Where difficulties have occurred, it has generally been as a result of a breakdown in communications arising from a lack of understanding and/or appreciation as to the roles and responsibilities of the other.

Recommendations 30 to 34 set forward a range of structures that can be applied to improve the communications process.

In particular, the continuing role of the Nature-Based Tourism Advisory Committee is seen as being a key component of the overall NBT management structure.

The creation of a DEC/Tourism WA Senior Officers Group will also improve the day-to-day operational requirements for NBT.

The roles and relationships of DCE, Tourism WA, tourism operators in the provision of visitor information in regard to protected areas;

Recommendations 26, 27 and 38 provide for a total review of the relationship between DEC and Tourism WA and the future tourism activities to be undertaken by DEC.

There are particular challenges for DEC as a front line tourism operator, e.g. Tree Top Walk, which will require a readjustment of its current role to more reflect its relationship with the tourism industry.

This readjustment will need to be resourced by government if the proposed changes are to take place and be effective.

As commented elsewhere in this review, the relationship between each of the issues and recommendations is such that they need to be implemented as a package, not on an individual basis, if the desired outcomes are to be achieved.

The communication and representation mechanisms between DEC (including the Tourism Industry Reference Group), Tourism WA (including the Nature-Based Tourism Advisory Committee), tourism operators, the Conservation Commission and the MRPA regarding nature-based tourism; and

Recommendations 30 to 37 address the communication needs between the key NBT stakeholders.

This is a key area of the review as the communication process has, in the past, not been adequate to suitably address the planning, policy and day–to–day management needs of NBT.

In particular, the ongoing role of Nature-Based Tourism Advisory Committee and the creation of a DEC/Tourism WA Seniors Officers Group will greatly facilitate the communication process.

The opportunities to improve and accelerate the integration of 'whole of government' delivery of opportunities for nature-based tourism (including specific initiatives such as "Landbank").

This review has provided a number of observations and recommendations based on a 'whole of government' approach to NBT.

The relationship between DEC and Tourism WA is critical. However, other government agencies such as the Conservation Commission, MRPA, Fisheries Department and Department for Planning and Infrastructure are key stakeholders in the future of NBT.

For NBT to progress, all of these agencies will need to work together towards their common goals, which for all intents and purposes, have compatible outcomes as their objective.

The Government's Landbank initiative is a demonstration of the 'whole of government' approach, with recommendation 43 seeking to increase the pace of the planning and development processes.

As stated earlier, NBT requires a 'whole of government' approach, with public endorsement by the government of the importance of NBT to the State's economic and social wellbeing.

The adoption of the recommendations of this review will require additional resourcing of DEC by government, which will be a further 'whole of government' commitment to NBT.

Outcome

This review has been conducted in close consultation with senior officers of DEC and Tourism WA in order to achieve an outcome that is sought by both agencies.

The Steering Committee has played an invaluable role in 'brokering' outcomes that have led to the formulation of recommendations in this report, which, it is believed, meet the goals of both agencies.

The wider consultation process with representatives of the tourism industry and conservation groups has provided important input in determining the directions for NBT, as provided in this report.

Throughout the review, it was extremely encouraging to observe the strong partnership that has developed between the tourism and conservation interests over the past 10 to 20 years. There is now a strong recognition of the mutual interests and compatibility of both sectors.

NBT is a major platform for the State's tourism industry and as such, needs to be protected and nurtured for the long–term benefits of all.

The purpose of this review is to maximize the values of NBT.

5

Focusing on Economics of Nature–Based Tourism: Select Case Studies from India

FOCUSING ON ECONOMICS OF NATURE–BASED TOURISM IN SOUTH ASIA

Introduction

Tourism is an important economic activity all over the world and also in South Asia. It contributes around 10 per cent of the export receipts in India and much more in Nepal, Maldives, etc. (Gossling, 1999). Nature–based tourism is an expanding segment of tourism (Tisdell, 1996). It is argued that nature–based tourism, if properly managed, can be a sustainable mechanism for transfer of global environmental values to developing countries to protect their natural resources (Boo, 1990; WWF, 1995; Brown *et al*, 1993). Given the fact there are not many studies analysing the economic and institutional issues of nature–based tourism, this study was proposed and accepted for funding by SANEI. This study started in November, 2002 has the following two major objectives: (*a*) to assess how far nature-based tourism can perform the role as mechanism to transfer the global environmental values for the protection of natural resources; and (*b*) to evaluate the effectiveness of existing institutional framework and property rights to utilize tourism as a source of income generation for the conservation of natural assets. It was proposed that case studies, of sites where tourism depends on natural resources such as forests, would be taken up in Bangladesh, India and Nepal. However, the recent political problems and the sharp decline in tourists to Nepal have discouraged us to carry out the study in that country. Thus primary–level case studies were confined to two sites in India (Sikkim and Periyar Tiger Reserve in Kerala) and Cox Bazar and Sundarbans in Bangladesh. In addition, we plan to look into the experience of other countries in the region based on secondary data and information, so that final write up reflects the issues of South Asia as a whole.

Status of the Study

The following activities were carried out so far:

1. Collection of secondary data and one–stage primary survey were completed in the Periyar Tiger Reserve of Kerala. Insights based on the analysis of this data form the core part of this progress report.
2. Data collection has started in Sikkim but the completion of this work will take some more time. However some insights based on collected data, and some issues of tourism in Sikkim are discussed as part of this progress report.
3. Data collection could not be started in Bangladesh. It will be carried out and analysis completed by December, 2003.

Completion of collection and analysis of data from Sikkim and Bangladesh and the writing of the final report are the activities in the remaining part of the study.

A Schedule for the Remaining Part of the Work

The following activities have to be carried in next six months so as to complete this study:

1. The analysis of the data collected from Kerala has to be completed, mainly on two aspects. First of all, the relationship between the income, educational, occupational and other social information on the one hand and the WTP has to be analysed in detail. Moreover, the joint nature of tourist activities and its impact on the stated values of WTP

also need to be examined (for example, to see whether those who have quoted higher WTP for entry have also quoted a higher value for boating, and then for trekking, etc.). A detailed analysis of the institutional aspects of management of PTR also has to be completed. It is expected to complete these activities by December 2003.

2. The complete analysis of the data thus far (first phase of survey) collected and to be collected (second phase of survey) from Sikkim during October to December 2003 has to be completed. Consumer surpluses based on TCM and CVM are to be estimated. Policy implications of the estimated consumer surpluses are to be explored. Detailed analysis of the institutional aspects has to be undertaken and completed. It is expected that these remaining works will be completed by the end of December 2003.
3. Because of the passing of tourist season in Bangladesh when we have started our study, it could not progress much in Bangladesh. We plan to study tourism in two sites namely Sundarbans and Cox Bazar in Bangladesh. It is expected that the study will be complete by December 2003.
4. The insights of these primary studies, in combination with secondary data and review of literature on tourism on countries in the region such as Bhutan, Maldives, Nepal and Sri Lanka will be used to write a monograph on the economic and institutional aspects of nature–based tourism in South Asia. This is expected to be complete by March 2004.

CASE STUDY OF PERIYAR TIGER RESERVE IN KERALA, INDIA

Tourism in PTR and Issues for Analysis

Periyar Tiger Reserve (PTR) located near Thekkady of the Idukki and Pathanamthitta districts of Kerala is probably the only such forest reserve attracting a large number of foreign and domestic tourists in the state. This wildlife sanctuary covers an area of 777 sq. km (with 430 reckoned as core, 347 buffer and 55 sq. km considered as tourist zone) (Mallick and Veeramani, 2002). It is a large forest block in Western Ghats of India, with three–fourths of area under tropical evergreen and semi–evergreen forests supporting species such as tiger, sloth bear, elephant, guar, lion–tailed macaque, great Indian hornbill, etc. It has attracted more than 0.3 million domestic tourists and around 25000 foreigners in 2000–01 (Table 1), and this number is growing significantly every year. Apart from entering the reserve, tourists carry out activities such as boating (in the reservoir of a dam located inside the forests), trekking, etc. There is a fee for entry and also for each of these tourist activities. These fees contribute revenue of about Rs. 75 million per year to the management of PTR (Table 2). The income from tourism comes to about 50 per cent of the annual expenditure incurred by the forest department for managing and protecting the wildlife sanctuary. The remaining part of the expenditure to conserve PTR comes mainly from the budgetary allocation of state government (Table 3). (It may be noted that this does not include all direct and indirect cost of conserving PTR and providing tourist services to visitors.) The PTR is a state property under the Government of Kerala and reserve management is fully under the control of its department of forests. However some tourist services such as guidance for trekking are provided by local people (under an organizational set up guided by the forest department) or other public sector organizations such as Kerala Tourism Development Corporation (KTDC). There are many privately owned hotels and shops located outside but close to PTR, catering mainly to the tourists.

Table 1: Total number of Tourists to PTR

Year	*Domestic Visitors*	*Foreign Visitors*
1995–96	252473	9911
1996–97	277278	10145
1997–98	319984	22253
1998–99	432396	23883
1999–00	320973	24347
2000–01	303895	37038
2001–02	363690	26044

Source: Mallik, A and Veeramani, A (2002)

Table 2: Revenue Collection at PTR

Year	*Total Revenue: Visitors*	*Total Revenue: Vehicles*	*Total Revenue: Boat Landing*	*Grand Total*
1995	953322	576105	3055171	4584598
1996	1450868	573220	3583491	5607579
1997	1508976	518965	3881340	5909281
1998	1708842	540120	4074954	6323916
1999	1808412	623975	5112142	7544529
2000	1978872	761330	4825498	7565700

Source: Equations (2000)

Table 3: Allotment and Expenditure of PTRM

Year	*Budget Allotment (Rs.)*	*Expenditure (Rs.)*
1994–95	20364600	21963913
1995–96	14864000	14444510
1996–97	18883000	13545430
1997–98	6829500	7631816
1998–99	12759800	13332228

A number of people belonging to Scheduled Tribes (ST) who live in the fringe area depend on PTR for collecting non–timber forest products, fuel wood, etc. and fishing in the reservoir, under the supervision and licensing of the forest department (Table 4). Some of them have been inducted into the provision of tourist services under an organizational framework of 'eco–development committees'. However there are many among this dependent population whose access to the forest resource has been restricted for its conservation but at the same time not benefited much from the growth of tourism.

Table 4: Number of ST Families depended on Forests for Livelihood

Activity–wise Category	*Number of Families*					
	1996–97		1998–99		1999–2000	
	Own use	Sale	Own use	Sale	Own use	Sale
Firewood collection	354	100	335	66	337	49
Fishing	43	93	37	87	28	45
Honey collection	138	206	121	175	96	110
Channa collection	–	160	–	5	–	5
Thelli collection	–	33	–	3	–	3

Source: Equations (2000)

On the other hand there are global environmental benefits of protecting forests such as those in PTR. These include the use–value benefits of bio–diversity conservation, carbon sequestration, etc., most of which is gained by the global population of which tourists form only a very small subset. However, the burden of conservation cost is mainly on the state government of Kerala, which like other Indian states, is under severe financial crisis. Tourism is a source that eases the financial burden of the state in conserving forests such as PTR.

There is a widespread feeling that PTR cannot accommodate the growing number of tourists, without compromising the conservation objectives (Equations, 2000). The large number of tourists also creates crowding, noise and waste–disposal problems within the reserve. Thus different strategies to control the growing number of tourists are under consideration.

Thus the central issues in the management of tourism in PTR are the following: (1) Is it possible to increase the revenue from tourism in order to further reduce the financial burden of the state government to conserve PTR, without affecting the environmental quality of the forests? (2) Is the institutional framework of PTR conducive for realising the potential of tourism on a sustainable basis? These are the issues addressed in the case study conducted here as part of SANEI–funded project on 'economics of nature–based tourism on south Asia'.

Theoretical Issues

There are a number of reasons, such as the following, why the governments of developing countries that conserve its natural resources such as forests, which provide global environmental benefits, should extract a rent or income from people who use it for services such as tourism.

1. It is the citizens of developed countries who derive a greater part of the benefits of conserving natural resources such as forests in developing countries (for example, through biodiversity conservation, and carbon sequestration). For example, such global benefits form the major part of the environmental value of a typical forest similar to PTR in Kerala (Santhakumar and Chakraborty,

2003). Moreover, it is also under the pressure from these people and their governments (driven by the use values of environment such as bio–diversity conservation or carbon sequestration, and/or the non–use values) that the governments of developing countries take the efforts to protect their natural resources. However, these governments cannot tax citizens of other countries, and cannot extract global environmental benefits to meet the cost of conservation (even though some inter–governmental transfer through global financial agencies does take place on an *ad–hoc* basis). Under such circumstances, if tourism that depends on these natural resources can be levied, it would provide an added incentive for the developing country governments to protect its natural resources.

2. There are related macro–economic and other reasons to extract a rent from nature–based tourists for enhancing the welfare of the people of host countries. Copeland (1991) who analysed the impact of tourism on the welfare of small open economies and the potential problems of 'dutch disease', notes that one condition that would enhance the benefits of tourism to local people is to extract `some additional rent from unpriced natural amenities enjoyed by tourists'. Otherwise local people may not benefit much from tourism growth, especially if the goods and services consumed by tourists are tradable.
3. It may also be important for reducing the revenue gap of governments of developing countries that bear the cost burden of conserving natural resources. The shadow price of their budget constraint can be positive and significant (which is normally considered in the pricing policy of public goods as in Wilman, 1988). There can be competing claims on limited public finance, and there can be more beneficial public investments for domestic economy such as in education and health, which may encourage even a welfare–maximizing domestic government not to invest in conservation of its natural resources to the level desired by the global society.
4. In a context, where adequate finances are not there to conserve natural assets, developing country governments

may shirk certain responsibilities of conservation. If the enforcement of environmental quality of protect areas is reasonably effective, such shirking is less likely here. However under such conditions, it is highly possible that conservation agencies may not fully bear the other costs of conservation such as compensation for those local people whose access to natural resource has to be curtailed for its preservation. This can have serious distributional consequences.

5. As noted by writers on the economics of nature–based tourism such as Tisdell (1987) and Chase *et al.* (1998), the levy imposed on tourist (for extracting rent by conservation agency) can also work as a regulatory tool on the number of tourists. The uncontrolled growth in the number of tourists can damage natural resource or can lead to the increase of conservation costs. This is yet another reason for levying or taxing nature–based tourists.

For a given natural asset such as tiger reserve, the environmental benefits far outweigh the direct cost of conservation. However there are indirect costs too. One component of this indirect cost is the losses for the local people who were using forests for consumptive use (such as the collection of timber that has a bearing on the quality of forests) or using forested land for agriculture, and whose use has to be restricted for keeping up the environmental quality of forests.

From the decision of the state government to conserve PTR, one can deduce that the total benefits of its conservation outweigh the costs. However the government of Kerala bears the cost of conservation. Let us take total benefits as TB and be it equal to the sum of domestic benefits DB (i.e., derived by Kerala society) and GB (global benefits). If C is the cost of conservation and if C<DB, then there is no net drain on the part of Kerala in conserving PTR. However, if C>DB [and C<(DB+GB)] there is a positive net loss for Kerala, even though it is beneficial globally to preserve PTR. If this is the case, then the argument for extracting a rent from non–domestic tourists is somewhat obvious. However, even if C<DB, there may be a case for taxing all tourists so that at least a part of the cost of conservation is collected from the direct

users. This is so since government has to use taxes, or tax the population for this purpose, to meet the cost of conservation in the absence of such collection. This can lead to deadweight losses for the society (and distortions in resource allocation), and it may be less costly to the society to collect revenue from the direct users such as tourists rather than taxing Kerala population for this purpose.

Thus we can presume that the conservation agency or the Government of Kerala can have an objective function of minimizing the uncovered cost (i.e., cost of conservation minus revenue from direct users such as tourists) of conserving PTR of a given quality. This is based on the assumption that the level of quality of conservation will be determined with global considerations, and is to some extent exogenous to the decision–making authority here.

This is graphically presented in Figure 1:

Figure 1

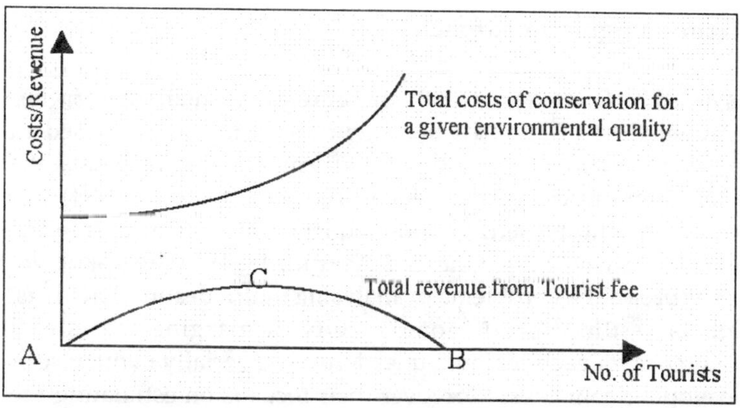

Total costs of conservation for a given environmental quality might follow an increasing pattern as the number of tourists increase because of the need for more resources to manage larger number of tourists as well as to alleviate the impact of increased pollution. (There can be an initial phase of non–increasing cost, where some fixed cost is any way necessary to manage some level of the number of tourists.) However total revenue might follow a pattern as shown in Figure 1, since larger number of tourists is usually associated with a smaller fee, and *vice versa* (under some assumptions of price elasticity).

With respect to tourism, there are two possibilities of sub–optimal equilibrium. At A (in figure 1), the potential revenue from tourism is not realized because entry is made very costly (usually associated with prohibition of tourism in forests). At B, where entry is free of cost, it is not only that potential revenue is not realized, but also the conservation cost is increased due to congestion and pollution. In a given context of nature–based tourism, it would be interesting to know the position of equilibrium in relation to cost and revenue functions, and to see how far it deviates from the position determined by the objective of minimizing uncovered costs. This would give insights into (*a*) the gap between the potential and actual income that can be realized from tourism, as a way of minimizing the direct and indirect cost of conservation, and (*b*) the institutional reason for the gap, if any, between the actual and potential revenue.

Methodological Approach

As noted by Chase *et al.* (1998), there are two primary approaches – Travel Cost (TC) and Contingent Valuation (CV) – used in literature to value nature–based tourism. TC approach uses the information on visitor's travel cost (i.e., direct and indirect) and the corresponding length and frequency of visit to derive the demand curve (Mungatana and Navrud, 1994). As well-known, this approach has problems in analysing multi–destination visits, and its assumption of homogeneity of marginal costs and preferences of each region is questionable especially in the case of developing countries. Moreover their focus is on estimating the consumer surplus than analysing the user fee strategies to minimize the cost of conservation. Thus this approach is not used here.

The CV exercise generating hypothetical values for non–marketed goods have also been used for valuing nature–based tourism (Chase *et al.*, 1998). It has some advantages that it will incorporate the non–use values of the visitors, and has more flexibility in generating service–specific or activity-specific values. The more clear the characteristics of the service, the more reliable will be the hypothetical value quoted by the user. Since the tourist service is a well–defined one, it is highly likely that CV generates less unreliable values. Since the focus of the case study in Kerala is to generate hypothetical user fees as a way of assessing the potential revenue from visitors, and the target study group is the actual visitors who have enjoyed the tourist amenity of PTR, we felt that a CV exercise is a more appropriate method in this context.

However there are some issues of concern in carrying out CV exercise in this regard. It is noted that the existing fees may have an influence on the hypothetical values of Willingness to Pay due to possibility of reckoning the actual fee as a reference point (Chase *et al.*). However we could not do much to avoid this bias. This seems to be of little policy significance since any move to change the fee would eventually go through a step-by-step approach from the existing one. Ideally one should also be analysing the substitution possibilities in such an exercise. This also could not be achieved here because of the fact that there are no other such developed sites offering similar type of nature–based tourism in the state of Kerala. Moreover we felt that since we have carried out CV exercise among the visitors who have just enjoyed their trip, their stated willingness to pay a different fee for the service that they have just enjoyed would also be based on a consideration of substitutes, and hence an explicit questioning on the possibility of using a substitute is not needed.

There are many other problems in carrying out a reliable CV exercise, which would be described in many standard textbooks on environmental economics such as Russell (2002). These include the possibilities of strategic responses (the respondent may not reveal his actual willingness to pay for strategic reasons), people's inability to know their true WTP for unfamiliar goods, the sensitivity of the response to the mode of survey and features of survey instrument and so on. There is also the fairly long debate on the discrepancy between 'Willingness to Pay' and 'Willingness to Accept' estimates (Hanemann, 1991; Brown and Gregory, 1999). Though aware of these methodological problems, we felt that CV exercise could provide some insights in this case since the characteristics of the 'service' in question are more or less clearly known, and also due to the fact that there are no better methodological approaches applicable in this context.

Collection of Empirical Data

Available secondary data on Periyar Tiger Reserve was collected from different sources. The number of domestic and foreign visitors, the revenue collected from them for different tourist activities (such as boating, trekking, etc.), and the budgetary allocation and expenditure for maintaining the reserve are available with the forest department or the statistical reports of Government of Kerala. PTR has also commissioned an agency (namely Equations, Bangalore) in 2002 to carry out a primary assessment of the state of tourism, conservation and other related issues. They have brought out data on certain issues including the current dependence of various stakeholders on PTR, and qualitative insights on the status of environmental quality and problems created by tourists.

A survey was carried out as part of this study among the domestic and foreign visitors of PTR in the months of December 2002, and January and February 2003, with the main focus on assessing their willingness to pay more for tourist services provided there. There are mainly four services that attract varying number of tourists. All the tourists pay a fee and enter the reserve, which gave them the right to walk or drive (with an additional fee for motor vehicle) about 3 km inside. Most of the tourists take a boating trip (on payment) within the Periyar Lake inside PTR (and boating is the most important tourist attraction here). A small percentage (i.e., around 5000 people in the year 2000) of tourists pay and use the service of guides to walk inside the forests for about two to three hours. There is also a night camping programme inside used by a very small number of tourists by paying a charge of around 150 USD. Our survey focused on the willingness to pay more for each of these services than the current fee. A set of higher values were listed in the questionnaire and they were asked to pick up maximum one, at which they would use and beyond which they are unwilling to use the service. This question is posed to the person who actually used a particular service. (Thus the question whether they would be willing to use a particular service at a fee less than the current one was not asked because of the assumption that the current rate is low and is probably just adequate to meet the direct cost of that service.) The reason for not using a particular service, if any, was ascertained. The questionnaire also collected information on origin/income/education of each interviewee, and their qualitative assessment of the type of service provided by PTR.

Regarding the sample of tourists interviewed, a distinction was made between foreign and domestic tourists. During the three months period of survey, investigators were posted at a central location in PTR for about 40 days. Since almost all the tourists take a boating trip, investigators approached around first five people who were coming out of the gate of boating land. This was the main way of approaching domestic tourists. However, as many foreign tourists as possible were approached during the survey days, and a rough estimate is that we could get hold of around 40 per cent of the total foreign tourists in these days. Altogether 360 tourists were surveyed. Among them 160 were foreigners and the rest domestic tourists from different states of India including Kerala.

Preliminary Insights from Empirical Data

An exhaustive analysis of data and presentation of results are not attempted in this progress report, and will be presented in the final report. However certain indications from primary data on the central issue of the study are presented here. This is about the position of potential revenue (based on the willingness to pay) for each tourist activity such as entry, boating and trekking. The gap between potential and actual revenue, and its implications for (recovering) the cost of conserving Periyar Tiger Reserve are also analysed preliminarily. With reference to Figure 1, it would be interesting to know (*a*) whether the potential total revenue function follows a pattern somewhat similar to the one hypothesized and (*b*) whether *status quo* is closer to A or B or C. We have considered the willingness to pay of domestic and foreign visitors separately.

Potential and Current Revenue from Entry by Domestic Tourists

All domestic tourists enter PTR by paying a fee of 2 Rupees. Their willingness to pay a higher charge based on sample survey is given in Table 5. The potential revenue by charging an amount higher than the current fee (and also based on the WTP) is also worked in Table 5. The potential revenue versus number of tourists is graphically represented in Figure 2. Though no curve fitting exercise is carried out here for the time being, some observations can be made from this scatter diagram itself. By and large, the shape of the total revenue function follows the hypothesized pattern. The more interesting aspect is that the current position, which is closer to B in Figure 1, is much inferior not only in terms of revenue, but also in terms of the potential cost of conservation due to the large number of tourists. Marginal revenue near the point reflecting *status quo* is negative. Whatever be the exact nature of the cost function (that means whether there is some flat portion at the initial phase or not), a reduction in the number of tourists associated with an increase in entry fee has the twin benefit of increasing revenue and reducing the cost of conservation. If we presume a flat portion of total cost curve over the peak of total revenue curve, then the minimization of cost recovery position (becomes closer to revenue maximization) occurs when the entry fee is around 10 rupees for domestic tourists.

Table 5: Potential Total Revenue from Entry by Domestic Tourists

Amount	*No. of Tourists WTP in Sample*	*No. of Tourists Willing to Pay in Population*	*Potential Total Revenue (Rupees)*
2 (Current fee)	**200**	**363690**	**727380**
4	122	221851	887404
5	116	210940	1054701
6	82	149113	894677
7	81	147294	1031061
10	80	145476	1454760
15	13	23640	354598
20	9	16366	327321
25	7	12729	318229
30	6	10911	327321
50	5	9092	454613

Figure 2

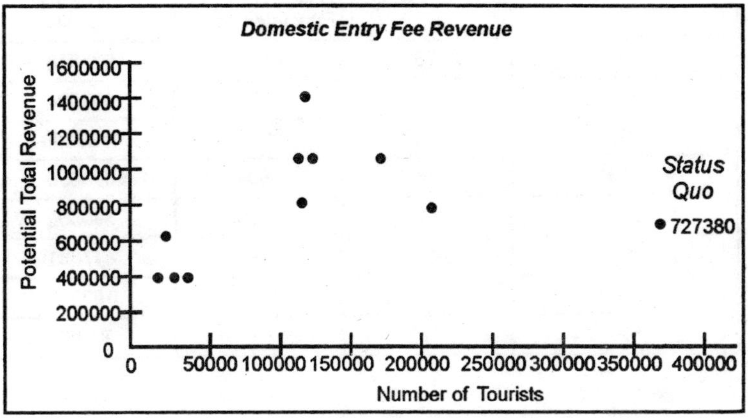

Potential and Current Revenue from Entry by Foreign Tourists

However the situation is somewhat different in the case of foreign tourists. The present position as evident from Table 6 and Figure 3, seems to be most favourable. However we did not evaluate the position of revenue when entry fee is reduced further, since all foreign tourists coming to PTR currently enter, and any reduction in this entry fee alone may not attract any more tourists as the decision to travel to PTR might be unaffected by it. However the majority of foreign tourists think that fee is high enough so that any further increase is unacceptable. This can be partially due to the situation in which they see discrimination in the current dual fee (of Rupees 2 for domestic visitor and 50 for foreigner) structure. Anyhow the WTP data does not show that any further increase in revenue can be achieved through enhancing the entry fee for foreign tourists.

Table 6: Potential Total Revenue from Entry by Foreign Tourists

Amount	*No. of Tourists WTP in Sample*	*No. of Tourists Willing to Pay in Population*	*Potential Total Revenue*
50 (Current fee)	**160**	**26044**	**1302200**
60	80	13022	781320
70	77	12534	877357

(contd.).

Amount	No. of Tourists WTP in Sample	No. of Tourists Willing to Pay in Population	Potential Total Revenue
75	76	12371	927818
80	72	11720	937584
100	69	11231	1123148
150	16	2604	390660
200	12	1953	390660
250	11	1791	447631
300	4	651	195330
500	1	163	81388

Figure 3

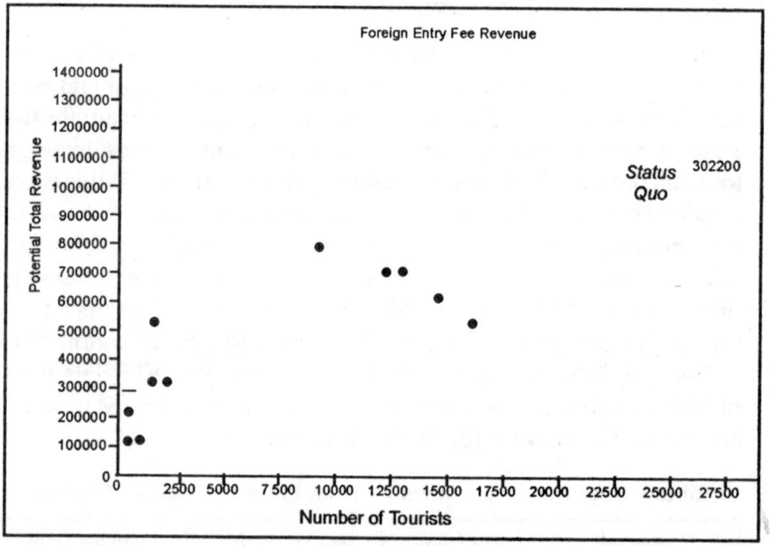

Potential and Current Revenue from Boating by Domestic Tourists

In the case of boating and trekking, the data shows a different picture. Currently people pay different charges for boating. This is mainly due to the fact that there are three agencies operating boats and they have different charges. Except in the case of one agency, which charges a differential pricing for lower deck and upper deck users, the services provided by different agencies are more or less same. Moreover, there is not much choice for visitors, since the number of boats run by each agency is fixed, the time of operation is fixed, and most visitors use that boat in which seat is available and which operates around their arrival time. Since visitors have paid different charges for boating, and some of them have reported their willingness to pay a charge higher than that they have paid, the WTP is estimated on the basis of the actual charge paid for those who are not ready to pay anything more, and the basis of stated WTP by others. This is estimated in Table 7.

If we take boating as an independent activity, then the current revenue (which is based on different prices for different subsets of visitors) seem to be the highest compared to a single charge based revenue (Table 8 and Figure 4). However, as evident from Figure 4, the number of visitors can be significantly reduced with a small proportional reduction in revenue. For example, the number of domestic visitors can be reduced to half if the charge is 100, instead of the multiple fee system today. This must be seen in the light that excessive boating creates the maximum pollution and disturbance to the animals (Equations, 2000) and this might be resulting in a sharp increase in the cost of conservation (for a given environmental quality), though we have not attempted any estimation of such cost function here.

The boating for domestic tourists can also be seen jointly with their entry. In the section dealing with the entry of domestic tourists we saw that a fee of around 10 Rupees maximizes revenue but can reduce the number of visitors by about 60 per cent. A similar reduction in visitors can be expected by charging 100 Rupees for boating rather than the current multi–fee structure. Moreover the change in entry fee structure would enhance revenue by 3 million rupees, which is equivalent to the loss in revenue by charging 100 Rupees for boating. In essence, the total revenue from entry and boating from domestic visitors is unlikely to change even if their number is reduced by more than half, through a different price structure. This reduction in the number of visitors would have significant gains in terms of environmental conservation.

Table 7: WTP for Boating by Domestic Tourists

		No. of People		
Amount	*Paid this Amount but not WTP more (a)*	*Haven't paid but WTP this Amount (b)*	*(a) + (b)*	*WTP up to this Amount*
250	0	2	2	2
200	0	1	1	3
150	0	5	5	8
125	0	1	1	9
120	0	1	1	10
100	48	24	72	82
75	0	2	2	84
60	0	3	3	87
50	36	17	53	140
25	26	0	26	166

Table 8: Potential Total Revenue from Boating by Domestic Tourists

Amount	*No. of Tourists WTP in Sample*	*No. of Tourists willing to pay in Population*	*Potential Total Revenue*
		301863	***18002673*** *(Current Revenue)*
25	166	301863	7546568
50	140	254583	12729150
60	89	161842	9710523
75	86	156387	11729003
100	84	152750	15274980
120	11	20003	2400354
125	10	18185	2273063
150	9	16366	2454908
200	3	5455	1091070
250	2	3637	909225

Figure 4

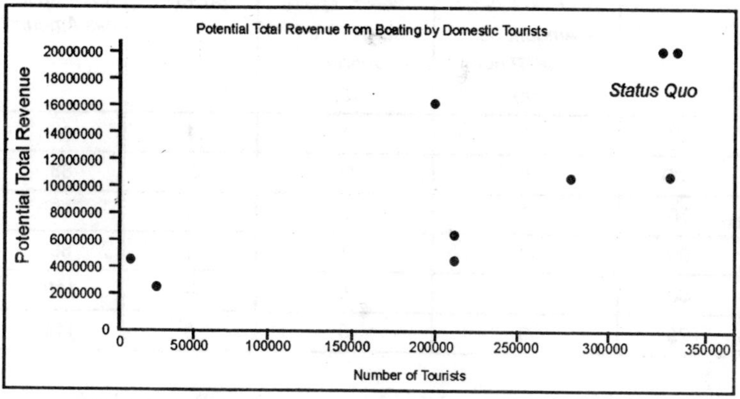

Potential and Actual Revenue from Boating by Foreign Tourists

Regarding the revenue from boating by foreign tourists, it is unlikely to change widely if the current fee structure is retained or a uniform fee of 100 Rupees is charged (see Table 10 and Figure 5). But there may be about 25 per cent reduction in the number of foreign tourists who would engage in boating if its charge is enhanced to 100. Since this number is only a very small percentage of the total number of tourists coming to PTR, it is unlikely to cause any significant effect on cost of conservation.

Table 9: WTP for Boating by Foreign Tourists

Amount	*No. of People*			
	Paid this Amount but not WTP more (a)	*Haven't paid but WTP this Amount (b)*	*(a) + (b)*	*WTP up to this Amount*
500	0	4	4	4
400	0	1	1	5
300	0	2	2	7
250	1	4	5	12
200	0	12	12	24
150	1	20	21	45

(contd.).

Amount	No. of People			
	Paid this Amount but not WTP more (a)	Haven't paid but WTP this Amount (b)	(a) + (b)	WTP up to this Amount
120	0	1	1	46
100	22	15	37	83
70	0	2	2	85
60	0	1	1	86
50	19	5	24	110
25	3	0	3	113

Table 10: Potential Total Revenue from Boating by Foreign Tourists

Amount	No. of Tourists WTP in Sample	No. of Tourists willing to pay in Population	Potential Total Revenue
	113	**18394**	**1361587**
25	113	18394	459839
50	110	17905	895263
60	86	13999	839919
70	85	13836	968511
100	83	13510	1351033
120	46	7488	898518
150	45	7325	1098731
200	24	3907	781320
250	12	1953	488325
300	7	1139	341828
400	5	814	325550
500	4	651	325550

Figure 5

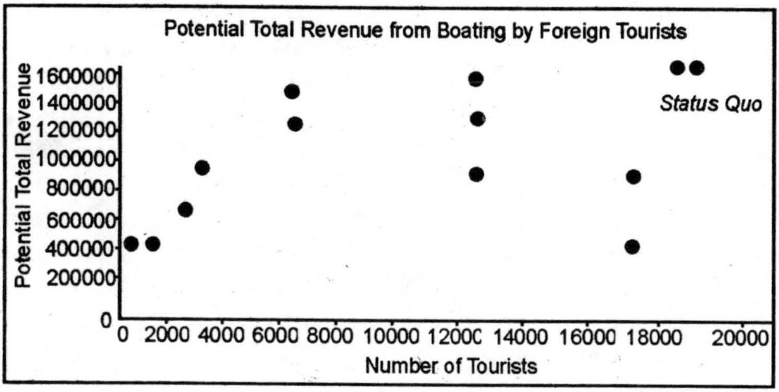

Potential and Actual Revenue from Trekking

The analysis of data on trekking by domestic tourists (Tables 11, 12 and Figure 6 in Appendix 1) and by foreign tourists (Tables 13 and 14, and Figure 7 also in Appendix 1) does not indicate that any significant improvement in revenue can be made through changing the fee structure for trekking. Instead of considering entry, boating and trekking separately, these can also be taken together and their potential and actual revenues can also be calculated. The corresponding figures are also given in Appendix 1. The basic insights are not different from the ones discussed above. The revenue loss is proportionally smaller even if the number of domestic tourists can be reduced by more than half through charging a higher fee for entry (and boating). However, since the number foreigners and those who participate in trekking as a whole are of a small proportion to the total number of tourists, no significant gains in terms of enhancement of revenue or reduction in the number of tourists can be obtained through changing the corresponding fees.

Institutional Analysis

Based on the discussions in the theoretical section, there are three hypothetical outcomes, depending on the position of total revenue being closer to A, B or C in Figure 1. Each of these outcomes corresponds to an institutional state. At A, the tourist use of natural asset is made very costly (similar to that of having a prohibition on entry to the natural area for recreation). This is visible in many cases where state property right is combined with the prohibition of use by others. The point C, which is at the peak of TR curve is one corresponding to the objective of minimizing the uncovered cost of conservation (if TC curve is flat over this range and otherwise somewhere more close to origin if MC is positive even from the beginning), which one would expect from a conservation agency owning the asset with 'right' incentives. The point B corresponds to one where rent is dissipated and marginal social cost due to externality (i.e., additional cost on conservation for having one more visitor to the natural asset) is high. This is somewhat similar to the open access situation analysed by Gordon (1954).

The analysis of the potential and actual revenue from tourism, as a whole, indicates that the natural asset is used somewhere near C, where a large number of tourists are allowed in without considering the additional revenue that can be realized from them and the additional cost imposed on conservation (or environmental quality). Thus, though PTR is under state ownership, and conservation is taking place with the presence of a direct enforcement agency, the situation is somewhat closer to an open access situation in the case of tourism.

Legally, the forests in India are 'owned, by the state more explicitly after the institution of Indian Forest Act, 1927. Forest Conservation Act, 1980 has made any use of forests for non–forest activity requiring prior permission from the Government of India. The consumptive use of forest should be based on the working plan of the state government. In addition to the Forest Conservation Act, areas such as PTR are governed by the Wildlife (Protection) Act, 1972. This rule in spirit is one of prohibitive in nature, where public entry is restricted as per its sections 27 and 35(8). Tourism oriented to study and research is permitted in wildlife sanctuaries under this Act. However it has stricter regulations in terms of vehicular entry into reserve, protection and avoidance of disturbance to animals and the introduction of exotic species into the area.

Regarding the mechanisms to enforce laws, the forest department of Kerala state through its wildlife warden is the custodian and is in charge of enforcing these regulations. The chief wildlife warden has some discretionary powers in allowing entry of people and vehicles into the reserve, and probably the legal status of allowing tourism might be founded on these powers. It is the wildlife warden who is authorized to give permission to visiting tourists based on the clause in Wildlife (Protection) Act, 1972, that 'the chief wildlife warden of a state may authorize any person to enter the sanctuary for the purpose of the study, research, tourism or related activity either free of charge or on payment of a prescribed fee'. The state government decides the entry fees and other charges on the basis of recommendations. The forest department controls and manages the entry of tourists to PTR. However, some tourist facilities inside PTR are provided by other agencies. The public sector organization namely, Kerala Tourism Development Corporation (KTDC) runs three hotels inside PTR, and operates boat service in Periyar Lake. KTDC has taken land and buildings on long–term lease from forest department. Forest department also owns and operates boats. Some sections of local people, mainly from tribal groups are organized as Environmental Development Committees, and they provide a number of services within PTR. Private sector operates outside the PTR in providing accommodation and other facilities to tourists.

Thus the lack of ownership or lack of an agency to enforce the property right is not the reason for the 'near open access' situation in PTR with regard to tourism. In fact the regulation and the motives of the enforcement agency is to restrict tourism to minimum possible extent. However, the system of ownership is unable to manage the system with either their own objectives, or that of 'minimizing uncovered cost to conserve the reserve at given quality' – an objective reasonable for 'welfare enhancing conservation agency'. There seems to be an inability, to decide appropriate entry charges, and this does not seem to be based on any explicit or clearly articulated concerns of equity. The forest department not only regulates the use of PTR but also provides tourist facilities, along with other public sector agencies. Such provision of tourism does not seem to have been done with either a conservation objective (minimizing the number of tourists) or with that of revenue maximization. (There are indications that the running of old boats by the forest department and the operation of hotels by the public sector unit are unfriendly to environment.) Moreover, the *status quo* seems to be falling on both grounds. There is a feeling among conservationists that the objective of revenue enhancement is against conservation. However, the situation in PTR is that not following revenue maximization is against the interest of conservation. Moreover, the possibility of achieving conservation through revenue enhancement from tourism is left unexplored.

Conclusions and Policy Implications of the Study in PTR, Kerala

The PTR is visited by around 0.4 million of tourists and there are indications that presence and management of these many tourists cause environmental damage and/or enhance the cost of conservation to keep the environmental quality desired by the global society. Thus there is a need to reduce the number of visitors to PTR. However tourism currently contributes around 50 per cent of the direct cost incurred for conservation. The remaining part of the direct cost is borne by the state government. There are also indirect costs mainly due to the need to restrict the access of local people who were using the forest areas for their livelihood and they would need adequate compensation. Thus income from tourism is needed to reduce the burden of the state government to conserve PTR, which faces financial crises, and encounters competing demand for its resources for other public requirements. Income from tourism is also required to meet albeit partially the indirect cost borne by the local people.

Thus this study analysed the possibility of using an enhanced user fee for tourist activities such as entry into PTR, boating in Periyar Lake and trekking into the forests to meet the twin objectives of enhancing the revenue from tourism (so as to recover a greater part of the costs of conservation) and also for reducing the number of tourists (so as to reduce environmental pollution and cost of conservation). Thus a willingness to pay survey was conducted among a sample of foreign and Indian tourists who visited PTR between December 2002 and January 2003.

Preliminary data analysis reveals that the current entry fee for domestic tourists (2 Rupees per person) is associated with a large number of tourists and the revenue is significantly lesser than the potential one based on visitor's willingness to pay. It is seen that potential revenue would be maximum when the entry fee is around 10 Rupees for these tourists, and by charging that the number of tourists can be reduced by more than 50 per cent. Thus an entry fee for domestic tourists is likely to lead to the achievement of the twin objective, i.e., increase in revenue and reduction in number of visitors. Reduction in number of domestic visitors by half would significantly reduce the burden created by congestion, pollution and the need for higher conservation cost to maintain the environmental quality of PTR. However, with regard to foreign tourists, there seems to be, based on their state willingness to pay, little possibility of enhancing revenue by charging a higher entry fee. Thus the current fee seems to be somewhat optimal. It may also be possible to charge 100 Rupees for boating for all types of tourists, whose total number would be reduced through an entry fee of 10 Rupees, thereby collecting total revenue, which is by and large equal to the present level. Thus there is a potential to reduce the number of tourists by more than half without reducing the total revenue. If there are well-defined equity objectives, such as providing students or children from poorer families opportunities to visit PTR at a lower cost, this need to be built in with an effective strategy.

However this requires changes at the institutional level of managing resources. First of all there need to be more clarity of objectives. Currently the objective of neither enhancing conservation, nor revenue seems to be working. At the conceptual level, revenue enhancement should not be seen as contradictory to the objective of conservation. Instead it should be seen as an effective tool for conservation. The provision of tourist facility by the state or public sector organization need not be aiding the objective of conservation. Organizations that carry out the task of preserving environmental quality with minimum cost to the society, and firms that maximizes revenue from tourists in an environment-friendly manner should be functioning in a broad state ownership structure, given the externality and public good nature, of conserving natural assets such as PTR.

APPENDIX 1—RELEVANT PTR RELATED DATA

Table 11: WTP for Trekking by Domestic Tourists

Amount	No. of People			
	Paid this Amount but not WTP more	*Haven't paid but WTP this Amount*	*Total*	*WTP up to this Amount*
500	2	2	4	4
400	0	2	2	6
300	0	9	9	15
250	13	0	13	28
200	1	0	1	29
150	1	2	3	32
100	0	0	0	32

Table 12: Potential Total Revenue from Trekking by Domestic Tourists

Amount	*No. of Tourists WTP in Sample*	*No. of Tourists willing to pay in Population*	*Potential Total Revenue*
		1692	**420092**
150	32	1692	253800
200	29	1533	306675
250	28	1481	370125
300	15	793	237938
400	6	317	126900
500	4	212	105750

Figure 6

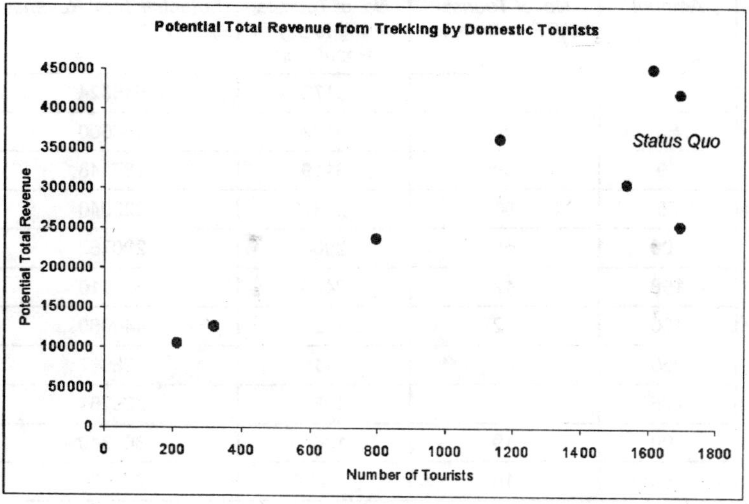

Table 13: WTP for Trekking by Foreign Tourists

Amount	*No. of People*			
	Paid this Amount but not WTP more (a)	*Haven't paid but WTP this Amount (b)*	*(a)+(b)*	*WTP up to this Amount*
500	2	10	12	12
400	1	1	2	14
350	0	2	2	16
300	1	2	3	19
275	1	0	1	20
250	20	0	20	40
200	0	2	2	42
150	1	4	5	47
100	2	6	8	55
75	1	0	1	56
60	3	0	3	59
50	1	0	1	60

Table 14: Potential Total Revenue from Trekking by Foreign Tourists

Amount	*No. of Tourists WTP in Sample*	*No. of Tourists willing to pay in Population*	*Potential Total Revenue*
		3172	**646824**
50	60	3172	158600
60	59	3119	187148
75	56	2961	222040
100	55	2908	290767
150	47	2485	372710
200	42	2220	444080
250	40	2115	528667
275	20	1057	290767
300	19	1004	301340
350	16	846	296053
400	14	740	296053
500	12	634	317200

Figure 7

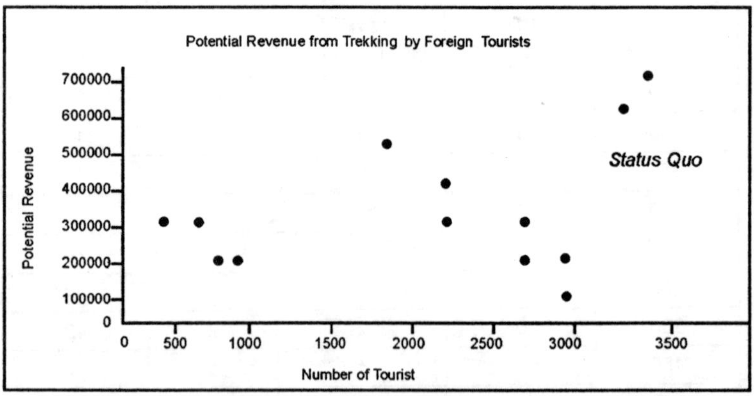

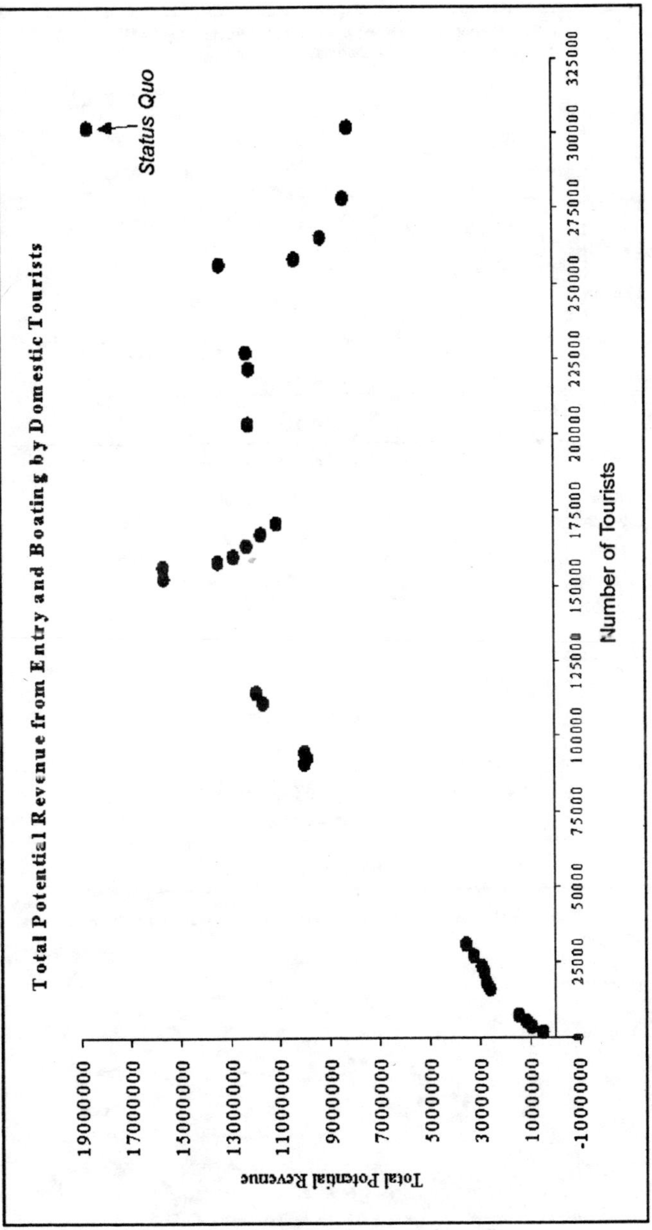

Figure 8

Total Potential Revenue from Entry and Boating by Domestic Tourists

Figure 9

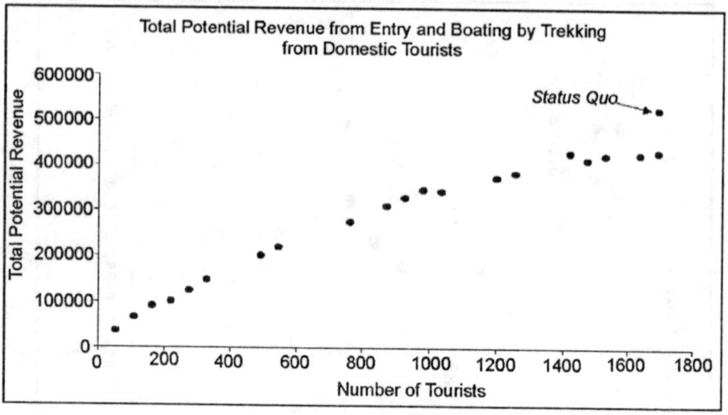

Figure 10

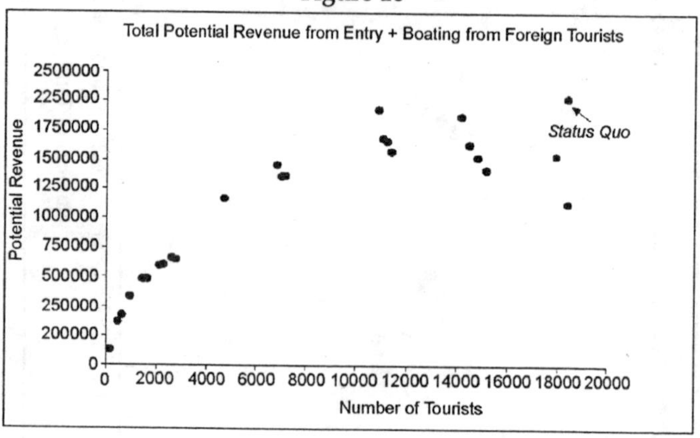

Figure 11

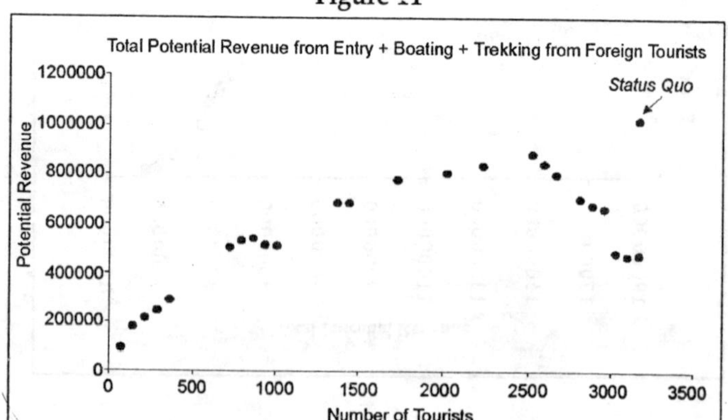

Case Study of an Ongoing Study in Sikkim, India

Tourism in Sikkim

The state of Sikkim in India, known for snow-clad mountains, spectacular valleys, beautiful streams, sacred lakes and dense forests is among the most attractive tourist destinations in India[2]. Sikkim gets about 1.6 lakh tourists including about 10,000 foreign tourists per year at present. The present growth rate of tourists to Sikkim is around 13 per cent per year. The Government of Sikkim has developed a 'master plan' for tourism and Sikkim is one of the first states in India, which has enforced the ban on plastic bags successfully. Although Sikkim is capable of achieving still higher rate of growth in tourism, it is claimed that Sikkim tourism has consciously maintained a growth rate so that the carrying capacity of the destination is not suddenly exceeded (Government of Sikkim, Tourism Department, 2001). Table 1 shows the tourist arrivals during 1990–2002.

Tourist arrival in Sikkim has seasonal pattern. Analysing the pattern of tourist visits according to the data available (Tata Economic Consultancy Services, New Delhi–110008) for nine years 1987–95, it is seen that 59 per cent of the domestic tourists and 64 per cent of the foreign tourists visit Sikkim during the five peak months, beginning mid–March and including April, May, September, October and up to mid–November.

---

2 The area of Sikkim is 7096 sq. km. and measures approximately about 110 km. in North to South and about 64 km. in East–West. The elevation ranges from 224 meters to over 8590 meters above the sea level that gives Sikkim its incomparable range of flora and fauna and a hot bed of bio–diversity rarely found anywhere else. The little state is flanked by Bhutan, Nepal, China (Tibet) and West Bengal state of India on its east, west north and southern boundaries respectively. It has a unique cultural diversity and is inhabited by Nepalese, Bhutias and Lepchas having close Tibetan cultural links. Sikkim is divided in four districts – East, West, North and South. The state capital Gangtok is situated at the heart of the East district, at the elevation of 5800 ft. (1700 meters). The nearest railway station is the New Jalpaiguri in West Bengal which is 125 km. from Gangtok. Bagdogra airport of West Bengal the nearest airport is 124 km. from Gangtok.

Table 1: Tourists' Arrival in Sikkim

Year	*Domestic*	*International*	*Total*
1990	56706	4719	61425
1991	61360	6187	67547
1992	68146	6761	74907
1993	75091	7132	82223
1994	92435	6888	99323
1995	98555	5866	104421
1996	145256	8642	153898
1997	116500	8068	124568
1998	133158	6111	139269
1999	139085	8563	147648
2000	144203	8794	152997
2001	14693	7757	154680
2002	150000	9000	159000

Source: Department of Tourism, Government of Sikkim (2002)

Months of March–April and October–November are the main tourist seasons for foreigners and the months of April, May, June and October are the tourist months for domestic tourists. Seasonality indexes computed, with an annual average of 100 for both domestic and foreign tourists for the years 1987 to 1995 are presented in Table 2.

Table 2: Average Seasonal Index

Month	*Domestic Tourists*	*Foreign Tourists*
January	43	53
February	89	59
March	128	75
April	167	115
May	93	192
June	44	119
July	37	65
August	62	62
September	83	84
October	228	196
November	150	93
December	76	87

Source: Tata Economic Consultancy Services, New Delhi & Department of Tourism, Government of Sikkim

The foreign tourist visits peak in April–June and October, which are the best months to visit Sikkim as the Rhododendron and Orchids bloom in March–April and the climate is pleasant and dry. On the other hand, domestic tourists' visits peak in May and October, not surprisingly in the line with the school holidays, because they tend to travel in families. This is fortuitous for the tourist industry because, it extends the 'peak season' after the climate peak is over. Seasonality is an important factor in determination of viability of investment in hotels and transport vehicles given that the duration of use is limited to short period. Occupancy rates for hotels are very low during the off seasons.

Domestic tourist is the main stay of Sikkim tourism. It constitutes more than 90 per cent of the total tourist traffic. The major sources of domestic tourists are from West Bengal (61%), Maharashtra (11%), and Delhi (10%). Other important markets are Gujarat, Tamil Nadu, Andhra Pradesh and Karnataka. In a way it reflects the negative relationship between travel cost and tourist arrival. Of the international markets, the major ones are the U.K. (14%), Germany (13%), France (10%), U.S.A. (9%) and Japan (5.5%) with certain year to year variations. The domestic tourists visiting Sikkim are predominantly in the site seeing segment, whereas foreign tourists visit for nature and culture-oriented tours including adventure tours like trekking, camping etc. The average length of stay of tourists in Sikkim is around 5 days. The tourist traffic is concentrated almost exclusively in Gangtok. About 94 per cent of tourists to Sikkim visit Gangtok. As a result Gangtok is overcrowded and congested during peak months. In the absence of remedial actions the situation in Gangtok is sure to become chaotic with the potential increase in tourist traffic in future (Government of Sikkim, Tourism Department).

To visit different tourist locations/sites tourists pay some permit charges and entry fees. For example to visit Flower Exhibition Centre tourists have to pay Rs. 5 per person. For Nathula visit, there is no entry fee, but a type of 'Environmental Tax' is being collected from the tourists at the rate of Rs. 150 per person. For visiting Tsomgo Lake and Baba Mandir the permit charge per vehicle is Rs. 10. A conservative estimate (done by the Master Plan) indicates a turnover of Rs. 40 crore per year (2.0 lakh tourists x Rs. 2000 per capita expenditure in Sikkim = Rs. 40 crore). This amount will go higher every year with the growth in number of tourists and number of days spent in Sikkim.

Table 3: Composition of Tourist Expenditure in Sikkim

	Foreign (%)	*Domestic (%)*
Accommodation and food	43.7	48.0
Transport	35.4	32.9
Shopping	15.5	16.7
Entertainment	5.4	2.9

Source: Tourism Department, Government of Sikkim, 2001

Sikkim Hotels and Restaurant Association has estimated employment of 3000 persons in hotels and Travel Agents Association of Sikkim has estimated employment of 150 persons in travel agencies. There are about 2500 taxis running on the road at present in Sikkim. That means about 2500 drivers and may be 1000 cleaners that is, about 7000 persons are directly employed in the various sectors of tourism. However, it is the indirect employment and benefits generated by tourism which is high and interesting. For instance, photo studios, photo film and camera industry reaps great benefits from tourism because more than 50 per cent photography is done by people while they are on vacation. Similarly, souvenir industry does more business with tourists than with local people.

Table 4: Financing Pattern of Sikkim Tourism

Institutions	*Investment Rs. in Lakhs*	*% share*
Government Institutions	7566	25
Financial Institutions	11778	39
Multilateral Agencies	4320	14
Private Sector	6854	22

Source: Department of Tourism, Government of Sikkim, 2001

Tourism Department of the Government of Sikkim has adopted some medium and long-term strategies. Taking increased tourism and development of certain additional infrastructure into consideration, the Master Plan for tourism has estimated Rs. 30.5 lakhs at 1996–97 price level for implementing various development works for the tourists spread over a period of 15 years. The suggested financing pattern is shown in Table 4.

Thus, participation of private sector in the development of tourism in Sikkim has been emphasized in the Master Plan.

Hotels and restaurants in Sikkim are almost exclusively privately owned. Out of these hotels about 60 per cent are located in Gangtok. Site–seeing and other recreational activities of the tourists are mostely conducted by the authorized travel agents of Travel Agents Association of Sikkim (TAAS). These agents are private agents. The Government of Sikkim and Defence Department of the Government of India (in some cases) are the legal owners of the different tourist locations. The tourism department of Government of Sikkim acts as a facilitator without itself conducting tours and travels and owning hotels and restaurants. However, they (along with other departments) remain responsible for development and maintenance of these locations and transport infrastructure. Thus, the institutional structure of tourism in Sikkim has a dual character where both private and public sector have a certain roles to play.

Issues for Analysis

In certain locations like Khecheopalri Lake and Bcarsey in West Sikkim local communities have also a stake in the surrounding natural environments. They exploit the natural resources by extracting fuel, fodder and timber and by livestock grazing. To prevent over–extraction of such resources efforts are in operation in these areas to involve local communities into preservation and promotion of economic–friendly tourism. However, there are many among this dependent population whose access to these resources has been restricted for conservation needs. But they have not always benefited much from the growth of tourism.

On the other hand, there are national and global environmental benefits of preserving such areas in Sikkim. These include the use value benefits of biodiversity conservation, preservation of scenic beauty, carbon sequestration etc., most of which is gained by the national and global population of which tourists form only a very small subset. On the other hand, the burden of conservation is borne mainly by the Government of Sikkim and the Government of India. Tourism being the most important source of revenue of the Government of Sikkim, it has the potential to ease the financial burden of the state in conserving places of tourist attraction in Sikkim.

There is a widespread apprehension (Government of Sikkim, Tourism Department, 2001) that Sikkim at its present state cannot accommodate the growing number of tourists without compromising the conservation activities. The large number of tourists also creates crowding, congestion, noise and waste–disposal problem within the tourism locations.

For many assets such as Barsey, Yumthang, Chopta Valley in Sikkim the direct cost of conservation may be substantial. There are indirect costs too. One such indirect cost is the sacrifice of the local people who were using some resources for consumptive uses and whose use has to be restricted for keeping up environmental quantity of natural resources.

Methodological Approach

There are two primary approaches that can be used to evaluate the value of the nature–based tourism – Travel Cost Method (TCM) and Contingent Valuation Method (CVM). The TCM has been widely used in valuing nature–based tourism (Dixon *et al.* 1994). It is an indirect valuation method where visitors' travel costs to a site are used as a proxy for the price of the tourism activity, together with participation rates and visitor attributes to estimate the visitation value of the site. It is well known that this approach has several problems including the problem in analysing multidestination visits (Bell & Leeworthy, 1990). Our approach here is not really a true TCM because the dependent variable we will be using is the number of days spent in Sikkim, not the number of trips or visitation rate. Further, to avoid dividing the costs of stay among the sites we assume that there is only one site (Sikkim) or that the different sites can be grouped because they satisfy identical recreational need. For the first phase of our study we have tumped 3 sites together. They are (*i*) Gangtok centric sites like Tsamgo, Nathula; (*ii*) Yumthang and (*iii*) Pelling and Yuksum. One of the weaknesses of this model is that it ignores multiple destination trips. However, adopting such means is not rare (see for example Bell & Leeworthy,1990). Thus we estimate a demand function, not as a function of each natural area on site price, but as a function of an aggregate expenditure for all areas. We recognize like many others (Maille, P. & R. Mendelsohn,1993; Navrand, S. & E.E. Mungatana, 1996) the difficulty of assigning a value to each site but use the travel costs as the price of a visit to a particular site and assume that most visitors come to these tourist destinations primarily for nature–based tourism. This enables them to calculate the entire value of nature–based tourism. There is further consideration for considering Sikkim as an aggregate. Many of the visits are packaged by TAAS covering various sites of tourist destinations of Sikkim. Hence we consider number of days spent by a given individual 'j' to a group of sites as the dependent variable with explanatory variables becoming specific to that individual. We have also attempted a CVM exercise in our study.

Collection of Empirical Data

Available secondary data on tourism in Sikkim was collected from different sources. Some missing links have to be plunged in. For example, in spite of our repeated attempts we are yet to receive official information on revenue earned from tourism over a span of time and we are also yet to receive the budgetary allocation and expenditure for maintaining various tourists' sites. However, we are optimistic about having access to this dataset soon.

We carried out a survey as part of the study among the domestic and foreign visitors of Sikkim during the months of March to May 2003. Prior to that we undertook a pilot survey in the month of February 2003. Sikkim, as noted earlier, has two peak tourist seasons (March to May and October to December). We could cover only the first season as yet. The objective of our survey was to assessing the tourists' willingness to pay for nature–based tourism provided in Sikkim. Tourists most often pay a hidden charge or pay a fee to enjoy different locations in Sikkim. Most of the tourists take package tours. The packages are like local site seeing in Gangtok, Pelling, Yumthang, Dzongri & Goechala. Our survey focused on assessing the willingness to pay more for these services as a whole. For TCM, respondents were asked about the costs of current trip, reasons for coming to Sikkim and a series of socio-demographic and economic questions. For CVM, a set of higher values were listed in the questionnaire and tourists were asked to pick up the maximum one up to which they would visit Sikkim. A dichotomous choice was also offered. Questionnaires were administered to a person who actually visited the sites. The reason for not willing to pay was ascertained. Qualitative assessment of the type of services provided at different sites was also collected.

Regarding the sample of tourists interviewed distinction was made between foreign and domestic tourists. To obtain variations among the tourists' interviews were conducted in different types of hotels (Luxury to Economy). Only adult visitors who had a defined source of personal income or family income were interviewed. During the three–month period of survey, investigators were posted at Gangtok and Pelling–Yuksum where we expected to meet most of the tourists who had already visited different sites of Sikkim.

Unfortunately the period of the first peak tourist season, when we conducted our first phase of survey coincided with the war in Iraq. Coupled with this was the post 11th September travel warnings for the US and European citizens and the panic related to SARS. Thus we could interview only 46 foreign tourists at this phase. Altogether 265 tourists were surveyed. Thus the domestic and foreign tourist composition that we could include in our survey was 219 and 46 respectively.

Preliminary Observations on Survey Data

Since at this stage we have an incomplete set of data, the analysis of data and presentation of results are somewhat tentative. An exhaustive analysis will be presented in the final report. However, certain indicative exercises on the basis of primary data collected thus far are presented here. The indications are about the potential revenue (based on travel cost incurred and willingness to pay) for tourist activities in Sikkim. We have used TCM and CVM for the domestic and foreign visitors taken together and separately too.

Tourist Characteristics and Tour-related Issues

Majority of the tourists (219) in the combined sample (265) were domestic tourists (82.64%). The remaining 17.36 per cent were foreigners. Respondents in our survey had average age of 38 years and sufficiently educated. 84.5 per cent of the domestic tourists had graduate and higher degrees and 44 per cent of the foreign tourists had the same level of education. Mean household income per month of the total tourists was Rs. 35043.00 of which mean monthly household income of the foreign tourists was Rs. 114708.00 and that of the domestic tourists was Rs. 18310.00. Mean per head trip cost to visit Sikkim was Rs. 5479.00 for domestic tourists and Rs. 24550.00 for foreign tourists. Average days spent by the tourists in Sikkim were around 5 days. Overwhelming number of tourists (157 domestic and 24 foreigners) opted for Sikkim to enjoy Scenic Beauty. Summary statistics of these and other related variables are provided in Appendix III in the form of tables and charts.

Preliminary Exercises for Estimation of Consumer Surplus

Initially we estimated the demand equation for nature-based tourism in Sikkim based on data collected for using TCM. We used OLS. We adopted a Log linear form. The estimated results of two alternative specifications are as follows:

1: LGDAYS = 1.154 – 0.0288 LGAGE – 0.440 LGEDU + 0.190LGHHS
(3.708) (–0.270) (–1.987) (6.511)
+ 0.140 LGSCB – 0.232 LGTCD
(1.11) (–7.988)
$R^2 = 0.318$ F = 21.895 N = 240

2: LGDAYS = 1.330 – 0.107 LGAGE + 0.222LGHHS – 0.358 LGSQEDU
(4.299) (–0.963) (7.039) (–3.071)
– 0.197 LGTCHD
(–5.650)
$R^2 = 0.236$ F = 18.183 N = 240

Where LGDAYS represents the log of number of days spent in Sikkim; LGAGE is the log of age of the respondents; LGEDU is the log of years of schooling; LGHHS is the log of household income; LGSCB is the log of scale values of scenic beauty; LGTCD is the log of travel cost per day; LGSQEDU is the log of square of the years of schooling and LGTCHD is the log of travel cost per head per day.

In both the exercises travel costs have the expected negative signs and are highly significant. Household income has also the expected positive sign with highly significant t value. The other significant variable is Education (years of schooling) which in both the exercises shows negative sign. One reason for the negative sign could be the higher opportunity cost of time of more educated persons. Though R^2 in both the cases is not high, F statistics are highly significant implying that these fits are not bad enough.

On the basis of estimated Equation (1) we worked out the willingness to pay curve of the visitors, taking travel cost per day per head as the price and the number of days spent as the demand for visits to Sikkim.

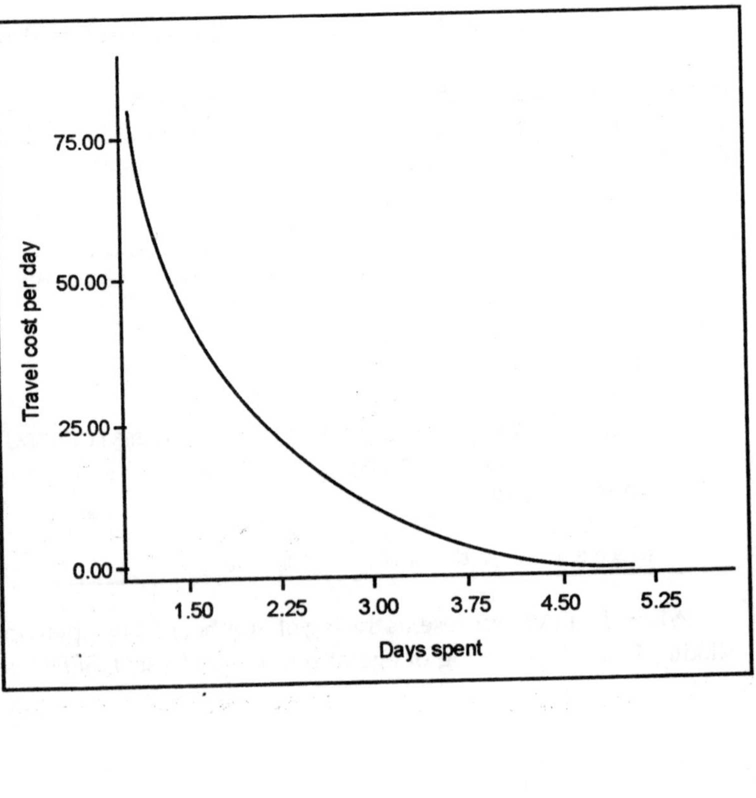

The area under this curve (which we have not yet estimated) will give us the total willingness to pay. If we deduct the actual current payments made by tourists we will have a measure of consumer surplus. These values can then be compared with the costs of conserving the various sites and used as an aid in public policy decisions. This analysis will be an integral part of the second phase of the project.

A Rudimentary CVM Exercise

We have also attempted a preliminary exercise using CVM. In the CVM exercise we adopted a Double Bounded Dichotomous Choice (DBDC) formulation, as it is more information intensive (Hanemann *et al.* 1991) as well as an open ended choice. From a policy perspective, the two most important questions are whether or not:

(1) Tourists are willing to pay more than the current permit cum entrance fee if measures are taken to improve the protection and management of the sites and
(2) If yes, how much more the tourists are willing to pay.

For open ended choice the interviewer started the bidding by a particular amount. For the dichotomous choice a particular amount was quoted uniformly to all respondents and their willingness to pay that particular amount was recorded in Yes – No format. While NOAA panel recommends use of DBDC format (Arrow *et al.* 1993) some recent studies report a preference for the first approach (Reaves *et al.* 1999).

Assuming a Random Utility Model (RUM) we perform a Logit Maximum Likelihood Estimation in the case of DBDC format. The results of the estimated Logit exercise (two alternative forms) are shown below:

Logit Maximum Likelihood Estimation
The estimation method converged after 6 iterations

Dependent variable is WTP
164 observations used for estimation from 1 to 164

Regressor	Coefficient	Standard Error	T–Ratio[Prob]
C	–3.7076	1.6770	–2.2109[.028]

AGE	−.0081262	.015519	−.52363[.601]
EDU	.019092	. 032138	.59408[.553]
PI	.1848E–4	.7253E–5	2.5484[.012]
SEB	.74622	.30436	2.4517[.015]

Factor for the calculation of marginal effects =.23658

Maximized value of the log–likelihood function =–102.4175

Akaike Information Criterion =–107.4175

Schwarz Bayesian Criterion =–115.1671

Hannan–Quinn Criterion =–110.5635

Mean of WTP =. 56098

Mean of fitted WTP =.73171

Goodness of fit =.63415

Pesaran–Timmermann test statistic = –1.8940[.058]

Pseudo–R–Squared =.089247

Logit Maximum Likelihood Estimation
The estimation method converged after 6 iterations

Dependent variable is WTP

164 observations used for estimation from 1 to 164

Regressor	Coefficient	Standard Error	T–Ratio[Prob]
C	–3.6574	1.6715	–2.1881[.030]
AGE	–.0082019	.015414	–.53210[.595]
EDU	.020771	.034898	.59518[.553]
HI	.1763E–4	.7060E–5	2.4979[.014]
SEB	.73061	.30038	2.4323[.016]

Factor for the calculation of marginal effects =. 24166

Maximized value of the log–likelihood function =–103.2231

Akaike Information Criterion =–108.2231

Schwarz Bayesian Criterion =–115.9727

Hannan–Quinn Criterion =–111.3691

Mean of WTP = .56098

Mean of fitted WTP = .72561

Goodness of fit = .64024

Pesaran–Timmermann test statistic = –1.8592[.063]

Pseudo–R–Squared = .082083

Where EDU stands for the years of schooling of the respondent; PI stands for personal income; SEB stands for scenic beauty; HI stands for household income.

Our exercise on open-ended bidding game type of response data using OLS on Logarithmic bid function (two alternative specifications) shows the following two estimated equations:

Model Summary

Model	R	R Square	Adjusted R Square	Std. Error of the Estimate
1	.358[a]	.128	.104	—

[a] Predictors: (Constant). LGTCPD, LGPI, LGSB, LFEDU

ANOVA[b]

Model		Sum of Squares	df	Mean Square	F	Sig.
1	Regression	4.079	4	1.020	5.391	.000[a]
	Residual	27.804	147	.189		
	Total	31.882	151			

[a] Predictors: (Constant), LGTCPD, LGPI, LGSB, LFEDU

[b] Dependent Variable: LGWTP

Coefficients[a]

Model		Unstandardized Coefficients		Standardized Coefficients	t	Sig.
		B	Std. Error	Beta		
1	(Constant)	–.356	.914		–.390	.697
	LFEDU	.359	.762	.040	,471	.638
	LGPI	.283	.079	.297	3.601	.000
	LGSB	1.414	.589	.187	2.403	.018
	LGTCPD	–.122	.083	–.118	–1.470	.144

[a] Dependent Variable: LGWTP

Model Summary

Model	R	R Square	Adjusted R Square	Std. Error of the Estimate
1	.356[a]	.126	.103	—

[a] Predictors: (Constant), LGAGE, LFEDU, LGSB, LGPi

ANOVA[b]

Model		Sum of Squares	df	Mean Square	F	Sig.
1	Regression	4.041	4	1.010	5.353	.000[a]
	Residual	27.936	148	.189		
	Total	31.977	152			

[a] Predictors: (Constant), LGAGE, LFEDU, LGSB, LGPI

[b] Dependent Variable: LGWTP

Coefficients[a]

Model		Unstandlardized Coefficients		Standardized Coefficients	t	Sig.
		B	Std. Error	Beta		
1	(Constant)	.322	1.048	.305	.308	.759
	LGPI	.291	.078	.007	3.712	.000
	LFEDU	6.515E–02	.734	.164	.089	.929
	LGSB	1.241	.587	–.108	2.114	.036
	LGAGE	–.429	.308		–1.395	.165

[a] Dependent Variable: LGWTP

Where LGTCPD stands for log of travel cost per day, LGPI stands for log of personal income and LGSB stands for log of scenic beauty.

Interpretations of the results obtained by these procedures are yet to be completed.

Institutional Questions

Based on our first phase of survey and communications with local administration, it seems that tourism in Sikkim is a type of joint venture endeavour. Whereas the state government provide access to the different sites and maintain and develop the tourist sites, private hoteliers, tour operators and transport operators use those infrastructures to provide the tourists with the requirements of actually visiting and staying in Sikkim. It seems that private hoteliers, tour operators and transport operators have a kind of tacit collusion to run the whole show. This may lead to a rent seeking behaviour (actually some respondents expressed such experiences) on the part of this collusion. It is true that they have to pay a license fee to the government for these activities but it seems that in the absence of any regulatory mechanism to monitor their activities the state government cannot realize at least a part of this rent. Had there been proper monitoring mechanism in operation, either this rent seeking behaviour could be curtailed or a part of the rent could be realized by the government and devoted to development and maintenance activities of the various tourist sites.

To avoid congestion externalities, which during peak tourist seasons become very high, some policy designs need to be adopted to control number of vehicles plying to these sites. In fact for trips to Nathula, currently there is a practice that it is open for only four days a week. The number of vehicles cannot cross generally 25. In the absence of such regulatory or other devices, access to the sites may be used as free access resources.

These observations are based just on our preliminary experiences. Further exploration awaits second phase of study.

APPENDIX II: RELEVANT SIKKIM RELATED DATA

Tables based on Primary Data collected from Sikkim

Table 1: Classification of Tourists on the basis of their Nationality

Tourists	*Number*	*%*
Domestic	219	82.64
Foreigner	46	17.36
Total	265	100.00

Table 2: Level of Education of the Respondents

Level of Education	*Domestic*	*%*	*Foreigner*	*%*
Secondary	14	6.39	0	0
Higher Secondary	20	9.13	2	4.35
Graduate	135	61.64	29	63.04
Post Graduate	50	22.83	15	32.61
Total	219	100.00	46	100.00

Table 3: Years of Schooling of the Respondents

Years of Schooling	*No. of Domestic Visitors*	*%*	*No. of Foreign Visitors*	*%*
Below 12 years	34	15.53	2	4.35
Above 12 years	185	84.47	44	95.65
Total	219	100.00	46	100.00

Table 4: Monthly Personal Income of the Domestic Tourists

Income Level	*No. of Visitors*	*%*
Less than 10000	112	51.14
10001 – 20000	64	29.22
20001 – 30000	26	11.87
30001 – 40000	8	3.65
40001 – 50000	6	2.74
50001 & above	3	1.37
Total	219	100.00

Table 5: Monthly Personal Income of the Foreign Tourists

Income Level	*No. of visitors*	*%*
Less than 50000	22	47.83
50001 – 100000	15	32.61
100001 – 150000	3	6.52
150001 & above	6	13.04
Total	46	100.00

Table 6: Number of Nights spent in Sikkim

No. of Nights	*Domestic*	*%*	*Foreigner*	*%*
Two	15	6.85	2	4.35
Three	58	26.48	4	8.70
Four	52	23.74	8	17.39
Five	47	21.46	3	6.52
Six	19	8.68	0	0.00
Seven	18	8.22	2	4.35
Eight & more	10	4.57	27	58.70
Total	219	100.00	46	100.00

Table 7: Length of Stay in Sikkim

No. of Nights	*Domestic*	*%*	*Foreigner*	*%*
1 – 3	73	33.33	6	13.04
4 – 6	118	53.88	11	23.91
7 – 9	25	11.42	5	10.87
10 & above	3	1.37	24	52.17
Total	219	100.00	46	100.00

Table 8: Nature of Visit in Sikkim

	Domestic	*%*	*Foreigner*	*%*
First Visit	174	79.45	44	95.65
Repeat Visit	45	20.55	2	4.35
Total	219	100.00	46	100.00

Table 9: Was the Travel to Sikkim Individual or Package?

	Domestic	*%*	*Foreigner*	*%*
Individual	188	85.84	36	78.26
Package	31	14.16	10	4.57

Table 10: Average Night Stay in Gangtok and other Places in Sikkim

Places	*Night Stay*
Gangtok	3.52
Pelling	2.07
Lachung	1.2
Rabangla	2.11
Yaksham	5.5
Lachen	1.75

Table 11: Average Night Stay in the Visited Places – Domestic

Places	*Night Stay*	*Max.*	*Min.*	*Coff. of Variations*
Gangtok	3.52	30	1	81.82
Pelling	2.07	7	1	44.44
Lachung	1.2	3	1	35.00
Rabangla	2.11	3	1	28.44
Yaksham	5.5	20	1	87.64
Lachen	1.75	4	1	85.71

Table 12: Monthly Household Income of the Domestic Tourists

Income Level	*No. of Visitors*	*%*
Less than 10000	91	41.55
10001 – 20000	70	31.96
20001 – 30000	34	15.53
30001 – 40000	9	4.11
40001 – 50000	10	4.57
50001 & above	5	2.28
Total	219	100.00

Table 13: Monthly Household Income of the Foreign Tourists

Income Level	*No. of Visitors*	*%*
Less than 50000	18	39.13
50001 – 100000	15	32.61
100001 – 150000	4	8.70
150001 & above	9	19.57
Total	46	100.00

Table 14: Activities carried out in Sikkim

Activities	*Domestic*	*%*	*Foreigner*	*%*
Enjoying scenic beauty	157	71.69	24	52.17
Trekking	0	0.00	14	30.43
Enjoying local flora & fauna	12	5.48	5	10.87
Enjoying local culture	12	5.48	10	21.74
Learning Buddhist Culture	9	4.11	9	19.57

Table 15: Average per capita Travel Cost

	Travel Cost (1)	*F&L Charge (2)*	*(2) as a % of (1) (3)*
Domestic	5470.47	1923.77	35.17
Foreigner	24550.27	6406.41	26.10

Table 16: Descriptive Statistics of Travel Cost

Nationality	*Minimum*	*Maximum*	*Mean*	*Std. Deviation*	*Coeff. of Variation*	*Median*
Domestic	660.00	180000.00	21395.26	26381.46	123.30	15000
Foreigner	3000.00	300000.00	37429.45	59870.01	159.95	10400
Total	660.00	300000.00	24178.56	34967.31	144.62	13000

Table 17: Descriptive Statistics of per head Travel Cost

Nationality	*Minimum*	*Maximum*	*Mean*	*Std. Deviation*	*Coeff. of Variation*
Domestic	330.00	42000.00	5479.1472	5624.7882	102.6581
Foreigner	888.89	173800.00	24550.2657	36366.6882	148.1315
Total	330.00	173800.00	8789.60	17433.60	198.34

Table 18: Whether the charge is reasonable for visiting Sikkim

	Domestic	*%*	*Foreigner*	*%*
Reasonable	183	83.56	41	89.13
Not reasonable	36	16.44	5	10.87
Total	219	100	46	100

Table 19: Present State of Conservation in Sikkim

	Domestic	*%*	*Foreigner*	*%*
Adequate	169	77.17	29	63.04
Inadequate	50	22.83	17	36.96
Total	219	100	46	100

Table 20: Willing to pay more for the Nature

	Domestic	*%*	*Foreigner*	*%*
Yes	137	62.56	28	78.26
No	82	37.44	18	21.74
Total	219	100	46	100

Table 21: Reasons for Unwillingness

	Domestic	*%*	*Foreigner*	*%*
Not worth it	51	62.20	14	87.5
Not enough income	26	31.71	2	12.5
Charges are OK	5	6.10	0	0
Total	82	100.00	16	100

Table 22: Total Willingness to pay of Tourists

WTP (in Rs.)	*Domestic*	*%*	*Foreigner*	*%*
Less or equal to 50	87	63.50	7	25.00
51 – 100	33	24.09	10	35.71
101 – 150	3	2.19	1	3.57
151 & above	11	8.03	10	35.71
Total	137	100.00	28	100.00

Table 23: Descriptive Statistics of WTP of Tourists

	Domestic	*Foreigner*
Number	137	28
Maximum	1180	1920
Minimum	4	15
Standard Deviation	176.25	77.5
Median	45	77.5

Table 24: Willing to pay more for the Nature

	Domestic	*%*	*Foreigner*	*%*
Yes	137	62.56	28	78.26
No	82	37.44	18	21.74
Total	219	100	46	100

Table 25: Reasons for Unwillingness

	Domestic	*%*	*Foreigner*	*%*
Not worth it	51	62.20	14	87.5
Not enough income	26	31.71	2	12.5
Charges are OK	5	6.10	0	0
Total	82	100.00	16	100

Table 26: Willingness to pay of the Domestic Tourists

Income Group	*Total Respondents*	*WTP*			
		Yes	*%*	*No*	*%*
Less than 10000	91	51	56.04	40	43.96
10001 – 20000	70	46	65.71	24	34.29
20001 – 30000	34	23	67.65	11	32.35
31000 – 40000	9	3	33.33	6	66.67
40001 – 50000	10	9	90	1	10
50001 – 60000	2	2	100	0	0
60001 & above	3	3	100	0	0

Table 27: Willingness to pay of Foreign Tourists

Income Group	*Total Respondents*	*WTP*			
		Yes	*%*	*No*	*%*
Less than 49999	16	8	50	8	50
50000–99999	16	10	62.5	6	37.5
100000–149999	2	2	100	0	0
150000 & above	12	8	66.67	4	33.33

Table 28: Reasons for coming to Sikkim

Reasons	*Not at all Important*	*Important*	*Very Important*	*Extremely Important*
Scenic Beauty	3	15	66	181
Trekking	228	18	3	16
Local flora & fauna	150	66	32	17
Local culture	129	79	35	22
Quality of services	168	46	36	15
Buddhist culture	179	50	17	19

Table 29: Justification of Charges

	Yes	*%*	*No*	*%*
Domestic	183	83.56	36	16.44
Foreigner	41	89.13	5	10.87

Table 30: Justification of Charges – Incomewise (Domestic)

Income level	*Yes*	*%*	*No*	*%*	*Total*
Less than 9999	49	80.33	12	19.67	61
10000 – 19999	59	86.76	9	13.24	68
20000 – 29999	37	84.09	7	15.91	44
30000 & above	22	84.62	4	15.38	26

Table 31: Perception of Domestic Tourists on the Justification of Travel Cost in Sikkim

Monthly Household Income	Justified (No.)	%	Average per capita Travel Cost	Average No. of Nights spent	Unjustified (No.)	%	Average per capita Travel Cost	Average No. of Nights spent
Less than 9999	49	80.33	3674.49	4.53	12	19.67	3660.78	4.66
10000 – 19999	59	86.76	4334.61	4.66	9	13.24	2842.96	5.22
20000 – 29999	37	84.09	5397.28	3.7	7	15.91	8678.57	4.57
30000 & above	22	84.62	12810.08	4.72	4	15.38	4698.33	3.75
Total/Wt. Average	167		5492.89		32		4658	

Table 32: Justification of Charges – Incomewise (Foreigner)

Income level	*Yes*	*%*	*No*	*%*	*Total*
Less than 49999	17	100.00	0	0.00	17
50000–99999	14	87.50	2	12.50	16
100000–149999	2	66.67	1	33.33	3
150000 & above	7	100.00	0	0.00	7

Table 33: Distribution of Domestic Tourists on per capita Travel Cost

Per capita Budget	*Visitors (In no.)*	*%*	*Per capita income (Rs.)*	*Willing-ness to pay*	*%*	*Average Willingness to pay*	*No Willingness to pay (No. of Tourists)*	*%*
Less than 2000	31	14.16	2943.33	19	61.29	88	12	38.71
2001 – 4000	94	42.92	3906.63	47	50	62	47	50
4001 – 6000	45	20.55	7127.85	36	80	81.25	9	20
6001 – 8000	22	10.05	8242.42	16	72.73	64	6	27.27
8001 – 10000	4	1.83	7770.83	2	50	130	2	50
10001 & above	23	10.5	10408.69	17	73.91	205	6	26.09
Total/Wt. Average	219		5621.16	137		89.54	82	

Table 34: Distribution of Foreign Tourists on per capita Travel Cost

Per capita Budget	*Visitors (In no.)*	*%*	*Per capita Income (Rs.)*	*Willing-ness to pay*	*%*	*Average Willing-ness to pay*	*No Willing-ness to pay (No. of Tourists)*	*%*
Less than 2000	1	2.17	9444.44	1	50.00	1060.00	0	0
2001 – 4000	7	15.22	210509.52	3	42.86	47.50	4	57.14
4001 – 6000	11	23.91	51561.81	5	45.45	153.18	6	54.55
6001 – 8000	4	8.70	103000	2	50	47.50	2	50
8001 – 10000	3	6.52	138000	2	66.67	173.33	1	33.33
10001 & above	20	43.48	80059	15	75	474.33	5	25
Total/Wt. Average	46	100	97334.15	28		340.18		

6

Tourism Policy of Guyana and Select State of India: An Insight

TOURISM POLICY OF GUYANA: AN INSIGHT

I. Basic Features of the Sector

A. Guyana's Current Tourism Product

Tourism takes diverse forms, each with appeal to a particular class of tourist and with its own implications for the country's infrastructure and revenue earnings from tourism. Guyana is ideally placed to take advantage of eco–tourism, which is currently the fastest growing segment of the tourism industry. The potential of eco–tourism today parallels the potential of the "sun, sea and sand" locations in the Caribbean when the tourism market was emerging forty years ago. However, eco–tourism is an entirely different industry and Guyana is uniquely placed to take full advantage of it because of two basic comparative advantages. First, the diversity of Guyana's flora and fauna, the virgin rainforests and the vast array of waterfalls, rivers and creeks are unique factors that set Guyana apart from her Caribbean neighbours who rely heavily on tourism. These are in a virtually pristine state on a scale that is rare in today's world. The second advantage is the fact that Guyana is the only English–speaking country in the South American Amazon Basin. This advantage cannot be underestimated in terms of its appeal to markets such as Europe, the United States and Canada, which are the main markets connected with eco–tourism.

However, eco–tourism development must be pursued in with extreme care and consideration for the natural environment. This is the eco–tourism dilemma, to find a balance in exploiting a natural site for eco–tourism activities without destroying the very location that the activity depends on. Any eco–tourism venture undertaken has to take this into account.

Current eco–tourism operations in Guyana are listed in Appendix 1, which summarizes all of Guyana's current tourism offerings, based on information supplied by the Tourism Association of Guyana (TAG).

B. Pertinent Characteristics of Visitor Travel to Guyana

The recently conducted Visitor Survey of Guyana by the Caribbean Tourism Organization in cooperation with the Guyana Statistical Bureau and the Ministry of Trade, Tourism and Industry provides many insights into the basic features of the sector.[1] The survey shows that the main distinguishing feature of the Guyana visitor profile is a relatively high proportion of business visitors and persons visiting friends and relatives. The peak season for Northern visitors to Guyana is in the winter months (see Appendix 2). Most other characteristics of visitor traffic reflect these basic facts.

Of the total of 112,751 non–Guyanese who visited in 1994, it is estimated that the overwhelming majority are Guyanese who have acquired other nationality, returning to visit family; business persons; international volunteers and members of NGOs; and visitors on official business. It is estimated that of the arriving foreigners no more than 2,000 come primarily for tourism, as the term is commonly understood. These persons would spend, on average, the equivalent of a few hundred US dollars per stay, certainly less than US$1,000. Therefore, in very approximate terms, it may be calculated that the sector at present generates between 1 and 2 million US dollars per year in foreign exchange earnings. However, the potential would be considerably more than that with a systematic effort to improve the country's infrastructure and develop an appropriate tourism programme.

C. The Opportunity

Some pertinent facts about tourism that demonstrate its potential impact are:

- The economies of other countries, not unlike Guyana, have been transformed in short order by tourism.
- Travel and tourism are on the brink of becoming the world's largest single industry.
- Even in a highly-developed economy like Britain's with industries of vast size, tourism is the second biggest industry.
- Worldwide tourism receipts are projected to grow by anything from 3 per cent to 6 per cent annually for the next ten years; the industry is estimated to be worth over US$3 trillion in 1996.

The overall benefit of tourism is that most of the steps which a developing country needs to take in order to improve its standard of living are exactly those which are required to develop tourism within a country. Some of the benefits of tourism are:

(1) A larger tax base for national development
(2) The generation of foreign exchange
(3) The provision of national employment
(4) The promotion of rural and interior development
(5) Human resources development.

Tourism is not simply an attempt to save the environment; it is also an important opportunity for Guyana's economic development. Properly managed, it is a non–depleting, non–consumptive industry that provides ever–increasing economic benefits in a sustainable manner.

II. Policies of the Sector

There is little evidence to suggest that a tourism policy existed prior to the 1990s, either implicitly or explicitly. Several factors may have been responsible for this. First, the Government may have felt that Guyana does not possess what it takes to be a tourist destination. Second, the apprehension that impacts associated with tourism would exacerbate social problems, discouraged the development of tourism. However, in recent years the emergence of eco–tourism as an alternative to resort–based mass tourism has generated an awareness of Guyana's potential for a more beneficial, less intrusive type of activity.

A. Tourism Policies from 1989 to 1992

In 1989 a study funded by the European Community (EC)[2] formulated a policy framework for the sector. The study recognized the importance of tourism in the generation of employment and the creation of income. A number of recommendations were made, including:

1. The maintenance of effective consultation with all sectors of the tourism industry to create a harmonious relationship between the public and private sectors.
2. The provision of fiscal and other incentives to attract foreign investment and entrepreneurial skills to accelerate new development and to obtain a critical mass in the range of accommodation and attractions.
3. The identification and removal of obstacles and deterrents to new investment and the expansion of existing businesses with tourism potential.
4. The improvement of both internal and international airline connections to foster tourism.
5. The protection of the natural beauty of the country through legislative and other Government measures.

These recommendations were accepted and ratified by the Government, but most have not been translated into practice. Most of the recommendations remain applicable today.

B. Current Policies

While a written tourism policy does not exist, certain policy decisions have been instituted to give guidance to the tourism industry. These are as follows:

1. Removal of the visa requirement for the major tourist generating markets, in Japan, North America, Western Europe and Scandinavian and Commonwealth countries, as of 1993.
2. The introduction of a 10 per cent room tax on all establishments with a capacity of fifteen (15) or more rooms. However, the funds raised from this tax are not channeled back into the industry.

3. A tourism incentive package that granted duty free concessions to a number of items was prepared for the sector in 1995. Investors have expressed total frustration at the bureaucratic bottlenecks in accessing these concessions. These concessions in their present form do not offer any meaningful incentives to the industry.
4. The Government's decision to commission the Organization of American States (OAS) to develop an Integrated National Eco–Tourism Development Plan, of which a Management Plan for Kaieteur National Park is a component.
5. The promotion of 1996 as "Visit Guyana Year" with the aim of attracting 250,000 visitors to Guyana; this effort has been perceived by the industry as poorly conceived and premature, with no input from the private sector.

At the same time, Government has strengthened the Tourism Division of the Ministry of Trade, Tourism and Industry. There have been attempts at enhancing the image of the Timehri International Airport and sensitizing Immigration and Customs Officers to their new obligations in a tourist destination. Efforts are being made to educate the general population about the new tourism initiatives through the media and other initiatives such as the 1996 Tourism and Environmental Exposition.

III. Description of Principal Issues and Constraints facing the Sector

A. Issues

1. Clear Definition of Tourism Products in Guyana

Before any real and meaningful development of tourism in Guyana can take place, it is necessary to have an understanding of the type of tourism products that are both suited to and suitable for Guyana. Efforts to develop these products and Guyana's image as a destination must be done in accordance with what Guyana determines to be its needs. This requires a precise definition of the types of tourism that are compatible not only with the product that Guyana has to offer, but also with what the country hopes to achieve from tourism development. It is also necessary to examine aspects of tourism which are undesirable for this country.

a. Forms of tourism suited to Guyana's natural product and development goals

The main tourism markets that are considered to be suitable or potentially suited to Guyana are:

Eco–tourism: Eco–tourism is a natural choice for Guyana for several reasons. First, Guyana's vast and pristine rainforest and savannahs, the abundant wildlife and spectacular natural attractions make Guyana a prime destination for eco–tourists. They are now looking for new, relatively untouched environments, and Guyana stands in a good position to take advantage of this as long as sustainable development techniques are used. Another signal advantage that Guyana has over many of its competitors in the region is that, as mentioned, it is the only English–speaking part of the Amazon Basin.

Eco–tourism is itself advantageous to Guyana because it endeavours to respect the natural environment and different cultures. It is a type of tourism which concentrates on small numbers of tourists paying relatively high prices, thus maximizing the economic benefits to the country (which is after all the major reason for tourism development) while minimizing the negative effects on the environment and society which are generally associated with traditional or mass tourism. Eco–tourism itself is a very broad classification and ranges from "soft" eco–tourism, which can include luxury accommodations, to "hard" eco–tourism, which focuses more on the surroundings in its natural form and less on personal comfort. To develop eco–tourism, more lodges are needed around the country in key locations, along with better transport and improvements in public health. In particular, it is essential to reduce drastically the incidence of malaria in the interior. A system of national parks and protected areas also needs to be established, preferably around these key attractions.

A basic element of eco–tourism is information and education. Most eco–tourists want to learn more about the environment, both physical and human, that they are visiting. On an international level this requires that adequate information be readily available and accessible to the potential visitor through literature (promotional and information–based) as well as through existing and emerging technologies such as the Internet and CD–ROM. On a local level, the transmission of information necessitates highly trained tourist guides who can communicate and interpret nature in a way that is entertaining and educational. The eco–tourist is typically a well educated, well travelled, professional (generally over 35–40 years old) with a high income and keen environmental, social and political awareness. He or she has probably travelled to several island destinations over the past 10 years and is now tired of the same routine. Eco–tourists are looking for new ways to escape the winter and big city pressures. At the same time, such persons easily see through operations that do not respect the environment or indigenous populations. If Guyana is serious about eco–tourism, it needs to embrace overarching environmental policies and ethics, so as not to be perceived as a "fake."

Adventure Tourism: Adventure tourism is another growing segment of the tourism sector and can also be divided into "hard" and "soft" categories. It is a sub–sector of eco–tourism. The safety of tourists undertaking this, as indeed all forms of tourism, is of paramount importance since negative publicity or perceptions in this area can have a negative effect on Guyana as a tourism destination in general. It is necessary to ensure that all operators work to high standards of safety and that there is adequate provision for emergency evacuation and medical facilities. The absence of national medical and emergency evacuation facilities is a major hurdle that must be overcome. Tour operators must also be encouraged to have and use appropriate equipment for the various adventure elements of a tour.

Multi–destination Tourism: This is a growing segment of the tourism industry, as more and more holiday makers are travelling further distances on vacation and visiting two to more countries. Given Guyana's distance from its main markets of Europe and America and its proximity to the Caribbean, joint destination packages make sense for Guyana, especially in the short term as Guyana builds and expands the products it offers. While eco–tourism is a natural tourism choice in itself for many people, the traditional form of "sun, sea and sand" tourism is still a major attraction for most tourists. Guyana has a unique product which is not widely available in the other Caribbean islands. Good flight connections to Trinidad, Barbados, Grenada and Curacao make these destinations good partners with which to team up to market a joint destination package.

Cruise Ship Tourism: There is a lot of controversy regarding cruise ship tourism in the Caribbean, and there is a school of thought in Guyana which maintains that cruise ship tourism on a large scale is not compatible with eco–tourism or in the interests of Guyana. This kind of tourism does not increase hotel occupancy rates and therefore much of the tourist expenditure is not spent in the destination country. Potentially large numbers of day tourists can bring detrimental influences to the country, such as increases in pollution, crime, drug trade and prostitution. In general, cruise ship tourism requires excellent shopping facilities, including duty free shops, speedy customs and immigration clearance, effective security and short, well coordinated tours. This type of tourism can bring revenue into the country in the form of a government head-tax and tourist expenditure on craft and other consumer items. However, tourist expenditure is often minimal in comparison to the costs. There is a rough estimate that average revenue obtained by Caribbean countries from cruise ship tourism is about US$5 per head. There is also no head–tax at present on cruise ship tourists to Guyana.

Cruise ship tourism should not be ruled out, but it should be carefully monitored and controlled to ensure that the detrimental effects of mass tourism do not occur. Cruise ship tourists that are here specifically as eco–tourists should be encouraged; there are such cruise ship tourists that visit South America. It is important to note, though, that cruise ship tourism of the wrong kind can destroy the very thing that Guyana is trying to sell.

The Business Market: A large captive tourism market associated with the business travel already exists. This market can generally be divided into three categories: short–term, long–term and conference travel. The long–term business traveller generally works in or around Georgetown during the week and has the weekend available for travel. The short–term business traveller generally has less time in the country and a less predictable time schedule. However, the country can only handle a small number of business visitors. To cater to large markets, much more infrastructure is needed; service has to be fast and efficient, with all necessary business and communication facilities available.

Heritage/Cultural Tourism: There is room for the promotion of Guyana's historical sites for their historical and architectural value. Sites suitable for this type of tourism include Georgetown, Fort

Island, Magdelenburg and Kyk–Over–Al. Amerindian culture is of potential interest to tourists. However, at the same time it is important to protect these communities from the negative impact which tourism can have on their traditional ways of life.

There are other types of tourism that are possible, such as *industrial* and *agricultural tourism,* which show potential. Tourists have expressed interest in visiting mining and forestry operations and facilities for rum and sugar production. In the case of the first two, these can be tourist attractions only if carried out under strict environmental controls.

While it is hardly likely that many tourists will travel to Guyana specifically to see Georgetown, the beauty of the capital city should not be underestimated in encouraging a tourist in Guyana to stay an extra night. This would have a positive spinoff for restaurants, taxi drivers, craft shops and other local businesses. Measures need to be taken to promote cultural offerings such as art exhibitions and presentations of traditional dance, and to preserve the traditional charm of the city, especially its rich architecture. The spate of concrete buildings being constructed where old Victorian style buildings once existed can only be viewed negatively.

b. Types of tourism not desirable for Guyana

Among the tourism products that are undesirable for development in Guyana are casino gambling and sex tourism, as well as hunting expeditions. Various agencies, such as TAG, have reported an increase in requests for *hunting* recreation but this contradicts the ethos of eco–tourism. The present hunting legislation lays down quotas, lists of protected species and hunting seasons that are questionable. In general, the wildlife trade seriously discredits eco–tourism efforts. In addition, due to Guyana's geography, demographics and human resource constraints, monitoring and enforcement of hunting regulations would be extremely problematic.

2. Eco–tourism

Because of its importance to Guyana eco–tourism deserves special attention. Eco–tourism cannot be simply classified as nature or adventure tourism. It usually denotes a particular type of tourism that is small in scale and in which local control and local benefits are of primary importance. As it is often closely linked to natural environments and habitats, it necessitates an understanding of the principles of environmental protection and sustainable development. One of the most widely accepted definitions of sustainable development is advanced in the Brundtland Report of 1987 which sees it as development that "meets the needs of the present without compromising the ability of future generations to meet their own needs."

The idea of sustainable tourism is linked to the notions of renewable and non–renewable resources, resource conservation and carrying capacity (i.e. the amount of human presence, both long and short-term, that specific natural environments and eco–systems can sustain without significant deterioration). It is a dynamic and evolving concept of partnership between humanity and nature and requires the strict management of each resource – land, air, water and wildlife – to ensure optimum value and continuity of supply. There is a convergence between long–term business interests and sustainable development that can be achieved without "cutting corners." At the same time, however, there are a number of socio–cultural, economic and environmental issues that impinge on eco–tourism and on the extent to which it is developed.

It should not be assumed that eco–tourism is a type of tourism in which tourists expect less than other forms of tourism. At the end of the vacation, they expect the same sense of satisfaction and leisure as they would find in other destinations; therefore, eco–tourism has to have fun elements built into it. Visitors must have rewarding and interesting things to do, and it is the responsibility of operators to provide these elements.

a. Lessons from other countries

In planning for eco–tourism, it is useful to learn from the leaders in this new industry, such as Costa Rica and Belize. Costa Rica and Belize have progressed well ahead of Guyana in eco–tourism and "rainforest travelism", and they have some significant advantages over Guyana. In the first place, they both have valuable sea and sand assets; Costa Rica has beaches on both its Atlantic and Pacific sides and Belize has, beside beaches, some of the world's best scuba diving.

Both these countries are closer to the North American markets than Guyana. This not only means cheaper and more frequent flights, but also more primary target cities from which direct flights depart, providing better marketing prospects. Guyana only has direct flight access to Miami, New York and Toronto in North America, and the frequency and quality of air service is well below optimal. Costa Rica (19,000 square miles) and Belize (8,000 square miles), though smaller in size and more advanced in development, also have more accessible interiors with cheaper transportation than Guyana has, with its 83,000 square miles. The consequence of these international and national transportation advantages is that many more potential customers can, conveniently and less expensively, leave home and arrive at a chosen eco–lodge in Costa Rica or Belize without losing an entire precious day of their vacation. It would take two days to get to Guyana from many of their target cities.

In addition to these broad advantages, those two countries have other miscellaneous advantages of varying importance and permanence. They have substantial archeological ruins to visit, active and inactive volcanoes, white water rafting, butterfly farms and well developed nature trails. They are also better able to handle medical emergencies. Costa Rica has long been a preferred retirement country for North Americans, and it has a very positive image compared to Guyana's "Jonestown" reputation. Both countries have established strong and supportive connections with prominent international environmental organizations. Their governments have also invested substantial sums of money into developing and promoting the tourism industry.

One of the most important lessons that can be learnt from the majority of tourism destinations in the Caribbean is the detrimental effect of mass tourism. Islands such as Jamaica, Barbados, and Antigua have regretted their attempts to attract large numbers of discount–rate tourists, who provide a much narrower margin of profitability and add pressure to the local infrastructure. The potential of eco–tourism is closely related to the carrying capacity of the land. Guyana needs to avoid falling into the trap of thinking that the more tourists that visit, the better it is for the industry and the economy. Emphasis should be placed on obtaining the maximum benefits from a minimum number of visitors. Elements of mass tourism that have crept into the industries of Belize and Costa Rica are damaging the very product that they are trying to sell. It is important to note that promotions such as price–cutting have the effect of attracting too many tourists and creating the perception of low quality. Policies therefore need to be adopted that orient the industry away from mass tourism.

Another important lesson to be learned is that the value of a country's offerings increases with time. In a generation or two, the worth of Guyana's natural attractions will multiply several times as such sites become fewer in the world and more people seek relief from choked up developed cities. This has been the experience of Belize and Costa Rica where people are willing to pay increasingly more for the opportunity to visit their attractions. In retrospect, it has also been the experience of Caribbean island destinations; few of these islands would have thought 40–50 years ago that their beaches would be worth what they are today.

b. Guyana's advantages

Guyana therefore needs to examine what it has to offer that is special in order to make it a competitive eco–tourism destination. Kaieteur is a terrific asset that should be used intelligently to maximize its value in developing this new industry. With the international language of English spoken by Guyanese, including Amerindians, the country has another major selling point.

But most of all, the singular advantage that Guyana has is that it possesses vast areas of interior that are still pristine compared to Costa Rica and Belize, and most of Panama, Venezuela and Brazil. Further, Guyana's virtually untouched forests are so diverse that they can show the entire spectrum of tropical rainforest at its best. Where most of Guyana's competitors have comparatively small pockets of rainforest, most of which have farms and rural developments nearby, Guyana has vast rainforests and savannahs with many beautiful waterfalls and very diverse flora and fauna that still are relatively intact. It is vital and intrinsic to the development of tourism to protect the integrity of Guyana's natural environment as a major selling point.

The beauty of the country's ninety miles of Shell Beach and Mangrove Swamp is unique. The four species of sea turtles laying eggs, the bird life, the tropical swamp life, the raw, wild flavour of this coast has to be experienced to be fully appreciated. The expansive southern savannahs are another entirely different tropical ecosystem; there, instead of sea turtles Guyana has unique river turtles. There is bird life such as the Harpy Eagle where the forested mountains meet the savannahs; to a bird enthusiast the Harpy alone provides more reason to visit Guyana than Kaieteur Falls itself. The petroglyphs (some of which are estimated to be over 6,000 years old), are indications of ancient civilizations. The cultural diversity and friendliness of the Guyanese people are also major advantages.

3. Protected Areas

The establishment of designated protected areas for Guyana is important for distinguishing between those areas to be protected and those to be utilized for extractive industries. Guyana is the only country in South America without a protected areas system. This is a major handicap for a country that is aiming to develop eco–tourism. To correct this situation, the Government has commissioned a team of scientists to prepare a project for a National Protected Areas System (NPAS) in Guyana. The NPAS project is being supported by the Global Environment Facility of the World Bank. Preparatory stages of the project involve collaborative efforts with Conservation International and the Smithsonian Institute. Additional work on protected areas is being conducted through the Amazon Co–operation Treaty (ACT), under which one project examines options for compatible economic development of the Amazon, through possible eco–tourism ventures. From the perspective of protected areas, eco–tourism may symbolize a new and promising way of protecting fragile ecosystems by enhancing their economic value in a sustainable manner.

The Iwokrama Rainforest Programme also offers potential for combining protected areas with tourism and this should be fully explored. The use of 360,000 hectares of virgin rainforest presents an opportunity for the development of eco–tourism and international cooperation based on the principles and practices of sustainable development. In fact, the Iwokrama project has already embarked on an undertaking that would train tourists on various aspects of the forests and surrounding ecosystems. It is expected that future protected areas would also allow for some form of eco–tourism including the education of tourists. Given the high educational element involved in eco–tourism, more international environmental agencies as well as scientific and medical research organizations could be vigorously encouraged to set up operations in protected areas that welcome visitors and study groups. This has been done successfully in many eco–tourism destinations. The Audubon project on Shell Beach is an example of such a combination of environmental research and protection operations, which should be actively sought by the Government as a definitive component of its tourism policy.

Linking tourism to conservation in National Parks requires that the economic gain by investors be coupled with at least two additional goals, benefiting the Amerindians. First, a tourism/conservation programme, as planned for the Kanuku Mountain range or the Kaieteur National Park, etc., ideally should extend the economic benefits of development to a broad base of the local human population through employment, compensation fees, or the development of social services. This was the approach taken in Kenya's Amboseli National Park, where it was demonstrated that local people were likely to protect lands and wildlife when they had an economic incentive to do so. The same would apply to the Makushi people who live at the foot of the Kanukus.

Second, tourism in these protected areas should be supported not only by research on the human impact of tourists on the ecosystem, but also by the creation of some mechanism that would allow visitors to contribute to the park following their visit. Excited by their experience, they may want to help, either through direct contributions to a conservation group working in the locality of their visit or though word–of–mouth advertising of the facility.

Private protected areas should also be encouraged. These areas need not be large; there are some in Costa Rica that are just 5,000 acres in size, although the weight of scientific evidence is increasingly in favour of larger areas.

4. Kaieteur National Park

Since Kaieteur Falls is the main tourist attraction in Guyana, its potential demands that it be given special attention in the development of the tourism industry. There is no doubt that the Kaieteur Falls and the surrounding Kaieteur Park constitute such a compelling attraction on a world scale that they could be Guyana's beachhead into the international tourism market.

Yet, Kaieteur, far from being world renowned, is scarcely known at all beyond a small circle of Guyanese and friends of Guyana, and a combination of circumstances has already put it in danger of being spoiled. Although only a few visitors go there, those few, wandering about at will on very fragile soils and in a fragile environment, are sufficient in present circumstances to pose a threat to the viability of the site and to its unique biosphere. Unregulated mining in the Potaro River watershed and the Kaieteur Gorge also poses a threat to the scenic beauty and ecosystem of the area. Thus, with Kaieteur Guyana has the worst of both worlds; it is not the major tourist destination it should be, yielding the great returns it is capable of but at the same time it is already an endangered site. Monitoring and management to protect it against unregulated visitation and illegal activities such as mining are urgently needed if its integrity as a protected area, and indeed Guyana's integrity as an eco–tourism destination, are to be kept intact.

An escape from this unfortunate situation will be found through well–managed tourism as a means of rationally exploiting and at the same time preserving this great natural resource. Tourist visitation to Kaieteur could increase significantly and entail less damage than is currently being done to the site. The key is the proper design and management of visitation. For example, by having sight–seeing visitors follow prescribed boardwalk trails, and by allowing others with more serious interests in exploring the area to move around only with skilled and licensed guides, many more people could enjoy the Kaieteur experience, and they could enjoy it vastly more, than at present. Managed visitation to Kaieteur would bring in the revenue required for financial sustainability of the site and would generate surpluses for general conservation and development purposes.

Fortunately, Government has commissioned a project funded by the Organization of American States to develop a master plan for the Kaieteur National Park. When complete, this plan will give details for the layout of the site, guidelines for construction on the site and rules for the limits of acceptable change. This plan would be an integral component of the broader Eco–tourism Development Plan mentioned above.

5. Amerindian Involvement in Tourism Development

Tourism is an economic imperative for Guyana that is likely to benefit Amerindians if properly pursued. It presents Amerindians with an opportunity to build an indigenous industry which is labour intensive and benefits the local communities.

For a start, English–speaking tourists, who make up the majority of visitors to Guyana, will find it easy to communicate with indigenous peoples in the interior. What could follow from this simple advantage is a best case scenario for the involvement of Guyanese Amerindians in eco–tourism ventures. Guyanese Amerindians are unsurpassed by any other ethnic group in Guyana when it comes to knowledge of the interior and can be trained to deliver that knowledge in a systematic way to tourists. This will contribute to a high quality experience, resulting in positive word–of–mouth advertising, which should lead to an increase in eco–tourist numbers.

The case of exploitation of wildlife is a good example of how an extractive industry could be turned into a sustainable economic venture for Amerindians. The trade does not earn a lot for the trapper, who gets a fraction of the exporter's profits and generally engages in trapping as a monetary supplement to subsistence practices. Jungle wildlife viewing, in contrast, could involve the same trapper, moving from marketing a consumptive, probably unsustainable activity to a non–consumptive, sustainable use for photo or adventure tours. Amerindian bird trappers could convert to guides if the option were available and if it proved to be a better financial deal for them.

When established, the National Protected Areas System could involve Amerindians in its eco–tourism activities. Amerindians could be trained as park rangers and guides, since they have an unrivaled knowledge of the local terrain and its natural resources. Further, they are more likely to remain in these areas in the long term than the average coastlander candidate filling such positions.

The impact of such measures on Amerindian communities can be significant because the industry is labour–intensive and can provide jobs for large numbers of unskilled workers. The industry can also stimulate local economies through increased local demands for transportation, lodging, food, materials and nature interpretation. Thus, even a relatively small share of tourism revenues can provide an extremely strong boost to the local economy. New job opportunities would stem the flow from villages to the coast, Brazil and Venezuela. There is great potential income for women and other less mobile Amerindians from the sale of handicraft to tourists, promoted by demonstrations and explanations of the craft processes.

On the other hand, jobs linked to eco–tourism could be seasonal and subject to world economic conditions. While eco–tourism is meant to be small in scale, it has the potential to make local communities too dependent upon it. These communities are likely to suffer much more from a decline in the tourism sector than the country as a whole would. For small communities that depend upon agriculture and other primary activities, eco–tourism has the potential to draw labour out of those sectors. For example, in indigenous communities, the craft industry may thrive at the expense of food production.

The influence of foreign cultures may also impact upon communities in such a way that many traditional values may be lost. Some theorists feel that commercialization of culture can lead to pseudo–culture, folklore specially devised for tourists, alteration of traditional crafts due to commercial pressures, and the replacement of traditional handicrafts by cheap souvenirs.

Before tourism can benefit Amerindians, therefore, there must be fundamental institutional strengthening. This requires a participatory approach that must be applied through direct discussion, education and practical training programmes. Amerindian groups should be empowered to start their own tourist ventures in a small and manageable way. These can grow as experience is gained.

6. Marketing

Guyana starts off as a difficult sell in the world of tourism. While it has no image in the world travel market, it also has to cope with the negative image of Jonestown and the perception of being a poor, fragile democracy. Compare this reputation to that of a West Indian island like Jamaica, with a history of greater political turmoil and violence, gun–crime and drugs; yet Jamaica, "where the nights are gay and the sun shines daily on the mountain top," benefits from helpful romantic images in the international marketplace. Guyana is even sometimes confused in name with Ghana in Africa, so one has to be sure that visitors do not get on the wrong plane, going to the wrong continent. Top priorities will have to be filling the gap in knowledge that exists in the world about Guyana and working to erase the current negative images.

Tourism is an export product, but unlike other exports of Guyana, tourism is intangible. To sell tourism is to sell a dream or fantasy, and such a product cannot be weighed or put into a box. The customer buying the tourism product cannot sample it before buying, nor can he or she take it home after purchase. Tourism is a singular and highly personal experience that is slightly different for every visitor. Factors that contribute to a sense of satisfaction with a tourism experience are many, but chief among them are physical beauty (the environment wildlife, etc.), cultural experiences (authenticity of life, historical locations, etc), and a friendly, helpful population.

In marketing tourism it is also important to examine what the overseas market wants. At present, visitors to Guyana can be grouped into the following categories:

- Business people and official visitors with a few days to spare
- Expatriate Guyanese returning on holiday or business
- Expatriate workers based in Guyana
- Tourists coming over for a few days as part of a multi–destination holiday
- Tourists coming currently to Guyana for eco–tourism holidays

The first two categories plus international volunteers currently make up the vast majority of all visitors to Guyana, in fact over 95 per cent of the total number. The total number of visitors to Guyana, a little more than 100,000 annually, is small compared to other tourist destinations, but the potential for growth and resulting foreign exchange is large. Guyana could market itself as part of multi–destination packages, but this requires cooperation with operators from other countries and detailed planning, especially in the coordination of flights, so it may be best left to a later stage in the sector's development.

Guyana needs to realize that marketing is a business and cannot be accomplished though embassies, a past common error among those trying to promote emerging tourism. A visitor looking for a tourist destination spot will not visit every nearby embassy or consulate and, in any case, Guyana does not have embassies and consulates in all of the major target cities. Professional representation in the markets that Guyana wishes to attract is vital. In marketing Guyana's tourism product, planners have to be prepared to spend money. Successful marketing is done through advertising and being sure that Guyana is listed in all travel guides and books. Government also needs to appreciate that tourism is an export industry and should therefore be eligible for benefits normally afforded to other export sectors.

7. Expansion and Improvement of the Product offered

A sudden shortage of fuel for internal aviation, which still occurs, means that a visitor's planned itinerary is ruined. Unregulated or badly managed access to prime sites like Kaieteur – or a failure to stop environmental degradation arising from mining in the wrong places – will destroy the assets on which the growth of tourism depends. Inadequately or inappropriately developed lodging facilities and attractions will send visitors home disappointed, never to recommend Guyana to their friends. Insufficient attention to the total quality of the experience that the market wants, from the moment of arrival to the moment of departure, will spoil the potential of Guyana.

It is obvious that there are a number of aspects of tourism that must be in place at the same time to make a successful industry. A failure of any one of the various requirements for the industry will mean the failure of the entire industry. If Guyana is going to be serious about tourism, then all aspects must be working properly at the same time.

Product improvement should be centered on the following areas:

- *General Information:* At present it is extremely difficult for the would–be visitor to Guyana to find any reasonable country information in existing literature and guide books. There is a total lack of generic advertising of the country.

- *Easier Access to Guyana and its Interior:* There are only a few airlines that serve Guyana and these only go to limited destinations. For example, in North America direct flights can only be made to Miami, New York and Toronto. In Europe, only London, Frankfurt, Zurich and Amsterdam are served through Trinidad or Barbados. Attention needs to be paid to upgrading facilities at Timehri so as to attract American and European airlines (see Chapter 38 of the National Development Strategy). The process for obtaining flight rights should be streamlined, so that the industry could work more with airlines to develop new markets.

The current Guyana Airways Corporation (GAC) service to the interior is totally inadequate to satisfy the needs of Guyanese, let alone tourism. For example, many tour operators' report being unable to obtain seats on GAC flights to Lethem, even though TAG holds six seats up to eleven days before flights. The number of locations served by GAC and the frequency of flights are not adequate for the development of the industry. And yet Government regulations restrict the number of commercial seats available on domestic flights. Coordinated efforts between private operators and GAC are required to ameliorate these problems, as well as a change in the regulatory framework (Chapter 38).

Because of the limited road infrastructure the only access to many of Guyana's remote areas suitable for tourism is via light aircraft. There is a shortage of such aircraft to meet the current and future needs of tourism in Guyana. In addition the costs associated with this kind of transportation are high and add to the overall price of Guyana's tourist product. The current high taxes that the private sector pays on aviation fuel, spare parts and aircraft (from which GAC is exempted) add to the cost of this type of transport. There is no level playing field between private airline operations and the Government-owned GAC. There is insufficient free competition in the market to properly develop the airline industry locally. This makes tourism in Guyana uncompetitive with other destinations with better infrastructure and better access to main tourism sites.

- *Improved Infrastructure:* Of all the productive sectors of the economy, tourism is the one that depends most on the physical environment and other ambient conditions that exist in the country. Infrastructure of such airport facilities, roads, water systems and medical facilities has to be improved to attract tourists. Tourists often wish to know that when they return from an exotic interior destination they will be comforted by the luxuries of a quality hotel in Georgetown. The importance of hot showers, quality restaurants, smooth roads and courteous airport officials, for example, cannot be underestimated even to the most intrepid backpacking adventure tourist.
- *Reliable Medical and Evacuation Services*: The nature of Guyana's industry is that tourists travel to remote areas often under arduous and sometimes risky conditions. Inevitably there will be accidents and the need for emergency evacuation. At present this recourse is not available, nor are medical treatment and facilities to the level that most tourists would consider adequate.
- *Professional Product*: Guyana's tourism product needs to be handled more professionally. This can be achieved through a number of changes such as regulation and monitoring and developing provisions for prosecuting those who fail to comply with the regulations and standards. It also requires further investment at both the private and public levels, especially in providing qualified and skilled staff and fostering a professional atmosphere that encourages a strong sense of commitment, pride and responsibility.
- *Security*: Georgetown in particular has a bad name internationally as a dangerous city. In reality, it is probably safer than many cities around the world, but Guyanese over–emphasize the problem instead of taking corrective measures. Extra police and lighting are needed in principal tourist locations in the city and on frequently–used walkways. Security needs to be increased in key tourism sites; the potential for illegal immigration and the movement of drugs and other restricted goods demands a tighter net of security in these places.

- *Streamlining the Procedure for obtaining Interior Permits and Visas*: An interior permitting procedure is standard policy to ensure that Amerindians are protected. However, the system should be streamlined so that applications to travel to the interior can be processed quickly. Tourists only have limited holiday time and will not tolerate sitting in a government office for hours; they will simply leave and visit a more organized country. To properly regulate visitation to the interior, permits should only be granted to tourism companies who have a proven track record and are willing to respect the communities they are working in.
- *Public Liability Insurance*: International wholesalers and operators often inquire as to whether local operators carry public liability insurance. This requirement often determines whether an international operator will sell the Guyanese tourist product. Most local operators would like to carry such insurance but it is either unavailable or too expensive. This is an important area of concern as the nature of Guyana's product means that there will always be a risk of accidents. In the absence of insurance, the operators themselves are subject to payment of claims made by tourists, in amounts which can severely damage a small-scale operation. Furthermore, the amount of compensation that would be awarded by a Guyanese court would not be internationally comparable. The repercussions for Guyana in such a case would be severe and wide–reaching due to the adverse international publicity and the fact that the country as a whole can be blacklisted as a high-risk destination.

8. Standards within the Industry

There is a strong feeling of responsibility among operators to maintain a good reputation for the industry in Guyana as a whole. This means a degree of self–regulation could work beneficially to prevent rogue operators from damaging the reputation of everyone, especially when the industry is in such an early stage of development. The Tourism Association of Guyana can play a role in assisting a national regulatory agency to monitor the industry and indeed it is currently developing standards for safety. There are also plans to develop guidelines to cover other aspects of quality control in the future. The Association cannot by itself function as a regulatory body; it can provide checks and send warning signals to relevant authorities, and it can help educate operators, but enforceable legislation and regulations are needed.

Areas in which standards and regulations are urgently needed include:

- Standards for licensing tour operators.
- Regulations for building eco–tourism resorts.
- Standards for other customer servers such as taxi drivers, boats, hotels, restaurants, employment of staff, etc.
- Land use.

The enforcement of these standards will be vital for a successful industry. The standards must be accompanied with stiff penalties that are compatible with the severity of the infringement.

9. Investment

First and foremost, it must be remembered that eco–tourism is a business. Investors and bankers will only support the industry if the profit potential justifies the high financial risk. The key to its success is achieving high occupancy rates and filling tours. Policies that protect the environment and promote safety, and the like, are irrelevant in the absence of policies that could attract investment.

The Guyanese tourism industry is currently considered to be a high-risk business by investors and bankers. The country is simply not perceived as a good investment in tourism because of the multiple risks involved. In addition to the financial risks normally associated with tourism itself, there are problems peculiar to Guyana related to the fact that the country's democracy is still in a stage of consolidation, to the uncertain overall investment climate and to the fact that Guyana is hardly known and that eco–tourism is still an emerging market. Investors are very skeptical: all things considered, the potential return often does not instil confidence, and investors would prefer to take their tourism investments elsewhere.

Relevant points for consideration when formulating investment policies for tourism are:

- Guyana has no track record with respect to tourism.
- Eco–tourism is itself still an infant industry.
- After opening a resort or a tour operation, it takes between eighteen months to two years of extensive marketing efforts before customers of any significant numbers can be attracted.
- Contingencies have to be built into each plan, providing for periods of low-occupancy rates, delays before a profitable level of business is achieved, natural disasters, etc.
- The investor has to periodically spend money bringing the press, tour operators, Caribbean owners or managers (for joint tours), interested travel agents, and to prepare brochures, video tapes, etc. These costs are considerably higher during the start–up period.
- Lodges and tours for eco–tourism are generally small. Thus there are high per capita overhead expenses.
- Because of the high risk involved, investors need higher returns to satisfy the bankers' payback period of 5 to 6 years.
- Twenty–five per cent of the gross selling price of a resort room has to be paid to the tour operator and be used to service bank charges such as the use of American Express, etc. Another 10 per cent has to be devoted to cover advertising costs. The resort then has to cover operational expenses and make a profit with the remaining 65 per cent.
- Bankers would like to know that they can recover and transfer all property and land of an eco–tourism resort, as an adequate means of collateral in the event of a failed operation.

At the same time, capital investment in eco–tourism in Guyana is between a quarter to a third of the per unit cost of a similar investment in the Caribbean. The typical capital investment cost per unit at an eco–lodge is about US$35,000 with appropriate fiscal concessions and infrastructure already in place (i.e., roads, air strip, etc.). A similar unit in a Caribbean destination is about US$100,000. Bankers may be willing to back such investments, provided the concerns mentioned above are mitigated.

10. Education and Public Awareness

The behaviour of eco–tourists can be an important issue. One does not become environmentally sensitive and responsible simply by booking onto an "eco-tourism" holiday or day trip. Tourists should not only be educated about their responsibilities to the environment, they should also be educated about the environment. In fact, the latter is a major component of an "eco-tourism" vacation whereby visitors have an opportunity to put their cameras down and engage in dialogue with their hosts. It is useful for native people in a host country or region to recognize the elements of the natural environment that may be new and of interest to the visitor. Natives guides in particular should be alert for the "teachable moment" that creates a bond between host and visitor. A true eco-tourist is also an "anthropotourist", deriving pleasure and satisfaction from learning how the environment is viewed through the eyes of local people.

Local people also need to be educated to the potential impacts of receiving tourists as well as the expectations of such visitors. While it is certainly most important for local peoples to take pride in their customs and culture, it is also important to have an understanding of the travellers and their perspective on activities that may give rise to what is termed as "culture shock."

There are also misguided perceptions about tourism among the wider Guyanese public that need to be dispelled such as:

- That Guyana lacks true beauty and has limited tourism potential. (On the contrary, the tourism product is not limited, rather it is specialized.)
- That applying the traditional image of tourism, largely based on the Caribbean model of sand, sea, and sun is the only valid one.
- That the tourism industry benefits only a few.
- That the industry is one of servitude. (Rather, there is an important difference between servitude and professional service.)

An informed and trained citizenry is the backbone of any successful development process; education is the key. Guyanese need to appreciate the great value that the interior represents to the peoples of the densely populated urban cities of the developed world. A community that understands tourism is one that would be better able to benefit from it. Its development demands that the industry be developed and fashioned in the best interest of both the visitor and the residents of the community. This can only be done by creating an appropriate attitudinal environment and educating persons within the local community to talk about tourism as a viable alternative in Guyana. This should eventually lead to a wider understanding to the benefits of tourism and the role of society in this new industry.

NGOs can be a valuable source of funding and training of guides and other tourism–related staff. The Tourism Studies Unit at the University of Guyana could be strengthened to play an important role in educating the general public and disseminating accurate information. It can work in coordination with the Government's tourism regulating body, TAG and other NGOs, as well as the Carnegie School of Home Economics, hotels, and other tourism agencies. It should, however, guard against teaching a generic tourism product as opposed to teaching about the uniqueness of Guyana. Thus it should incorporate practical, on–the–job experience in its programme.

11. Partnerships in the Industry

a. The Tourism Division

At present, Government regulation and support services for the tourism industry are provided through the Tourism Division in the Ministry of Trade, Tourism and Industry. This division was created in July, 1991, and emerged out of a reorganization of the Public Service in 1990. Its creation hinged on a policy decision to formally establish a tourism industry in Guyana. One of its major functions is to co–ordinate the activities of the industry.

This division is also responsible for:

- The execution of national policy related to tourism.
- The formulation and monitoring of tourism guidelines and regulations.
- The marketing of the country's tourism image.
- Human resource development for the industry.

The Tourism Division is also a member of the Caribbean Tourism Organization (CTO) and functions as the local coordinating agency for CTO activities. Much effort in the Division has also focused on international marketing and development of the product and the required human resources.

Despite its best efforts, the Division of Tourism is understaffed and lacks the internal systems and structures for the smooth facilitation of programmes and activities required for its work. It is affected by many of the same ailments that are prevalent in other Government departments, such as a shortage of skills, a lack of facilities and no legal mandate to perform many of the functions that are required of the department.

b. The Tourism Association of Guyana Limited (TAG)

The Tourism Association of Guyana represents its members' interests in a number of ways by providing them with advice and assistance on marketing their products and making available all information concerning the promotion of Guyana abroad. It also deals with enquiries about tourism and passes on information to its members and to interested parties abroad. The Association has tried to promote the interests of its members by ensuring that high standards of safety and product quality are maintained throughout the industry. Plans are underway to certify all members meeting the required levels of safety and standards required by TAG but this cannot, and should not, replace government regulation of the industry, as TAG cannot by its very nature function as a national regulatory body.

There have been questions about TAG's membership and how well it represents all the interests associated with Tourism. The list of potential members is quite long since tourism impacts on all sectors of the economy and the increase in tourist arrivals will ultimately benefit all business in Guyana.

B. Constraints

There are significant and serious obstacles to the development of eco–tourism. If incorrect perceptions and misunderstandings about the sector prevail, then the opportunity for the development of a sustainable industry will be lost. The principal constraints to the development of the industry can be summarized as follows:

1. Institutional Framework

There is a lack of the required institutional framework to effectively implement, develop, and sustain the eco–tourism industry. This framework involves laws and behaviour codes for both eco–tourism operators and eco–tourists as well as for monitoring activities.

2. Investment

There is a lack of investment guidelines for an industry in which all investment would have to come from the private sector. This has led to a reluctance on the part of investors to enter the industry.

The problems of investment are also related to the airline industry. The impediments to the development of the private aircraft industry, such as the substandard state of navigational facilities, lack of incentives for investment, regulations that create unequal competition (especially with regard to GAC), the reluctance of international airlines to come to Guyana, and policies that discriminate against new airline operations, among others, directly affect the tourism sector.

Other impediments to investment include high duties and consumption taxes, high interest rates and the generally high cost of doing business in Guyana because of the bureaucratic delays.

3. Land Use

There is a lack of mechanisms to coordinate the allocation of land to various users, which has led to land conflicts which hamper the desired image of eco–tourism. For example, in areas of potential tourist value, there may be unchecked mining and unsustainable forestry practices. Together with a questionable record on the part of Guyana on protecting and preserving its environment, this takes away from the "green" image that is necessary for the development of tourism.

There is also a lack of adequate land monitoring and regulating mechanisms. Few land use laws are realistically enforceable due to this lack of monitoring and regulating systems.

4. Quality and Variety of Product

Guyana's tourism product is not yet developed to the extent that it can competitively attract the typical eco–tourist, i.e. there are not enough lodges, tour sites, trained guides, etc. The sector currently runs the danger of disappointing visitors.

5. Infrastructure

There is a general lack of infrastructure to support the tourism industry. This is especially related to airstrip facilities in the interior such as refuelling nodes. The absence of medical evacuation facilities is also a deterrent to the development of the industry, as is the prevalence of malaria and deficiencies of the potable water systems.

6. National Parks

The lack of a national parks system with a framework for managing them does not help to create an appropriate image for Guyana.

IV. Objectives

The broad objective for a tourism strategy policy for Guyana is as follows:

The further development of a tourism industry that balances the economic, social and environmental needs of Guyana to create a sustainable and profitable dynamic tourism sector. Achieving this sectoral objective will contribute to the national objectives (Chapter 2) of rapid economic growth and poverty alleviation, the latter because of employment creation effects, especially among hinterland populations.

To achieve this sectoral objective, a number of sub–objectives can be defined as follows:

1. The promotion of an industry that makes appropriate use of what Guyana has to offer and takes full advantage of market trends in the tourism industry.
2. The development of the industry by placing the protection of its natural resource base as its highest priority through the use of sustainable practices.
3. The setting of standards and practices that are commensurate with the market that is being targeted.
4. The development of an industry which ensures that its operations benefit widely the people of Guyana, in particular the Amerindian community.

V. Policy Recommendations and their Technical Justifications

The central thrust of these new policies for tourism is a focused and unambiguous strategy of pursuing high quality, up–market eco–tourism in controlled numbers that do not exceed scientifically determined carrying capacities of interior sites. All other policies should follow from this central thrust.

A. Ministerial Responsibility

The Minister responsible for tourism should be the same Minister responsible for the Environment, Protected Areas and Amerindian Affairs in a separate Ministry. This restructuring is fundamental and would result in a single person being able to speak for interests that have a lot in common.

B. Need for a National Tourism Board

The idea for a National Tourism Board has been tabled for some time. It is absolutely vital that the creation of this Board be undertaken urgently. Such a Board would replace the Tourism Advisory Board and absorb most of the functions of the Tourism Division of the Ministry of Trade, Tourism and Industry. Its main responsibilities would be regulation, marketing, research and product development. This Board should be a semi–autonomous agency with the authority to hire, fire, set salary levels, etc. Funding should be supplied by Government with supplementary funding from licence fees on the industry and a diversion of the hotel room tax. This investment by Government would benefit the country several times over in a short period of time through increased corporate and income taxes, the generation of employment, foreign exchange inflows and through the spin–off effects on other industries.

The composition of the Board is critical for its success. The Board should be composed of no more than nine persons, with five representatives from TAG and four from the Government. This would result in a Board that is widely representative but not too large to manage the affairs of the industry. The Government should have the authority to pick the chairperson from among the nine members. The President of TAG should be an automatic choice as one of the five private sector representatives. Appointments to the

Board should be staggered so as to avoid the arbitrary replacement of members when the Executive of TAG or the Government changes hands.

It will be the Board's responsibility to overesee the implementation of many of the recommendations stated in this chapter.

C. The Role of the Tourism Association of Guyana

Currently, the Association is made up mostly of tour operators, resort owners and hoteliers, but it is being widened to include representatives from all sectors of the economy that have an impact on, or can benefit from, tourism. Consideration is already being given to including the mining and forestry private sector groups as associate members, and efforts are continuously being made to invite Amerindian representatives to join TAG.

The Association will continue to set minimum standards with which all members serving the industry must comply. Certification will be given only to those who meet or exceed these standards. The Association should develop classification and grading schemes for its members that can be based on physically measurable criteria. For example, in the case of tour operators, it can be based on the number of passengers the operator puts into a boat, the type of aircraft that is used, or the provision of education on the ecosystem etc. These classifications can make tourists aware that Guyana is serious about tourism and as the sector in Guyana grows it can assist international certifiers in grading Guyana's product. Standards set by TAG will not supersede those set by the Tourism Board.

D. Protected Areas

A large percentage of tourists can be expected to visit National Parks. Parks therefore need to be carefully regulated, and the lines of responsibility for these parks must be clearly delineated. For example, responsibility for protected areas should be removed from the Ministry of Health and placed in the hands of appropriate authorities, through the reorganization indicated in subsection A above.

It is important that certain criteria be established for each protected area in the interest of tourism. Among these are definitions for the carrying capacity of each and guidelines for visitation. Among the guidelines for visitation will be specifications regarding the length of stay, requirements for trained guides, means of access, controls on the removal of flora and fauna and the taking of pictures, visitation by individuals or groups, etc. Within the park itself there may be areas in which absolutely no one is allowed to go, for protection of the area's biodiversity.

(Guidelines for the sustainable management of the forests and the environmental soundness of mining operations are covered in Chapters 30 and 32, respectively, of this National Development Strategy.)

The boundaries of the Kaieteur National Park should be determined as a matter of urgency and all mining in the Kaieteur watershed and the gorge below the falls should be immediately stopped. Among the major tasks that must be accomplished as a matter of priority are to:

- Obtain a definitive boundary survey and posting the perimeter.
- Obtain a topographic survey with the appropriate contour intervals identified for a more detailed study.
- Develop consultative mechanisms for incorporating representatives of local Amerindian groups in the decision making concerning the site.
- Locate significant site features, e.g., trees, marshes, streams, existing structures (if any), archaeologically significant areas, etc.
- Obtain aerial photographs of the site to confirm survey information.
- Identify a sustainable power source on the site.
- Investigate soil conditions and bearing capacities for the number of tourists and any construction.
- Review the local watershed layout relative to the site, noting activities on adjacent property which may impact on drainage and water quality.
- Investigate present and planned uses for adjacent property.
- Study any significant archaeological sites on the property.

The OAS project for the Kaieteur National Park should be opened for private sector comment before its finalization and implementation.

International organizations such as the World Wildlife Fund and Conservation International must be invited by Government to conduct additional scientific and other environmental studies in parks, along the lines of the ones that they are currently doing. The support and stamp of approval of these groups is important. These organizations should also be able to attract funds for the parks' maintenance and upkeep. In any case, realistic charges will have to be paid by tourists to enter the parks so as to provide sufficient revenues to cover all costs.

Lessors of large tracts of private land in the interior could also be encouraged to convert these into protected areas. In allocating land among sectors, priority should be given to eco–tourism for the simple reason that the land can be used afterwards for other extractive industries if the tourism venture proves not to be in the best interest of the country. Land that is used for extractive industries cannot be used for other purposes afterwards.

After the initiation of the Guyana Rainforest Foundation (Chapter 18) linkages should be explored between its activities and programmes to support eco–tourism.

E. Amerindian Involvement in Tourism

In developing the tourism industry efforts must be made to ensure that Amerindians are involved. Tourism should be started at a slow and measured pace in Amerindian communities so as not to overwhelm local capacity and result in a sudden increase in social stresses. Aiming at once for state–of–the–art tourist lodges may not be the way to initiate eco–tourism ventures in Amerindian communities. There will of course be the need for good business management such as rigorous bookkeeping and accountability for funds received and the reliable supplies of goods and services for guests.

Due to the limited experience that Amerindians have with development projects, tourism ventures to be started and managed by Amerindians will have to be accompanied by:

- A local group with the initiative and willingness to maintain the level of effort that an eco–tourist venture entails.
- Intensive and extensive training of Amerindians in business management, account–keeping, accountability, etc.

- Start–up capital that is affordable and accessible to Amerindians.
- A commitment by Central Government and funding agencies to work to sustain Amerindian ventures in the eco–tourist field.
- The encouragement of partnerships between Amerindians, investors and nature and conservation NGOs in developing tourism sites.
- Continuous information–sharing and consultation with Amerindians in the development of tourism.

Clearly, all of these requirements cannot be fulfilled by Government or the tourism industry only. Non–governmental organizations and others will have to play a role. Other aspects of the National Development Strategy with respect to Amerindian affairs have to be incorporated. For example, given Government's fiscal constraints, it is unlikely that it can be depended on to provide subsidized loans. However, the establishment of an Amerindian Development Fund will provide a source funding. Chapter 22 of the National Development Strategy, Amerindian Policies, provides more details on the proposed Fund. The use of such funds for tourism ventures presents an ideal opportunity for the sustainable development of Amerindians.

Amerindian involvement may also provide the more affordable alternative that Guyanese need in order to visit the interior. This could have the spin–off effect of allowing other Guyanese to observe Amerindians in their interior environment and utilize their services as guides, teachers, etc., which would lead to a greater respect for the indigenous community.

With regard to tour operators entering Amerindian communities, guidelines need to be established for gaining permits. An overall code of conduct should be developed between tour operators and the Amerindians that all tourists must follow. Such a code should provide guidelines for taking photographs, access to sacred sites, times of visiting, etc. It will be the responsibility of tour operators to educate tourists about these regulations before visiting Amerindian communities. Failure to do so could result in licences being revoked. Individual Amerindian communities may develop stricter codes. The collection of head fees by Amerindian communities should be legislated.

Finally, of course, Amerindians will decide for themselves if eco–tourism ventures are worth the trouble or not. They would also have to find ways to limit or mitigate the stresses of this new industry. In each case, the community in question should decide on the soundness of eco–tourism on a project–by–project basis.

F. Investment

1. Tax Concessions and Exemptions

Since tourism is essentially a private sector enterprise, the right conditions to attract private investment must be in place. Investors must feel a sense of security about investing in a country and a sector that are perceived as high risk. By international standards of the industry, the first concession would be a tax holiday on all capital investments in the sector for five to seven years. This is below the ten–year concession that is commonly given to developers in Caribbean destinations. Secondly, until the more uniform tax code discussed in Chapters 13 and 36 is implemented, the industry should be given a waiver on duty and consumption taxes for the import of items necessary for the tourism industry. At present, in the absence of these concessions, the industry is stagnant and does not contribute as much as it could to the Government coffers. The returns from granting these concessions would be perceived soon afterwards, basically in the form of higher income tax revenues.

2. The Development of Lodges

As a practical measure, the Lands and Surveys Department must first of all embark on a special project to eliminate the existing backlog of all applications for land and institute mechanisms for the fast processing of land applications.

The development of lodges can be expected to occur on lands in two categories. The first category includes the obvious areas: next to or in proposed National Parks such as Kaieteur, in the Kanuku mountains, at Shell Beach, or around Orinduik Falls, for example. In the second category would be lands identified by investors at their own expense. Under current land policies, annual lease rates for all lands should be based on a percentage of the gross revenues, say between 2 to 3 per cent, or based on market lease rates, which ever is higher. (The reforms to land policy proposed in Chapter 29 would be as beneficial to the tourism sector as to agriculture.)

In the first category, there can be expected to be more potential investors than can be allowed, especially at places such as Kaieteur top. Therefore, mechanisms need to be put in place for selecting those who will be allowed to build a lodge there. As a first step, there must be minimum criteria set for these locations, such as the maximum number of units per lodge. This would ensure that several investors are allowed to invest; thus if it is determined that the area can support only 40 units, then Government may stipulate 5 lodges at 8 units per lodge. The minimum capital investment should also be specified. The locations will then be put up for auction to those who meet the minimum requirements. The bids will be judged on two criteria: the percentage of gross revenues that an investor is willing to pay to Government as annual rent for the land and the capital investment that is proposed for the site over a given period, such as five years. The winning bid will be the one with the highest product from the percentage of gross revenues and the capital investment. This would guard against the possibility of an investor losing the bid when the lease rate offered is smaller than another but the proposed investment is higher.

A portion of the lease rates should be turned over to nearby Amerindian communities. This is an innovative approach because it places the Government, the investor and the Amerindians on the same side of the equation; they would all like to see greater returns to the investment because they all have more to gain. At the same time, the Amerindians have an incentive to protect the land because in the long term it will represent a continuous source of income. Amerindians can also monitor the operations of the investors with respect to reporting requirements, such as the number of tourists that visit.[3]

In the second category of land, in which an investor identified the land needed for setting up a lodge, the investor must again meet certain minimum requirements before being granted a lease or freehold title to the land. Rights to the land should be given on a first come, first served basis provided the minimum requirements are met. In this case, the lease should be offered at market rates or as a fixed percentage of the gross revenues whichever is higher. The latter arrangement would, however, require careful monitoring because investors might tend to under–report visitation. Again, arrangements could be entered into whereby a portion of the lease payments is diverted for the benefit of nearby Amerindian communities.

In all cases, leases should be for 99 years, be freely transferable from one person to another and be available for use as collateral, as discussed in Chapter 29. Banks should have the authority to repossess land and property on which an eco–tourism site is built. Whenever possible, lands should be sold to investors in freehold.

Guidelines should also be developed to mandate buffer zones around lodges, the distance between lodges, etc. There should also be certain allocations allowed for Guyanese investors, especially at places such as Kaieteur.

The Government should embark on a project to list all the sites in the interior that have been identified as desirable areas for the development of lodges. Tourism site investment listings have been highly successful in a number of countries in encouraging the right type of investment suitable to the peculiarities and carrying capacity of the land identified.

3. *Financial Monitoring*

The new Tourism Board should insist that assessments and reports, financial and otherwise, be prepared by lodge owners in a consistent and timely manner. Bank reports should be copied to the Ministry responsible for Tourism. Severe penalties should be issued for fraudulent reporting and/or non–compliance. Computer–assisted accounting and reporting will help make the process easier and more efficient.

G. *Air Transport*

This sector needs to be opened up as soon as possible for effective functioning and to benefit all sectors of the Guyanese economy. With respect to tourism this necessitates the participation of private capital and management in the domestic operations of GAC. This should be accompanied by the freeing up of restrictions on general aviation to allow for more competition. Aircraft owners should also be allowed to decide what type of aircrafts they would like to buy. The management of Ogle aerodrome should be passed on to the Private Aircraft Owners Association and refuelling centres need to be set up in interior locations.

Other details for setting up a autonomous Air Transport Authority and adopting an open skies policy with respect to international airlines are given in Chapter 38, Transport Development. Such changes will provide tourists with more flight connections to visit Guyana and would be of enormous benefit to the sector.

H. Product Improvement

The following areas of Guyana's tourism product should be improved using the suggested guidelines.

1. Visitor Security

Visitor security should be an absolute priority throughout Guyana. This must be guaranteed on all levels simultaneously; it should include training for the police force on interaction with tourists as well as a permanent police presence in the major thoroughfares of main towns and cities. Street lighting needs to be improved. Procedures on crime reporting should be streamlined to enable the visitor to spend as little time as possible in police stations reporting crimes, and all efforts should be made to make the experience of crime reporting as hassle free and as comfortable as possible.

In addition to education for the police force on dealing with tourists, the best form of visitor protection can be achieved by educating the general public to look out for tourists and their safety and to discourage crimes against tourists within their own communities. This mind set already exists to some extent, as part of the genuine warmth and hospitality that most Guyanese have towards visitors. This attitude needs only to be enhanced through good public awareness campaigns showing how local Guyanese can benefit from tourism and visitor safety.

Due to the fact that certain areas of the interior are open to drug trafficking and other criminal activity (Kaieteur is a prime example), the efforts of the Guyana Defence Force, the police force and tour operators should be coordinated in these areas. Police stations should be set up in areas where tourist activity is high, in particular at Kaieteur Falls, where there have been many reported incidents of theft from tourists.

2. Search and Rescue

There must be a national search and rescue operation that can deal with all eventualities. This includes high–level detection methods, fast and effective evacuation procedures and top level medical training and equipment. This would require an established mechanism between the Tourism Board, TAG, the Government, the police and the army.

Tour operators must have adequate safety equipment for the tours they conduct. Training in first aid and CPR must be mandatory for all persons/guides conducting or in charge of tourists, and adequate emergency evacuation plans and procedures must be set for all tour operations and resorts. These safety procedures and equipment must be linked to the licensing of these operations, and failure to comply with the minimum safety standards set for the industry should carry severe and enforceable penalties for the failure in their observance.

A list of licensed operators should be made available to all tourists through hotels and other outlets.

3. Insurance

At present, many resorts, hotels and tour operations within the industry do not have public liability insurance. Steps should be taken to amend laws pertaining to insurance to give the industry access to adequate levels of insurance. In conjunction with this, adequate insurance for all resorts, hotels, charter airlines and tour operations should be made mandatory and linked to the licensing of these operations.

4. Financial Streamlining

While more retail outlets, restaurants, hotels and tour operations in Georgetown are beginning to accept credit cards, this acceptance is still not widespread in the capital city, let alone nationwide. Travellers' cheques are accepted as reliable currency, but since many outlets must wait 28 days for reimbursement, this discourages their use. All necessary steps must be taken to ensure that tourists can get easy access to money and that facilities for changing foreign exchange and travellers' are widespread and convenient.

5. Visas

Though there has been a relaxation on visa requirements for visitors to Guyana, pre–travel visa requirements for entry into Guyana should be completely eliminated.

6. Timehri International Airport

Plans for the expansion and upgrading of Timehri International Airport are underway and are described in Chapter 38 of this National Development Strategy. With regard to tourism, the airport is in urgent need of fully manned tourist arrival and departure booths. The departure booth will also be a place for lodging complaints about Guyana that should be channeled back to the relevant authorities.

I. Marketing Guyana as an Eco–tourism Destination

Marketing tourism can be expected to be expensive and the Tourism Board will have to enter into arrangements with the Government and industry to promote generic advertising for the country. As the industry and the economy grow this can be done through a mechanism of matching funds, whereby the Government agrees to match funds pledged by TAG at an agreed ratio, say of 1:2 (industry to Government).

Specific markets must be studied and targeted individually according to their needs and demands. There should be tourism representatives in key cities such as New York, Miami, Toronto, London and Frankfurt. Niche groups such as clubs for bird watching, nature tourism, biodiversity study and conservation that pre–qualify as eco–tourists should be targeted with information on Guyana. The advertising dollar should be carefully spent in appropriate magazines such as those that deal with nature and the environment. The country must also invite writers and specialised tour operators for visits to the national sites as a way of gaining publicity and marketing the product.

Guyana is currently featured in the South American Handbook, but efforts must be made to improve that information, produce more literature on Guyana itself and to include Guyana in a wider range of guide books featuring South American and Caribbean destinations. In addition, the use of existing and up–and–coming technologies should be explored as a way to convey information to the international traveller. While Guyana is marginally listed on the Internet, this facility has to be expanded and upgraded; given the profile of the average eco–tourist, computer based technology is an excellent way to convey information to this segment of the market.

J. Joint Destination Tourism

Joint destination packages should be developed with neighbouring countries. However, this does not mean that Guyana can expect to encourage operators in the Caribbean to send their visitors here. Joint destination tourism is about attracting tourists to Guyana in the first place and encouraging them here by offering them an extension trip to another destination. The industry should work closely with the Board in promoting this.

K. Regular Bulletin on the Industry

There is need for an adequate system for collecting information on visitor arrivals, visitor activities, and visitor feedback. This information must be collected and collated in a timely manner and must be made public. This would provide the industry with up–to–date information on the market and allow it to see where it stands with respect to overall trends. The published totals would also allow the comparison of figures by different agencies to keep track of the number of tourists that visit Guyana. For instance, the number of tourists that visit Kaieteur National Park can be compared to the number of visitors that are reported visiting there by tour operators. While the published figures would represent totals, figures for individual companies will be open for inspection by tax officials to ensure compliance with reporting requirements.

The bulletin could also include information on the world travel market, such as emerging tastes and visitor preferences. This would allow to Guyana to respond efficiently and effectively to changing patterns.

L. Regulations and Standards within the Industry

In regulating the industry, the Tourism Board will have the authority to license operators, resort owners, hoteliers, and other tourism–related operators. The Board will also set minimum standards to be met by those involved in the sector; meeting these standards would also be one of the criteria for obtaining a licence.

It is not expected that the Board will itself grade or classify facilities, but this responsibility will be left to independent certifiers. The Board will have the responsibility for writing and monitoring regulations and standards.

To ensure that the tourism industry can deliver on the promises it makes through its marketing campaign, strict standards need to be set within the industry with appropriate penalties for non-compliance, particularly standards pertaining to visitor safety and environmental integrity.

M. Tour Guides

Tour guides are an important part of interior resorts and tour operations. Areas of knowledge should include basic life saving procedures as well as a good information base on the geography of Guyana and the wildlife and eco–systems in the different regions of the country. Of primary importance would be the communication skills of such persons; it is not just what they know, it is the ability to impart it to tourists that matters. The Tourism Board in conjunction with the University of Guyana should develop short courses for tourist guides, and practical training with hoteliers and operators should be pursued. The use of guest lectures from the industry should be actively encouraged.

N. The Wildlife Trade

Severe restrictions and legislation governing the wildlife trade should be implemented. Breeding of these animals is an alternative for satisfying the needs of tourists and restaurants in Georgetown.

O. Georgetown

Strict zoning and building codes should be enforced in Georgetown. New buildings in the city should be made to conform to Georgetown's rich architectural heritage. The further construction of concrete buildings along Main Street and Avenue of the Republic should be proscribed. (See Chapter 23 of this Strategy for more on this topic.)

P. Continuity of Work in the Sector

Follow–up efforts in the sector, such as the Integrated Eco–tourism Development Plan by the OAS, must build upon the recommendations of this Strategy.

Q. Public Health

The Tourism Board and TAG must work with the Ministry of Health to ensure that an integrated and effective attack is carried out on malaria and other vector–borne diseases.

VI. Legislative Requirements[4]

A. Establishing the Tourism Board

Legislation needs to be enacted to establish a Tourism Board for the support of the tourism industry. This Board could be established through the Public Corporations Act (1988) or by completely new legislation.

B. Government Regulations

Following from the laws which establish the Tourism Board, a series of regulations should be prepared to implement those laws. It is not recommended that the regulatory framework of Guyana's tourism legislation should extend, in the present situation, to imposing qualitative classification or grading by law, but eventually that should be a goal.

C. Services to Tourism

1. International Transportation

It is recommended that Guyana should replace its applied civil aviation codes with local legislation. More details on the legislative changes required are given in Chapter 38. However, if resource constraints dictate the continued use of British legislation for Guyana's aviation law, then it is recommended that at least Guyanese legislation should be enacted to give the Minister the choice of when to adopt and apply new British regulations. In this way, the laws can be updated periodically based on trends in the world as reflected in updated British laws.

2. International Water Transportation

Guyana still depends on the United Kingdom's Merchant Shipping Act of 1894. Since a modern Caribbean–oriented model Shipping Act exists, which has been prepared by CARICOM in conjunction with the Caribbean Law Institute, it is recommended that Guyana should enact this legislation. For Guyana, the main advantage of such legislation would be to give some control of ships in its waters and sports.

Guyana's interest in maritime legislation should not be confined to passenger movements at sea. Maritime pollution could hurt the tourism product through, for example, the depletion of the sea turtles in the northwest. While Guyana is a party to the United Nations Convention on the Law of the Sea, and the Maritime Boundaries Act can be considered to allow for the exploitation of resources through jurisdictional allocation, this Act does not provide for environmental considerations. The fact that Guyana did not sign any of the leading International Maritime Organization Conventions except the constituent convention, does not auger well for the protection of the marine environment. Guyana should meet international obligations to have legislation in place to safeguard the marine environment under its jurisdiction, and should participate in MARPOL 1973/78[5] and SOLAS.[6]

With respect to inland water navigation, the River Navigation Act and Regulations and the Fisheries Act should be reviewed with regard to the standards they require for river navigation and to their exemptions of categories of craft from the application of those standards.

3. Accommodations, Restaurants and Places of Entertainment

a. General hotels regulation

It is recommended that a system of registration for hotels in the tourist sector be enshrined in law. This system would require that standards be met and maintained as a condition of such registration by the Tourism Board. These standards should be consistent with the best modern industry practice.

Reference to hotels in the laws of Guyana are found in the Provisions relating to Common Lodging Houses which form a part of the City's by–laws and made under powers contained in the Municipal and District Act. This has certain problems, such as: (1) it relates only to Georgetown, (2) it does not differentiate between hotels, apartments and guest houses, and (3) the standards are outdated.

The Common Lodging House By–Laws (Laws of British Guiana, 1953 Vol. VIII, p. 1609) apply across the country, but they do not appear to govern hotels. New laws in this area also need to re-examine the minimum number of rooms per hotel that make these liable for payment of the hotel room tax. Consideration should be given to removing the stipulation that only hotels in excess of 15 rooms are liable to pay the tax. Interior resorts should continue to be excluded from the hotel room tax, regardless of the minimum number of rooms they contain so as not to discourage the construction of lodges in the interior.

b. Protection of hotels from visitors' claims

A good precedent in law to protect hotel owners from claims from visitors is the English Hotel Proprietors' Act of 1956. This law allows an escape from being liable for losses suffered by guests unless they take advantage of the hotel's security system. Reasonable limits for losses are the equivalent of US$100 for any one item and US$200 as the aggregate loss. There should also be legislation to prevent guests who do not pay their hotel bills from leaving Guyana.

c. Food licensing and food safety

The legislative provisions for hotels and restaurants in Georgetown should be applied countrywide. Although there is provision against the employment of food handlers suffering from infection diseases, it is not clear that the current system of food handlers' permits is legislated. The current system of permits which must be renewed every six months also need to be reviewed, with the intent of extending the validity of the permit. Extending its validity would reduce the logistical problems and expense of bringing food handlers from the interior to Georgetown to be tested. A strengthening of the system of distributing these permits regionally could also be pursued.

Legislation should also be enacted that requires new restaurants and hotels, or those undergoing renovation, to have adequate toilet facilities and amenities for disabled persons.

d. Places of entertainment

The preparation of special legislation to regulate places of public entertainment, with rules governing matters such as capacity limitations, provision of sanitary facilities and fire exits, safeguards against noise nuisance, and other offences to neighbouring residents, is recommended. Similarly, legislation is needed that provides in detail the required fire safety criteria, or structural reliability, means of escape, fire–fighting equipment, fire detection, and restriction or suppression of the spread of fire.

D. Zoning

It would appear that the Town and Country Planning Act provides legal control over zoning and the quality and suitability of the construction of buildings in Georgetown, but these are not enforced. The law should be updated and areas in Georgetown such as Main Street and the Avenue of the Republic should be included. The Act should be amended to provide for its automatic application to newly developed areas.

The designation of a buffer zone of 66 feet inland from the low water mark of creeks as Government reserve should be maintained but legislative allowance should be made for restricted use of such zones by lodges that are adjacent to creeks. This should not prejudice the use of the zone for access.

E. Building Codes and Tourism Facilities

Building codes for interior lodges can be expected to vary from those for structures built from established building materials. It is impractical to develop codes for interior resorts because of the new and multitudinous/indigenous materials that may legitimately be used. The use of such materials is necessary if lodges are going to fit into the surrounding environment. Lodges must, however, be certified by a professional engineer.

There must also be minimum standards legislated for the disposal of sewerage and garbage. These should be included in the requirements for environmental impact statements for tourist facilities in the interior.

There should also be regulations for the distance between tourism lodges and buffer zones around lodges, etc.

F. National Parks

It is intended that legislation covering the establishment of National Parks and Protected Areas will be written as Guyana moves to establish a Protected Areas System. The new law should replace the Kaieteur National Park Act (Cap. 20:02) and National Parks Commission Act (1977–23). The powers of the Guyana Forestry Commission "to identify, establish, maintain and manage forests including national parks, wildlife areas, and natural reserves" should be removed from the Commission and place under the authority established to regulate National Parks.

The National Trust Act (Cap. 20:03) provides for the protection of national monuments but this needs adequate enforcement.

G. Protection of Wildlife and Fisheries

The Fisheries Act (Cap. 78:01) and accompanying Fisheries Aquatic Wild Life Regulations and the Wild Birds Protection Act (Cap. 71:01) allow for some protection of fisheries and birds. The scope of the Fisheries Act is not confined to fauna but is wide enough to include the protection of both marine and fresh water aquatic flora, as the result of the amendment of the Act in 1977.

Between these two acts, four–footed wildlife is excluded. The Wild Life Protection Act of 1987, which should have remedied this situation, is still not enacted. This Act should be enacted.

H. The Environmental Protection Act

The recent enactment of the Environmental Protection Bill should be followed expeditiously by the drafting of suitable regulations for the implementation of its various prescriptions.

Appendix 1a. Typical Offerings in the Guyanese Tourism Industry

RESORTS

Company	*Barakara Island*	*Emerald Tower*	*The Gazebo*	*Karanambu*	*Rockview*	*Shanklands*	*Timberhead*
Resort Location	Mazaruni River	Madawini Creek Linden Highway	Kaow Island, Essequibo	North Rupununi	Annai, North Rupununi	Essequibo River	Pokerero River
Land Area (Acres)		165	136	125 square miles	+/– 3	96	15
Land Tenures		25 year lease from Lands & Surveys	Transport land	25 year lease from Lands & Surveys	Amerindian or State has permission from both	Transport Land	Lease from Santa Amerindian Reservation
Activities	Swimming, volley ball, jet skies, jet boat tours to surrounding nature spots. Caters for groups, individuals, conference facilities	Swimming, boats, fishing, cycling, walking, bird watching, miniature golf, table tennis, conference facilities	Trails, fishing, water sports, swimming, sauna, visit to nearby historical sites	Boat trips, bird watching, trekking, fishing, Amerindian villages	Pony trekking, bird watching and nature tours, fishing, Amerindian villages, visit to Iwokrama	Jungle walks, water sports, boat tours to surrounding areas, croquet, golf	Day & Evening jungle walks and boat tours, cayman watching, bird watching, canoeing, swimming, volleyball and badminton
Cost All Inclusive	G $8000 (Day trip)	US $85 (day trip) US $155–245 o/n	US $120 per person o/n plus cost of transportation	US $120	US $95–115	US $125	US $90 (Day Trip) US $145 (Overnight)

(*Contd.*)

Company	*Barakara Island*	*Emerald Tower*	*The Gazebo*	*Karanambu*	*Rockview*	*Shanklands*	*Timberhead*
Target Group	Overseas Business and holidays, local	Overseas, local and overseas business persons. Expats based in Guyana	Overseas: holiday and business	Not specified	Guyanese, Brazilian, Overseas	Overseas and Local	Mainly overseas business persons and tourists, some local tourists
Start Date	1995	19/09/92	late 1989	1989	April 1993	May 1992	May 1991
Capacity		16–26	12	10	8	16–25	20
Expansion Plans		More resorts planned in the Interior. Head Falls resort opening	Yes	No	Yes, up to 20 persons	Yes – more cottages	Yes
Primary Land Use	Tourism	Tourism	Saw milling	Cattle ranching	Ranching and Farming	Tourism	Tourism
Government Liaison	Min. of Trade & Tourism Lands & Surveys	Min. of Trade & Tourism Min. of Finance	Min. of Trade; Guyana Natural Resources Agency	Min. of Trade & Tourism	Min. of Trade & Tourism	Min. of Trade & Tourism	Mins. of Trade & Tourism, Finance, Foreign Affairs
Amerindian Involvement		Yes, family live there and run facilities	Yes, employed on site	Yes, employed on site and visit Amerindian villages	Yes, employment, support from council	None, except support local schools and help out in emergencies	Yes, employment and close links with villages of Santa

Appendix 1b. Typical Offerings in the Guyanese Tourism Industry

HOTELS

Hotel	*Ariantze*	*Cara Lodge*	*Cara Suites*	*Embassy Club*	*Park Hotel*	*Campala Hotel*	*Pegasus Hotel*	*Queenstown Inn*	*Hotel Tower*
Location	176 Middle Street	293, Quamina Street	176, Middle Street	Pere Street	37, Main Street	10, Camp Street	Seawall Road	65, Anira & Peter Rose	74–75 Main Street
Rooms	8	14	15	22	45	22	134	6	56
Facilities	1, 2, 4, 5, 6, 8, 10	1, 2, 4, 5, 6, 7, 8	1, 2, 4, 5, 6, 7, 8	1, 2, 3, 4, 5, 6, 7, 8, 9	1, 2, 5, 6, 7, 4, 8	1, 2, 5, 6	1, 2, 3, 4, 5, 6, 7, 8, 9	1, 2, 5, 6	1, 2, 3, 4, 5, 6, 7, 8, 9
Target Group	Corporate	Business, leisure	Business	Business	Business/ Group Delegations	Business	Corporate/ Business	Business/ Locals	Business
Cost	$55	$85–130	$87–145	$80–130	$40– 60	$61– 82	$110–260	$55–80	$85–160
Start Date	1991	1996	1995	1994	1893	1988	1969	1994	circa 1866
Expansion Plans	Rooms 3–4 Rooms	Rooms 2 Executive Rooms	None	Create an interior resort	Yes	Upgrading facilities	None	None	14 Deluxe Rooms
Gvt. Liaison	Min. of Trade	Min. of Trade Min. of Finance	Min. of Trade Min. of Finance	Min. of Trade	Min. of Trade Min. of Finance	None	Min. of Trade Min. of Fin. Min. of F.A.	Min. of Trade	None

Services and Facilities

1. Private Bath/ Shower
2. Air Conditioning
3. Swimming Pool
4. Restaurant
5. Telephone
6. Television
7. Business Centre
8. Bar
9. Gym
10. Night Club

Appendix 1c. Typical Offerings in the Guyanese Tourism Industry

TOUR OPERATORS

Company	*Cattelya Rainforest*	*Cortours*	*Discover Tours*	*Shell Beach Adventures*	*White Water Adventures*	*Wilderness Explorers*	*Wonderland Tours*
Location of Tours	Kaiteur, Essequibo Region, Bartica, Linden	Orealla – Manituba, Corentyne River	Kaiteur, Orinduik Emerald Tower	Shel Beach, Kaieteur/ Orinduik, Essequibo and personalised activities anywhere	Mazaruni	Comprehensive standard and custom designed itineraries to all areas of Guyana	Kaiteur & Orinduik, Santa Mission, Essequibo, Mazaruni, G/T city tour, Berbice, Linden
Activities	City Tours, Overland trips, Nature walks, Trekking, fishing	Boat Tours, hiking (3–5 days)	Bird watching, Overland Camping, River Tours, Kaiteur & Orinduik	Kaiteur & Orinduik Falls by air, Rupununi Ranches & Kaiteur	Inland river trips	Nature and advent-ure based activities such as bird watch-ing, wildlife watching, hiking, canoeing, horse trekking, history tours and cultural tours	Essequibo Fiver, Santa Mission, Kaiteur & Orinduik

(*Contd.*)

Company	*Cattelya Rainforest*	*Cortours*	*Discover Tours*	*Shell Beach Adventures*	*White Water Adventures*	*Wilderness Explorers*	*Wonderland Tours*
Cost Range	$20 (City) $150/day (1–7 days)	$8140–$800/day	$175/day	$50 – $170	$60 US (G$8000) incl. Day trip $120 US(G$16800) o/n trip	From US$30 7 days –US$1,140 14 days–US$2,095	$25–300
Target Group	Local (w/discount) regional (W.I.) Germans &British	Intl. mostly	Local & Intl.	Local & Intl.	Local, overseas, business	International, regional and local	Overseas Guyanese
Start Date	1994, April		1974	1995, April	1995, March	1 August, 1994	1989
Group Size Min–Max	2–12	3–15	8– no maximum	4 – no max.	15–40	Minimum 1 person. No maximum	2–60
Expansion Plans	Resort site in Santa Mission	Building camps in Manituba	Great falls	Not Immediately	More Cabins (private) on island	Nature resort and itineraries to new areas	Shell Beach Overland Kamarang & area
Govt. Liaison	Min. of Trade			Min. of Trade/ Min. of A.A.	Min. of Trade	Min. of Trade; Min. of Amerindian Affairs	No liaison
Amerindian Iinvolve–ment	Amer. Boat guide; family inside mission, also overseas site	Very little, other than visiting settlements	Work sites run by Amerindians	All Amerindian involvement – family full time at Shell Beach – guides, drivers etc.	Amerindian staff on site and in Georgetown	Partnership with some Amerindian communities to conduct tours. Others employed for tours as necessary.	Interior – hired on freelance basis

Appendix 2a: Visitor Arrivals by Country of Origin 1992–1994

Country	1992	1993	1994	% Share 1994
USA	34566	57269	42143	37.4
Canada	13976	no data	17668	15.7
Europe	6763	7892	8104	7.2
Caribbean	14427	19514	21916	19.4
South America	5149	20553	20904	18.5
Other	no data	1899	2016	1.8
Total	74881	107127	112751	100

Appendix 2b: Monthly Arrivals of Visitors 1992–1994

Month	1992	1993	1994
January	4562	6251	7513
February	5463	7039	7322
March	4994	7567	9330
April	5990	8169	7974
May	5122	6933	6629
June	6261	8320	8278
July	9699	13972	14760
August	9136	12345	14692
September	4594	7233	7550
October	4538	7203	6715
November	5127	7236	6924
December	10395	14959	15064
TOTAL	74881	107227	112751

Source: Caribbean Tourism Organization, Caribbean Tourism Statistical Report 1993; 1994

1 Guyana Visitor Survey, 1993/94. Caribbean Tourism Organization in Cooperation with the Guyana Statistical Bureau and the Ministry of Trade, Tourism and Industry. Published in 1995.

2 Kelly, E., Developing Tourism for Guyana: Policy and Strategy Plan (1989).

3 As an alternative to the selection process outlined above, lessors could be selected based on two other criteria: the initial lease rental that an investor is willing to pay and the yearly

per cent increase in this rate that is offered. Similarly to the process outlined above, the winning bid would be the one in which the cumulative fees over the lease period will provide the highest returns to Government.

4 For this section, reference is made to *Guyana Tourism Legislation Project,* November 1995 by A. Ralph Carnegie and Ainsley M. O'Reilly. Published by the Caribbean Tourism Organization and the Guyana Ministry of Trade, Industry and Tourism.

5 International Convention for the Prevention of Pollution from Ships 1973, as amended by Protocol of 1978.

6 The International Convention for the Safety of Life at Sea, 1974.

WORLD TOURISM SCENARIO AND INDIA'S POSITION

In recent years tourism has emerged as a major economic activity that is employment oriented and earns foreign exchange. Its share in the world's GDP in 1994–95 was 10 per cent which is more than the world military budgets put together. In global terms, the investment in tourism industry and travel trade accounts for 7 per cent of the total capital investment. Today 21.2 crore people around the globe are employed in travel trade and tourism. In future, this industry is likely to see unprecedented growth. According to the World Tourism Council at Brussels, the revenues from travel and tourism in Asia Pacific region will grow at the rate of 7.8 per cent annually over the next decade.

Amongst the economic sectors, the tourism sector is highly labour intensive. A survey by the Government of India notes that the rate of employment generation (direct and indirect) in tourism is 52 persons employed per Rs.10 lakh investment (based on 1992–93 Consumer Price Index). This is much higher than the rates of employment generation in most other economic sectors.

India's tourism industry has also recorded phenomenal growth. The rate of international arrivals in India in recent years has been to the tune of about 19 lakh arrivals per year. The unprecedented growth in tourism in India has made it the third largest foreign exchange earner after gem and jewellery and ready–made garments. This is not surprising since India possesses a whole range of attraction normally sought by tourists and which includes natural attractions like Iandscapes, scenic beauty, mountains, wildlife, beaches, kajor rivers and man-made attractions such as monuments, forts, palaces and havelis. However, in global terms, in spite of such attractions, tourist arrivals in India are a mere 0.30 per cent of the world arrivals. Receipts are similarly low, just a 0.50 per cent of the world receipts. We are still quite far from the target of 50 lakh tourist arrivals per year.

Tourism in the State of Gujarat

A separate Tourism Department was established in 1973 to identify and develop the tourism potential in the State. This was followed by the creation of Tourism Corporation of Gujarat Limited in 1978 which was entrusted with the task of undertaking and developing tourism-related commercial activities. The Corporation is presently engaged in a variety of activities such as creation of lodging and boarding facilities for the tourists and other aspects of tourist attraction such as transportation, packaged tours, wayside catering along the National and State Highways, arranging cultural festivals, organizing exhibitions and producing and distributing maps, posters, brochures and pamphlets. The Corporation has set up accommodation facilities at Chorwad, Ahmedpur Mandvi, Porbandar, Veraval, Hajira, Ubharat and Tithal. Similar facilities at pilgrimage centres like Palitana, Somnath, Dwarka, Pavagadh and Dakor have also been set up by the Corporation. One of the recent tourist attractions introduced by the Corporation in collaboration with the Indian Railways is a special tourist train. The Royal Orient Train connects up various tourist destinations straddling the Gujarat and Rajasthan State. However, the Corporation has suffered losses due to a number of organizational constraints. In order to minimize these losses and also to provide better services to the tourists, the Government has undertaken privatisation of some of the commercial property units of the Corporation.

In spite of possessing a variety of tourist attractions such as wildlife, scenic beauty, pilgrimage centres, exotic traditional crafts and festivals, beaches, hospitality of the region and a varied healthy and tasteful cuisine, the State has not been able to accelerate the pace of tourism in comparison to other states. In 1991, the State did declare a tourism policy but it did not elicit adequate response from the private sector since the policy contained only a handful of benefits while the implementation was tardy due to legal and administrative constraints. This was at a time when the Government of India had already declared tourism as an industry and a large number of states had followed suit. This enabled the tourism industry to avail of incentives, reliefs, benefits available to the industry in those states.

While other State Governments made successful efforts in developing tourism within their states, the relative inability of the Gujarat State to harness and develop its full tourist potential may be attributed to a combination of factors such as lack of effective policies, inadequate infrastructure, ineffective marketing and lack of decent facilities for the tourists.

The main rationale for formulating a comprehensive tourism policy is rooted, on one hand, in the convergence of socio–economic spread benefits, environment–friendliness and employment potential of tourism industry and on the other, in the growing demand for tourism products in the State, brought by a rapid industrial growth in the State during the recent years that has led to tremendous increase in number of business travellers.

Objectives of Gujarat's Tourism Policy

The main objective of the State's Tourism Policy will be to undertake intensive development of tourism in the State and thereby increase employment opportunities. The following related objectives are dovetailed with main objectives:

- Identify and develop tourist destinations and related activities.
- Diversifications of tourism products in order to attract more tourists through a varied consumer choice.
- Comprehensive development of pilgrimage centres as tourist destinations.
- Create adequate facilities for budget tourists.
- Strengthen the existing infrastructure and develop new ones where necessary.
- Creation of tourism infrastructure so as to preserve handicrafts, folk arts and culture of the state and thereby attract more tourists.

Approach and Strategy of Gujarat w.r.t. Tourism

In addition to the facilitation role assigned to itself by the Government in the development of tourism, the Government will adopt the following strategy towards the private sector with the objective of securing its active involvement in leading the development of tourism in the State.

- The tourism will be given the status of industry in order that the facilities and benefits available to the industry are also made available to tourism projects.
- A special incentives package will be made available for encouraging new tourism projects as well as expansion of existing tourism units.
- Infrastructural facilities will be strengthened and developed within the State, particularly in Special Tourism Areas which will be notified latter and which will be developed by adopting an integrated area.
- Effective mechanisms will be set up to build meaningful co–ordination with the Central Government and the State Government's agencies, the local self–government bodies and the NGOs.
- Government will encourage building effective linkages with the relevant economic agents and agencies such as the national and international tour operators and travel agents of repute, hotel chains and global institutions connected with tourism such as WTO.

Policy Proposals by State of Gujarat

1. *Tourism as Industry*

1.1 Like other industrial projects, tourism projects too involve professional management, capital investment, special skills and training. The Government of India and a number of other states have declared tourism as an industry. Gujarat State which is at the forefront of the industrial development will also declare tourism as an industry. This will enable the tourism projects to be reliable to get benefits contained in the paras 1.2 and 1.3 below.

1.2 Availability of land is a primary requirement of any project. The process of grant of land will be facilitated in urban areas for the projects concerning setting up of hotels, restaurants and apartment hotels etc.

Existing arrangements for grant of government waste land to industrial units will be made applicable to various tourism projects.

Arrangements will be made to acquire private land under Land Acquisition Act for various tourism projects by companies registered under the Companies Act.

The existing commercial rates of NA assessment applicable to land involving tourism projects would be reviewed and rates of NA assessment for industrial purposes will be made applicable to them.

1.3 As one of the sets of infrastructural institutions, the State Financial Institutions have made an important contribution in creating conductive environment for industrial entrepreneurs. They will be called upon to do the same for tourism entrepreneurs in terms of making available adequate finance.

So far, the lending from the State Financial Institutions has been largely confined to hotels only. In reality, the range of activities for tourism projects is far larger than just hotels as can be seen from the following illustrative list:

Accommodation Projects:

- Hotels
- Resorts
- Motels
- Apartment Hotels
- Heritage Hotels.

Food-oriented Projects:

- Restaurants
- Wayside Facilities on the State Highways.

Other Tourism–related Projects:

- Amusement Parks and Water Sports
- Handicraft Village Complexes
- Fairs and Festivals

- Camps and Facilities encouraging Adventure
- Train Travel Projects
- Sea/River Cruise Projects
- Sound and Light Shows
- Museums
- Natural Parks/Zoos
- Safari Projects
- Ropeways
- Sports/Health Facilities Complexes
- Training Schools for the managerial expertise for Hospitality Industry
- Golf Courses.

Service-oriented Projects:

- Travel Agency
- Tour Operation
- Transport Operation
- Linkage with the International Hotel Chains (Franchise)
- Human Resources Development (HRD) for Tourism Industry and necessary training facilities.

Most of the projects on this illustrative list are not eligible for loans from the banks or the State Financial Agencies. It will be necessary to make suitable changes in the lending criteria for viable projects in the listed activities in order than their financial requirements are met.

The modification of the lending criteria of the State Financial Agencies will be made with regard to the financial ceiling, debt equity ratio, recovery period, moratorium etc.

Necessary arrangements will be made to ensure that the State Financial Agencies and the banks attach adequate priority to the financing requirements of tourism projects.

1.4 As referred to in para 4(b), a new incentive package will be made available to replace the existing incentive policy instituted in 1991. A tax holiday of 5–10 years in respect of following taxes will be made available up to 100 per cent of capital investment to various tourism projects located in Special Tourism Areas whether declared by the Central Government or the State Government, located in designated areas and located on National and State Highways. The scope and the extent of the benefits of tax holiday will vary according to certain considerations such as the admissible expenditure, the size of the capital investment etc. The benefit of tax holiday will also be made available for the purpose of expansion of the existing tourism projects in these areas:

- Sales Tax
- Purchase Tax
- Electricity Duty
- Luxury Tax
- Entertainment Tax.

Necessary administrative arrangements will be made at the State and District Level to operationalize the incentive schemes.

Suitable schemes will be designed to market tourism products, and particularly wide publicity will be secured in respect of various facilities being offered by the travel agents, tour operators etc.

Special paying guest scheme will be formulated for providing adequate and inexpensive lodging and boarding facilities to take care of seasonal flows of tourists to the pilgrimage centres during festivals.

Financial assistance will be provided for the preparation of feasibility reports by consultants in respect of tourism projects.

Structure of the taxes and tariffs, e.g. luxury tax, entertainment tax, sales tax, etc., will be reviewed with reference to developmental needs of tourism sector and necessary amendments will be made.

2. *Redefining the roles of the State and the Market*

Since the approach of the Tourism Policy focuses on market–led developments, the role of the State would be as follows:

2.1 The Government proposes to make commercial services available entirely through private sector or in association with it. The State's role will primarily focus on strengthening and upgrading existing infrastructure and development of new infrastructure. Reputed consultants will be hired to prepare area development master plans/feasibility studies in respect of important tourist destinations and areas of tourism potential, e.g.

Sardar Sarovar Project Area, Kutch, Beach sites and area covering Porbandar, Gir Forest, Veraval, Somnath, Ahmedpur–Mandvi, Saputara, Modhera etc.

Efforts will be made to get funding for development of infrastructure for these destinations/areas from national and international agencies.

2.2 To ensure timely provision of necessary funding, the Government will earmark funds in the annual budgets of the departments concerned for securing the purpose mentioned in 2.1.

2.3 In conformity with State's promotional role in the development of tourism sector, all competitive and commercial activities of Tourism Corporation of Gujarat Limited will be privatized except where no entrepreneur is coming forward to meet the existing need. This privatization would help strengthen the financial position of the Corporation and also help provide qualitative services to the tourists.

Tourism Corporation of Gujarat Limited will assume a catalytic role focused on acting as clearing house of information, production and distribution of promotional literature, policy advice etc.

The Tourism Corporation will assist entrepreneurs and agencies in tourism sector and will try to help alleviate their difficulties particularly *vis a vis* the Government and its agencies.

A Computerized Information Centre will be set up at the State level to make available necessary information to the agencies/ entrepreneurs who wish to set up tourism projects.

In addition to its existing offices in Bombay, Delhi and Madras, the Tourism Corporation will also open its offices in other major cities of India to give wide publicity and disseminate information on Gujarat Tourism and market tourism products through these offices and through reputed travel agents in other big cities. Thus, the information about Gujarat's tourist destinations and related information would be made available to tourists from outside the State in their own cities.

2.4 There is already a scheme of 50 per cent matching grant from the State Government to the local self–governing bodies for the development of local tourist destinations. This scheme will be made more effective and attractive and necessary provisions in the budget will be made. This will help centralize the process of developing tourist destinations.

The process of decentralization will be further strengthened by delegation of administrative and executive powers of approval of incentives to small tourism projects to District Level Bodies headed by the Collector. These bodies, in addition, will also secure co–ordination from other departments/agencies of the Government in development and promotion of tourism. Representation will be given on this body to the experts, individual agencies and individuals connected with the tourism.

2.5 A single window clearance system will be instituted for speedy clearance of various permissions, approvals required under different laws and rules. Necessary modification/ amendment will be made to various administrative arrangements and laws which are not consistent with the approach of this policy. Care will be taken to ensure that prospective investors do not have to suffer protracted and complex administrative process.

2.6 Intensive efforts will be undertaken to attract investors from outside the State as well as from other countries including non–resident Indians to invest in tourism sector on large scale. Tourism Corporation of Gujarat Limited and Directorate of Tourism will play active role to ensure that investors get various permissions easily and are provided with all the necessary facilities.

2.7 A High Powered Committee under the Chairmanship of Chief Secretary with Director of Tourism as the Member Secretary will be constituted with the objective of securing effective co–ordination among various Government departments and agencies as also to speed up decision-making proceeds concerning tourism. The committee will meet regularly and enjoy full powers of Government, provided the approval of the Chief Minister and the Council of Ministers will be obtained wherever required.

2.8 In order to create a particular forum for deliberation and discussion concerning tourism industry, a Tourism Advisory Council headed by the Chief Minister will be set up. The Ministers and Secretaries of administrative departments concerned will be the members. The representatives of tourism industry, experts and related organizations will be nominated as members. The Additional Chief Secretary (Tourism) will be the Member Secretary of this Council.

The Council will meet periodically to deliberate upon policy as well as individual issues and offer suitable advice to the Government.

3. *Perspective Planning*

Perspective plan for tourism development will be prepared in consultation with experts. An overview of possible tourism products is offered below:

3.1 *Religious (pilgrimage) and Archaeological Tourism*: Gujarat has a preponderance of pilgrimage centres as in some other states. Somnath and Dwarka – some of the well-known and revered sites of ancient Hindu temples are situated in the State. The temple architecture has reached heights of excellence in Jain temples at Shetrunji, Girnar and Taranga. The temple of Ambaji situated in Aravalli range in North Gujarat is an important religious centre for devotees in the country. Dakor, Pavagadh, Bahucharaji, Shamlaji, Narayan Sarovar, Sudama's Porbandar, Kabirvad Shuklatirth, Kayavarohan, Bhadrakali Temple Ahmedabad and Tankara – Maharshi Dayanand Saraswati's birth place are also important pilgrimage destinations which have kept alive the religious sentiments of the people. Lakhs of pilgrims visit these places every year.

These places are visited not only by the devotees from all over the country but also by non-resident Indians and travellers especially from the eastern part of the world. Necessary accommodation facilities and related services will be created on these sites. For ensuring orderly and planned development of pilgrimage centres, the State Government has constituted Pavitra Dham Vikas Board chaired by the Chief Minister. The Board will prepare and implement plans to provide necessary facilities to the devotees and also ensure conservation of cultural atmosphere consistent with sentiments of visiting devotees.

Shamlaji is an ancient site for Buddhists. The excavated relics of Buddhist period at the site are now kept in a museum at Baroda.

There are a number of places of archaeological importance such as the temple–town of Palitana, Modhera with its Sun temple, historical Ranki Vav at Patan with relics of an ancient capital, the Girnar Hills with Hindu and Jain temples, Junagadh with a historical fort, Dabhoi, Champaner, Pavagadh, Shaking Minarets, Gandhi Ashram, Siddi Sayed Jali etc. These can be developed by providing necessary infrastructural facilities and marketed as tourist destinations to attract tourists.

3.2 *Heritage Tourism*: A large number of old palaces, havelis, darbargadhs exist in the State. These historical buildings can be converted into hotels, restaurants or museums by providing suitable incentives to owners. Wildlife and Pilgrimage Tourism circuits can be linked to heritage properties exploiting the geographical congruity. Development of this sub–sector will not only attract foreign tourists but also provide encouragement and support to local art and craft.

Government will take necessary steps to promote Heritage tourism in the State.

3.3 *Wildlife Tourism*: There is substantial scope for development of tourism based on wildlife in the State. Gir Forest of Gujarat is the last stronghold of Asiatic Lions. The Bear Sanctuary at Ratan Mahal (District Panchmahal, Black Buch Sanctuary at Velavadar (District Bhavnagar), Bird Sanctuary at Nalsarovar (District Ahmedabad), Wild Ass Sanctuary at Kutch etc. can be effectively developed into tourist destinations by providing infrastructural facilities. In order to facilitate visitors to these areas, coordination among various agencies will be established.

3.4 *Coastal and Beach Tourism*: The Gujarat State has the longest coastline among Maritime States of the country. Identified stretches of coastline can be developed into beaches from tourism point of view. It will be the endeavour of the State to develop beach potential by providing such facilities as may attract foreign tourists.

Various tourist destinations easily accessible from the coast will be linked through coastal shipping circuits.

3.5 *Tourism based on Traditional Art and Craft and Cultural Activities*: Banni in Kutch, Khambhat, Junagadh etc. are known for their craftsmanship. Similarly, there are hundreds of fairs that are celebrated throughout the year with enthusiasm. Tarnetar Fair in Surendranagar District, Chitra Vichitra Fair at Poshina (Sabarkantha District), Kanwat Fair at Chhota Udepur (Panchmahals District), Dang Darbar in Dang. Bhavnath Fair of Junagadh, Vautha Fair of Ahmedabad etc. have immense tourism value. By developing accommodation, transport and other facilities, these fairs and festivals will be promoted nationally and internationally. The places of importance from art and craft point of view will be included in the tourist circuits and necessary facilities provided to tourists.

3.6 *Corporate Tourism*: Private sector will be encouraged to build the state of the art convention centres, seminar halls etc. so as to attract corporate events like seminar, workshops and annual general meetings. Participants in such events generally have high purchasing power and provide a boost to local economy.

3.7 *Adventure Tourism*: This is also a territory with possibility of development as a sub–sector which will be examined and new activities like Camel Safari in Kutch, Horse–riding in Aravalli hill ranges, Parachuting in Saputara, Trekking in Dang, Pavagadh, Palitana etc. will be promoted. Such activities will create large-scale employment opportunities for guides, coolies, traders for hire of tents and equipments etc. and will also encourage paying guest accommodation in such areas. Private entrepreneurs and institutions will be encouraged to develop such facilities.

3.8 *Highway Tourism*: There is a good network of State and national highways which criss–cross the State and a large number of travellers prefer road journey. Because of large geographical expanse of the State, these journeys tend to be quite long and boring. There is a need for creating necessary facilities like hotels, restaurants, picnic spots, water parks etc. along the highways at suitable intervals for the highway travellers to relax. In fact, travellers can be induced to follow certain traffic routes if such facilities are better developed. Highway facilities and wayside amenities are so well developed in some states that this has become the mainstay of tourism. State shall encourage private investors to create such facilities on highways.

3.9 Various sub–sectors of tourism activities listed above will be encouraged by marking new tourism units eligible for incentives under Tax Holiday incentive scheme in designated areas.

3.10 As mentioned earlier, the State Government intends to designate certain areas having significant tourist potential as Special Tourism Areas. To this end, reputed consultants and institutions will be engaged to prepare area development plans in respect of various areas such as Kutch District, areas around Sardar Sarovar project area, South Saurashtra areas covering Gir, Porbandar, Veraval, Somnath, beaches and areas of pilgrimage/ heritage towns. These areas will be developed by following integrated area development approach. The State Government will make efforts to tap all the source of national and international funding for development of these areas and provide special encouragement to tourism projects being established therein. For ensuring faster development of these areas, area development committees will be constituted.

4. *Human Resources Development*

1. Human Resources Development is an important aspect of service industries. Tourists depend upon travel agents, guides and hence trained manpower is a *sine qua non* of tourism industry. On the basis of available statistics, training facilities can be safely said to be totally inadequate. If trained manpower is not available locally, the objective of local employment will not be achieved.

2. Keeping in view the approach of market–led development, the State Government will encourage and support creation of training facilities in the private sector by private agencies/individuals. Hotel Management course, courses meant for guides, caterer and other supervisory and non-supervisory staff of hotel will be introduced in Industrial Training Institutes (I.T.Is). Approved hotel associations and private entrepreneurs will be encouraged to create new training facilities by making available land to them for this purpose and by giving other appropriate incentives. The Government will consider setting up a Hotel Management Training Institute at the State level preferably in private sector.

3. Residents of Gujarat, especially local youths, would be encouraged and facilitated to take part in such training courses.

4. The Institute of Hotel Management, Catering & Nutrition which is working under the administrative control of the Central Government will be utilized to start new training courses so that the residents of Gujarat can get admission and manpower requirement of this sector is met.

The residents of Gujarat undergoing such training will be reimbursed a part of the tuition fees through scholarships.

Feedback and Monitoring

To make the New Tourism Policy result-oriented, implementation will be monitored by a High Powered Committee under the Chairmanship of Chief Secretary.

A Management Information System will be set up to assist the Committee to make available information on various aspects of implementation on a continuous basis. The Committee will also review the policy from time to time.

TOURISM POLICY OF ANDHRA PRADESH

The Travel and Tourism industry is well on its way to becoming one of the most powerful growth engines in the coming millennium and is anticipated to generate nearly 338 million jobs by the year 2005 with an annual growth rate of 4.8 per cent.

Acknowledging the vast potential and spin–off tourism has other industries, the Government of Andhra Pradesh is focusing on tourism for generating greater employment and achieving higher economic growth.

We have a vision of making Andhra Pradesh the destination state of India, given its attractive diversity, natural endowments and friendly population. Andhra Pradesh has a rich tourist potential, which is yet to be exploited. "Bring the world to Andhra Pradesh, take Andhra Pradesh to the world", is our guiding spirit.

Andhra Pradesh has great potential for tourism with its temple towns, beach resorts, monuments and other tourist attractions. Hyderabad and Visakhapatnam airports are proposed to be expanded to receive international flights. Hyderabad has been identified as one of the 5 locations in the country for the establishment of a full–fledged international airport. Direct flights to Singapore have recently commenced from Hyderabad in addition to other destinations. Hyderabad is being developed as a major transit hub between Europe and the far East.

"Andhra Pradesh Unlimited", is the strategy of this policy. We recognize the advantage of offering the collective attractiveness of other places in the region with places in Andhra Pradesh. We plan to decentralize tourism development to districts and local bodies. This policy will also encourage private sector in the tourism industry and provide a framework for private–public partnership.

To encourage private investment in tourism and related industry, various incentives and concessions are being offered. In keeping with our objective and spirit, taxation has been attempted to be rationalized on the logic of intelligent taxation to enable private sector to expand tourism. While acknowledging the primacy of the private sector, the state retains with itself the responsibility of provision of public goods and for addressing issues related to safety, quality and regulation.

We view this new tourism policy as the product of a shared vision for the state. A series of consultations within the government and with the industry culminated in this policy, which stands enriched by the inputs of the industry. It is necessary that the state moves in a clear direction and consolidates its comparative advantage and realizes its tourist potential to the fullest. It is in this context that the tourism policy has to be evaluated.

Step Forward to the Next Millenium

Tourism policies are products of time, technology and needs of people. Secular growth trends in tourism witnessed all over are a result of social factors that boost demand for tourism and development in technology. Demand for tourism is propelled mainly by growth. Growing wealth and the rise of a middle class creates that demand. Technology, in turn, makes travel better, easier and hassle–free. Service technology makes leisure an activity which delivers memorable experiences.

Tourism provides opportunity for economic growth, employment generation and poverty alleviation. Tourism holds the key for creation of rural wealth, opportunity for the hitherto neglected segments of society, artisans and service providers in the backward areas. This sector employs 212 million people world wide, generates $3.4 trillion in gross output and contributes $655 billion towards government tax revenues. Travel and Tourism is the world's largest industry. By 2005, the industry is expected to grow to $7 trillion. The industry accounts for 10.7 per cent of the global work force and provides 1 in every 9 jobs. Between the years 1995 and 2000, the industry is adding a new job every 2.5 seconds. Andhra Pradesh is gearing itself for these opportunities with this policy.

This policy, while defining the direction of tourism development and providing a strategic action plan converging on 'Vision 2020' of the state, also articulates the express desire of the state to use it as a growth platform and charter a growth path which is sustainable and responsible. Sustainable because our people, history, culture and life styles are at the core of this policy. We accept competition as the driving force. We also accept our shared vision of protecting our common heritage and not straining our resources when they are fragile. Responsible because this policy defines responsibility of the state, private sector, people and tourists. Moreover, it is designed to be an instrument or a framework which will enable the state to catapult into a different platform and enable much needed private capital to flow into activities involving technology and enterprise. Eventually, together with the private sector, a champion will be created.

Objectives:

- To position tourism as a major growth engine and to harness its direct and multiplier effect for employment generation, economic growth and poverty alleviation in the State of Andhra Pradesh in an environmentally sustainable manner.
- To position Andhra Pradesh as the destination state of India and take advantage of the burgeoning travel and trade market on the demand side and vast untapped potential in heritage, pilgrimage, conventions and beach tourism on the supply side.
- To acknowledge the primacy of the role of the private sector with the government working as the facilitator and the catalyst.
- To bring into effect a co–operative endeavour of both public and private sectors on one hand and between and among different sectors of the government on the other.
- To reap the benefit of the increasing inter–relatedness of the world, which allows capital to move freely across countries and travellers, to cross borders for the benefit of the common man seeking wholesome, memorable and pleasurable experiences.
- To position tourist and tourism–friendly policies as a showcase to demonstrate the attractiveness of Andhra Pradesh as a destination as well as a fast developing business hub.

In the spirit of co–operative federalism, the efforts of the state will augment tourist arrivals in the country and provide larger opportunities for a win–win framework of operation, both among the states and between the federal government and the state of Andhra Pradesh rather than relying on imperial harmonization strategies. The policy's guiding spirit is: Bring the World to Andhra Pradesh and Take Andhra Pradesh to the World.

The Way Ahead: Where We Are And Where We Want To Be

The reform process has been in motion since 1991. Currently, India's near–complete integration with the global economy is witnessing:

- An upsurge with private capital in the forefront and government playing the crucial role of facilitator and catalyst.
- A fresh and meaningful look at the opportunities of travel, hospitality and leisure market which are growing rapidly.
- There is a growing realization that private investment should play a larger part in the constructive co–operation between private and public sectors in tourism development. Besides, when a market for leisure and tourism exists, there is a need for affirmative action to tap the market.

This new growth and conducive environment ought to have attracted sizeable private investments to the tourism sector of Andhra Pradesh, with its rich and varied heritage, an array of flora and fauna, and an extensive coast line of nearly 1000 kms. Tourism was declared as an industry in the state as far back as 1986, duly extending benefits and concessions to investors. In 1994, special tourist centres were notified and an incentive subsidy, tax concessions and electricity rebates were offered. The State Tourism Policy was documented and released in 1994. Despite all this, not too much progress has been made in attracting tourists and investors. This could be attributed mainly to low initial development, failure of the state to address the critical areas for kick–starting the tourism development in the state and poor marketing strategies to attract tourists and potential investors.

Tourism is emerging as the fastest growing industry all over the world with the potential to generate one of the highest returns on investments and providing large employment opportunities. Tourism is the second largest foreign exchange earner in the country even though India has a share as low as 0.4 per cent of world tourism with nearly 2.4 million international tourists arriving in 1997. Its importance can therefore be overlooked only at the cost of long–term possibilities.

Tourism is a sector with a tremendous multiplier effect in employment generation and has been a platform from which poverty can be combated and economic growth attained.

Some facts and figures are:

- In India alone, nearly 20.5 million jobs are in the tourism sector.
- Tourism creates 85 jobs with 47 direct against 13 direct in the manufacturing sector with every million rupees spent.
- Consequently, it has become necessary to have a re–look at the existing Tourism Policy parameters as well as to calibrate them to the need of the hour, with a view to attract sizeable private investment in the state, position the state in the travel and tourism market and to promote Andhra Pradesh as a destination state in India. While the potential of tourism as an invisible foreign exchange earner is undoubtedly an important consideration, it is its multiplier effect in large employment creation, its ability in bootstrapping economic growth and fostering poverty alleviation that makes it a prime candidate for governmental focus. India's inability to exploit a burgeoning market in tourism is a pointer to the fact that "imperial harmonization" of planned development is hardly the recipe for tourism promotion. Federal policies supplemented by focused, aggressive and market friendly approaches of the state are steps in the right direction.

Economic reforms and India's attempt to take the position in an inter–related world has created the right backdrop for the growth of tourism. Firstly, it is liberalization rather than controls that create a proper atmosphere for the growth of tourism. The entire world is our market. We cannot afford to overlook the capacity of tourism to generate employment. If the State's capacity is weak, new capacities can be created, as capacity is not destiny at all. We should also be able to take maximum advantage of the possibilities of tourism by consolidating or creating capacities.

7

Towards Developing Tourism Action Plans: Select Reviews

TOWARDS DEVELOPING A TOURISM ACTION PLAN IN CANADA

A tourism action plan defines the who, what, where, when and how of making tourism happen. It provides a framework for businesses, local government and other organizations to analyse tourism resources and concerns, and to encourage development and promotion within your community.

It covers the five key components of tourism:

- *Attractions*: natural and man–made features within and near your community that are of interest to tourists—lakes, mountains and wilderness, unique shops, historic sites, industries, fairs, conventions, competitions and tours.
- *Promotion*: marketing tools, such as advertisements, travel shows, magazine articles, brochures, maps, videos, commercial and promotional signs, auto tour guides and tourist information booths.
- *Infrastructure*: roads, airports, railways, parking areas, sewage dump stations, water and power services, boat launches, and location and distance signs. Community recreation facilities that can be used to host events and sports tournaments, such as ice arenas, curling rinks, baseball diamonds and community halls are also infrastructure elements. If access to your area is poor, and if basic services are lacking or in disrepair, tourists may go elsewhere.

Elements of a Tourism Action Plan

- An endorsement from your band council acknowledging the plan as your community's official tourism development and promotion strategy
- The plan's credentials: what it is, who developed it, under what authority and what it hopes to accomplish
- A description of the process: when and how the plan was prepared, when it will be monitored and reviewed; how it should be used and by whom, and how public input was obtained
- A definition of tourism
- The development policy for your community
- A summary of your present and potential tourism markets, assets, concerns about tourism, goals and objectives, and actions to be taken
- *Services*: hotels, motels, campgrounds, restaurants, service stations, shops and other retail businesses.
- *Hospitality*: This key element is the cement that holds the whole tourism package together. Involving everyone in your community, it determines whether tourists enjoy their stay, whether they will come back and whether they will encourage others to visit.

A committee approach to developing the plan ensures commitment from your community. It also takes advantage of the skills and experiences of community members who own businesses, work in tourism or have training in the industry.

A Band Council Resolution can formalize the committee by confirming its official name, mandate, number and selection of members and chairperson, procedures for meetings and reporting, frequency of meetings and meeting quorums.

The Committee Meeting

AGENDA
TOURISM DEVELOPMENT COMMITTEE
INAUGURAL MEETING
DATE
PLACE

Item

1. Selection of a chairperson
2. Selection of a secretary (if not provided by the First Nations Council)
3. Review of the committee's terms of reference
4. Review of *The Development of Tourism in Your Community*
5. Review of background information
6. Review of the development policy, including the tourism components
7. Other business
8. Date and agenda for next meeting.

During meetings, questions may arise that committee members cannot answer. Your chairperson, in consultation with the group, can designate members to collect whatever information is needed and report back to the committee by a specified deadline.

Meeting discussions and decisions should always be recorded:

- Your chairperson or an appointed member should record lists and group statements in point form on a flip chart for all to see. This can be done as the meeting proceeds to help keep the group focused on the topic.
- Your secretary should keep detailed minutes for subsequent distribution to committee members. The minutes will form a permanent record of what takes place at each meeting.
- As each step in an activity is accomplished, your secretary should record completion.

Identify Present Tourism Markets

Before any decisions can be made, you need reliable information on the present state of tourism in your area. To establish baseline information, your committee could look at the following:

- Reasons they come. Is it for business, pleasure, for local services, to visit friends and relatives or are they just passing through?
- Services they look for and whether the services are available.
- Time of year most people visit.

- Mode of transportation.
- Length of stay.
- Amount of money they spend.
- Age, sex, education, occupation, income class and place of origin of the tourists who come to your community now.
- New trends in travel, changes in types of people travelling.

The action plan should reflect the specifics of your own community, but other communities and regional tourist associations may have information to share.

Develop Tourism Market Profiles

The chart (see Appendix A) can be used to develop profiles for each type of tourist that comes to your community at present. As previously stated, there are five types of tourists, defined according to their reason for travel:

- business;
- personal business;
- vacation;
- visiting friends and relatives; and
- passing through.

Fill in the "present Tourism type" row for each tourism type by answering the questions along the top of the chart. There might be potential to attract tourists from all categories, but the importance of each type of tourist to your local tourism industry will vary.

By grading present tourism markets in the column, "Present Importance," your committee can best focus on where to concentrate its efforts.

Each committee member grades each tourist type on a scale of one to 10 in importance, in terms of number, length of stay and expenditures. Ten would be the highest grade. The consensus grade is arrived at by adding up the numbers assigned to each tourist type. The tourist type with the highest grade would be ranked first; the type with the second highest grade would be ranked second, and so on.

If there are tourism operators in or near your community that are not represented on the committee, talk to them to validate your committee's findings. These tourism operators could include:

- hotel/motels
- restaurants
- parks and campgrounds
- service stations
- tourist information booths
- hunting and fishing operations
- tours
- provincial departments of culture, tourism, parks and recreation, and transportation
- utility departments
- regional tourist associations
- retail businesses
- service clubs
- sport and cultural events
- tourist attractions (museums, cultural centres, etc.)

If you emphasize that the chart is still at draft stage, people will realize that their input is going to be used. This also gives you the opportunity to find out what tourism promotional activities are under way and what are planned.

At your next committee meeting, change the market profile charts according to what you have learned from these discussions.

List Tourism Assets

Tourism assets can be divided into five categories:

- attractions
- promotion
- infrastructure
- hospitality
- services.

For example, a new elementary school is a community asset but it would also be a tourism asset if its architecture reflected First Nations influences or if it could be used for major events or conventions for tourists.

First Nations have tourism assets which are not necessarily recognized as such. These include:

- Their history and their perspectives of that history;

- Aboriginal views on nature and the environment;
- Aboriginal arts, crafts and performing arts;
- On–reserve wildlife regulatory regimes which may differ from provincial/territorial regimes;
- Reserve and nearby lands, including archaeological and historic sites, lakes, wilderness areas, wildlife habitats, vegetation and geological structures;
- Native tourism sectoral organizations which could provide valuable central services and co–ordinate the activities of First Nation communities; and
- Unique industries.

Tourism Assets

Assets	*Rank*
Tourism Attractions	
Provincial park nearby	1
Wilderness areas nearby with good fishing lakes	2
Annual powwow	3
Annual hockey tournament	4
Community hall	5
Community craft store/workshop	6
Tourism Promotion	
Linkages with other First Nations	1
Tourism Infrastructure	
Good access to primary highway	1
Full sewer and water servicing, excellent–quality water	2
Tourism Hospitality	
Some friendly merchants	1
Tourism Services	
New outfitter camp	2
Service station	3
Campground near reserve	1
General store	5
Tow truck service	4

Once you have listed your assets, rank them in importance. Start with tourism attractions. Have each committee member grade attractions on a scale of one to 10. Then use the grade total for each asset to determine its rank. Once you have completed ranking the attractions, go on to look at infrastructure, hospitality, service and promotion.

Recognize Tourism Concerns

Tourism concerns can include:

- *Negative Assets*: Check your market profiles and list of assets for those items that may have negative aspects. Discuss how they can be improved.
- *Outright Liabilities*: A noxious pulp mill on your doorstep is definitely a concern. List all such liabilities—even those that seem insurmountable—because someone else may have a partial solution. Even if no solution is found, your discussion will have helped put it into perspective for the community.
- *Undeveloped Ideas*: List and discuss all ideas, no matter how off–the–wall they are. They may include great proposals that have not been acted upon. If a good suggestion is presented negatively, you then can list it as a concern, which then becomes motivation for action.

List tourism concerns the same way you listed assets.

Be explicit. For example, the statement, "Visitors just pass right through town; nobody ever stops here," is too general. It may be true, but it has to be more specific to be of use as a discussion point. Visitors may not be stopping in town because:

- There are few clean washrooms at local service stations (services).
- There are no parking spots (infrastructure).
- Tourists do not know about attractions (promotion).
- No interesting attractions are visible from the highway (attractions).
- Some merchants have not recognized the importance of being courteous to tourists (hospitality).

The more specific you are in categorizing a concern, the easier it will be to find a solution.

Rank the concerns as you did the assets. At the top of the list put obvious concerns that can be fixed easily, at little cost, and with highly visible results.

Determine Potential Tourism Markets

This exercise looks at the possibilities for increasing existing tourism and attracting an entirely new market. Using the Tourism Market Profile answer the questions along the top of the chart for the five categories of "potential new tourist types." Base your analysis on present tourism markets. For example, if existing facilities are at capacity during the summer, it might make sense to focus on winter tourists, such as snowmobilers, hockey tournament participants and spectators.

Tourism Concerns

Concerns	*Rank*
Tourism Attractions	
No major tourist attraction in community	1
No museum or cultural centre	2
Tourism Promotion	
No tourist literature	2
No welcome signs at edge of town	3
Businesses are not members of provincial and regional tourism association	6
No powwow or hockey tournament promotion outside of community	4
No community theme	1
Campers are not aware of all the goods and services available in community	5
Tourism Infrastructure	
Several good fishing lakes in the area without adequate access	1
No sewage dumping station for recreational vehicules in or near the community	2
Tourism Hospitality	
Some merchants and staff are unfriendly	1
Some residents are unfriendly or discourteous to visitors	2
Tourism Services	
Campground near reserve does not provide full service	1
No repair facilities for recreational vehicles and outboard motors in town	2
No recreational equipment rentals in town (canoes, boats, snowmobiles, etc.)	3

Rank all anticipated tourist markets in order of importance.

State Tourism Goals and Objectives

Tourism goals are clear, concise statements describing the kind of tourism wanted in your community. They must be compatible with the community's development policy and should provide direction for more specific objectives.

Tourism goals can be stated simply by inserting the phrase "to improve" in front of each of the five key components of tourism:

- to improve tourism attractions;
- to improve tourism promotion;
- to improve tourism infrastructure;
- to improve tourism hospitality; and
- to improve tourism services.

Each of these goals leads to a set of objectives which are simple, concise steps to achieving the relevant goal. They should be measurable and realistic.

How to develop Tourism Objectives

Look at how the needs and wants on your market profile charts relate to the tourism resources of your community. Focus on one tourism goal at a time. For each goal, display your charts on present and potential market profiles, assets and concerns. Then, assign an objective to each concern. For example, tour buses may travel through your community but do not linger. How do you encourage those travellers to stay longer or to come back? The concern is that you have tourism services and attractions but no one knows about them.

For the goal, "to improve tourism promotion," your committee then develops objectives that promote businesses and services by advertising special tour services in local newspapers, provincial or territorial tourism publications or by mailing information flyers to tour companies.

The following chart provides a detailed look at the process of developing objectives.

One well–worded objective may cover more than one concern. However, avoid wording so broad or general that the objective becomes difficult to focus on or fulfil.

Once all the concerns have been matched with objectives, the objectives can be ranked to highlight the priorities. A priority list of five objectives is recommended to provide direction on what is to be achieved.

The answers to three questions help focus the relative importance of each objective.

- What present and potential markets do the objectives relate to? How important are they?
- How long will it take to accomplish the objective?

(a) less than a year; (b) one to three years; or (c) more than three years.

What will it cost (approximately) to achieve this objective and where will the money come from?

Process for Developing Objectives

1. Display all charts completed to date.
2. Write the first goal at the top of the Tourism Goals and Objectives flip–chart.
3. Review your Tourism Market Profiles, Tourism Assets and Tourism Concerns lists related to the goal.
4. Taking the first concern on the list, ask: What can or should be done about it?
5. Write an objective related to this concern. Your first thoughts are often the best: once you have something on paper you can add, delete or amend at will. This is a time for creative thinking.
6. When everyone is satisfied with the objective, move on to the next concern and develop the next objective.
7. When all concerns relating to your first goal have been dealt with, repeat the process for the other four goals.
8. Keep a record of all proceedings.
9. After a break or at a subsequent meeting, carry out a critical review of your objectives. Make changes if you are not happy with what has been produced to this point.

The top–priority objectives should be feasible, compatible with the development policy, have highly visible results and appeal to your community members.

An example of a tourism goals and objectives chart is on the next page.

Develop Action Steps

Tourism action steps are specific, detailed directives on how to achieve each objective.

They must be realistic. If a proposed step leads nowhere or needs additional activities to make it work, either alter or abandon it. Otherwise, the individuals responsible for supervising its co–ordination and implementation will have an impossible task.

Tourism Action Step Work Sheet summarizes all the previous work and the elements needed to turn planning into reality. Take the information from the work sheets and lists already completed, then list action steps in the order in which you expect them to be accomplished.

If action steps are difficult to develop for a certain objective, that objective might be unrealistic and have to be changed or abandoned.

Tourism Goals and Objectives

Goal	*Objectives*	*Rank*
To improve tourism attractions	To determine what major new attraction should be pursued by the community	2
	To have the Hudson's Bay store declared a provincial historic resource	12
	To provide tourist literature	7
	To provide welcome signs on the promotion edge of town	8
To improve tourism promotion	To encourage local businesses to join the regional and provincial tourism associations	9
	To ensure that event organizers are aware of any funding available to assist in tourism promotion	5
	To establish a town theme	1
To improve tourism infrastructure	To ensure that campers know about the goods and services available in town	10
	To investigate means of ensuring good access to fishing lakes	6
	To encourage businesses to use hospitality training programmes	4
To improve tourism hospitality	To establish a training programme for tourist information staff	14
	To establish a programme to ensure that all residents appreciate the need to be friendly and courteous to visitors	13
	To encourage the establishment of a full–service campground	3
To improve tourism services	To encourage the establishment of the following businesses in town: recreation vehicle service centre, 24–hour convenience store, recreation equipment rentals	11

Tourism Action Step Work Sheet

Goal:
To improve Tourism Promotion
Objective:
To establish a Community Theme
Concern(s)
Addressed: No Community Theme

Justification

What are we known for? What is our main claim to fame? Tourists will be more **Rank No. 1** inclined to visit if we portray a single interesting theme.

Markets implicated

Ecotourism. Campers. Visiting friends and relatives.

Time Frame

Less than a year **Expense:** $500.00

Action Steps by Whom When Results

1. Develop a proposal to come up with a community theme including:
   - what criteria should be used in deciding upon it;
   - who should make the final decision;
   - how to get residents interested and involved; and
   - how the theme can be portrayed to visitors.
2. Seek assistance for the proposal from the First Nations Council and local businesses (businesses may be willing to provide prizes for the winning theme in a contest).
3. Decide on the theme.
4. Determine how best to portray the theme.
5. Institute other ways to support and promote the theme.

At this point, your committee can assign responsibility and realistic deadlines for the completion of each step. Individuals and local organizations should be encouraged to participate, but the assigned committee member is the supervisor who manages the process and reports on activities. Throughout the process, your committee is the lead player.

Involve Your Band Council and Community

Your draft tourism action plan is now ready for submission to the band council and then to the community. The draft gives both groups the opportunity to review and discuss the plan before the committee seeks input from parties outside the community.

The resulting additions or changes can be incorporated into a second draft and resubmitted to the council.

Community Input

After the band council approves the draft plan in principle, your committee can seek input from entrepreneurs, local tourism associations and government departments outside the community. The band council may have advice on when, where and how to obtain public feedback. There are various ways, including open house meetings and workshops, an open band council meeting, and presentations to local interest groups with follow–up discussion and a questionnaire. The plan can also be mailed to designated individuals with a request for feedback or can be published in the local newspaper with a request for comments or date of a public meeting. Committee members can also hold one–on–one discussions with others in the community.

Those most likely to be affected by the plan should be included at this stage. For example, if it recommends improving highway directional signs, ask the provincial highway department for comments. If key people fail to respond, have committee members visit them to explain the plan and obtain feedback.

Implement the Action Plan

The plan can be implemented only after it has received support from the band council, the community and outside private and public agencies. During this process, regular committee meetings will allow members to:

- report on the status of action steps and develop new or alternative ones if needed;
- undertake tasks to help accomplish objectives; and
- deal with problems as they arise.

If you apply for advice or financial support from outside organizations, attach a copy of the plan. It will lend substance and credibility to your application.

Outside Expertise

There are three major sources of outside expertise: consultants, published material and private tourism associations.

Use consultants only for those tasks you cannot do yourselves. Your committee is certainly in a better position to initiate the project by doing the early legwork of gathering and reviewing available information. Not only is it cheaper, but the knowledge and contacts will remain in your community.

If you do go outside your community for expertise, government tourism consultants should be able to provide sound initial advice.

When hiring consultants, be as explicit as possible in detailing the requirements. Your tourism action plan process is a good information tool for the consultant and saves briefing time.

Books are available on how to select and use consultants; how to start and run tourism businesses; and how to execute business functions, such as preparation of business plans, accounting and marketing. These books contain excellent advice at a fraction of the cost of consultants.

Private hotel and restaurant associations as well as provincial, territorial and regional tourism associations provide services to tourism businesses. Through them you can develop a network of association members who have dealt with problems similar to your own.

Monitor the Results

The procedures for monitoring the success or failure of your plan should be in place before implementation begins. Base these procedures on specific action steps and objectives.

For example, your community stages an annual powwow and you plan to promote it. Monitoring procedures need to be in place well before the event. If your objective is to attract more visitors through direct-mail promotion, newspaper and radio advertising, or a combination of these and other promotional activities, try to gauge the success of these efforts by comparing attendance figures for previous powwows with attendance figures after advertising was introduced.

Such monitoring could come in the form of sampling. Committee members or volunteers could survey a sampling of people attending the powwow with a checklist of questions, such as how they heard about the powwow, whether they have friends or relatives in the community, and where they are staying. The more people questioned, the better the sample. Encourage people to take the time to answer questions by offering such incentives as free tickets, discount coupons, pins or balloons.

Other sampling activities include questionnaires by mail and telephone interviews, but for these, you will need information on who attended and how to reach them.

Monitoring could include a status report once every six months from the committee member responsible for each objective. The report—no more than one or two pages long—could describe:

- The action steps that have been taken;
- The most significant results of these steps;
- The extent to which the objective has been accomplished;
- Proposed revisions, if necessary; and
- A personal comment on the validity of the objective.

After the committee reviews all the reports, they can be compiled as one document for presentation to the First Nation Council. It is also a good idea to schedule a detailed annual review to evaluate objectives. The findings of this review can be presented to the First Nation Council for consideration and endorsement.

Your community should be made aware of your committee's successes. Toot your own horn because it's a safe bet no one else will. For instance, an annual tourism night with guest speakers, films and presentations would give your chairperson an opportunity to report on achievements, to discuss what is still to be accomplished and where help is needed.

ACTION PLAN FOR TOURISM: A CASE STUDY OF ANGLESEY, UK

1. Introduction

Anglesey is a rural island with a population of 66,000. It's *tourism* industry attracts 2 million visitors to the island per annum, accounting for £181 million into the local economy and supports 19 per cent of employment. It is considered to be an important sector in the island's economic base and is recognized as one sector which is capable of sustainable growth and thus a vital element of future economic well-being.

However the present industry is based on a relatively short season of traditional family holidays providing low income and limited reinvestment. This situation is compounded by a fragmented sector of small and micro businesses competing for an ever declining volume of visitors as the global *tourism* market and variety of holiday opportunities expands.

Anglesey has a very diverse nature, a characteristic that can be harnessed to provide new and additional *tourism* opportunities and benefit from developing *tourism* trends for short break and special interest holidays. It is geologically an ancient island, with a variety of recognized natural assets, its coastline is all designated an Area of Outstanding Natural Beauty or Heritage Coast which provides the basis for beach and coastal holidays. It has, at present, 22 award winning beaches. It is rich in heritage and culture with a wealth of prehistoric, Roman, mediaeval, and industrial artefacts, and traditionally has a range of manmade tourist attractions mainly geared to the family holiday sector.

Recent *tourism* projects, mainly developed through the Leader II initiative, aimed at developing niche markets within the special interest sectors such as walking, cycling, golf fishing and farm holidays, have illustrated that modest investment in such areas can provide significant benefits. The challenge is to ensure that such projects do not develop in isolation but in such a way as to be sustainable and provide benefits to the widest possible range of local businesses and communities.

Whereas the *tourism* sector demonstrates many of the characteristics of other SMEs, the industry possesses unique characteristics which cannot always be addressed comfortably within mainstream business support. It also impacts considerably on the environment and local communities and has considerable implications for infrastructure. The *Action Plan* for *Tourism* will therefore identify the needs and aspirations of the *tourism* trade on the island and balance them with the requirements of the visitor to maximize benefits to the SMEs and increase employment opportunities.

This will be done by maximizing the synergy with the broader regional and local programmes and providing sector specific assistance where these programmes are not appropriate for the special needs of this business sector.

2. Strategic Objective

To develop a range of ***tourism*** *strategies and programmes which ensure the sustained development of* ***tourism*** *on the Island and maximise the benefits it provides to the local economy.*

This will be achieved through:

Exploiting training and business development mechanisms to create high–quality employment opportunities and enable existing *tourism* SMEs to develop.

Improving the overall standard and variety of the *tourism* product/ service that is provided.

Enabling the industry to prosper from the island's natural diversity.

Developing marketing and promotional activities together with information provision in a manner which meets the needs and expectations of the customer.

3. Links to other Strategies and Documentation

The economic importance of *tourism* has been recognized by the National Assembly for Wales within the recently approved National *Tourism* Strategy – "Achieving our Potential". The strategy was produced by the Wales Tourist Board (WTB) following extensive consultation with the public sector and establishments that are operating within the industry and the main objectives of the strategy are to:

To market Wales more effectively as an attraction all year round *tourism* destination.

To exceed the expectations of visitors to Wales by providing high standards and ensuring that investment in *tourism* is responsive to changing needs.

To improve professionalism and innovation by raising the profile of the industry and by enhancing skills, training and motivation within the industry.

To embrace a sustainable approach to *tourism* development which benefits society, involves local communities and enhances Wales' unique environmental and cultural assets.

The Regional *Tourism* Strategy – "Co–operating to Compete", co–funded by the WTB and covering the six unitary authority areas of North Wales is a key component within the national strategy.

It's overall strategic aim is to:

Contribute to winning a bigger market share for Wales as a whole from both domestic and overseas markets. This will be achieved by extending the North Wales vision 'Co-operating to Compete' so that both product development and marketing campaigns are carefully planned and targeted to work in a complementary way.

On a local level, the Isle of Anglesey Economic Development Strategy, Unitary Development *Plan* (Draft version), which recognize the local importance of tourism have been paramount to the plan's development.

In addition, results from the 'Ynys Môn Visitors Survey' (1997–98) have provided valuable information and customer profiles/ expectations in relation to the *tourism* product on Anglesey. It has illustrated that the *tourism* industry on Anglesey, while providing for traditional holidays, is not adapting to the changing *tourism* market and is thus losing market share. The undertaking of the 'Scarborough *Tourism* Economic Activity Model' which was begun last year is also providing information on the economic value of *tourism* and an insight into changing trends.

Analysis of the available information, together with the strategic framework provided by wider policies and programmes, has provided the strong foundation upon which this *Plan* has been based.

4. Links with other Local Action Plans

Many of the issues which underpin the *tourism* industry are also commonplace in other sectors and industries. The support, development, training and skills issues are uniform. As a result, it is envisaged that businesses operating within the *tourism* industry will benefit directly from the programmes outlined within the Business *Action Plan*. Additionally, rural and community development issues are also relevant to the future growth of *tourism* on Anglesey.

These clear and important links represent the need to synergize and co–ordinate activities and programmes which are outlined in other strands of the Local *Action Plan* with the needs of the *tourism* industry. This approach will also reduce duplication of both effort and resources.

5. Links with the Single Programme Document (SPD)

This *Plan* relates closely to the Aims and Objectives which are outlined within the SPD. The wide ranging nature and requirements of the industry make it likely that the programmes outlined within this *plan* will seek funding assistance from a number of Measures within Priorities 1, 2, 4, 5 and 6.

6. Tourism Action Plan Projects

Name: Developing Local Knowledge

Aims and Objectives

To develop a wider knowledge of Anglesey and its attractions by local businesses and residents.

To provide a knowledge base that can be passed on to visitors and potential tourists to:

- To increase the numbers of visitors to the island and encourage them to stay on the island.
- To increase *tourism* activity across the island.
- To increase the spread of economic and (social) benefits to local businesses and communities.
- To create ambassadors for the island within both business and *tourism*.

To develop better networking and the opportunity for mutual support and joint business initiatives.

To undertake a pilot research project that can be used to test and evaluate a range of methodologies with a view to developing a more comprehensive range of activities to support future development and promotion of *tourism* on the Isle of Anglesey.

To encourage residents and local people to take more leisure visits in their own locality.

To establish a database for the development and implementation of the *Tourism Action Plan*.

Project Description

The project will undertake three related pilot schemes that will target different sectors of business and the community to raise the level of local awareness and knowledge of tourist related businesses.

Each scheme will allow access to *tourism* related businesses to:

- gain first hand knowledge of the business e.g. enabling local people to pass on information to visitors
- provide the opportunity for developing networking and mutual support activities e.g. pass on business to local providers etc.
- provide the opportunities for developing joint business activities and marketing.

Scheme 1 – Island wide and provide the opportunity for residents and the staff of businesses to experience tourist attractions.

Scheme 2 – Sector based, providing business to business support and experience to encourage networking and best practice.

Scheme 3 – Community based providing different businesses and specific local people based in the locality to learn more about each other and encourage mutual support and networking opportunities.

The schemes will test different methodologies including voucher schemes over a fixed period of time, informal targeted invitations, and formal tours and presentations. It will include the employment of a dedicated project officer and administration staff to ensure the support and encouragement that small and micro businesses will need to enable them to participate.

The main purpose is to be as inclusive as possible and raise the awareness of *tourism* to a wide audience. This will then provide a receptive base for the development of other *tourism* projects to raise the quality of the *tourism* product on Anglesey and develop a sustainable *tourism* industry spreading benefits to a wide range of businesses and communities.

Outputs

If implemented it is envisaged that the project in total will involve and assist up to 200 businesses and enable 2000 visits to be made. Scheme 3 includes the involvement of 5 communities across the island.

Funding

Funding will be secured via the businesses themselves in the form of agreed levels of goods and services and via the local authority in the form of financial assistance and office time.

Name: Green and Clean

Aims and Objectives

To provide a range of opportunities to upgrade the general image of the island to the visitor.

To raise the awareness of local businesses, communities and individuals of the need to clean up and enhance their locality.

Encourage, facilitate and market clean up campaigns, develop environmental awareness, encourage recycling.

Develop the use of rural skills such as stone walling and hedge laying and reintroduce the concept of lengths men to provide opportunities for local employment.

Develop local footpaths and bridle ways.

Link activities to job creation and skills development programmes.

Link administration and funding to local communities to encourage community development and ownership.

Provide for project managers and co–ordinators.

Project Description

To develop a range of co–ordinated activities that will link with training and community development schemes to increase the quality of life within communities and develop local initiatives and pride.

Provide a range of job opportunities and economic benefits to rural areas. Increase the quality of *tourism* and support other activities to increase visitor numbers to the island.

Outputs

Funding

Name: An Island for All Seasons

Aims and Objectives

To provide a range of *tourism* trails, based on sectoral, thematic and geographic areas to encourage visitors to travel around the area or the island.

To encourage use of different means of travel including cycling, walking, horseback and boats.

To support the development of new and existing attractions and facilities to provide for a range of attractive, themed trails.

To provide the mechanisms for an integrated tourist information network across the island utilizing new and existing print, information technology, TICs and the development of new tourist information points within local businesses and communities.

To provide opportunities for businesses to gain knowledge and training in relation to *tourism* and local product knowledge.

Project Description

To develop, support and market a range of niche *tourism* products which will build on the existing diversity of the Isle of Anglesey as a *tourism* product to provide economic benefits and employment opportunities to businesses and geographic areas of the island. To undertake a series of co–ordinated activities to support these developments and develop the tourist potential of the island. cFacilitate the development of co–ordinated information utilizing local businesses to supplement national and strategic activities including the development of a local pocket guide, the development of auto and audio tours and multilingual print and information. Work within developing national and regional training programmes to provide a scheme of opportunities to develop and support businesses on Anglesey. Provide additional training to add value through knowledge of a local perspective.

COMMONWEALTH TOURISM ACTION PLAN

Commonwealth tourism ministers, who met for the first time in Kuala Lumpur, Malaysia, last week (19 to 21 March 2004) have developed an action plan to promote tourism and information exchange. The plan includes the establishment of a Commonwealth Centre for Tourism Promotion (CCTP) and the organization of workshops to identify joint marketing and promotional activities between the public and private sector. A task force formed at the meeting will study the role of the CCTP and work out its functions as well as identify the sources of financing to run it.

"The task force will consist of representatives from all regions of the Commonwealth and be chaired by the Commonwealth Secretariat," said Malaysia's Minister for Culture, Arts and Tourism Dato' Paduka Abdul Kadir Sheik Fadzir, who chaired the meeting.

> "The members will have until the end of the year to recommend to governments the terms of reference and the work plan of the proposed centre. It will create an information database and co–ordinate an information exchange, which will contribute towards a collaborative approach to tourism marketing and promotion."

The tourism ministers also agreed to work closely with the World Tourism Organization and the World Travel and Tourism Council on trade liberalization issues. They underscored the importance of tourism in reducing poverty and promoting investment, exports and jobs. Socio–cultural understanding and peace are also enhanced by tourism.

The ministers supported the international community's fight against terrorism and other criminal activities affecting the tourism sector. They noted the impact of these actions on trans–border movement of people, transport and economic flows. They also recognized the problems faced by some member countries in complying with international standards of safety and security, and called on donor agencies to assist.

The importance of sustainable tourism was highlighted, particularly for small and vulnerable states, and the ministers stressed the need for concrete actions to strengthen this sector. They agreed to incorporate tourism as a priority in development and poverty reduction strategies.

Secretary–General Don McKinnon said tourism can play a key role in transforming the lives of the poor as it is one of the key instruments of economic development. Speaking at the opening ceremony in Kuala Lumpur last week, he said, "For many nations in the Commonwealth, including small states and developing countries, tourism is not only an important source of income, it plays an essential part in their efforts to lift themselves out of poverty. A vibrant tourism industry brings inward investment, foreign exchange earnings and stimulates employment. It is often a boon for small and medium enterprises. For them, tourism is one of the key access routes into the global economy."

8

Code of Ethics for Tourism and Tourists: An Overview

GLOBAL CODE OF ETHICS FOR TOURISM

Tourism's Contribution to Mutual Understanding and Respect between Peoples and Societies

1. The understanding and promotion of the ethical values common to humanity, with an attitude of tolerance and respect for the diversity of religious, philosophical and moral beliefs, are both the foundation and the consequence of responsible tourism; stakeholders in tourism development and tourists themselves should observe the social and cultural traditions and practices of all peoples, including those of minorities and indigenous peoples and to recognize their worth;
2. Tourism activities should be conducted in harmony with the attributes and traditions of the host regions and countries and in respect for their laws, practices and customs;
3. The host communities, on the one hand, and local professionals, on the other, should acquaint themselves with and respect the tourists who visit them and find out about their lifestyles, tastes and expectations; the education and training imparted to professionals contribute to a hospitable welcome;
4. It is the task of the public authorities to provide protection for tourists and visitors and their belongings; they must

pay particular attention to the safety of foreign tourists owing to the particular vulnerability they may have; they should facilitate the introduction of specific means of information, prevention, security, insurance and assistance consistent with their needs; any attacks, assaults, kidnappings or threats against tourists or workers in the tourism industry, as well as the wilful destruction of tourism facilities or of elements of cultural or natural heritage should be severely condemned and punished in accordance with their respective national laws;

5. When travelling, tourists and visitors should not commit any criminal act or any act considered criminal by the laws of the country visited and abstain from any conduct felt to be offensive or injurious by the local populations, or likely to damage the local environment; they should refrain from all trafficking in illicit drugs, arms, antiques, protected species and products and substances that are dangerous or prohibited by national regulations; and
6. Tourists and visitors have the responsibility to acquaint themselves, even before their departure, with the characteristics of the countries they are preparing to visit; they must be aware of the health and security risks inherent in any travel outside their usual environment and behave in such a way as to minimize those risks.

Tourism as a Vehicle for Individual and Collective Fulfilment

1. Tourism, the activity most frequently associated with rest and relaxation, sport and access to culture and nature, should be planned and practised as a privileged means of individual and collective fulfilment; when practised with a sufficiently open mind, it is an irreplaceable factor of self–education, mutual tolerance and for learning about the legitimate differences between peoples and cultures and their diversity;
2. Tourism activities should respect the equality of men and women; they should promote human rights and, more particularly, the individual rights of the most vulnerable

groups, notably children, the elderly, the handicapped, ethnic minorities and indigenous peoples;

3. The exploitation of human beings in any form, particularly sexual, especially when applied to children, conflicts with the fundamental aims of tourism and is the negation of tourism; as such, in accordance with international law, it should be energetically combatted with the cooperation of all the States concerned and penalized without concession by the national legislation of both the countries visited and the countries of the perpetrators of these acts, even when they are carried out abroad;
4. Travel for purposes of religion, health, education and cultural or linguistic exchanges are particularly beneficial forms of tourism, which deserve encouragement; and
5. The introduction into curricula of education about the value of tourist exchanges, their economic, social and cultural benefits, and also their risks, should be encouraged.

Tourism, a Factor of Sustainable Development

1. All the stakeholders in tourism development should safeguard the natural environment with a view to achieving sound, continuous and sustainable economic growth geared to satisfying equitably the needs and aspirations of present and future generations;
2. All forms of tourism development that are conducive to saving rare and precious resources, in particular water and energy, as well as avoiding so far as possible waste production, should be given priority and encouraged by national, regional and local public authorities;
3. The staggering in time and space of tourist and visitor flows, particularly those resulting from paid leave and school holidays, and a more even distribution of holidays should be sought so as to reduce the pressure of tourism activity on the environment and enhance its beneficial impact on the tourism industry and the local economy;
4. Tourism infrastructure should be designed and tourism activities programmed in such a way as to protect the natural heritage composed of ecosystems and biodiversity

and to preserve endangered species of wildlife; the stakeholders in tourism development, and especially professionals, should agree to the imposition of limitations or constraints on their activities when these are exercised in particularly sensitive areas: desert, polar or high mountain regions, coastal areas, tropical forests or wetlands, propitious to the creation of nature reserves or protected areas; and

5. Nature tourism and ecotourism are recognized as being particularly conducive to enriching and enhancing the standing of tourism, provided they respect the natural heritage and local populations and are in keeping with the carrying capacity of the sites.

Tourism, a User of the Cultural Heritage of Mankind and Contributor to its Enhancement

1. Tourism resources belong to the common heritage of mankind; the communities in whose territories they are situated have particular rights and obligations to them;
2. Tourism policies and activities should be conducted with respect for the artistic, archaeological and cultural heritage, which they should protect and pass on to future generations; particular care should be devoted to preserving and upgrading monuments, shrines and museums as well as archaeological and historic sites which must be widely open to tourist visits; encouragement should be given to public access to privately–owned cultural property and monuments, with respect for the rights of their owners, as well as to religious buildings, without prejudice to normal needs of worship;
3. Financial resources derived from visits to cultural sites and monuments should, at least in part, be used for the upkeep, safeguard, development and embellishment of this heritage; and
4. Tourism activity should be planned in such a way as to allow traditional cultural products, crafts and folklore to survive and flourish, rather than causing them to degenerate and become standardized.

Tourism, a Beneficial Activity for Host Countries and Communities

1. Local populations should be associated with tourism activities and share equitably in the economic, social and cultural benefits they generate, and particularly in the creation of direct and indirect jobs resulting from them;
2. Tourism policies should be applied in such a way as to help to raise the standard of living of the populations of the regions visited and meet their needs; the planning and architectural approach to and operation of tourism resorts and accommodation should aim to integrate them, to the extent possible, in the local economic and social fabric; where skills are equal, priority should be given to local manpower;
3. Special attention should be paid to the specific problems of coastal areas and island territories and to vulnerable rural or mountain regions, for which tourism often represents a rare opportunity for development in the face of the decline of traditional economic activities; and
4. Tourism professionals, particularly investors, governed by the regulations laid down by the public authorities, should carry out studies of the impact of their development projects on the environment and natural surroundings; they should also deliver, with the greatest transparency and objectivity, information on their future programmes and their foreseeable repercussions and foster dialogue on their contents with the populations concerned.

Obligations of Stakeholders in Tourism Development

1. Tourism professionals have an obligation to provide tourists with objective and honest information on their places of destination and on the conditions of travel, hospitality and stays; they should ensure that the contractual clauses proposed to their customers are readily understandable as to the nature, price and quality of the services they commit themselves to providing and the financial compensation payable by them in the event of a unilateral breach of contract on their part;

2. Tourism professionals, insofar as it depends on them, should show concern, in co-operation with the public authorities, for the security and safety, accident prevention, health protection and food safety of those who seek their services; likewise, they should ensure the existence of suitable systems of insurance and assistance; they should accept the reporting obligations prescribed by national regulations and pay fair compensation in the event of failure to observe their contractual obligations;
3. Tourism professionals, so far as this depends on them, should contribute to the cultural and spiritual fulfilment of tourists and allow them, during their travels, to practise their religions;
4. The public authorities of the generating States and the host countries, in cooperation with the professionals concerned and their associations, should ensure that the necessary mechanisms are in place for the repatriation of tourists in the event of the bankruptcy of the enterprise that organized their travel;
5. Governments have the right – and the duty – especially in a crisis, to inform their nationals of the difficult circumstances, or even the dangers they may encounter during their travels abroad; it is their responsibility however to issue such information without prejudicing in an unjustified or exaggerated manner the tourism industry of the host countries and the interests of their own operators; the contents of travel advisories should therefore be discussed beforehand with the authorities of the host countries and the professionals concerned; recommendations formulated should be strictly proportionate to the gravity of the situations encountered and confined to the geographical areas where the insecurity has arisen; such advisories should be qualified or cancelled as soon as a return to normality permits; and
6. The press, and particularly the specialized travel press and the other media, including modern means of electronic communication, should issue honest and balanced information on events and situations that could influence the flow of tourists; they should also provide accurate and reliable information to the consumers of tourism services;

the new communication and electronic commerce technologies should also be developed and used for this purpose; as is the case for the media, they should not in any way promote sex tourism.

Right to Tourism

1. The prospect of direct and personal access to the discovery and enjoyment of the planet's resources constitutes a right equally open to all the world's inhabitants; the increasingly extensive participation in national and international tourism should be regarded as one of the best possible expressions of the sustained growth of free time, and obstacles should not be placed in its way;
2. The universal right to tourism must be regarded as the corollary of the right to rest and leisure, including reasonable limitation of working hours and periodic holidays with pay, guaranteed by Article 24 of the Universal Declaration of Human Rights and Article 7.d of the International Covenant on Economic, Social and Cultural Rights;
3. Social tourism, and in particular associative tourism, which facilitates widespread access to leisure, travel and holidays, should be developed with the support of the public authorities; and
4. Family, youth, student and senior tourism and tourism for people with disabilities, should be encouraged and facilitated.

Liberty of Tourist Movements

1. Tourists and visitors should benefit, in compliance with international law and national legislation, from the liberty to move within their countries and from one State to another, in accordance with Article 13 of the Universal Declaration of Human Rights; they should have access to places of transit and stay and to tourism and cultural sites without being subject to excessive formalities or discrimination;

2. Tourists and visitors should have access to all available forms of communication, internal or external; they should benefit from prompt and easy access to local administrative, legal and health services; they should be free to contact the consular representatives of their countries of origin in compliance with the diplomatic conventions in force;
3. Tourists and visitors should benefit from the same rights as the citizens of the country visited concerning the confidentiality of the personal data and information concerning them, especially when these are stored electronically;
4. Administrative procedures relating to border crossings whether they fall within the competence of States or result from international agreements, such as visas or health and customs formalities, should be adapted, so far as possible, so as to facilitate to the maximum freedom of travel and widespread access to international tourism; agreements between groups of countries to harmonize and simplify these procedures should be encouraged; specific taxes and levies penalizing the tourism industry and undermining its competitiveness should be gradually phased out or corrected; and
5. So far as the economic situation of the countries from which they come permits, travellers should have access to allowances of convertible currencies needed for their travels.

Rights of the Workers and Entrepreneurs in the Tourism Industry

1. The fundamental rights of salaried and self–employed workers in the tourism industry and related activities, should be guaranteed under the supervision of the national and local administrations, both of their States of origin and of the host countries with particular care, given the specific constraints linked in particular to the seasonality of their activity, the global dimension of their industry and the flexibility often required of them by the nature of their work;

2. Salaried and self–employed workers in the tourism industry and related activities have the right and the duty to acquire appropriate initial and continuous training; they should be given adequate social protection; job insecurity should be limited so far as possible; and a specific status, with particular regard to their social welfare, should be offered to seasonal workers in the sector;
3. Any natural or legal person, provided he, she or it has the necessary abilities and skills, should be entitled to develop a professional activity in the field of tourism under existing national laws; entrepreneurs and investors – especially in the area of small and medium–sized enterprises – should be entitled to free access to the tourism sector with a minimum of legal or administrative restrictions;
4. Exchanges of experience offered to executives and workers, whether salaried or not, from different countries, contributes to foster the development of the world tourism industry; these movements should be facilitated so far as possible in compliance with the applicable national laws and international conventions;
5. As an irreplaceable factor of solidarity in the development and dynamic growth of international exchanges, multinational enterprises of the tourism industry should not exploit the dominant positions they sometimes occupy; they should avoid becoming the vehicles of cultural and social models artificially imposed on the host communities; in exchange for their freedom to invest and trade which should be fully recognized, they should involve themselves in local development, avoiding, by the excessive repatriation of their profits or their induced imports, a reduction of their contribution to the economies in which they are established; and
6. Partnership and the establishment of balanced relations between enterprises of generating and receiving countries contribute to the sustainable development of tourism and an equitable distribution of the benefits of its growth.

Implementation of the Principles of the Global Code of Ethics for Tourism

1. The public and private stakeholders in tourism development should cooperate in the implementation of these principles and monitor their effective application;
2. The stakeholders in tourism development should recognize the role of international institutions, among which the World Tourism Organization ranks first, and non–governmental organizations with competence in the field of tourism promotion and development, the protection of human rights, the environment or health, with due respect for the general principles of international law; and
3. The same stakeholders should demonstrate their intention to refer any disputes concerning the application or interpretation of the Global Code of Ethics for Tourism for conciliation to an impartial third body known as the World Committee on Tourism Ethics.

GLOBAL CODE OF ETHICS FOR TRAVELLERS

1. Travel in a spirit of humility and with a genuine desire to learn more about the people of your host country. Be sensitively aware of the feelings of other people, thus preventing what might be offensive behaviour on your part.
2. Cultivate the habit of listening and observing rather than merely hearing and seeing.
3. Realize that often the people in the country you visit have time concepts and thought patterns different from your own. This does not make them inferior, only different.
4. Acquaint yourself with local customs. What is courteous in one country may be quite the reverse in another – people will be happy to help you.
5. Instead of the western practice of 'knowing all the answers', cultivate the habit of asking questions.
6. Do not make promises to people in your host country unless you can carry them through.

7. Remember that you are only one of thousands of tourists visiting this country and do not expect special privileges.
8. If you really want your experience to be a 'home away from home', it is foolish to waste money on travelling.
9. Spend time reflecting on your daily experience in an attempt to deepen your understanding.

Specifically

- Always ask permission before photographing people.
- When you are shopping, remember that the bargain you obtained may only be possible because of the low wages paid to the maker.
- Understand that there can be no guarantees when it comes to wildlife, all sightings are a bonus.
- Ensure that your behaviour has no impact on the wildlife you so enjoy and remember that picking flowers, removing seeds and buying souvenirs such as shells and skins can only cause harm in the long run.
- Conservation begins with keeping an eye on your own consumption of such base necessities as water and energy.

9

Sustainable Tourism: Charter and Principles on Implementation

CHARTER FOR SUSTAINABLE TOURISM

The Charter for Sustainable Tourism was developed at the World Conference on Sustainable Tourism, in Lanzarote, Canary Islands, Spain on 27–28 April 1995. The following is a transcript of the findings of the participants:

Mindful that tourism is a worldwide phenomenon and also an important element of socio-economic and political development in many countries, and that tourism touches the highest and deepest aspirations of all people.

Recognizing that tourism, as an ambivalent phenomenon, since it has the potential to contribute positively to socio-economic and cultural achievement, while at the same time it can contribute to the degradation of the environment and the loss of local identity, should be approached with a global methodology.

Mindful that the resources on which tourism is based are fragile and that there is a growing demand for improved environmental quality.

Recognizing that tourism can afford the opportunity to travel and to get to know other cultures, and that the development of tourism can help promote closer ties and peace among peoples, creating a conscience that is respectful of the diversity of culture and life styles.

Guided by the principles set forth in the Rio Declaration on the Environment and Development and the recommendations that emanate from Agenda 21.

Recalling declarations in the matter of tourism, such as the Manila Declaration on World Tourism, the Hague Declaration and the Tourism Charter and Tourist Code.

Recognizing the objective of developing a tourism that meets economic expectations and environmental requirements, and respects not only the social and physical structure of the location, but also the local population.

Taking into account the priority of protecting and reinforcing the human dignity of both local communities and visitors.

Mindful of the need to establish effective alliances among the principal actors in the field of tourism so as to build the hope of a tourism that is more responsible towards our common heritage.

Appeal to the international community, and, in particular, Urge governments, other public authorities, decision-makers and professionals in the field of tourism, public and private associations and institutions whose activities are related to tourism, and tourists themselves, to adopt the principles and objectives of the Declaration that follows:

1. Tourism development shall be based on criteria of sustainability, which means that it must be ecologically bearable in the long term, as well as economically viable, and ethically and socially equitable for local communities. Sustainable development is a guided process which envisages global management of resources so as to ensure their viability, thus enabling our natural and cultural capital, including protected areas, to be preserved. As a powerful instrument of development, tourism can and should participate actively in the sustainable development strategy. A requirement of sound management of tourism is that the sustainability of the resources on which it depends must be guaranteed.
2. Tourism has to contribute to sustainable development and its integration with the natural, cultural and human environment; it must respect the fragile balances that characterize many tourist destinations, in particular small islands and environmentally sensitive areas. Tourism should ensure an acceptable solution as regards the influence of tourism activity on natural resources, biodiversity and the capability for assimilation of any impacts and residues produced.

3. Tourism must consider its effects on the cultural heritage and traditional elements, activities and dynamics of each local community. Recognition of these local factors and support for the identity, culture and interests of the local community must at all times play a central role in the formulations of tourism strategies, particularly in developing countries.
4. The active contribution of tourism to sustainable development necessarily presupposes the solidarity, mutual respect, and participation of all the actors, both public and private, implicated in the process, and must be based on efficient cooperation mechanisms at all levels: local, national, regional and international.
5. The conservation, protection and appreciation of the worth of our natural and cultural heritage afford a privileged area for cooperation. This approach implies that all those responsible must take upon themselves a true challenge, that of cultural, technological and professional innovation, and must also undertake a major effort to create and implement integrated planning and management instruments.
6. Quality criteria both for the preservation of the tourist destination and for the capacity to satisfy tourists, determined jointly with local communities and informed by the principles of sustainable development, should represent priority objectives in the formulation of tourism strategies and projects.
7. To participate in sustainable development, tourism must be based on the diversity of opportunities offered by the local economy. It should be fully integrated into and contribute positively to local economic development.
8. All options for tourism development must serve effectively to improve the quality of life of all people and must entail a positive effect and inter–relation as regards socio-cultural identity.
9. Governments and the competent authorities, with the participation of NGOs and local communities, shall undertake actions aimed at integrating the planning of tourism as a contribution to sustainable development.

10. In recognition of economic and social cohesion among the peoples of the world as a fundamental principle of sustainable development, it is urgent that measures be promoted to permit a more equitable distribution of the benefits and burdens of tourism. This implies a change of consumption patterns and the introduction of pricing methods which allow environmental costs to be internalized.

Governments and multilateral organizations are called upon to reorient aid related to tourism, particularly aid which leads to negative effects on the environment. Within this context, it is necessary to explore thoroughly the application of internationally harmonized economic, legal and fiscal instruments to ensure the sustainable use of resources in tourism.

11. Environmentally and culturally vulnerable spaces, both now and in the future, should be given special priority in the matter of technical cooperation and financial aid for sustainable tourism development. Similarly, special treatment should be given to zones that have been degraded by obsolete and high impact tourism models.
12. The promotion of alternative forms of tourism that are compatible with the principles of sustainable development, together with the encouragement of diversification, participate in medium– and long–term sustainability. In this respect there is a need for many small islands and environmentally sensitive areas in particular, to actively pursue and strengthen regional cooperation.
13. Governments, industry, authorities, and tourism–related NGOs should promote and participate in the creation of open networks for research, dissemination of information and transfer of appropriate tourism and environmental knowledge on tourism and environmentally sustainable technologies.
14. The establishment of a sustainable tourism policy necessarily requires the support and promotion of environmentally–compatible tourism management systems, feasibility studies for the transformation of the sector, as well as the implementation of demonstration

projects and the development of international cooperation programmes.

15. Bodies, particularly associations and NGOs whose activities are related to tourism, shall draw up specific frameworks for positive and preventive actions for sustainable tourism development and establish programmes to support the implementation of such practices. They shall monitor achievements, report on results and exchange their experiences.
16. Particular attention should be paid to the role and the environmental repercussions of transport in tourism, and to the development of economic instruments designed to reduce the use of non–renewable energy and to encourage recycling and minimization of residues in resorts.
17. The adoption and implementation of codes of conduct conducive to sustainability by the principal actors involved in tourism, particularly industry, are fundamental if tourism is to be sustainable. Such codes can be effective instruments for the development of responsible tourism activities.
18. All necessary measures should be implemented in order to sensitize and inform all parties involved in the tourism industry, at local, regional, national and international level, with regard to the contents and objectives of the Lanzarote Conference.

Final Resolution

The World Conference on Sustainable Tourism considers it vital to make the following public statements:

1. The Conference recommends State and regional governments to draw up urgently plans of action for sustainable development applied to tourism, in consonance with the principles set out in this Charter.
2. The Conference agrees to refer the Charter for Sustainable Tourism to the Secretary–General of the United Nations, so that it may be taken up by the bodies and agencies of the United Nations system, as well as by international organizations which have cooperation agreements with

the United Nations, for submission to the General Assembly.

PRINCIPLES ON THE IMPLEMENTATION OF SUSTAINABLE TOURISM

While some agreement has been reached on what sustainable tourism is, the key question is how to put sustainable development into practice in all tourism activities – from mass tourism to nature–based and specialist tourism.

The proposed UNEP principles for implementation of sustainable tourism were presented at UNEP's 20th Governing Council Session.

The Objectives

The objectives for developing the UNEP Principles for Implementation of Sustainable Tourism are:

- To help governments and inter-governmental, private sector and other organizations apply the general concept of sustainable tourism in practice, and minimize environmental impacts from tourism.
- To facilitate the development of more specific guidelines at the regional level or in relation to specific issues, such as coral reefs and biodiversity.
- To provide a framework for the work programmes of the Convention on Biological Diversity, the Framework Convention on Climate Change, the Regional Seas Action Plans, and other international agreements that address tourism issues.

Consultation Processes

Consultation processes were conducted in three ways: through active input collection at three regional events, on the Web, and through comments received by UNEP's regional offices.

In early 2000, the principles were produced in final form, and have been used as reference by many inter–governmental organizations and agreements such as the Convention on Biological Diversity.

UNEP's Governing Council at its 20th Session (February 1999, Decision UNEP/GC.20/L.4/Rev.1) and the UN Commission on Sustainable Development (CSD Decisions and resolutions, E/CN.17/1999/L.6) requested UNEP to 'further develop, through a consultative process involving Governments and other relevant partners, guiding principles for sustainable tourism in accordance with the mandate of the United Nations Environment Programme and taking into account the draft principles on sustainable tourism....'

MANAGEMENT OF TOURISM DESTINATIONS

Managing tourism destinations is an important part of controlling tourism's environmental impacts. Destination management can include land use planning, business permits and zoning controls, environmental and other regulations, business association initiatives, and a host of other techniques to shape the development and daily operation of tourism–related activities.

The term "destination" refers broadly to an area where tourism is a relatively important activity and where the economy may be significantly influenced by tourism revenues. Destination management is complicated by the fact that a single, recognizable destination may include several municipalities, provinces, or other government entities – in island environments it may be the entire country.

Participating governance structures led by local authorities, with the involvement of local NGOs, community and indigenous representatives, academia, and local chambers of commerce, make up what are known as "Destination Management Organizations" (DMOs). Often DMOs take the form of local tourism boards, councils, or development organizations. The network of local tourism businesses (hotels, attractions, transportation services, service providers such as guides and equipment rentals, restaurants, etc.) are also a significant part of a destination.

Destination Management Approach

The needs, expectations and anticipated benefits of tourism vary greatly from one destination to the next, and there is certainly no "one size fits all" approach to destination management. As local communities living in regions with tourism potential develop a vision for what kind of tourism they want to facilitate, a comprehensive planning framework such as Local Agenda 21 has proved useful and is being used more and more often. For UNEP, promoting sustainable tourism within Local Agenda 21 processes is a way to strengthen local stewardship of the environment. UNEP works with the International Council of Local Environmental Initiatives (ICLEI) to build local capacity and to disseminate tools and useful approaches to local destination governance.

THE LOCAL AGENDA 21 APPROACH

Agenda 21 binds local authorities to implementing at local level the commitments made towards sustainable development by the international community. It was drawn up in 1992 at the "Earth Summit" in Rio de Janeiro – and has since become the main mechanism for community planning for sustainability.

A local Agenda 21 is an approach through which a local community defines a sustainable development strategy and an action programme to implement it. A local authority initiates and provides leadership for the process; its success hinges on close cooperation between the population, NGOs, and economic and social players.

ICLEI estimates that more than three thousand local communities worldwide are now implementing local Agenda 21. In the coming years their numbers will continue to rise, thanks to inter–community networking and to the information campaigns being conducted by international organizations, states and NGOs. The approach is also spreading through teaching tools and methodologies for communities, in particular, through training and guides produced by ICLEI.

Experience has proven that the success of a local Agenda 21 depends directly on the involvement of the population, and on the partnerships between the various players. Such partnerships encourage a balance between economic development, social development and the protection of natural resources and the environment.

UNEP has produced a study called Promoting Sustainable Tourism within Local Agenda 21 that looks at how tourism has been taken into account in local Agenda 21 programmes. It is partly based on a study of the hands–on experience gained by local communities that are involved to varying degrees in tourist activity, and that have adopted a local Agenda 21 approach. It examines:

- The position of tourism within local Agenda 21 programmes;
- The usefulness of the local Agenda 21 process in dealing with problems posed by tourism and in defining a tourism strategy;
- The possible limits to the local Agenda 21 approach to tourism; and
- Recommendations for improving the way in which specific tourism–related aspects are taken on board in local Agenda 21 processes.

10

Tourism and Biodiversity: Process and Guidelines

BIOLOGICAL DIVERSITY AND TOURISM: ILLUSTRATING THE PROCESS

Tourism is one of the world's fastest growing industries as well as the major source of foreign exchange earning and employment for many developing countries, and it is increasingly focusing on natural environments. However, tourism is a double–edged activity. It has the potential to contribute in a positive manner to socio–economic achievements but, at the same time, its fast and sometimes uncontrolled growth can be the major cause of degradation of the environment and loss of local identity and traditional cultures. Biological and physical resources are in fact the assets that attract tourists. However, the stress imposed by tourism activities on fragile ecosystems accelerates and aggravates their depletion. Paradoxically, the very success of tourism may lead to the degradation of the natural environment: by depleting natural resources tourism reduces the site attractiveness to tourists, the very commodity that tourism has to offer.

As far as economic benefits are concerned, tourism certainly constitutes an opportunity for economic development, economic diversification and the growth of related activities, in developing countries especially, contributing around 1.5 per cent of world gross national product. Tourism is also a major source of income and employment. Tourism based on the natural environment (ecotourism) is a vital growing segment of the tourism industry and, despite the negative impacts, and given the fact that tourism generates a large proportion of income and that a growing percentage of the activities are nature–based, tourism does present a significant potential for realizing benefits in terms of the conservation of biological diversity and the sustainable use of its components.

Among the benefits are direct revenues generated by fees and taxes incurred and voluntary payments for the use of biological resources. These revenues can be used for the maintenance of natural areas and the contribution of tourism to economic development, including linkage effects to other related sectors and job–creation. Sustainable tourism can make positive improvements to biological diversity conservation especially when local communities are directly involved with operators. If such local communities receive income directly from a tourist enterprise they, in turn, increase their evaluation of the resources around them. This is followed by greater protection and conservation of those resources as they are recognized as the source of income. Moreover, sustainable tourism can serve as a major educational opportunity, increasing knowledge of and respect for natural ecosystems and biological resources. Other benefits include the provision of incentives for maintaining traditional arts and crafts, traditional knowledge, and innovations and practices that contribute to the sustainable use of biological diversity.

In considering the role of tourism in the sustainable use of biological resources and their diversity, it is important that the potential adverse impacts of tourism are fully considered. These are roughly divided into environmental impacts and socio-economic impacts, the latter generally being those imposed on local and indigenous communities. Although such impacts on biological resources may be less easy to quantify and analyse systematically, they may be at least as important as, if not more important than, environmental impacts in the long run.

Direct use of natural resources, both renewable and non–renewable, in the provision of tourist facilities is one of the most significant direct impacts of tourism in a given area. Land use for accommodation and infrastructure provision, the choice of the site, the use of building materials are all essential factors. Deforestation and intensified or unsustainable use of land also cause erosion and loss of biodiversity. Direct impact on the species composition and on wildlife can be caused by incorrect behaviours and unregulated tourism activities (e.g. off–road driving, plant–picking, hunting, shooting, fishing, scuba diving). Moreover, tourists and tourist transportation means can increase the risk of introducing alien species and the manner and frequency of human presence can cause disturbance to the behaviour of animals. Construction activities related to tourism can cause enormous alteration to wildlife habitats and ecosystems.

Tourism has for many years been focused on mountain and coastal areas. Pressures from tourism activities on biological resources and their diversity are enormous and includes: erosion and pollution from the construction of hiking trails, bridges in high mountains, camp sites, chalet and hotels. Tourism activities have a major impact also on the marine and coastal environment, the resources they host and the diversity of those resources. Most often, those impacts are due to inappropriate planning, irresponsible behaviour by tourists and operators and/or lack of education and awareness of the impacts by, for example, tourist resorts along the coastal zones.

Tourism is also a water–intensive activity with a large production of waste. The extraction of groundwater by some tourism activities can cause desiccation, resulting in loss of biological diversity. Moreover, the disposal of untreated effluents into surrounding rivers and seas can cause eutrophication and it can also introduce a large amount of pathogens into the water body. Disposal of waste produced by the tourism industry may cause major environmental problems.

Socio-economic and cultural impacts of tourism include influx of people and related social degradation, impacts on local communities and on cultural values. Increased tourism activities can cause an influx of people seeking employment or entrepreneurial opportunities, but who may not be able to find suitable employment, thus causing social degradation. Sudden loss of income and jobs can also be experienced in times of downturn, if the economy is not diversified and it heavily relies on tourism. When tourism development occurs, economic benefits are usually unequally distributed among members of local communities. In the case of foreign direct investment, much of the profit may be transferred back to the home country. Therefore, tourism can actually increase inequalities in communities, and thus relative poverty.

Tourism has a highly complex impact on cultural values. Tourism activities may lead to intergenerational conflicts and may affect gender relationships. Traditional practices and events may also be influenced by the tourist preferences. Tourism development can lead to the loss of access by indigenous and local communities to their land and resources as well as sacred sites.

Sustainable tourism is therefore in everybody's interest. Given that a high percentage of tourism involves visits to naturally and culturally distinguished sites, generating large amounts of revenue, there are clearly major opportunities for investing in the maintenance and sustainable use of biological resources. Along with the efforts to maximize benefits, efforts must be made to minimize the adverse impacts of the tourism industry on biological diversity.

In this context, one of the challenges for the Convention on Biological Diversity is to develop, promote and disseminate guidelines for the sustainable planning and management of tourism activities in vulnerable terrestrial, marine and coastal ecosystems and habitats of major importance for biological diversity.

The Process

At its fourth meeting in 1999 the Conference of the Parties decided to consider "Sustainable use including tourism" as one of the three themes for in–depth consideration at its fifth meeting (Annex II of decision IV/16). Accordingly, a note was prepared by the Executive Secretary for the fourth meeting of the Subsidiary Body on Scientific, Technical and Technological Advice (SBSTTA 4), in order to assist SBSTTA in its consideration of the development of approaches and practices for the sustainable use of biological resources, including tourism.

In adopting decision IV/16, the Conference of the Parties took note of the Programme for the further implementation of Agenda 21, adopted at the nineteenth special session of the United Nations General Assembly, held in June 1997. With regard to sustainable tourism, the General Assembly specifically directed the Commission on Sustainable Development (CSD) to develop an action–oriented international programme of work to be defined in cooperation with the Conference of the Parties together with other relevant organizations, including the World Tourism Organization (WTO), the United Nations Conference on Trade and

Development (UNCTAD) and the United Nations Environment Programme (UNEP). Accordingly, the seventh session of the CSD considered tourism and sustainable development and adopted an international work programme on sustainable tourism development. In its decision, the CSD invited the Conference of the Parties to further consider existing knowledge and best practice on sustainable tourism development and biological diversity with a view to contributing to international guidelines for activities related to sustainable tourism development in vulnerable ecosystems and habitats.

At its fourth meeting, in June 1999, SBSTTA focused on tourism as one example of sustainable use and developed and recommended for adoption by the Conference of the Parties an assessment of the interlinkages between tourism and biological diversity (SBSTTA Recommendation IV/7, annex and Final Report).

In decision V/25, the Conference of the Parties accepted the invitation to participate in the international work programme on sustainable tourism development under the Commission on Sustainable Development process with regard to biological diversity, in particular, with a view to contributing to international guidelines for activities related to sustainable tourism development in vulnerable terrestrial, marine and coastal ecosystems and habitats of major importance for biological diversity and protected areas, including fragile riparian and mountain ecosystems, bearing in mind the need for such guidelines to apply to activities both within and outside protected areas, and taking into account existing guidelines.

The Conference of the Parties further requested the Executive Secretary "to prepare a proposal for the contribution on guidelines, for example, by convening an international workshop".

A workshop on tourism and biodiversity was subsequently held in Santo Domingo in June 2001. The workshop resulted in the "International Guidelines on Sustainable Tourism in Vulnerable Ecosystems", which have been forwarded to the tenth session of the Commission on Sustainable Development serving as the Preparatory Committee for the World Summit on Sustainable Development, as requested by SBSTTA Recommendation VII/5. With the same recommendation SBSTTA also requested the Secretariat to submit the draft guidelines to the preparatory process for the World Summit on Eco–tourism (WES) to be held in Quebec

City, in May 2002 and to open an electronic consultation inviting further reactions to the guidelines. Comments received have been compiled and made available to the sixth Conference of the Parties. They are contained in document UNEP/CBD/COP/6/12/Add 2.

As requested by decision IV/14 of the Conference of the Parties, the draft guidelines were revised by the Secretariat of the Convention on Biological Diversity taking into account comments submitted to the Secretariat by Parties and Organizations through two rounds of electronic consultations as well as the outcome of the World Ecotourism Summit, which took place in Quebec City in May 2002.

The revised version of the guidelines was submitted to the eighth session of the Subsidiary Body on Scientific, Technical and Technological Advice in March 2003 for its consideration. SBSTTA 8 forwarded it to the seventh meeting of the Conference of the Parties for final adoption. The seventh meeting of the Conference of the Parties adopted the CBD Guidelines for Biodiversity and Tourism Development (Decision VII/14).

The Conference of the Parties also requested the Executive Secretary, in order to increase clarity and facilitate the detailed understanding of the guidelines and the implementation by Parties and to identify and address specific stakeholders to:

a. Develop a user's manual, checklists and, on the basis of experience gained, including the contribution of indigenous and local communities, produce and make available a streamlined and user–friendly core set of improved voluntary guidelines;
b. Prepare a glossary and definitions of terms used in the Guidelines;
c. Promote the use of the clearing–house mechanism to collect and disseminate information on:
   i. Specific case–studies on the implementation of the Guidelines that make clearer reference to the use and application of specific analytical management tools; and
   ii. Best practices, lessons learned and case–studies on the involvement of indigenous and local communities embodying traditional lifestyles in sustainable–tourism and ecotourism activities and projects.

Further to the request, the Secretariat, with the financial support from the Government of Germany, brought together a number of experts to assist the Secretariat in drafting a users' manual on the CBD Guidelines on Biodiversity and Tourism Development in the Bahamas from 24 to 28 January 2005. The Secretariat subsequently prepared a draft version of the manual and, by notification 2005–072, invited Parties, Governments and relevant stakeholders to submit their comments by 30 September 2005.

The Secretariat also prepared a glossary and definitions of technical terms used in the Guidelines and, by notification 2005–072, invited Parties, Governments and relevant stakeholders to provide their views and comments no later than 30 September 2005. The final versions of the Users' Manual on the CBD Guidelines on Biodiversity and Tourism Development and the technical glossary will be submitted to the eighth meeting of the Conference of the Parties.

CBD GUIDELINES ON BIODIVERSITY AND TOURISM DEVELOPMENT

Scope

International guidelines for activities related to sustainable tourism development in vulnerable terrestrial, marine and coastal ecosystems and habitats of major importance for biological diversity and protected areas, including fragile riparian and mountain ecosystems.

1. The present Guidelines are voluntary and represent a range of opportunities for local, regional, national governments, indigenous and local communities and other stakeholders to manage tourism activities in an ecological, economic and socially sustainable manner. They can be flexibly applied to suit different circumstances and domestic institutional and legal settings.
2. The Guidelines will assist Parties to the Convention on Biological Diversity, public authorities and stakeholders at all levels, to apply the provisions of the Convention to the sustainable development and management of tourism policies, strategies, projects and activities. They will provide technical guidance to policy makers, decision

makers and managers with responsibilities covering tourism and/or biodiversity, whether in national or local government, the private sector, indigenous and local communities,[1] non–governmental organizations or other organizations, on a process for working together with key stakeholders involved in tourism and biodiversity.

3. The Guidelines cover all forms and activities of tourism. These activities should be consistent with the principles of conservation and sustainable use of biological diversity. These include, but are not limited to, conventional mass tourism, ecotourism, nature– and culture–based tourism, heritage and traditional tourism, cruise tourism, leisure and sports tourism. Although the primary focus of the Guidelines is vulnerable ecosystems and habitats, they are also appropriate for tourism with impact on biodiversity in all geographical locations and tourist destinations. The Guidelines on Biodiversity and Tourism Development can also play a crucial role in incorporating sustainable use and equity strategies within and around protected areas. Furthermore the Guidelines recognize the need for collaboration between originating and receiving countries and should be used to balance local interests and national, regional and international policies.

The Policy–making, Development Planning and Management Process

4. The main elements considered in developing the Guidelines are:
   a. Framework for management of tourism and biodiversity;
   b. Notification process in relation to such a management framework; and
   c. Public education, capacity–building and awareness–raising concerning tourism and biodiversity.
5. Policy–making, development planning and the management process need to be undertaken through a multi–stakeholder process. Governments will normally coordinate this process at national level. This process may also be undertaken at more local levels by local

government, and should ensure strong involvement of indigenous and local communities throughout the management and decision–making process. In addition, those responsible for tourism development and activities are encouraged to consult with and involve all relevant stakeholders, and especially those who are or may be affected by such developments and activities. The process applies to both new tourism development and the management of the existing tourism operations.

6. In order to ensure coordination between the levels of decision–making in government departments and agencies concerned with management of biological diversity and tourism as well as agencies responsible for broader national economic development, inter– and intra–departmental and inter–organizational structures and processes should be established, if they do not already exist, to guide policy development and implementation.
7. There is a need to improve awareness and exchange of knowledge between those responsible for and affected by tourism and nature conservation at a national, subnational and local level. In addition, national biodiversity strategies and action plans should include consideration of tourism issues, and tourism plans should likewise include full consideration of biodiversity issues. Existing documents, strategies and plans should be coherent or revised and amended to that effect as applicable.
8. A consultative process should be established to ensure ongoing and effective dialogue and information–sharing with stakeholders, as well as to resolve conflicts that might arise in relation to tourism and biological diversity and build consensus. To assist in this process, a multi–stakeholder body should be established including government departments, the tourism sector, non–governmental organizations, indigenous and local communities and other stakeholders, to ensure their engagement and full participation in the whole process, and encourage the establishment of partnerships.
9. The institutional arrangements should provide for the comprehensive involvement of stakeholders in the management process described in these Guidelines.

10. Authorities and managers of protected areas have a special role for the management of tourism and biodiversity. To this end, there is a need for government support and resources for managers, including training to perform their role effectively. In addition, it is necessary to establish and review mechanisms and funding policies to ensure the availability of adequate resources for maintaining biodiversity and promoting sustainable tourism. International institutions and development agencies should be involved as appropriate.
11. To be sustainable, tourism development in any destination requires coordinated policy–making, development planning and management. The policy–making, development planning and management process comprises the following steps:

    a. Baseline information and review;
    b. Vision and goals;
    c. Objectives;
    d. Reveiw of legislation and control measures;
    e. Impact assessment;
    f. Impact management and mitigation;
    g. Decision-making;
    h. Implementation;
    i. Monitoring and reporting; and
    j. Adaptive management.

Baseline Information

12. Baseline information is necessary to enable informed decisions to be taken on any issue. A minimum of baseline information is needed to enable impact assessment and decision–making and it is recommended that its compilation follows the ecosystem approach.
13. For tourism and biodiversity, the baseline information should include information, as appropriate, on:

    a. Current economic, social and environmental conditions at national and local level, including current and planned tourism development and activities and their overall positive and negative impacts, as well as development and activities in other sectors;

b. Structure and trends within the tourism sector, tourism policy and tourism markets and trends, at national, regional and international level, including information based on market research as necessary;
c. Environmental and biodiversity resources and processes, including any special features and sites of particular importance and protected areas, and identifying those resources that may be off bounds to development due to their particular fragility and those resources identified by existing analysis of threats;
d. Culturally sensitive areas;
e. Benefits from, and costs of, tourism to indigenous and local communities;
f. Information on damage done to the environment in the past;
g. National biodiversity strategies, action plans and reports and other sectoral plans and policies relevant for tourism development and biodiversity; and
h. National, subnational and local sustainable development plans.

14. Baseline information should take into consideration all sources of knowledge. The adequacy of the baseline information available will need to be reviewed, and where necessary, further research and information–gathering can be undertaken to fill gaps that may be identified.
15. All stakeholders may contribute relevant information to this process, including indigenous and local communities. To this end, there is a need for capacity–building and training to assist stakeholders in documenting, accessing, analysing and interpreting baseline information.
16. Collation and synthesis of information provided will need to be undertaken by an appropriately qualified team, drawing on a range of expertise, including expertise in tourism and in biodiversity issues, and in traditional knowledge and innovation systems.

17. In order to ensure that all relevant information, its credibility and reliability are considered, all stakeholders should be involved in review of the collated baseline information available, and in the synthesis of this information.
18. Baseline information should include maps, geographical information systems and other visual tools, including already identified zoning schemes.
19. The baseline information–gathering and review process should make full use of the clearing–house mechanism under the Convention on Biological Diversity, as well as other relevant networks such as the World Network of Biosphere Reserves, World Heritage sites and Ramsar sites.
20. Requirements for site–specific information in relation to proposals for tourism development and activities at particular locations are set out in the notification process, and its compilation should follow the ecosystem approach. To enable impact assessment and decision making, the basic information required includes:

a. Site–specific aspects:

i. The various laws and regulations and plans that may be applicable to the specific site, including overviews of:
   a. Existing laws at local, subnational and national levels;
   b. Existing uses, customs and traditions; and
   c. Relevant regional and international conventions or agreements and their status, and cross–boundary agreements or memoranda of understanding (MoUs)

ii. Identification of various stakeholders involved in or potentially affected by the proposed project – including stakeholders in governmental, non–governmental, and private sectors (particularly those from the tourism sector), and indigenous and local communities – along with details concerning their participation in and/or consultation on the proposed project during its design, planning, construction and operation.

b. Ecological aspects:

i. Detailed indication of the protected and biodiversity significant areas;

ii. Specifications on the ecosystems, habitats, species;
iii. Quantitative and qualitative information on the loss of habitats and species (main reasons, trends);
iv. Indexing of species;
v. Identified threats;
vi. Existing zones, ecological zones and existing tourism zones within the ecological zones; and
vii. Ecologically sensitive zones and zones where ecological disasters have or will most likely take place.

c. Development aspects:

i. Summary of the proposed project, why and by whom it is proposed, estimated outcomes and possible impacts (including impacts on the surrounding areas and transboundary impacts), and quantitative and qualitative data on these aspects;
ii. Description of the stages of development and the various structures and stakeholders that may be involved at each stage; and
iii. Description of current land–uses, infrastructures, tourism facilities and services and their interaction with proposed operations.

Vision and Goals

Vision

21. An overall vision for sustainable tourism development in harmony with the goals and objectives of the Convention on Biological Diversity and other related conventions, such as the World Heritage Convention, is important for the effective management of tourism and biodiversity, and for ensuring that this also contributes to income generation and poverty reduction and a reduction of threats to biodiversity. The vision developed at the local level, while reflecting local priorities and realities, should take into account, as appropriate, national and regional tourism development strategies, policies and plans for economic and social development and for land–use, as well as the

baseline information and review. It should be based on a multi–stakeholder process including indigenous and local communities that are or may be affected by tourism development.

Goals

22. The main goals are established to maximize the positive benefits of tourism to biodiversity, ecosystems, and economic and social development, and of biodiversity to tourism, while minimizing negative social and environmental impacts from tourism, and can cover, *inter alia*:
    a. Maintenance of the structure and functioning of ecosystems;
    b. Sustainable tourism compatible with biodiversity conservation and sustainable use;
    c. Fair and equitable sharing of benefits of tourism activities, with emphasis on the specific needs of the indigenous and local communities concerned;
    d. Integration and interrelation with other plans, developments or activities in the same area;
    e. Information and capacity–building;
    f. Poverty reduction through the generation of sufficient revenues and employment to effectively reduce threats to biodiversity in indigenous and local communities;
    g. Protection of indigenous livelihoods, resources and of access to those resources;
    h. Diversification of economic activities beyond tourism to reduce dependency on tourism;
    i. Prevention of any lasting damage to biological diversity, ecosystems, and natural resources, and of social and cultural damage, and restoration of past damage where appropriate;
    j. Supporting the effective participation and involvement of representatives of indigenous and local communities in the development, operation and monitoring of tourism activities on lands and waters traditionally occupied by them;

k. Zoning and control of tourism developments and activities, including licensing and overall targets for and limits to the scale of tourism, to provide a range of activities for user groups that meet overall visions and goals;
l. Empowerment through participation in decision–making;
m. Access by indigenous and local communities to infrastructure, transport, communications and healthcare provisions laid on for tourists;
n. Increased safety for indigenous local communities;
o. Increased social pride; and
p. Control of tourism development and activities including licensing and clear indication on the limits to the scale and type of tourism development.

23. In relation to sharing of benefits arising from tourism and the conservation of biodiversity with indigenous and local communities, it should be noted that benefits may take various forms, including: job creation, fostering local enterprises, participation in tourism enterprises and projects, education, direct investment opportunities, economic linkages and ecological services. Appropriate mechanisms need to be established/evolved to capture the benefits.
24. The vision and goals will form the basis of national strategies or master plans for sustainable development of tourism in relation to biodiversity. Such plans should also incorporate consideration of biodiversity strategies and plans. In addition, biodiversity strategies and plans should include consideration of tourism issues.
25. Governments will normally coordinate this process at national level. This process may also be undertaken at more local levels by local government, and by communities at community level. Where local and community level vision and goals for tourism and biodiversity have been set, these may be taken into account by governments when preparing the national level vision and goals, for example, through workshops at the local level.

Objectives

26. The objectives focus on actions to implement specific elements of the overall vision and goals, and may include clear activities and the time by which these will be achieved. Objectives should be performance–based (e.g., construction of an interpretative trail to aid development of local guide services) and process–based (e.g., establishment of an operational management system for tourism and biodiversity). As with the vision and goals, it is important to involve and consult with all relevant stakeholders, and especially the tourism industry and indigenous and local communities that are or may be affected by tourism development, in the process for setting objectives.
27. Objectives should be specific and should include specific areas identified in clearly delineated zones listing the types of activities and infrastructure that would be acceptable and should be developed. It should also outline the impact management measures that would be appropriate, and intended markets (with greater detail, as set out in the notification process, being required for proposals for tourism development or activities at specific locations).
28. Governments may also wish to consider:
    a. Measures to ensure that sites designated at international level, such as Ramsar or World Heritage sites or Biosphere Reserves, are accorded appropriate legal recognition and government assistance at the national level;
    b. Establishing reserves based on the biosphere reserve concept and incorporating sustainable development objectives, generating income and employment opportunities for indigenous and local communities, and promoting appropriate product development;
    c. Measures to ensure that sites, at the national level, such as national parks, reserves and marine conservation areas are accorded appropriate legal recognition, have management plans and are provided necessary government support;

d. Strengthening the protected area network and encouraging the role of protected areas as key locations for good practices in the management of sustainable tourism and biodiversity, taking into account the full range of protected area categories;
e. Use of political and economic tools and measures to encourage the channelling of part of total tourism revenues towards supporting the conservation and sustainable use of biodiversity, such as conservation of protected areas, education, research programmes, or local community development; and
f. Encouraging all stakeholders, as well as the private sector, to actively support the conservation of biodiversity and the sustainable use of its components.

29. Governments will normally coordinate this process at national level. This process may also be undertaken at more local levels by local government, and by communities at community level. Where local– and community–level objectives for tourism and biodiversity have been set, these may be taken into account by governments when preparing national level objectives.

Legislation and Control Measures

30. Respect for existing national legislation and appropriate regulatory mechanisms and tools, such as land–use planning, protected area management plans, environmental assessment, building regulations and standards for sustainable tourism, are essential for the effective implementation of any overall vision, goals, and objectives. A review of legislation and control measures could consider, as appropriate, the legislation and control measures available for implementation of the overall vision, goals and objectives for tourism and biodiversity, their effectiveness, including enforcement, and any gaps that may need to be addressed, for example, by revision of—or the development of additional—legislation and control measures.
31. The review of legislation and control measures may include, *inter alia*, assessment of the effectiveness of any

provisions for resource management, access, and/or ownership by communities, especially indigenous and local communities in relation to tourism development or operations on lands and waters traditionally occupied or used by them; addressing legally established rights of indigenous and local communities; and enabling these groups to make decisions about tourism development and activities, amongst other forms of development and activities, in these areas.

32. Legislation and control measures considered could include measures for:
    a. Effective enforcement of existing laws, including the participation of all stakeholders;
    b. Approval and licensing processes for tourism development and activities;
    c. Controlling the planning, siting, design and construction of tourism facilities and infrastructures;
    d. Management of tourism in relation to biodiversity and ecosystems, including vulnerable areas;
    e. Application of environmental assessment, including assessment of cumulative impacts and effects on biodiversity, to all proposed tourism developments, and as a tool to develop policies and measure their impacts;
    f. Setting national standards and/or criteria for tourism that are consistent with overall national or regional plans for sustainable development and national biodiversity strategies and action plans:
        i. Environmental quality and land–use criteria in and around tourism sites;
        ii. Development of a decision–making process with environmental and cultural sustainability guidelines for new and existing tourism development within the designated goals and objectives of the site's different zones and within the limits of acceptable change;
    g. Integrated land–use management;
    h. Ensuring inter–linkages between tourism and cross–cutting issues, including agricultural development, coastal zone management, water resources, etc.;

i. Mechanisms to resolve any inconsistencies between policy objectives and/or legislation in a manner that takes into account the interests of all stakeholders;

j. Application of economic instruments, including tiered user fees, bonds, taxes or levies, for the management of tourism and biodiversity;

k. Creating incentives for sustainable tourism development in line with the provisions of the Convention on Biological Diversity and Agenda 21 through relevant economic mechanisms;

l. Supporting private sector voluntary initiatives consistent with these Guidelines, such as certification schemes and providing opportunities for the private tourism sector to contribute to management initiatives through direct donations, in–kind services, and other voluntary initiatives consistent with these Guidelines, and relevant policies;

m. Avoiding tourism development or activities outside those areas set out in the objectives; and

n. Monitoring, control of and provision of information on activities related to collection and trade of biological and related cultural resources within tourism sites.

33. Governments will normally coordinate this process at the national level. It is important to involve and consult with all relevant stakeholders, and especially indigenous and local communities that are or may be affected by tourism development, in the process for reviewing legislation and control measures, assessing their adequacy and effectiveness, and proposing development of new legislation and measures where necessary.

Impact Assessment

34. Impact assessment for sustainable tourism development in ecosystems should be based on the "Guidelines for incorporating biodiversity–related issues into environmental impact assessment legislation and/or processes and in strategic environmental assessment" developed by the Convention on Biological Diversity and

contained in the annex to decision VI/7 A (paras. 1 24) as well as on the Akwe: Kon voluntary guidelines for the conduct of cultural, environmental and social impact assessment regarding developments proposed to take place on, or which are likely to impact on, sacred sites and on lands and waters traditionally occupied or used by indigenous and local communities (as contained in Annex to Decision VII/14).

35. At national level, Governments should normally undertake assessment of impacts associated with the overall vision, goals and objectives for tourism and biodiversity. In addition, this process may also be undertaken at more local levels by local government, and by indigenous and local communities.
36. Proposers of tourism developments or activities should assess the potential impacts of their proposals and provide information on this through a notification process.
37. Governments will normally undertake evaluations of the adequacy of impact assessments submitted by proposers of tourism development or activities. These evaluations will need to be undertaken by an appropriately qualified team, drawing on a range of expertise, including expertise in tourism and in biodiversity management, and also involving those indigenous and local communities that would be affected by the proposals. There should be public access to the documentation.
38. If the information provided is not sufficient, or the impact assessment inadequate, then further impact assessment studies may need to be undertaken. The proposer may be requested to undertake such studies, or the Government may decide to undertake these studies, and may request funds from the proposer for this purpose, as appropriate. Other stakeholders, including biodiversity managers and indigenous and local communities that may be affected by a proposed development, may also provide their assessments of impacts associated with specific proposals for tourism development or activities, and provisions may be needed to ensure that any such assessments are taken into account by decision–makers.

39. Indigenous and local communities concerned should be involved in impact assessment. Their traditional knowledge should be acknowledged and considered for impact assessment in particular tourism projects that affect their sacred sites or lands and waters traditionally occupied or used by them.
40. Sufficient time should be allowed considering the different conditions and circumstances to ensure that all stakeholders are able to participate effectively in the decision–making process for any project using information provided by the impact assessment. Such information should be provided in forms that are accessible and comprehensible to all the various stakeholders involved.
41. Impacts of tourism in relation to the environment and biological diversity may include:
    a. Use of land and resources for accommodation, tourism facilities and other infrastructure provision, including road networks, airports and seaports;
    b. Extraction and use of building materials (e.g., use of sand from beaches, reef limestone and wood);
    c. Damage to or destruction of ecosystems and habitats, including deforestation, draining of wetlands, and intensified or unsustainable use of land;
    d. Increased risk of erosion;
    e. Disturbance of wild species, disrupting normal behaviour and potentially affecting mortality and reproductive success;
    f. Alterations to habitats and ecosystems;
    g. Increased risk of fires;
    h. Unsustainable consumption of flora and fauna by tourists (e.g., through picking of plants; or purchase of souvenirs manufactured from wildlife, in particular such endangered species as corals and turtle shells; or through unregulated hunting, shooting and fishing);
    i. Increased risk of introduction of alien species;
    j. Intensive water demand from tourism;
    k. Extraction of groundwater;

l. Deterioration in water quality (freshwater, coastal waters) and sewage pollution;
m. Eutrophication of aquatic habitats;
n. Introduction of pathogens;
o. Generation, handling and disposal of sewage and waste–water;
p. Chemical wastes, toxic substances and pollutants;
q. Solid waste (garbage or rubbish);
r. Contamination of land, freshwater and seawater resources;
s. Pollution and production of greenhouse gases, resulting from travel by air, road, rail, or sea, at local, national and global levels; and
t. Noise.

42. Socio–economic and cultural impacts related to tourism may include:
 a. Influx of people and social degradation (e.g. local prostitution, drug abuse, etc.);
 b. Impacts on children and youth;
 c. Vulnerability to the changes in the flow of tourist arrivals which may result in sudden loss of income and jobs in times of downturn;
 d. Impacts on indigenous and local communities and cultural values;
 e. Impacts on health and the integrity of local cultural systems;
 f. Intergenerational conflicts and changed gender relationships;
 g. Erosion of traditional practices and lifestyles; and
 h. Loss of access by indigenous and local communities to their land and resources as well as sacred sites, which are integral to the maintenance of traditional knowledge systems and traditional lifestyles.

43. The potential benefits of tourism may include:
 a. Revenue creation for the maintenance of natural resources of the area;
 b. Contributions to economic and social development, for example:

i. Funding the development of infrastructure and services;
ii. Providing jobs;
iii. Providing funds for development or maintenance of sustainable practices;
iv. Providing alternative and supplementary ways for communities to receive revenue from biological diversity;
v. Generating incomes;
vi. Education and empowerment;
vii. An entry product that can have direct benefits for developing other related products at the site and regionally; and
viii. Tourist satisfaction and experience gained at tourist destination.

Impact Management and Mitigation

44. Impact management is essential to avoid or minimize any potential damage to biodiversity conservation and sustainable use that tourism development or activities might cause. Proposals for tourism development or activities may incorporate proposals for impact management, but these may not necessarily be judged sufficient to deal with potential impacts on biodiversity. Therefore all stakeholders, and especially Governments that exercise overall control over tourism development and activities, will need to consider the various impact management approaches that may be necessary in any given situation. In particular, Governments should be aware that the tourism industry could provide a direct impetus for conservation of vulnerable ecosystems by supporting sustainable tourism activities that have a direct commercial interest in maintaining the vulnerable ecosystem in a good condition.
45. Tourism should be planned and managed using the internationally accepted planning methodologies (such as the Recreation Opportunity Spectrum and the Limits of Acceptable Change). In vulnerable ecosystems, based on these methodologies and relevant background

information, tourism should be restricted and where necessary prevented.

46. Impact management can include, *inter alia*, measures for the siting of tourism development and activities, including establishing appropriate activities in different designated zones, differentiation between the impacts of different types of tourism, and measures to control tourist flows in and around tourist destinations and key sites, to promote appropriate behaviour by tourists so as to minimize their impacts, and to establish limits to numbers of visitors and their impacts within Limits of Acceptable Change at any site.
47. Impact management in relation to transboundary ecosystems and migratory species requires regional cooperation.
48. There is a need to identify those who will be responsible for implementing impact management and the resources that will be required for impact management.
49. Impact management for tourism development and activities can include the adoption and effective implementation of policies, good practices and lessons learned that cover, *inter alia*:
    a. Controlling impacts of major tourist flows including excursions, cruise ships, etc., which can cause serious effects on destinations even though they are visited for only short periods;
    b. Reducing impacts of activities outside tourism areas on adjacent and other ecosystems of importance for tourism (e.g., pollution from nearby farming activities or extractive industries may affect areas of tourism development);
    c. Responsible use of natural resources (e.g., land, soil, energy, water);
    d. Reducing, minimizing and preventing pollution and waste (e.g. solid and liquid waste, emissions to air, transport);
    e. Promoting the design of facilities that are more eco–efficient, which adopt the cleaner production approach, and use environmentally sound

technologies, in particular, to reduce emissions of carbon dioxide and other greenhouse gases and ozone–depleting substances, as set out in international agreements;

f. Conserving flora, fauna and ecosystems;
g. Preventing the introduction of alien species as a result of the construction, landscaping and operating of tourism activities, including for example from shipping associated with tourism;
h. Conserving landscapes, cultural and natural heritage;
i. Respecting the integrity of local cultures and avoiding negative effects on social structures, involving, and cooperating with Indigenous and local communities, including measures to ensure respect for sacred sites and customary users of these sites, and to prevent negative impacts on them and on lands and waters traditionally occupied or used by them, as well as on their subsistence resources;
j. Using local products and skills, and providing local employment;
k. Promoting appropriate behaviour by tourists so as to minimize their adverse impacts, and to promote positive effects through education, interpretation, extension, and other means of awareness raising;
l. Alignment of marketing strategies and messages with the principles of sustainable tourism;
m. Contingency plans for handling accidents, emergencies or bankruptcies that may occur during construction and use of facilities and which may threaten the environment and the conservation and sustainable use of biodiversity;
n. Environmental and cultural sustainability audits and review of existing tourism activities and development and of the effectiveness with which impact management is being applied to existing tourism activities and development; and
o. Mitigation measures for existing impacts, and appropriate funding to support them. Such measures should include development and implementation of

compensation measures in cases when tourism has resulted in negative environmental, cultural, and socio–economic effects, taking into consideration the range of redress and compensation measures.

50. Governments, in cooperation with biodiversity managers, those communities that would be affected by the proposals, and other stakeholders, would normally assess the need for impact management in addition to any management measures included in the proposals under consideration. All stakeholders should understand the importance of such impact management.
51. The tourism industry can assist in promoting corporate policies on sustainable tourism and biodiversity, with defined goals, monitoring and reporting their progress publicly on a regular basis.

Decision–Making

52. Decisions will be made concerning approval or otherwise of, *inter alia*:
    a. National strategies and plans for tourism and biodiversity;
    b. Proposals for tourism development and activities at particular locations in relation to biodiversity, which are to be submitted through the notification process;
    c. Adequacy of impact management measures in relation to anticipated impacts from tourism development and activities; and
    d. Adequacy and frequency of monitoring and reporting.
53. Such decisions will ultimately be taken by Governments (or specific authorities designated by Governments). It is recognized, however, that effective consultation with and participation of the communities and groups affected, including specific input from biodiversity managers, and from indigenous and local communities as well as the private sector in a broad sense, is an important foundation of the decision–making process and critical to sustainable development. Decision makers should consider using multi–stakeholder processes as a tool for the decision–making process.

54. The decision–making process should be transparent, accountable, and apply the precautionary approach. Legal mechanisms should be put in place for notification and approval of tourism development proposals and for ensuring implementation of the conditions of approval of development proposals.
55. For proposals for tourism development and activities at particular locations, the proposers will normally be required to provide the information set out in the notification process. This should apply equally to public sector development and infrastructure projects, as well as to private sector development. Impact assessment should be a component of any decision–making process.
56. Measures should be taken to ensure full and timely disclosure of project information concerning tourism development proposals. Consistent with Article 8(j), decision–making should include meaningful consultation with indigenous and local communities affected by projects in order to ensure, *inter alia,* respect for the customs and traditional knowledge, innovations and practices of indigenous and local communities, and adequate funding and technical support for effective participation. Where the national legal regime requires prior informed consent of indigenous and local communities with respect to decisions identified in paragraph 52, such prior informed consent must be obtained.
57. Decisions should include a review of the adequacy of information available, that could cover, *inter alia,* baseline information, impact assessment, and information on the proposed tourism development or activity, its nature and size, the type(s) of tourism involved, and information on human settlements and communities that may be affected.
58. In cases where there is no sufficient contextual/baseline information available at the time, or where the overall vision, goals and objectives for tourism and biodiversity have not been developed sufficiently to make a decision, decisions may be deferred pending sufficient information being obtained, and/or completion of overall plans/goals.
59. In making a decision, conditions may be attached to any approvals that may be granted, including conditions

regarding management of tourism in relation to avoidance or minimization of adverse impacts on biodiversity, and for appropriate decommissioning of tourism activities should the development cease. Decision makers may also, as appropriate, request further information from a proposer; defer a decision pending further baseline research by other agencies; or refuse a proposal.

Implementation

60. Implementation follows a decision to approve a particular proposal, strategy or plan. Unless otherwise stated, the developer and/or operator will be responsible for complying with the conditions for granting the approval; and, as part of this process, they can also be required to notify the designated government authority of any failures to comply with conditions attached to an approval, including conditions for decommissioning, and/or of any changes in circumstances, including unforeseen environmental conditions and/or biodiversity issues (e.g., detection of rare or endangered species not recorded in the original proposal and impact assessment).
61. Any revisions or changes to an approved project, including additions and/or variations of activities, must be approved by the designated authorities before construction.
62. Implementation plans should recognize that indigenous and local communities and other relevant stakeholders may require assistance as actors in implementation, and should ensure that sufficient resources are available for implementation and for effective participation.
63. Local stakeholders should be given an ongoing opportunity to express their wishes and concerns to those managing tourism facilities and activities. As part of this process, clear and adequate information regarding implementation should be provided for review by the stakeholders, in forms that are accessible and comprehensible to them.
64. Availability of information on policies, programmes, projects, and their implementation, including information on existing and future guidelines, should be ensured and

exchange of information fostered, for example, through the clearing house mechanism of the Convention on Biological Diversity.

Monitoring and Reporting

65. It is necessary to establish a monitoring and control system for the management of tourism activities and biological diversity. Long–term monitoring and assessment are necessary in relation to the impacts of tourism on biodiversity, and will need to take into account the timescale for ecosystem changes to become evident. Some effects may develop quickly, while others may take place more slowly. Long–term monitoring and assessment provide a means for detecting adverse effects that may arise from tourism activities and development in relation to biodiversity, so that action can be taken to control and mitigate such effects.
66. Monitoring and surveillance in relation to management of tourism and biodiversity include, *inter alia*, the following main areas:
    a. Implementation of approved tourism development or activities, and compliance with any conditions attached when approval was granted, and taking appropriate actions in cases of non–compliance;
    b. Impacts of tourism activities on biodiversity and ecosystems, taking appropriate preventative actions as necessary;
    c. Impacts of tourism on the surrounding population, especially indigenous and local communities;
    d. General tourism activities and trends, including tour operations, tourism facilities, and tourist flows in originating and receiving countries, including progress towards sustainable tourism;
    e. Clearly defined objectives, actions and targets for conservation or mitigation of threats to biodiversity, maintenance or restoration of ecosystems and for tourism; and
    f. Compliance with, and enforcement as necessary, of conditions attached to any approval. Communities

and other interested stakeholders may also monitor and report their findings to the designated government authorities.

67. Developers and operators of tourism facilities and activities should be required to report periodically to designated authorities and to the public on compliance with conditions set out in approvals, and on the condition of biodiversity and the environment in relation to the tourism facilities and activities for which they are responsible.
68. Prior to the commencement of any new tourism development or activities, an inclusive monitoring and reporting system should be put in place, with indicators to track how tourism actions are mitigating threats to biodiversity, along with agreed upon quantifiable standards indicating thresholds of acceptable change. These should be developed in conjunction with all key stakeholders including indigenous and local communities.
69. Indicators to cover aspects of management of biodiversity and sustainable tourism, including socio economic and cultural aspects, should be identified and monitored at global, national, and local levels, and should include, but not be limited to, the following:
    a. Conservation of biodiversity;
    b. Generation of income and employment from tourism (long–term and short–term);
    c. Proportion of tourism income retained in the local community;
    d. Effectiveness of multi–stakeholder processes for management of biodiversity and sustainable tourism;
    e. Effectiveness of impact management;
    f. Contribution of tourism to the well–being of the local population; and
    g. Visitor impacts and visitor satisfaction.
70. Monitoring results depend largely on the appropriate set of data to be collected. Guidelines on how to collect data in a way that can be used to evaluate change over time should be developed. Monitoring could follow a standard process and format, and be based on a framework

including parameters on social, economic, environmental and cultural impact.

71. Monitoring and surveillance in relation to biodiversity impacts should include activities undertaken to ensure respect for endangered species under relevant international agreements, prevention of the introduction of alien species as a result of tourism activities, compliance with national rules concerning access to genetic resources, and prevention of illegal and unauthorised removal of genetic resources.

72. In relation to indigenous and local communities, monitoring and evaluation should include development and use of appropriate tools to monitor and evaluate tourism impacts on the economy of indigenous and local communities, particularly their food and health security, traditional knowledge, practices and customary livelihoods. Use of indicators and early warning systems should be developed as appropriate, taking into account traditional knowledge, innovation and practices of indigenous and local communities, and guidelines developed under the Convention on Biological Diversity relating to traditional knowledge. Measures should also be taken to ensure that indigenous and local communities involved in, or affected by tourism, have the opportunity to be involved effectively in monitoring and evaluation.

73. Monitoring of general environmental and biodiversity conditions and trends, as well as tourism trends and impacts, can be undertaken by Governments, including designated biodiversity managers. Management measures may need to be adjusted, as appropriate, where adverse impacts on biodiversity and ecosystems are detected. The need for and nature of such adjustments will be based on the results of monitoring, and it is important for these to be determined in dialogue with all relevant stakeholders, including the developers and/or operators of tourism facilities and activities, communities affected by those facilities and activities, and other interested stakeholders. The monitoring process needs to be multi–stakeholder and transparent.

Adaptive Management

74. The ecosystem approach requires adaptive management to deal with the complex and dynamic nature of ecosystems and the absence of complete knowledge or understanding of their functioning. Ecosystem processes are often non–linear, and the outcome of such processes often shows time–lags. The result is discontinuities, leading to surprise and uncertainty. Management must be adaptive in order to be able to respond to such uncertainties and contain elements of "learning–by–doing" or research feedback. Measures may need to be taken even when some cause–and–effect relationships are not yet fully established scientifically.
75. Ecosystem processes and functions are complex and variable. Their level of uncertainty is increased by the interaction with social constructs, which need to be better understood. Therefore, ecosystem management must involve a learning process, which helps to adapt methodologies and practices to the ways in which these systems are being managed and monitored. Adaptive management should also take the precautionary approach fully into account.
76. Implementation programmes should be designed to adjust to the unexpected, rather than to act on the basis of a belief in certainties.
77. Ecosystem management needs to recognize the diversity of social and cultural factors affecting natural–resource use and sustainability.
78. Similarly, there is a need for flexibility in policy–making and implementation. Long–term, inflexible decisions are likely to be inadequate or even destructive. Ecosystem management should be envisaged as a long–term experiment that builds on its results as it progresses. This "learning–by–doing" will also serve as an important source of information to gain knowledge of how best to monitor the results of management and evaluate whether established goals are being attained. In this respect, it would be desirable to establish or strengthen capacities of Parties for monitoring. In addition, adaptive

management learning portfolios should be developed between different sites so that comparison can be made and lessons learned.

79. Implementing adaptive management in relation to tourism and biodiversity will require the active cooperation of all stakeholders in tourism, and especially those in the private sector, with biodiversity managers. Impacts on biodiversity at a particular location may require rapid curtailment of visits by tourists to prevent further damage, and to allow for recovery, and in the longer term, may necessitate an overall reduction in tourist flows. It may be possible for tourists to be redirected to less sensitive areas in such cases. In all cases, maintenance of the balance between tourism and biodiversity will require close interaction between tourism managers and biodiversity managers, and appropriate frameworks for management and dialogue are likely to need to be established.
80. Governments, including designated biodiversity managers, in conjunction with all other stakeholders will therefore need to take actions, as appropriate, to address any problems encountered and to keep on track towards agreed goals. This may include changes and additions to conditions set in the original approval, and will require participation of and consultation with the developer and/or operator of the tourism facilities and activities concerned, and with local communities.
81. Adaptive management can also be undertaken by all those who have management control over any specific site, including local governments, indigenous and local communities, the private sector, non–governmental organizations and other organizations.
82. Where necessary, legal frameworks may need to be reviewed and amended to support adaptive management, taking into account experience gained.

Notification Process and Information Requirements

83. Proposals for tourism development and activities at particular locations in relation to biodiversity are to be submitted through the notification process. As such, this

process provides the link between proposers of tourism activities and development, and the management process steps outlined above. In particular, the notification process makes specific links to the steps in the management process for impact assessment and decision–making and should take into account local, regional and national impacts. Proposers of tourism projects, including government agencies, should provide full and timely advance notice to all stakeholders who may be affected, including indigenous and local communities, of proposed developments.

84. Information to be provided as part of the notification could include:
    a. Scale and types of tourism development or activities proposed, including a summary of the proposed project, why and by whom it is proposed, estimated outcomes and possible impacts, and a description of the stages of development and the various structures and stakeholders that may be involved at each stage;
    b. Analysis of market for proposed tourism development or activities, based on market conditions and trends;
    c. Geographical description including recreation opportunity zones, outlining tourist activities and infrastructure development, and location of the site of tourism development or activities, the identity and any special features of the surrounding environments and biodiversity;
    d. Nature and extent of human–resource requirements and plans for their procurement;
    e. Identification of various stakeholders involved in or potentially affected by the proposed project – including stakeholders in governmental, non-governmental, and private sectors, and indigenous and local communities – along with details concerning their participation in and/or consultation on the proposed project during its design, planning, construction and operation;
    f. The perceived roles of local stakeholders in the proposed development;

g. The various laws and regulations that may be applicable to the specific site, including overviews of existing laws at local, subnational and national levels, of existing uses and customs, of relevant regional and international conventions or agreements and their status, and cross–boundary agreements or memoranda or understanding and any proposed legislation;
h. The proximity of the site to human settlements and communities, sites used by people from those settlements and communities as part of their livelihoods and traditional activities, and heritage, cultural or sacred sites;
i. Any flora, fauna and ecosystems that could be affected by the tourism development or activities, including keystone, rare, endangered or endemic species;
j. Ecological aspects of the site and its surroundings, including indication of any protected areas; specifications on the ecosystems, habitats, and species; quantitative and qualitative information on the loss of habitats and species (main reasons, trends), and indexing of species;
k. Training and supervision of personnel carrying out the tourism development or activities;
l. Likelihood of impacts beyond the immediate area of the tourism development or activities, including transboundary impacts and effects on migratory species;
m. A description of current environmental and socio–economic conditions;
n. Expected changes to environmental and socio–economic conditions as a result of the tourism development or activities;
o. Proposed management measures to avoid or minimize adverse impacts from the tourism development or activities, including verification of their functioning;
p. Proposed measures for mitigation, decommissioning and compensation in the event of problems arising with the tourism development or activities;

q. Proposed measures to maximize the local benefits of the tourism development or activities on surrounding human settlements and communities, biodiversity and ecosystems, which may include, but are not limited to:
   i. Using local products and skills;
   ii. Employment;
   iii. Restoration of biodiversity and ecosystems;

r. Relevant information from any previous tourism development or activities in the region, and information on possible cumulative effects; and

s. Relevant information from any previous tourism development or activities by the proposer.

85. Categories of responses that Governments may wish to consider making in response to notification of proposals for, and requests for permission to undertake, tourism development, include, *inter alia*:
   a. Approval without conditions;
   b. Approval with conditions;
   c. Request for further information;
   d. Deferral pending further baseline research by other agencies; and
   e. Refusal of the proposal.

Education, Capacity–building and Awareness–raising

86. Education and awareness–raising campaigns need to be addressed to both the professional sectors and the general public and should inform them about the impacts of tourism on biological diversity, and good practices in this area. The private sector, and, especially, tour operators, could provide information more widely to their clients—the tourists—about tourism and biodiversity issues, and encourage them to conserve, and avoid adverse impact on biodiversity and cultural heritage to respect national legislation of the visited country, as well as traditions of indigenous and local communities of that country, and to support actions in conformity with the present Guidelines.

87. Awareness campaigns explaining the link between cultural diversity and biological diversity will need to be tailored

for various audiences, particularly stakeholders including consumers of tourism, developers and tourism operators.

88. Education and awareness–raising is required at all levels of government. This should include processes for increasing mutual understanding between relevant ministries, including joint and innovative approaches for dealing with tourism and environmental issues.
89. Awareness should also be increased within and outside government that vulnerable ecosystems and habitats are often located within lands and waters occupied or used by indigenous and local communities.
90. The tourism sector as a whole along with tourists should be encouraged to minimize any negative impacts and maximize positive impacts on biodiversity and local cultures associated with their consumption choices and behaviour, for example, through voluntary initiatives.
91. It is also important to raise awareness within the academic sector responsible for training and research on issues regarding the interaction between biological diversity and sustainable tourism of the role that they can play concerning public education, capacity–building and awareness–raising on these issues.
92. Capacity–building activities should aim to develop and strengthen the capacities of Governments and all stakeholders to facilitate the effective implementation of the present Guidelines, and may be necessary at local, national, regional and international levels.
93. Capacity–building activities can be identified through the adaptive management process and can include strengthening human resources and institutional capacities, the transfer of know–how, the development of appropriate facilities, and training in relation to biological diversity and sustainable tourism issues, and in impact assessment and impact management techniques.
94. Such activities should include ensuring that local communities are equipped with the necessary decision–making abilities, skills and knowledge in advance of future tourist in–flows, as well as with relevant capacity and training regarding tourism services and environmental protection.

95. Capacity–building activities should include, but not be limited to:
    a. Capacity–building and training to assist all stakeholders, including Governments, and indigenous and local communities, in accessing, analysing and interpreting baseline information, undertaking impact assessments and evaluations, impact management, decision–making, monitoring and adaptive management;
    b. Development or strengthening of mechanisms for impact assessment with the participation of all stakeholders, including for the approval of the approach, content and scope of impact assessment;
    c. Establishment of multi–stakeholder processes involving government departments, tourism sector, non–governmental organizations, indigenous and local communities and other stakeholders; and
    d. Training of tourism professionals in conservation and biodiversity issues.
96. Information exchange and collaboration regarding sustainable tourism implementation through networking and partnerships between all stakeholders affected by, or involved in tourism, including the private sector, should be encouraged.

CBD SUSTAINABLE TOURISM DEVELOPMENT GUIDELINES FOR VULNERABLE ECOSYSTEMS

With a total of 692.7 million international arrivals, and international receipts of $462.2 billion in 2001, tourism is one of the biggest industries in the world. Biodiversity is one of its main assets. Tourism, on the other hand, can impact biodiversity both in negative and in positive ways. For this reason, the Convention on Biological Diversity, in decision V/25, has accepted a recommendation of CSD to produce a set of guidelines. These guidelines were based on a number of existing documents, and on an expert workshop. (Please find, "the compilation and analysis of existing codes, guidelines, principles and position papers on sustainable tourism", on the bottom of the page under "Information Documents").

The CBD is the most successful Multilateral Environment Agreement ever, with 156 signatories. Along with GATS/WTO, it may become one of the most efficient intergovernmental agreements to regulate tourism.

The CBD Guidelines focus specifically on biodiversity but do refer to much broader topics such as water and waste pollution, energy consumption, coastal resource management, participation of local communities, biological diversity, including economic, social and environmental impacts. The introduction refers to "impacts of tourism on biological diversity, including economic, social and environmental impacts." The document clearly acknowledges that biodiversity is just one of the many important aspects of sustainability. The guidelines cover all forms and activities of tourism, which all come under the framework of sustainable development, in all geographic regions. These include conventional mass tourism, ecotourism, nature and culture–based tourism, cruise tourism, leisure tourism and sport tourism.

For these reasons, and given the significant political support, the CBD Guidelines enjoy in the process on CoP7, UNEP DTIE collaborates closely with the CBD Secretariat to support the guidelines and implement them on the ground based on practical projects.

Appendix–I

UN Economic and Social Council Resolution Declaring the Year 2002 as the International Year of Ecotourism

The Economic and Social Council,

Recalling its resolution 1980/67 of 25 July 1980 on international years and anniversaries in which the Council recognized the contribution of international years to the furtherance of international cooperation and understanding,

Recalling also Agenda 21[1] which was adopted by one hundred and eighty–two Governments at the United Nations Conference on Environment and Development (Earth Summit), on 14 June 1992, and the conclusions of the General Assembly at its nineteenth special session relative to sustainable tourism,

Stressing that the implementation of Agenda 21 requires the full integration of sustainable development in the tourism industry in order to ensure, *inter alia,* that travel and tourism provide a source of income for many people; that travel and tourism contribute to the conservation, protection and restoration of the Earth's ecosystem; that international trade in travel and tourism services takes place on a sustainable basis; and that environmental protection is an integral part of tourism development,

Stressing also the need to promote the implementation of international conventions on environment and development, including those on biodiversity and climate change,

Bearing in mind the need for international cooperation in promoting tourism within the framework of sustainable development so as to meet the needs of present tourists and host

---

[1] Report of the United Nations Conference on Environment and Development, Rio de Janeiro, 3–14 June 1992, vol. I, Resolutions Adopted by the Conference (United Nations Publication, Sales No. E.93.I.8 and corrigendum), resolution 1, annex II.

countries and regions while protecting and enhancing opportunities for the future, managing resources to fulfill economic, social and aesthetic needs, and maintaining cultural integrity, essential ecological processes, biological diversity and life–support systems,

Recognizing the support of the World Tourism Organization for the importance of ecotourism, and particularly of the designation of the year 2002 as the International Year of Ecotourism, in fostering better understanding among peoples everywhere, in leading to greater awareness of the rich heritage of various civilizations and in bringing about a better appreciation of the inherent values of different cultures, thereby contributing to the strengthening of world peace,

Considering that the designation of the year 2002 as the International Year of Ecotourism will encourage the intensification of cooperative efforts by Governments and international and regional organizations, as well as non–governmental organizations, to achieve the aims of Agenda 21 in promoting development and the protection of the environment,

1. Recommends to the General Assembly that it declare the year 2002 as the International Year of Ecotourism;
2. Invites States' Members of the United Nations, and members of the specialized agencies and pertinent intergovernmental and governmental organizations, to exert all possible efforts on behalf of the success of the Year, in particular regarding ecotourism in developing countries;
3. Requests the Commission on Sustainable Development, in the framework of its discussion of tourism during its seventh session, to recommend to the General Assembly, through the Economic and Social Council, supportive measures and activities which will contribute to a successful Year;
4. Requests the Secretary–General to provide, in accordance with the guidelines for future international years as contained in the annex to Economic and Social Council resolution 1980/67, necessary support to ensure the success of the Year, including widespread dissemination of pertinent information;

5. Requests the Secretary–General, in cooperation with all relevant entities of the United Nations system, including the United Nations Environment Programme as well as the World Tourism Organization and the World Travel and Tourism Council, to submit to the General Assembly at its fifty–eighth session a report containing:
   (a) Programmes and activities undertaken by Governments and interested organizations during the Year;
   (b) An assessment of the results achieved in realizing the aims and objectives of the Year, particularly in terms of encouraging ecotourism in developing countries;
   (c) Recommendations to further advance the promotion of ecotourism within the framework of sustainable development.

Appendix–II

Report of the International Association of Antarctica Tour Operators 2008–2009

Introduction

The International Association of Antarctica Tour Operators (IAATO) is pleased to present a report of its activities to ATCM XXXII in Baltimore, Maryland, USA from April 6–17, 2009, in relation to Article III (2) of the Antarctic Treaty.

IAATO is a member organization founded by seven companies in 1991 to advocate, promote and practice safe and environmentally responsible private–sector travel to the Antarctic.

During the 2008–2009 fiscal year, IAATO maintained its total membership level at 108 companies and organizations. A Membership Directory, regularly updated, can be found on line at www.iaato.org.

As an organization, IAATO provides an online and central office resource for its members. Comprehensive operational guidelines and procedures are stored in the *Members Only* section of the website for reference, research purposes and downloading by its members (www.iaato.org). Regular updates and information are shared with members throughout the year, both in the field and home offices. The aim is to encourage the highest possible operating standards for IAATO companies by providing them with the information needed for a safe and environmentally responsible operation.

Coinciding with the start of the new 2008–2009 fiscal year, a new Executive Director was appointed to manage the IAATO Secretariat. IAATO Secretariat offices were relocated in July 2008 to 179 Wayland Avenue in Providence, Rhode Island, USA, and a full–time office manager was hired. In addition, the position of IAATO Environmental Operations Manager became full–time. All members of the Antarctic community are welcome to visit the new IAATO offices.

Primary Activities & Developments

IAATO continues to focus its activities in several key areas. The following is a brief synopsis of organizational activities:

1. *Seasonal Instructions*: The Seasonal Instructions to operators provide a comprehensive resource of materials and guidelines adopted by both IAATO and the Antarctic Treaty System. In addition to the annually amended Instructions, current updates are circulated to operators throughout the season as necessary, and are posted to the *Members Only* section of the IAATO website.
2. *Field Operations Manuals*: For the 2008–2009 season, IAATO produced and distributed for the first time to its members a standardized Field Operations Manual (FOM) for use by expedition leaders (ELs) and staff, captains and officers and by staff in members' home offices. A comprehensive, 800–page, two–binder compendium, the FOM is based on the traditional expedition leader's handbook previously created independently by operators for their own vessel or operation. By incorporating guidelines and operating procedures established over the years by experienced ELs into a standard new format, IAATO is taking steps to ensure consistency in the transmittal of the latest information on regulations and guidelines. The FOM will also serve as the "course manual" in the IAATO Field Staff Training and Certification Scheme (see #19 below).
3. *Ship Scheduler*: The web–based IAATO Ship Scheduler continues to serve a vital management function of the organization, allowing for the pre–scheduling of visits to sites prior to the season. This not only ensures the presence of not more than one ship at one site at one time, but also implements the requirements laid out under the 45 IAATO Site Guidelines and the 18 ATCM Site Guidelines. In addition to noting each vessel's day–to–day schedule, the Ship Scheduler also stores a named contact for each voyage (the expedition leader, vessel Master or Ice Master) and departure dates and ports.

Member–operators input data into the Ship Scheduler prior to the season (July), with the resulting spreadsheet available as a planning tool in September. Once the Antarctic operating season begins, the Ship Scheduler is "locked" and ELs further coordinate their landings in the field as needed. IAATO members have coordinated their schedules consistently since 1991, and the online database and creation of a master schedule have facilitated this effort in recent years. Prior to and during the season, the master schedule is available to non–IAATO vessel operators on a request basis. The resulting coordination with other non–IAATO vessels helps assure compliance with the intention of only one ship at one site at one time.

Access to the Ship Scheduler during the 2008–2009 season was also made available to RCCs, COMNAP and national programmes that interact with IAATO on a regular basis with respect to station visits. The master schedule was circulated to numerous Antarctic Treaty Parties, the Antarctic Treaty Secretariat, IHO/HCA, AMVER and others at the beginning of the Antarctic season. This facilitates further scheduling, transport of scientists, and the coordination of logistics and contingency planning.

The Ship Scheduler allows for an effective exchange of information between operators, the coordination of station visits and ship itineraries in advance, and ensures compliance with requirements under adopted Site Guidelines. It also assists the IAATO Secretariat and IAATO members in their pre–planning to address potential cumulative environmental impact issues and site usage at the various landing sites. The tool also has proven useful as a multiyear planning tool for ships' arrivals and departures in port cities such as Ushuaia, Argentina.

4. *Vessel and Member Database*: IAATO's Vessel Database is a comprehensive web–based data programme that maintains detailed information on all member–operated vessels and the companies who operate them. Each IAATO member is responsible for uploading detailed vessel and company information. This online programme was created primarily as an aid to the management of the IAATO Emergency Contingency Plan, and to maintain an accurate, up–to–date database on company and vessel specifications. For example, a contact information sheet for IAATO's fleet of vessels is generated through the database each season.

Components of this database and contingency plan were tabled at ATCM XXIX IP 29 *IAATO Vessel Emergency Contingency Plan–An Update* (2006). MRCCs and COMNAP have full access to the vessel database; this enables them to assess the assets they have available should an emergency occur.

5. *Vessel Tracking*: It was agreed during IAATO 19th Annual Meeting (2008, Punta del Este, Uruguay) that it would be desirable for all IAATO member vessels to be tracked on a single website. This would assist in both contingency response but also, in due course, become an additional management tool for day–to–day operations. During 2008–2009 season, sixty per cent of IAATO vessels took part in the scheme, and its usefulness was proven during both the *MV Ushuaia* and the *MV Ocean Nova* incidents. Efforts are underway to bring the remainder of IAATO vessels onboard with the satellite tracking initiative. Full information on the tracking scheme can be found on the IAATO website.
6. *Post–Visit Report Database*: IAATO continues to maintain a single electronic database to store information downloaded from all members' Post Visit Reports (PVRs), using the PVR template approved at ATCM XXVIII Resolution 6 (2005) *Antarctic Post Visit Report Form*. Established in 2003, this database provides a detailed digital record of all member activities. Reports from the database, plus tourism statistics compiled by the US National Science Foundation since 1989, are openly available under *Tourism Statistics* on the IAATO website at www.iaato.org. The 2008–2009 data is estimated to be available in May 2009.

   IAATO welcomes submission of non–IAATO member PVRs for inclusion in the database. A blank PVR form is posted on *Operational Procedures* on the IAATO website (www.iaato.org).
7. *Site Guidelines and Field Staff Interviews*: During the 2008–2009 intersessional period, the IAATO Site Guidelines Committee assisted in the development of seven additional site guidelines with several Antarctic Treaty Parties. In addition, field staff were interviewed through

the season to discuss operational issues and provide an opportunity for practical feedback on the effectiveness of the ATCM endorsed Site Guidelines. This feedback will be discussed within the IAATO Site Guidelines Committee, and at IAATO's 20th Annual Meeting in Providence, Rhode Island (June 2009).

8. *IAATO Observers*: IAATO requires new member–operators to carry an appointed observer on one cruise during their initial season of operation as an IAATO member. Guided by a detailed checklist, the observer reports on critical aspects of an operation and provides an unabridged report to the IAATO Membership Committee for analysis and approval. These reports are then presented at the next IAATO Annual Meeting, where they are instrumental in providing information for Members on which to base their voting decisions to accept or reject a new member into IAATO. During the 2008–2009 season, five new members carried IAATO observers. For further information on the IAATO Observer programme, see Section 12 of this Annual Report.
9. *Safety and Conservation Briefing*: IAATO continues to rely on the use of its *Safety and Conservation Briefing*. This is a PowerPoint presentation based on Recommendation XVIII–1 (1994) and is mandatory for all passengers and crew landing in Antarctica. A Quicktime slide show version of this can be found on iaato@iaato.org under *Guidelines*.
10. *Introduced Species or "Aliens"*: Operational procedures were updated to continue to support all methods necessary to eliminate the potential spreading of Antarctic diseases and translocation of non–native species. During the 2008–2009 season, an IAATO member field staff person reported the discovery of a non–native plant species at Whalers Bay, Deception Island.
11. *Discovery of High Mortality Events*: IAATO High Mortality Procedures were followed on two occasions as members remain vigilant regarding the potential discovery and reporting of high mortality events in both the Antarctic and sub–Antarctic Islands. During the 2008–2009 season, IAATO members alerted British Antarctic Survey (BAS),

the US National Science Foundation (NSF) and sub–Antarctic island groups to two possible high mortality events. In each instance, evidence indicates that these were due to low food supplies rather than pathogen–related mortalities. Nonetheless, full High Mortality Procedures were followed as a precaution. *IAATO Procedures for the Discovery of a High Mortality Event* is in the IAATO Field Operations Manual (section 6b), and posted on the *Members Only* page of the IAATO website (www.iaato.org).

12. *Station Visits*: IAATO continued to closely coordinate schedules for station visits and landings with the United States Antarctic Programme (Palmer, McMurdo and South Pole Stations), British Antarctic Survey (Rothera, Halley and Signy Stations) and Port Lockroy. "IAATO Standard Procedures for Station Visits" is in the IAATO Field Operations Manual (section 12b) and posted on the *Members Only* page of the IAATO website (www.iaato.org).
13. *Science News Sheet*: During the IPY, IAATO has provided its field staff with information on various research projects that are of interest to both tourists and field personnel. The Science News Sheets provide a dedicated channel for this information and aim to support the IPY, promoting relations between the scientific and tourist community. Recently published Science News Sheets can be found on the *Information Papers* page of the IAATO website (www.iaato.org). IAATO welcomes input from national programmes in order to provide education and outreach to tourists travelling to Antarctica and the general public who visit IAATO's website.
14. *Seabird Landings Poster and Report Form*: Prior to the 2008–2009 Antarctic season, IAATO coordinated efforts with one of its members to develop and distribute a new poster/flyer on seabird landings at sea. The poster outlines measures designed to reduce the likelihood of nocturnal bird landings resulting from unnecessary or overly bright lights on vessels. A report form was also distributed to members for use in the field. The poster and additional information can be downloaded from the *Information Papers* page of the IAATO website (www.iaato.org).

15. *Education and Outreach*: IAATO member–operators continue to use four large format size posters for display aboard vessels and in member company offices as educational tools entitled:
    Guidance for Visitors to the Antarctic, Recommendation XVIII–1 (1994)
    http://www.iaato.org/docs/Visitor-Guidelines–1.pdf
    Marine Wildlife Watching Guidelines (Parts 1&2)
    http://www.iaato.org/wildlife.html
    IAATO Boot and Clothing Decontamination Guidelines for Small Boat Operations
    http://www.iaato.org/docs/Boot-Washing07.pdf
16. *Yacht Package*: In an effort to promote understanding of safe and environmentally responsible private sector travel to the Antarctic, the one–off Yacht Package, which includes comprehensive operating information, continues to be made available for private one–off yacht visitors who are not IAATO members. This package was detailed in *IP 110 IAATO Information Outreach to Private One–Off Non–Member Expeditions,* ATCM XXX (2007), and is available on the *Information Papers* page of the IAATO website (www.iaato.org).
17. *Emergency Response*: Continued use was made of the IAATO Member Emergency Medical Evacuation Response (EMER) action plan. Information on the number of IAATO medevacs during the 2008–2009 season will be available once end–of–season reports are finalized and tabulated. *IAATO Emergency and Medical Evacuation Response (EMER)* is in the IAATO Field Operations Manual (section 4c) and is posted on the *Members Only* page of the IAATO website (www.iaato.org).
18. *IAATO Exchange of Information*: In addition to distributing the IAATO Field Operations Manual, coordination with all new members in their start–up operations was provided. Support and advice is offered on an ongoing basis to all member companies. In recent years, an introductory information session has been added to the IAATO Annual Meeting for new members to assist in this effort.
19. *IAATO Field Staff Training and Certification Scheme*: The pilot phase of a new field staff training and certification

programme has begun. Using the new IAATO Field Operations Manual (FOM) as a course book, expedition leaders and staff can be assessed online at their convenience, with assessment results available to IAATO, the field staff and their operating company. A new IAATO Field Staff Logbook is also being developed, enabling field staff to record their work histories and credentials into a standardized, recognized format that will facilitate their employment opportunities with IAATO member–operators. It will also assist member–operators to hire the most qualified personnel available, in their goal of ensuring safe and environmentally responsible travel to Antarctica.

1 ***IAATO Membership and Activities***

1.1 IAATO member offices are located worldwide, including in the following Antarctic Treaty Parties: Argentina, Australia, Belgium, Canada, Chile, France, Germany, Italy, Japan, The Netherlands, New Zealand, Norway, Sweden, United Kingdom and the United States. A full Membership Directory can be found on the IAATO website at www.iaato.org.

1.2 ***Membership during the 2008–2009 Season***

IAATO's total membership numbers for the 2008–2009 season remain unchanged at 108 from the previous season, with one new member and one member dropping out due to lack of any cruise operations in Antarctic waters during the season just ended. Several new applications for membership are currently under review.

The breakdown of the 108 IAATO companies that are members from July 1, 2008–through March 6, 2009 includes the following categories of membership:

Members: 44 Member companies. These included one land-based operator, ship operators, companies that charter ships and/or organize groups to Antarctica and companies that reserve space from other ship operators.

Associate B1 members: Formerly known as Provisional, this category includes 12 ship operators, small vessel/yacht operators, and companies that charter vessels from existing members. Following a season of operation as an IAATO Associate B1 member, these companies are eligible to be approved as Members, contingent upon meeting certain requirements.

Associate B2 members: This category includes 35 tour operators, travel agents or organizers that do not operate Antarctic tour programmes themselves, but book into other members' programmes.

Affiliate members: This category includes 17 companies, organizations or individuals with an interest in supporting Antarctic tourism and the IAATO objectives.

1.3 *Membership by Operational Activities*

During the 2008–2009 period (July 1, 2008 – June 7, 2009) IAATO members were categorized by the following types of operational activities:

1. Organizers of expedition ships that carry less than 200 passengers or small sailing vessels that carry less than 12 passengers. The limit of 100 passengers ashore at one site at one time applies. (40 Members or Associate B1 members)
2. Organizers of vessels carrying 200–500 passengers who are making passenger landings. Stringent restrictions on landing activities of time and place apply. The limit of 100 passengers on shore at one site at one time also applies. (Nine Members or Associate B1 members)
3. Organizers of cruise ships making no landings (cruise only). Cruise ships carrying more than 500 passengers are not permitted to make any landings. (Five Members or Associate B1 members)
4. Organizers of land–based operations. (One Member)
5. Organizers of air operations with over–flights only. (One Associate B2 member)
6. Organizers of air/cruise operations. (One Member)

1.4 *IAATO Bylaws*

IAATO Bylaws and Objectives can be found on line at www.iaato.org under *About IAATO*.

2 2008–2009 *Statistics*

2.1 *Overview of Tourist Numbers*

Because of the early timing of ATCM XXXII, it has not been possible to compile or analyse the statistical data for the just–concluded 2008–2009 season. It is expected that this information will be available in June 2009, and will be posted on the IAATO website (www.iaato.org) under *Information Pages*.

It is, however, possible to give an estimated general picture of the 2008–2009 Antarctic tourism season relative to the previous season and to earlier estimates for the season just ended. Overall, total visitors in all categories of operational activities for the 2007–2008 season were previously reported by IAATO to be 46,265 (ATCM XXXI IP 85 *IAATO Overview of Antarctic Tourism 2007–2008 Antarctic Season and Preliminary Estimates for 2008–2009 Antarctic Season)*. For the season just ended, this number is expected to drop 16 per cent to approximately 38,900 including over–flights and cruise–only visitors (counting IAATO member passengers only). It is worthwhile noting that this number is eight per cent below the 42,298 that IAATO members had projected in June 2008 for the 2008–2009 season. Estimates for the 2009–2010 season can be found in ATCM XXXII IP 86 *IAATO Overview of Antarctic Tourism 2008–2009 Antarctic Season and Preliminary Estimates for 2009– 2010 Season.*

3 *Participation in Organized Meetings during 2008–2009 and IAATO 20th Annual Meeting*

During the year, IAATO members participated in several internal IAATO and external international meetings, liaised with National Antarctic Programmes, government agencies of the sub–Antarctic island groups, and scientific and environmental organizations.

3.1 IAATO's 20th Annual Meeting is scheduled for June 8–11, 2009 in Providence, Rhode Island. Interested parties that would like to attend or participate should contact IAATO at iaato@iaato.org.

3.2 IAATO sent a representative to the COMNAP XX Meeting in St. Petersburg, Russia in late June, 2008. IAATO appreciates the opportunity to work cooperatively with COMNAP where mutual interests lie in both air and ship operations. IAATO supports further cooperation between its operators to ensure there is little or no disruption to science or station activities.

3.3 IAATO was pleased to send two representatives to the International Hydrographic Organization/Hydrographic Committee on Antarctica (IHO/HCA) Meeting in Rio de Janeiro, Brazil in October 2008. IAATO strongly supports and encourages the work of the HCA. This is the 6th year where IAATO has sent a representative to this meeting and appreciates the cooperative working relationship with the HCA. At the meeting, IAATO representatives invited officials of Treaty Party Hydrographic Offices (HO) to visit IAATO "ships of opportunity" to look at equipment onboard and advise masters and navigators on best practices in collecting hydrographic data in Antarctic waters. IAATO was appreciative of Argentina and Chile's expression of willingness to make information available on their respective Ice Navigation training courses.

3.4 IAATO sent two representatives to the *Workshop Towards Improved Search and Rescue (SAR) Coordination and Response in the Antarctic,* held in Valparaiso/Vina del Mar, Chile, August 12–14, 2008. The workshop was hosted by the Chilean Navy's Directorate General of the Maritime Territory and Merchant Marine (DIRECTEMAR) in collaboration with COMNAP. As a result of the meeting, significant improvements have been made in the coordination and communication between the relevant Regional Control Centres (RCCs), COMNAP and IAATO.

3.5 IAATO and several of its UK–based vessel operators participated in an Antarctic Shipping Workshop, September 11, 2008 at the Foreign and Commonwealth Office in London, UK. This workshop was designed to review the tasks sent to IMO's Design and Equipment (D&E) Sub–Committee Correspondence Group, which is considering amendments to the guidelines for ships operating in Arctic ice–covered waters to make them applicable to ships operating in similar conditions in the Antarctic Treaty Area.

3.6 IAATO and several of its UK–based members took part in a workshop sponsored by the Foreign and Commonwealth Office's Polar Regions Unit, January 29, 2009 in London,

UK. The workshop furthered the intersessional discussion on a *Strategic Vision for Tourism and Non–Governmental Activities in Antarctica over the Next Decade.* IAATO appreciates the opportunity to have shared in the process that resulted in the submission by the UK of ATCM XXXII WP 10, *Strategic Vision of Antarctic Tourism for the Next Decade.*

3.7 IAATO's Marine Committee co–sponsored with Cruise Lines International Association (CLIA) a two–day workshop to discuss vessel operations, safety and related issues, February 10–12, 2009 in Arlington, VA, USA. Twenty–four participants attended, including IAATO vessel operators and invited experts. The outcomes of the meeting will be presented to IAATO members at the IAATO Annual Meeting, Providence June 8–11, 2009. These outcomes will include proposed: advice on forward–looking echo–sounders; advice on vessel operations in the vicinity of ice cliffs, icebergs and bergy bits; and advice on shore–stranding equipment. In addition, a detailed proposal will be tabled for the IAATO Marine Committee and invited experts to launch the second phase of development of a geographical and seasonal approach to management of ship–based tourism. This geographical and seasonal approach would be based on a tiered–risk assessment, a concept that received considerable support and sympathy at the recent IMO D&E Sub–Committee Meeting (see 3.8 below), relative to the proposed amendments of the Guidelines for Ships Operating in Arctic Ice–Covered Waters.

3.8 IAATO sent a representative to the International Maritime Organization (IMO) Design and Equipment Subcommittee 52nd meeting in March 2009, in London, UK, participating as a member of the Cruise Lines International Association (CLIA) delegation.

3.9 Numerous other meetings took place between IAATO members, IAATO Committees and their representative governments throughout the year. IAATO continues to maintain a policy of availability for discussions on topics of tourism with Treaty Parties and others.

4 Field Coordination

4.1 IAATO compiles seasonal documents including vessel call data, a comprehensive ship scheduler, emergency contact information, expedition leader schedules, and important instructional procedures for responsible operations. This information is included in the IAATO Field Operations Manual (FOM). In addition IAATO maintains for its members an archive of relevant guidelines, standard operating procedures, past papers and articles relating to Antarctic Tourism.

4.2 IAATO's comprehensive directory of Vessel Call Data and the Master Ship Schedules are shared with COMNAP, MRCCs and other government offices to encourage improved communication and operational coordination. COMNAP's MINIATOM is an extremely useful tool for tour operators trying to contact stations or government vessels. As IAATO vessels transport numerous scientists and support personnel to Antarctica each year, in addition to requesting tourist visits to stations, it is important that station contact information be kept current for communication, planning and emergency purposes.

4.3 Expedition leaders and ship's officers on member vessels circulate advance day–to–day itineraries and maintain regular contact throughout the season to coordinate site visits and exchange general information such as ice conditions, weather, landing recommendations, and note concerns about potential environmental impacts, etc. At 1930 hrs local time, expedition staff monitor agreed on radio frequencies to change itineraries if needed or report on ice conditions, weather or wildlife sensitivities. This constant cooperation and coordination between members is a key part of the IAATO Emergency Contingency Plan.

4.4 IAATO's Emergency Medical Evacuation Response plan (EMER), in place since 1998, continues to underpin medical evacuations.

5 *Environmental Impact Assessment and Advance Notification*

5.1 IAATO members are required to submit Environmental Impact Assessments (EIAs), Advance Notification and/or operational documents that substitute for EIAs to their national authorities pending each countrys' legal processes. Not all governments require EIAs or yearly updates.

5.2 A comparison of the various EIAs and the level of EIAs that individual operators are required to submit to their respective national authorities reflect some notable variations among documents and requirements. IAATO endeavours to bridge these variations in required documentation for ship–based members, in particular to ensure that mitigation measures and procedures are in place to avoid environmental impacts.

6 *Procedures to Prevent the Introduction of Non–Native Species*

6.1 For the past nine seasons, IAATO's Boot and Clothing Decontamination Recommended Guidelines and Translocation of Diseases Protocol have been in place and have been shown to be very effective. These guidelines can be found in the IAATO Field Operations Manual (FOM) and also on the *Members Only* page of the IAATO website (www.iaato.org).

7 *Reporting of Tourism and Non–governmental Activities and Database*

7.1 As noted previously in this paper, IAATO requires its members to submit to IAATO the ATCM approved Post–Visit Reports (PVRs) on the conclusion of their activities.

7.2 IAATO continues to support the use of this single form, which reduces the burden of paperwork and facilitates the study of the scope, frequency and intensity of tourist activities. Should any Parties wish to send IAATO a copy of Post Visit Report forms received from non–IAATO operators in order for the data to be incorporated into the electronic database, IAATO would be pleased to include this data and believes this will further the ability by all to address cumulative impact issues, monitor site guidelines compliance and assess trends in use.

8 *Implementation of Recommendation XVIII–1 (1994) Guidance for those Organizing and Conducting Tourism and Non–governmental Activities in the Antarctic and Guidance for Visitors to the Antarctic, and other Guidelines*

Recommendation XVIII–1 (1994) *Guidance for those Organizing and Conducting Tourism and Non–governmental Activities in the Antarctic,* is provided to all members in order to inform them of key obligations and procedures to be followed.

IAATO urges Parties to consider formally adopting Recommendation XVIII–1 for Visitors and Tour Organizers.

8.1 IAATO remains concerned about tourists travelling on non–IAATO operated yachts visiting the Antarctic who may not be aware of the Environmental Protocol and its obligations. Every visitor and operator must be ever vigilant regarding their responsibilities for landing sites and the marine environment.

8.2 IAATO's standard operating procedures for implementing Recommendation XVIII–1 include the following:

Mandatory briefings on each tour ship prior to arrival in the Antarctic, a presentation consisting of the IAATO PowerPoint presentation. This presentation can be viewed on line at www.iaato.org under *Guidance for Visitors* on the home page. Most expedition leaders will enhance the presentation with additional slides and commentary.

Passengers, ships' command, crew and expedition staff receive paper copies of Recommendation XVIII–1 *Guidance for Visitors to the Antarctic.* Some companies distribute this document in pre–season materials in advance of departure, some on board the ship. In addition to receiving copies of the Recommendation, all passengers and ship's personnel (crew) are required to attend the briefing.

The Recommendation document is available on the *Guides & Resources* page of the IAATO website (www.iaato.org) in

English, Chinese (Mandarin), Dutch, French, German, Italian, Japanese, Russian and Spanish.

8.3 In addition, IAATO members continue to use IAATO and/or company adopted guidelines which include: marine wildlife watching, site specific information, assessment checklist for visiting 'new' sites, kayak, mountain climbing, camping, scuba, helicopter, Zodiac, Remote Operated Vehicle (ROV), and boot and clothing decontamination and more. See ATCM XXV IP 72 *Guidelines for Tourist Operations in Antarctica* and ATCM XXXI IP 83 *Regulation of Antarctic Tourism—A Marine Perspective.*

9 ***Update on Marine Incidents 2007–2008, and Marine Incidents 2008–2009***

9.1 **Marine Incidents 2007–2008 – Final Report on *MS Explorer* Incident:** With respect to the loss of the *MS Explorer* in November, 2007 and analysis of the final report from the Republic of Liberia, Bureau of Maritime Affairs, IAATO has not seen the report at the time that this Information Paper was submitted. Consequently, IAATO has confined its discussions to issues related to the IAATO-wide response and consideration of potential enhancements to current management practices. Once the final investigative report is made public, IAATO's Marine Committee will analyze it in detail, with the intention of assessing any further steps that can be taken to enhance vessel safety.

In the meantime, IAATO marine operators have held two multi–day meetings since the incident to deliberate critical issues pertaining to vessel operations and safety. The results of the first meeting, in February, 2008, were detailed in ATCM XXXI IP081 *Summary Report and Outcomes of IAATO's Marine Committee Meeting on Vessel Operations, Safety and Related Issues,* which summarized the immediate steps which were taken as well as longer term strategies. These strategies were revisited and refined in a recent joint meeting in February 2009 of IAATO and CLIA (Cruise Lines International Association) vessel operators. Central to the discussion of the 2009 meeting was the proposal to develop a tiered–risk assessment proposal based on a geographical and seasonal sector to aid both regulation and management of polar vessel operations.

9.2 **Marine Incidents 2008–2009**: Two separate vessel incidents occurred during the recently concluded Antarctic season. The first involved the *MV Ushuaia*, which grounded at the entrance of Wilhelmina Bay, near Cape Anna, on December 4, 2008 with 82 passengers and 40 crew. The operator of the vessel, Antarpply Expeditions, immediately notified the relevant MRCCs. Another IAATO vessel, the *MV Antarctic Dream*, was seven nautical miles away at the time of the incident, and quickly came to the assistance of the *MV Ushuaia*. The Chilean Navy vessel *AP Aquiles* and Chilean naval tug *ATF Lautaro* were also on the scene within hours. As a precautionary measure requested by Chile, the passengers of the *MV Ushuaia* were transferred the following morning using Zodiac landing craft of the *MV Ushuaia* and *MV Antarctic Dream* to the *AP Aquiles*, which then proceeded to Eduardo Frei Station, King George Island. Passengers were flown from King George Island by Argentine aircraft to Ushuaia on December 6, 2008. Two days later, the *MV Ushuaia* was floated free with the assistance of the *ATF Lautaro*. IAATO would like to thank Chile for this effort, which made unnecessary the alternative response arrangements that had been planned using other IAATO vessels.

Despite the puncture of two fuel tanks of Marine Gas Oil (MGO), leakage was minimal and dissipated quickly. The *MV Ushuaia* proceeded under her own power to an anchorage in the South Shetland Islands to await good weather for the northbound crossing of the Drake Passage. The Drake Passage crossing occurred in close proximity and frequent communications with two other IAATO vessels. Following repairs in dry dock in Punta Arenas, the *MV Ushuaia* returned to scheduled service on January 27, 2009.

9.3 A second grounding incident, on February 17, 2009, involved the Quark Expeditions' vessel, *MV Ocean Nova* in Marguerite Bay, west of Debenham Island and approximately two kilometers from the Argentine research

> station San Martin. The captain of the vessel contacted the Argentine MRCC to notify them of the incident. As a result, the Spanish naval vessel *B.I.O. Hesperides* was soon on the scene. Onboard *MV Ocean Nova* were 64 passengers and 41 crew. When initial attempts that evening failed to refloat the vessel, all passengers were transferred the following afternoon to another Quark vessel, the *MV Clipper Adventurer*. The Spanish naval vessel *B.I.O. Hesperides* continued to stand by, ready to assist if needed.

On February 18, the *MV Ocean Nova* was freed of her position. There was no serious damage to the hull and no leakage of fuel. Following an underwater inspection by divers from *B.I.O. Hesperides*, the *MV Ocean Nova* headed north, crossing the Drake Passage in close proximity to the *MV Clipper Adventurer*. Both vessels arrived in Ushuaia on February 22. The *MV Ocean Nova* cancelled her last voyage of the season, in order to undergo further inspections and repairs in Ushuaia before returning to Europe.

At the time of both incidents, frequent updates were forwarded to the Antarctic Treaty Secretariat and posted on the IAATO website, www.iaato.org. Additional details regarding both incidents can still be viewed on the website.

During both incidents, the IAATO Emergency Contingency Plan and Incident Report template, which had been reviewed following the *MV Explorer* incident, was used to underpin the response.

10 ***Scientific and Information Support***

Members continue to provide logistic and scientific support to National Antarctic Programmes and to the sub–Antarctic Islands facilities providing a cost–effective resource for the scientific community. During the 2008–2009 season, scientists, support personnel and equipment for various National Antarctic and sub–Antarctic Programmes were provided transport to and from stations, field sites and gateway ports. Because of the timing of ATCM XXXII, prior to the submission of most IAATO operator End of Season Reports, a detailed listing of scientific support provided by IAATO members is not yet available. This information will be available in May, and will be posted on the *Information Papers* page of the IAATO website (www.iaato.org), adjacent to this Annual Report. It will also be forwarded to the Antarctic Treaty Secretariat for further distribution to Treaty Parties.

Specific requests for logistic or other support can be made directly with members or via the IAATO Secretariat.

11 ***Conservation Research, Academic and Scientific Support***

Members and their passengers continued the tradition of direct financial contributions to many organizations active in Antarctica. Because of the timing of ATCM XXXII, prior to the submission of most IAATO operator End of Season Reports, a detailed listing of financial contributions by IAATO members and their passengers is not yet available. This information will be available in May, and will be posted on the *Information Papers* page of the IAATO website (www.iaato.org), adjacent to this Annual Report. It will also be forwarded to the Antarctic Treaty Secretariat for further distribution to Treaty Parties.

12 ***Observers on Board Member Vessels***

As noted in point 8 under Primary Activities & Developments, IAATO requires B1 Associate and Probationary members to carry an appointed observer before they are eligible to apply for Member status. There were no Probationary members during the past season.

IAATO considers using a qualified National Programme observer from the country in which the company is registered. When not available, IAATO will appoint an appropriate person with broad experience in Antarctic and/or related matters. IAATO's *Checklist for Observers* form (version October 2007) is used by all observers, providing for a consistent reporting of all operations. In addition, ATCM XIX Resolution 5 (1995), *Antarctic Treaty Inspection Checklist B – Vessels within the Antarctic Treaty Area* is also provided to the appointed observer. IAATO–operated vessels have been carrying observers since 1991.

Furthermore, IAATO members operating from New Zealand to the Ross Sea region carry New Zealand–assigned observers on all voyages, as per New Zealand requirements.

13 ***With Thanks – Cooperation with National Programmes, the Antarctic Treaty Parties and all Stakeholders***

IAATO appreciates the opportunity to work cooperatively with Antarctic Treaty Parties, COMNAP, SCAR, CCAMLR, IHO/HCA,

ASOC and others towards the long-term protection of Antarctica. In particular we appreciate being able to contribute towards the ATCM–agreed ICGs, discussion groups, other intersessional meetings etc.

The following provided assistance and operational guidelines to IAATO during the 2008–2009 season for which members are grateful:
To all Stations in the Antarctic and Sub–Antarctic who welcomed tourists and broadened their views on the value of science and provided friendly, educational and rewarding experiences for tourists.
United Kingdom: United Kingdom Foreign and Commonwealth Office, British Antarctic Survey, U.K. Antarctic Heritage Trust, Port Lockroy staff, sub–Antarctic Islands' personnel and others for making visits an extremely educational and enjoyable experience and for providing members with comprehensive guidelines for visits to BAS stations and their process for arranging visit applications.
New Zealand: Ministry of Foreign Affairs and Trade of New Zealand, Antarctic New Zealand, and Department of Conservation for assistance with Scott Base and the New Zealand Sub–Antarctic Islands. And to New Zealand Antarctic Heritage Trust for their assistance with visits to Ross Sea Huts.
Chile and Russia: For the use of the runway at Marsh/Frei for medical emergencies in conjunction with Aerovias DAP and to Bellingshausen Station for accommodation and taking last minute requests during medevacs.
United States: Palmer, McMurdo and South Pole Station personnel for hosting organized visits throughout the season and providing operational guidelines to operators in advance of the season.
Chile, Argentina and Spain: For assisting by air, land and sea with regard to the *MV Ushuaia* and *MV Ocean Nova* groundings.

14 ***Update: IMO Heavy Fuel Oil Discussion***

After the initial submission of this IAATO Annual Report, information has been brought to IAATO's attention about which we would like to ask the ATCM for clarification. This is in regards to recent discussions within the IMO to Decision 8 (2005,

Stockholm) *Use of Heavy Fuel Oil (HFO) in Antarctica.* Since this Decision was adopted in 2005, there has not been, to our knowledge, any update from IMO to ATCM as to progress within the IMO on this matter.

We have recently learned that the IMO sub–committee that deliberated this issue (Bulk Liquids & Gases) has put forward in March 2009 an amendment to MARPOL that will ban not only HFO, but will also ban Intermediate Fuel Oil (IFO). In addition, the amendment bans not only the use of these fuel oils, including IFOs, but also their carriage in Antarctic Treaty waters. Reference to banning "the use and carriage of heavy grade oil in Antarctic waters" was noted by ASOC in IP034 *Managing Antarctic Vessels – Avoiding Future Disasters,* submitted to this Meeting.

It appears to IAATO that the Decision taken in 2005 by ATCM and sent to IMO has now been expanded to a much broader set of issues, with wide–ranging implications.

Appendix–III
Conservation Areas of India: A Listing

Conservation Areas in India refer to well-demarcated large geographical entities with an established conservation plan, and were part of a joint Indo-US project on "landscape management and protection." The project ran from 1996 to 2002. These areas are home to many Conservation reliant species.

Locations

Four Conservation Areas were selected for this project:

- Annamalai Conservation Area in Tamil Nadu
- Garo Hills Conservation Area in Meghalaya
- Satpura Conservation Area in Madhya Pradesh and Maharashtra
- Terai Conservation Area in Uttar Pradesh

Participants

The participating entities in the project were;

- Ministry of Environment and Forests, Government of India
- Wildlife Institute of India
- United States Forest Service

Goals

The primary goal was to develop experience in "landscape protection"- protection of large geographical entities as a whole, only parts of which may be under federal control and protection. Each of the conservation areas contained *fully protected areas* like *national parks* and *wildlife sanctuaries*, managed resources like reserved forests and communal forests, as well as privately held land. The size of the selected regions constituted more than one forest division and in one case was spread over two states.

External Sources

A complete documentation of the project reports is available at the Wildlife Institute of India website.

Appendix–IV
List of Related Environmental Organizations

Intergovernmental Organizations

- European Environment Agency (EEA)
- Intergovernmental Panel on Climate Change (IPCC)
- UNEP (United Nations Environment Programme)
- Earth System Governance Project
- GLOBE Europe

There are also environmental Intergovernmental Organizations that group governments at the regional and local level, as distinguishable from the national level. Examples are the network of regional governments for sustainable development [1], the ICLEI-Local governments for sustainability [2] and the Partnerships in Environmental Management for the Seas of East Asia (PEMSEA) [3]. These organizations use the method of open coordination to share policy best practice and provide assistance and counsel to partners on issues related to environmental development following the UN Millennium Agenda. These networks can be seen as international organizations and have observer status in the different UN environmental organizations.

Europe

- Regional Environmental Center for Central and Eastern Europe
- Milieukontakt International

Government Organizations

The governments of all developed countries, as well as the majority of developing countries have government departments or agencies devoted to monitoring and protecting the environment.

Australia

- Australian Environment Portal

Each State and Territory also has a Department dealing with the environment: New South Wales, Queensland, Victoria, Western Australia, South Australia, Tasmania, Northern Territory, Australian Capital Territory

Brazil

- IBAMA
- Ministry of Environment

Canada

- ECO Canada
- Environment Canada
- Wildlife Rehabilitation and Conservation Association

India

- Central Pollution Control Board
- Environmental Organizations and Resource Persons in Tamil Nadu
- Eco-wrist Watch
- Gujarat Pollution Control Board
- Ministry of Environment and Forests

Ireland

- Environmental Protection Agency (Ireland)

Isle of Man

- Manx National Trust

Japan

- National Institute for Environmental Studies (NIES)

New Zealand

- Department of Conservation

- Ministry for the Environment
- Parliamentary Commissioner for the Environment

Norway

- Norwegian Ministry of the Environment
- Norwegian Directorate for Nature Management
- Norwegian Pollution Control Authority

United Kingdom

England

- English Heritage
- Environment Agency (England & Wales)
- Natural England

Scotland

- Historic Scotland
- Scottish Natural Heritage
- Scottish Environment Protection Agency

Wales

- Cadw
- Countryside Council for Wales
- Environment Agency Wales

Northern Ireland

- Northern Ireland Environment Agency

United States

- United States Environmental Protection Agency
- United States Fish and Wildlife Service

Native American Nations

- Inter-Tribal Environmental Council
- *All US states have fish and game departments that regulate local hunting and other taking of wild animals.* Spencer's Invention *http://alternatepowerssourcemagneticdonations.web.officelive.com/default.aspx*

Private Organizations (Environmental NGOs)

These organizations are involved in lobbying, advocacy, or conservation efforts.

International

- 350.org refers to the level in parts per million of carbon dioxide in the atmosphere that is deemed to be a safe upper limit in order to avoid a climate tipping point. [4]
- African Wild Dog Conservancy
- Aga Khan Trust for Culture
- American Consumer Council http:// www.americanconsumercouncil.org
- American Indoor Air Quality Council
- Antinea Foundation
- Antipoisoner International [5]
- ATWA (ATWA International)
- Bellona Foundation
- Biofuelwatch
- Biosphere Expeditions
- BirdLife International
- Center for International Environmental Law
- Coal River Mountain Watch
- Conservation Foundation
- Conservation International
- Conservation Law Foundation
- Earth Charter Initiative
- Earth First!
- Earth Island Institute
- Earth Liberation Front (ELF)
- Earth Liberation Prisoner Support Network (ELPSN)
- Earth Policy Institute
- EarthLink e.V.
- Earthwatch
- Environmental Law Foundation (ELF) (UK)
- Environmental Investigation Agency
- Equiliberate
- Forests and the European Union Resource Network (FERN)

- Forest Stewardship Council
- ForestEthics
- Friends of Nature
- Friends of the Earth
- Gaia Mater (the mother Earth)
- Global Footprint Network
- Global Water Policy Project
- Global Witness
- Global Vision International
- Great Transition Initiative
- Green Cross International
- Greenpeace
- International Union of Conservation (IUCN)
- International Analog Forestry Network
- International Council on Monuments and Sites (ICOMOS)
- International Institute for Sustainable Development
- International Network for Sustainable Energy (INFORSE)
- Legacy Foundation
- The Mountain Institute
- NatureServe
- Nicodemus Wilderness Project
- Regenesis—the Global Movement for Environment Sustainability, Liberty & Social Justice
- Tellus Institute
- The Climate Project
- The Nature Conservancy
- Sea Shepherd Conservation Society
- Stockholm Environment Institute (SEI)
- Surfrider Foundation
- Wetlands International
- Whale and Dolphin Conservation Society
- Wildlife Conservation Society
- Wolf Preservation Foundation (WPF)
- World Business Council for Sustainable Development
- Worldchanging
- World Conservation Union (IUCN)
- World Resources Institute (WRI)
- World Union for Protection of Life (WUPL)
- Worldwatch Institute

- World Wide Fund for Nature (WWF)
- Xerces Society
- Yellowstone to Yukon Conservation Initiative
- youthNoise

Regional

Africa

- African Conservation Foundation
- Environmental Foundation for Africa
- Tropical Wildlife and Environment Conservation.. www.tropicalwildlifeandenvironmentconservation.org

Europe

- Climate Action Network - Europe (CAN-Europe)
- European Biomass Association
- European Eco-Forum
- European Environmental Bureau (EEB)
- INFORSE-Europe

North America

- Association of Environmental Professionals
- Defensores del Medio Ambiente de los Tuxtlas, AC (in Mexico)
- North American Native Fishes Association
- International Joint Commission
- Rivers Without Borders

National

Australia

- Australian Conservation Foundation
- Australian Coal Alliance
- Australian Koala Foundation
- Australian Student Environment Network
- Australian Wildlife Conservancy
- Birds Australia
- Environment Victoria

- Greening Australia SA
- Gaia Foundation
- Landcare Australia
- Public Transport Users Association
- Rainforest Rescue
- Sustainable Behaviours
- The Wilderness Society (Australia)
- Wildlife Watch Australia

See also Category: Environmental organisations based in Australia.

Austria

- Transitforum Austria Tirol
- Global 2000

Bulgaria

- Gorichka

Canada

- Canadian Association of Physicians for the Environment
- Canadian Environmental Law Association
- Canadian Environmental Network
- Canadian Institute for Environmental Law and Policy
- Canadian Parks and Wilderness Society
- David Suzuki Foundation
- Ecojustice Canada (formerly Sierra Legal Defence Fund)
- Earth Liberation Army (ELA)
- Green Tomorrow
- International Institute for Sustainable Development
- Manitoba Eco-Network
- Nature Canada
- Pollution Probe
- Raging Grannies
- Sierra Club of Canada
- Sierra Legal Defence Fund
- Toronto Environmental Alliance (TEA)
- Toronto Environmental Coalition

See also Category: Environmental organizations based in Canada.

Croatia

- Ekološko društvo Zeleni Osijek

Zelena akcija/Friends of the Earth Croatia www.zelena-akcija.hr

Czech Republic

- Hnutí DUHA - Friends of the Earth Czech Republic

Denmark

- Danmarks Naturfredningsforening (Danish Nature Protection Association
- DIB
- Danish Organisation for Renewable Energy (OVE)
- OOA (Danish Antinuclear Movement)
- NOAH
- Natur og Ungdom (Nature and Youth)
- Nepenthes (Defending Rainforest)
- Nordic Folkecenter for Renewable Energy
- 92-gruppen (92-group, a coalition of Danish environmental NGOs)

Egypt

- Habi Center for Environmental Rights

France

- CLER
- GERES
- Helio International

Germany

- BOS Deutschland e.V. (Borneo Orangutan Survival Germany)
- Bund für Umwelt und Naturschutz Deutschland (BUND) = Friends of the Earth, Germany

- BUNDjugend (BUND's Youth organization)
- Naturschutzbund Deutschland (NABU) - German Nature Conservation Society
- Robin Wood

Hungary

- Energy Club Hungary
- E-misszio
- ETK

Hong Kong

- Action Blue Sky Campaign
- Clear the Air (Hong Kong)
- Friends of the Earth (HK)
- Green Power
- Greeners-action
- Hong Kong Dolphinwatch
- Lights Out Hong Kong
- Society for Protection of the Harbour
- The Conservancy Association
- WWF Hong Kong

India

- Green Coalition Network[4]

Green Coalition Network is an environmental NGO devoted to improving public health standards, promoting sustainable development and protecting the environment.

- Environment and Food Security Concerns[5]

green wariors of tamilnadu agricultural engineering college and research institute, agriuniversity tamilnadu

- Indian Institute of Ecology and Environment[6]

Studies, training, research and consultancy in the areas of ecology, environment, disaster management, sustainable development, remote sensing, eco-tourism at the bachelor's and master's levels besides encyclopedic publications on environment related subjects carried out at A 15, Paryavaran Complex, South of Saket, New Delhi-110030, India 24 hrs Helpline: +91-9810162127

Iran

- Earth Watchers Center (EWC)

Ireland

- Environmental Conservation Organisation
- Gluaiseacht
- Irish Natural Forestry Foundation
- Irish Peatland Conservation Council (IPCC)

Israel

- Israel Union for Environmental Defense (IUED), Adam Teva V'Din
- Green Movement (Israel), Green Movement (external link), HaTnua HaYeruka

Italy

- Ministero Dell'Ambiente E Tutela Del Territorio Ministry of Environment
- Istituto Superiore per la Protezione e la Ricerca Ambientale Environmental Protection Agency
- Lega Italiana Protezione Uccelli
- Legambiente
- Wwf
- Terra! onlus
- Greenpeace

Kenya

- Green Belt Movement

Laos

- Sustainable Laos Education Initiatives (SLEI)

Lebanon

- Green Orient

Macedonia

- Macedonian Ecological Society

Madagascar

- L'Homme et L'Environnement

Malta

- BirdLife Malta

Nepal

- ICIMOD
- CRT

The Netherlands

- Both ENDS environment and development service
- ICCO
- Milieudefensie - Friends of the Earth Netherlands
- (Dutch)(English) Justice for the World

New Zealand

- Buller Conservation Group
- Environment and Conservation Organisations of Aotearoa New Zealand (ECO)
- Greenpeace Aotearoa New Zealand
- Kiwis Against Seabed Mining
- Native Forest Restoration Trust
- New Zealand Ecological Restoration Network
- Royal Forest and Bird Protection Society of New Zealand
- Save Happy Valley Campaign
- TerraNature
- Trees for Survival
- Waipoua Forest Trust
- Climaction [15]

Norway

- Balyena Foundation
- Eco-Agents
- Norwegian Society for the Conservation of Nature (Friends of the Earth Norway or Norges Naturvernforbund)
- Green Warriors of Norway (Norges Miljøvernforbund)
- Natur og Ungdom
- Zero Emission Resource Organisation

Pakistan

- Rehbar Development Foundation
- Safwan Foundation

Poland

Polish Ecological Club (PKE) 14 regional branch

Portugal

- Quercus (organization)
- Maria Hloist (organization)

Philippines

- Haribon Foundation

Slovakia

- Foundation for Alternative Energy (FAE)
- SZOPK

South Africa

- Earthlife Africa
- Koeberg Alert
- Cape Town Ecology Group
- South Africa Water Action

Taiwan

- Taiwan Environmental Action Network
- Tzu-Chi Foundation - A Buddhist organization, similar to the American Red Cross, dedicated to serving disaster-stricken areas and environmental "activism".

- Wild at Heart (environmental group)

Tanzania

- Sand County Foundation

United Kingdom

- Association for Environment Conscious Building
- Camden Green Fair
- Campaign for Better Transport
- Camp for Climate Action
- Campaign to Protect Rural England
- CEEQUAL
- Centre for Alternative Technology (CAT)
- The Corner House
- Down to Earth
- Earth First!
- Earth Liberation Front (ELF)
- Eco Hive [16]
- Forest Peoples Programme
- Friends of the Earth England Wales and Northern Ireland
- Friends of the Earth Scotland
- Groundwork UK
- The Institution of Environmental Sciences
- Marine Conservation Society
- John Muir Trust
- Plane Stupid
- Rising Tide UK
- River of Flowers [17]
- RSPB (Royal Society for the Protection of Birds)
- Sea Shepherd Conservation Society
- The Wildlife Trusts
- Town and Country Planning Association
- UK Environmental Law Association (UKELA)
- World Wildlife Fund
- Woodland Trust

United States

- Abalone Alliance (historic)
- Adirondack Mountain Club

- African American Environmentalist Association
- Allegheny Land Trust
- Alliance for Climate Protection
- Alliance to Save Energy
- America the Beautiful Fund[18]
- American Bird Conservancy
- American Farmland Trust
- American Wind and Wildlife Institute
- Appalachian Voices
- Association of Environmental Professionals
- Baywatch
- Californians for Population Stabilization
- Center for a New American Dream
- Center for Progressive Reform
- Center for Biological Diversity
- Citizens Campaign for the Environment
- Citizens Environmental Coalition [19]
- Citizens League for Environmental Action Now [20]
- Clamshell Alliance
- Clear the Air (United States)
- Defend Oahu Coalition [21]
- Defenders of Wildlife
- Defense of Place [22]
- Earth First!
- Earth Island Institute
- Earth Liberation Army (ELA)
- Earth Liberation Front (ELF)
- EarthLab
- Ecologyfund.com
- Environmental Defense Fund
- Environmental Law Institute
- Environmental Life Force (ELF)
- Forest Guardians
- Global Green USA
- Greystone Nature Preserve [23]
- High Uintas Preservation Council
- Institute of Environmental Sciences and Technology
- I Plant Trees [24]
- Izaak Walton League
- Keep America Beautiful

- Kids Ecology Corps [25]
- League of Conservation Voters
- National Audubon Society
- National Geographic Society
- National Wildlife Federation
- National Wildlife Refuge Association
- Native Forest Council
- Natural Resources Defense Council
- Nature's Classroom
- NatureServe
- Negative Population Growth
- Neighborhood Parks Council
- New Jersey Audubon Society
- New York City Audubon
- New York Student Sustainability Coalition
- Go Green Florida
- Go Green USA
- Our Earth
- Partner Engineering and Science, Inc.
- Trees Instead
- Population Connection
- Population-Environment Balance
- Rainforest Action Network
- Republicans for Environmental Protection
- Rising Tide North America
- Sand County Foundation
- Save the Redwoods League
- Sea Shepherd
- Sierra Club
- Silicon Valley Toxics Coalition
- Student Conservation Association
- Student Environmental Action Coalition (SEAC)
- Texas Campaign for the Environment
- The Marine Mammal Center
- The Nature Conservancy
- The School for Field Studies
- The Wilderness Society
- TreePeople (founded by Andy Lipkis)
- Trees for a Change
- Union of Concerned Scientists

- Waterkeeper Alliance
- Worldchanging
- Worldwatch Institute
- Youth Earth Savers (Y.E.S.)

Other (to be categorized)

- The Resource Foundation
- The Civic Trust
- GREENGUARD Environmental Institute
- Environmental Desk to Elate the Nature (EDEN)
- The Green Atom
- Groundwork
- Industrial Workers of the World
- Essential Information
- Environmental Working Group
- Bird Protection Quebec
- Montana Wilderness Association
- Mothers Organized to Stop Environmental Sin (MOSES)
- The Earth Organization
- Earth Rangers
- Earth Share
- People & Planet
- Applied Environmental Research Foundation - AERF
- Association of Environmental and Resource Economists (AERE)
- Banksia Environmental Foundation
- Bonneville Environmental Foundation (BEF)
- Chartered Institution of Water and Environmental Management
- Confederation of European Environmental Engineering Societies
- Creative Environmental Networks (CEN)
- Federation of Environmental Trade Associations
- ENFORAC (Environmental Forum for Action)
- Environment California
- Environmental and Energy Study Institute (EESI)
- Environmental Centre ARCTUROS
- Environmental Design Research Association (EDRA)
- Environmental groups and resources serving K–12 schools
- Environmental Justice Foundation

- Environmental Law Service (ELS)
- Environmental Protection UK
- Environmental Services Association
- Environmental Transport Association
- European Association of Environmental and Resource Economists (EAERE)
- Green Camel Bell
- Green Life DC
- Institute for Energy and Environmental Research (IEER)
- National Council for Science and the Environment (NCSE)
- National Registry of Environmental Professionals (NREP)
- New Zealand Institute of Environmental Health (NZIEH)
- Pacific Environment
- Palestinian Environmental NGOs Network
- Public Employees for Environmental Responsibility (PEER)
- Science & Environmental Policy Project (SEPP)
- The Environmental Institute (O Instituto Ambiental [OIA])
- The Ocean Conservancy
- West Harlem Environmental Action (WEACT)
- 41pounds.org
- Albatross Foundation USA
- Arlington Coalition on Transportation (ACT)
- Asociación pola defensa da ría
- ATREE
- Bhutan Trust Fund for Environmental Conservation
- Blue Wedges
- Builders for the Bay
- CERE India
- Clean Ocean Foundation
- Committee for a Constructive Tomorrow
- Earth Force (Environmental group)
- Ecotrust
- Energy Probe
- Environment 2004
- Friends of the Environment
- Green Actors of West Africa (GAWA)
- Green Alliance
- International Council on Nanotechnology (ICON)
- London Islamic Network for the Environment (LINE)

- Preserve Our Island
- Project AWARE
- Resources for the Future (RFF)
- Riverkeeper
- Sibuyanons Against Mining
- Sierra Youth Coalition/Coalition Jeunesse Sierra
- Society for the Environment (SocEnv)
- Stop Climate Chaos
- Sustainable Silicon Valley (SSV)
- Tasmanians Against the Pulp mill Inc.
- Water Environment Research Foundation (WERF)
- WILD Foundation
- Green hopes Kashmir
- Animal Protection and Rescue League (APRL)
- Honor the Earth
- Zalul Environmental Association
- Energy Action Coalition

Fictional

- Campaign to Save The Humans, in *So Long And Thanks For All The Fish* by Douglas Adams
- GreenWorld, in the *Trancers* II film
- Reds, in the Mars Trilogy by Kim Stanley Robinson

Bibliography

Aderhold, P. 1996. The Integrated Commitment of the Adventure Travel and Ecotourism Community: Defining the Role of the Visitor. *Proceedings of the 8th PATA Adventure Travel and Ecotourism Conference.*

Allcock, A., B. Jones, S. Lane, and J. Grant. 1994. *National Ecotourism Strategy.* Canberra: AGPS. Also at: http://tourism.gov.au/publications/nes/nes_toc.html

Alvares, C. 1993. "Fish, Curry and Rice: A Citizen's Report on the State of the Goan Environment." *Ecoforum.* Goa, p. 260.

Arrow, K., R. Solow, P. Portney, E. Learner, R. Rander, H. Schuman 1993: Report of the NOAA Panel of Contingent Valuation: Federal Register; 58: pp. 4601–4614.

Bailey, M. 1995. China. *EIU International Tourism Reports* (I): 19–37.

Ballantine, J.L., and P.F.J. Eagles. 1994. Defining Canadian Ecotourists. *Journal of Sustainable Tourism* 2(4):210–214.

Basiuk, R. 1996. Accreditation: The Case For. *Proceedings of the 8th PATA Adventure Travel and Ecotourism Conference.*

Bell, F. and V.R. Leeworthy 1990: Recreational Demand by Tourists for Salt Water Beach Days; *Journal of Environmental Economics and Management,* No. 18.

Blamey, R. 1995. *The Nature of Ecotourism.* Bureau of Tourism Research Occasional Paper No. 21. Canberra: Bureau of Tourism Research.

Boo, E. (1990) 'Eco–tourism: The Potentials and Pitfalls', Washington, D.C.:WWF.

Bottrill, C.G. and D.G. Pearce. 1995. Ecotourism: Towards a key elements approach to operationalising the concept. *Journal of Sustainable Tourism* 3(1):45–54.

Braatz, S. (1992). *Conserving Biological Diversity: A Strategy for Protected Areas in the Asia–Pacific Region.* World Bank technical paper no. 193. Washington: World Bank.

Brandon, K. 1993. Basic Steps Toward Encouraging Local Participation in Nature Tourism Projects. In Lindberg, K. and D. Hawkins, eds. *Ecotourism: A Guide for Planners and Managers.* Bennington, VT: The Ecotourism Society.

Brandon, K. 1996. *Ecotourism and Conservation: A Review of Key Issues.* World Bank Environment Department Paper No. 033. Washington, DC: World Bank.

Brohman, J. 1996. New Directions in Tourism for Third World Development. *Annals of Tourism Research* 23 (I): 48–70.

Brown, K., Agdar, W.N., and Turner, R.K. (1993) 'Global Environmental Change and Mechanisms for North–South Resource Transfer, *Journal of International Development*, 5(6), 571–589.

Brown, T.C. and Gregory, R. (1999), 'Why the WTA–WTP disparity matters', *Ecological Economics,* 28: 323–335.

Brunson, M.W. 1996. Human Dimensions in Silviculture. In A.W. Ewert, ed. *Natural Resource Management: The Human Dimension.* Westview: Boulder, CO, pp. 91–108.

Buckley, R. and J. Pannell. 1990. Environmental impacts of tourism and recreation in national parks and conservation reserves. *Journal of Tourism Studies* 1(1):24–32.

Buckley, R. 1994. A framework for ecotourism. *Annals of Tourism Research* 21(3):661–665.

Bushnell, S. 1994. *Pacific Islands Ecotourism: A Business Planning Guide.* Honolulu: Pacific Business Center, University of Hawaii/Manoa.

Campbell, D. 1994. Ecotourism Booms in South East Asia. *The Ecotourism Society Newsletter* 4(4):1–3.

Carneiro, J.R.L. 1996. Use of Hydrochemical Techniques for Detection of Sea Water Intrusion in Coastal Aquifers between Fort Aguada and Fort Chapora, North Goa. Msc. Thesis. Goa University, p. 130.

Carter, R.W.G. 1988. Coastal Environments—An Introduction to Physical, Ecological and Cultural Systems of Coastlines. London: Academic Press, p. 607.

Ceballos–Lascurin, H. 1993. Ecotourism as a Worldwide Phenomenon. In Lindberg, K. and D. Hawkins, eds. *Ecotourism: A Guide for Planners and Managers.* Bennington, VT: The Ecotourism Society, pp. 12–14.

Ceballos–Lascurin, H.C. 1996. *Tourism, Ecotourism, and Protected Areas.* Gland, Switzerland: IUCN.

Center for Monitoring of the Indian Economy. 1995. *Basic Statistics of the India Economy.*

Chapman, D.M. 1996. *Ecotourism in State Forests of New South Wales: Who Visits and Why?* Report to the State Forests of New South Wales.

Chase, L.C., Lee, D.R., Schulze, W.D. and Anderson, D.J. (1998) 'Eco–Tourism Demand and Differential Pricing of National Park Access in Costa Rica', *Land Economics,* 74(4), 466–82.

Choegyal, L. 1996. Catering to the Special Needs/Requirements of Adventure and Eco–Travellers. *Proceedings of the 8th PATA Adventure Travel and Ecotourism Conference,* pp. 58–59.

Christ, C. Forthcoming. Community Planning & Involvement. In Lindberg, K., M.E. Wood, and D. Engeldrum, eds. *Ecotourism: A Guide for Planners and Managers,* 2nd ed. Bennington, VT: Ecotourism Society.

Chudintra, S. 1993. Nature Tourism Profile: Thailand. In J. Nenon and P.B. Durst, eds. *Nature Tourism in Asia: Opportunities and Constraints for Conservation and Economic Development.* Washington, DC: Forestry Support Programme, pp. 31–41.

Clark, R.N. 1987. Recreation Management: A Question of Integration. *Western Wildlands* Spring.

Cochrane, J. 1996. Reconciling Tourism and Conservation: A Small–scale Approach in the Bada Valley, Central Sulawesi. Paper presented at the conference on Tourism and Heritage Management. Yogyakarta, Indonesia.

Cole, D.N., M.E. Petersen, and R.C. Lucas. 1987. *Managing Wilderness Recreation Use: Common Problems and Potential Solutions.* USDA Forest Service Gen. Tech. Rep. INT–230. Ogden, UT.

Commonwealth Department of Tourism [CDOT]. 1995. *Best Practice Ecotourism.* Canberra: CDOT. Also available at: http://tourism.gov.au/publications/BPE/Start.html

Costanza, R. *et al.* 1997. The value of the world's ecosystem services and natural capital. *Nature.* WWW version at: http://www.nature.com/Nature2/serve?SID=27218758&CAT=NatGen&PG=ecosystem/ecosystem3.html#refs1–10

Cotterill D. 1996. Developing a sustainable ecotourism business. In Richins H., A. Crabbe, and J. Richardson (eds.), *Proceedings of the 1995 Ecotourism Association of Australia Conference.*

D'Souza, E. 1997. Economy and Institutions: Essays on Goa. Bombay: Himalayan Publishing House.

D'Souza, J.A. *et al.* 1988. The Regional Plan for Goa, 2001 A.D. India, Government of Goa, Department of Town and Country Planning, October, p. 108.

Department of Conservation and the Environment [DCE]. 1992. *Ecotourism: A Natural Strength for Victoria.* Melbourne: DCE.

Department of Wildlife and National Parks (Malaysia) [DWNP]. 1996a. *Annual Report 1995.* Kuala Lumpur: Department of Wildlife and National Parks.

Department of Wildlife and National Parks (Malaysia) [DWNP]. 1996b. *Taman Negara Annual Report 1995.* Kuala Lumpur: Department of Wildlife and National Parks.

Dixon, J.A., L.F. Scura, R.A. Karpenter and P.B. Sherman 1994; *Economic Analysis of Environmental Impacts,* London, UK; Earth Scan.

Driml, S. and M. Common. 1995. Economic and financial benefits of tourism in major protected areas. *Australian Journal of Environmental Management* 2(1):19–29.

Dwivedi, O. 1992. Satyagraha for conservation: awakening the spirit of Hinduism. In J.R. Engel and J.G. Engel (eds.) *Ethics of Environment and Development: Global Challenge and International Response*. London: Belhaven.

Eagles, P.F.J. 1995. Key Issues in Ecotourism Management. Paper presented at the Western Australia Annual Tourism Conference, Perth, WA.

Eagles, P.F.J., J.L. Ballantine, and D.A. Fennell. 1992. Marketing to the Ecotourist: Case Studies From Kenya and Costa Rica. Mimeo, Dept. of Recreation and Leisure Studies, University of Waterloo, Ontario, Canada.

Ecologically Sustainable Development Working Groups [ESDWG]. 1991. *Final Report – Tourism*. Canberra: AGPS.

Empau, E. and C. Ayim. 1994. The Use of Forest in Tourism: Sabah. In T.C. Ti (ed.) *Issues and Challenges in Developing Nature Tourism in Sabah*. Sabah: Institute for Development Studies.

Equations (2000) India Ecodevelopment Project: Visitor Management and Participatory Eco–Tourism Strategy for Periyar Tiger Reserve and Surrounds. *Equations*, Bangalore, India.

FAS Online. 1996. Market Brief: China's Forest Products Market. Web site at: http://ffas.usda.gov/ffas/fas–publ...or–rep/mar–focus–rep/ chforest.html

Fazio, J.R. and Gilbert, D. L., 1986, *Public Relations and Communications for Natural Resource Managers*. Iowa: Kendall/Hunt Pub. Co.

Field, C. 1995. Journey amongst Mangroves. International Society for Mangrove Ecosystems. Okinawa, Japan. Australia: John Witzig and Company, p. 140.

Figgis, P.J. 1996. Issues in Protected Area Policy in Australia. Paper presented at the 1996 EAA Ecotourism Conference, Kangaroo Island.

Furze, B., T. De Lacy, and J. Birckhead. 1996. *Culture, Conservation and Biodiversity: The Social Dimensions of Linking Local Level Development and Conservation through Protected Areas*. Chichester: Wiley.

Gadgil, M. and S. Chandran. 1993. "Konkan Lessons—A Railway Project and Environment." *Frontline*. 26 March, p. 62.

Giongo, F., J. Bosco–Nizeye, and G.N. Wallace. 1994. *A Study of Visitor Management in the World's National Parks and Protected Areas*. Colorado State University, The Ecotourism Society, and the World Conservation Monitoring Centre.

Gordon, H.S. (1954) 'The Economic Theory of a Common Property Resource: the Fishery', *Journal of Political Economy,* 62: 124–142.

Gossling, S. (1999) 'Eco–tourism: A Means to Safeguard Biodiversity and Ecosystem Functions?', *Ecological Economics,* 29(2), 303–20.

Government of Sikkim, Tourism Department, 2001; Invitation to Investment in the Tourism Sector in Sikkim.

Gramopadhye, A. 1997. "Earth Day Special: Think Big." *The Herald,* 21 April, p. 8.

Gregersen, H., S. Draper, and Elz, D. (eds.) 1989. *People and Trees: The Role of Social Forestry in Sustainable Development.* Washington: World Bank.

Gurung, C. 1996. A Case Study Presentation on Providing the Quality Experience. *Proceedings of the 8th PATA Adventure Travel and Ecotourism Conference,* pp. 11–15.

Ham, S.H. 1992. *Environmental Interpretation.* North American Press: Golden, Colorado.

Hammitt, W.E. and D.N. Cole. 1987. *Wildland Recreation: Ecology and Management.* New York: Wiley.

Han, N. and Z. Guo. 1995. An Investigation into the current situation of China's Nature Reserves. *China's Biosphere Reserves – Special English Issue.* Beijing: Chinese National Committee for Man and the Biosphere Programme.

Hanemann, M., J. Loomis and B. Kannianen, 1991: Statistical Efficiency of Double Bounded Dichotomus Choice Contingent Valuation; *American Journal of Agricultural Economics,* No. 73 pp. 1255– 1263.

Hanemann, W.M. (1991), 'Willingness To Pay and Willingness To Accept: How Much Can They Offer?', *The American Economic Review* 81: 635–647.

Harroun, L. and E. Boo. 1996. *Managing People in Parks: A Guide to Visitor Use in Natural Areas.* Washington, DC: World Wildlife Fund (US).

Hawkins, D.E., M.E. Wood, and S. Bittman. 1995. *The Ecolodge Sourcebook for Planners and Developers.* N. Bennington, VT: The Ecotourism Society.

Healy, R. 1994. Tourist merchandise as a means of generating local benefits from ecotourism. *Journal of Sustainable Tourism* 2(3): 137–151.

Herath, G. 1996. Ecotourism in Asia and the Pacific: Potential, Problems and an Integrated Planning Model. In Prosser, G. (ed.) *Proceedings from the Australian Tourism and Hospitality Research Conference.* Canberra: Bureau of Tourism Research.

Hitchcock, M., V.T. King, and M.J.G. Parnwell. 1993. *Tourism in South–East Asia.* London: Routledge.

Hodgson, G. and J.A. Dixon. 1988. *Logging Versus Fisheries and Tourism in Palawan: An Environmental and Economic Analysis.* EAPI Occasional Paper No. 7. Honolulu: East–West Center.

Hunter, C. and H. Green. 1995. *Tourism and the Environment: A Sustainable Relationship?* London: Routledge.

Hurst, P. 1990. *Rainforest Politics: Ecological Destruction in South–east Asia.* London: Zed.

India Institute of Social Sciences. 1989. *Tourism in Goa: Socio–Economic Impacts.* New Delhi.

India, Government of Goa, Department of Tourism. 1987. Master Plan for Tourism Development in Goa (Draft Report). July, p. 130.

India, Government of Goa, Department of Tourism. Personal Communications.

India, Government of Goa, Department of Town and Country Planning. 1996a. Coastal Zone Management Plans for Goa, p. 69.

India, Government of Goa, Department of Town and Country Planning. Personal Communications.

India, Government of Goa, Department of Statistics and Evaluations. Personal Communications.

India, Ministry of Environment and Forests. 1991. The Gazette of India. Notification; S.O. No. 114(E), February 20.

Inglehart, R. 1990. *Culture Shift in Advanced Industrial Society.* Princeton, NJ: Princeton University Press.

Inskeep, E. 1991. *Tourism Planning: An Integrated and Sustainable Development Approach.* New York: Van Nostrand Reinhold.

IUCN Bulletin (1993) The Asia–Pacific Region: crisis and challenge, Number 2, pp. 12–23.

Jagtap, T.G., V.S. Chavan and A.G. Untawale. 1993. "Mangrove Ecosystems of India: A Need for Protection." Ambio. v22, pp. 252–254.

Jarvie, L. 1993. Trends and Challenges in Developing Responsible Tourism. *Proceedings of the 5th PATA Adventure Travel and Ecotourism Conference.*

Johnson, R. 1996. Improving the quality of Information: Options on the Information Superhighway. *Proceedings of the 8th PATA Adventure Travel and Ecotourism Conference.*

Kalavampara, G. 1994. Preliminary Assessment of Salt Water—Fresh Water Interface between Fort Aguada and Candolim Coast, North Goa. Msc. Thesis. Goa University, p. 130.

Kearsley, G.W. 1995. Managing the consequences of over–use by tourists of New Zealand's Conservation Estate. Paper presented to the Geography of Sustainable Tourism symposium. Canberra.

Kellert, S.R. 1996. *The Value of Life: Biological Diversity and Human Society.* Washington, DC: Island Press.

King B, A. Pizam, and A. Milman. 1993. Social impacts of tourism: Host perceptions. *Annals of Tourism Research* 20:650–665.

Kinnaird, M.F. and T.G. O'Brien. 1996. Ecotourism in the Tangkoko Duasudara Nature Reserve: Opening Pandora's Box. *Oryx* 30(1):65–73.

Kirloskar Consultants Ltd. 1994. Report on Study of Tourism Industry in Goa. December.

Knight, R.L. and K.J. Gutzwiller (eds.) 1995. *Wildlife and Recreationists: Coexistence through Management and Research.* Washington, DC: Island Press.

Knudston, P. and D. Suzuki. 1992. *Wisdom of the Elders.* Sydney: Allen and Unwin.

Kumar, P. 1996. Accreditation: The Case Against. *Proceedings of the 8th PATA Adventure Travel and Ecotourism Conference,* pp. 52–55.

Laarman, J.G. and Durst, P.B. 1993. Nature Tourism as a Tool for Economic Development and Conservation of Natural Resources. In J. Nenon and P.B. Durst, eds. *Nature Tourism in Asia: Opportunities and Constraints for Conservation and Economic Development.* Washington, DC: Forestry Support Programme, pp. 1–19.

Laarman, J.G. and H.M. Gregersen. 1996. Pricing policy in nature–based tourism. *Tourism Management* 17(4): 247–254.

Lankford, S.V. and D.R. Howard. 1994. Developing a tourism impact attitude scale. *Annals of Tourism Research* 21:121–139.

Lew. A.A. 1997. The Ecotourism Market in the Asia Pacific Region: A Survey of Asia Pacific and North American Tour Operators. WWW site at: http://www.for.nau.edu/~alew/ecotsvy.html.

Lindberg, K. 1991. *Policies for Maximizing Nature Tourism's Ecological and Economic Benefits.* Washington, DC: World Resources Institute.

Lindberg, K. 1994. Quantifying Ecotourism: Are Reliable Statistics in Sight? *The Ecotourism Society Newsletter,* vol. 4, n. 2, pp. 1–2, 7.

Lindberg, K. and B. McKercher. 1997. Ecotourism: A Critical Overview. *Pacific Tourism Review* 1(1): 65–79.

Lindberg, K. and J. Enriquez. 1994. *An Analysis of Ecotourism's Economic Contribution to Conservation and Development in Belize.* Report to the World Wildlife Fund (WWF–US) and the Ministry of Tourism and the Environment (Belize).

Lindberg, K. and R.L. Johnson. 1997. Modeling resident attitudes toward tourism. *Annals of Tourism Research* 24(2): 402–424.

Lindberg, K. and R.M. Huber, Jr. 1993. Economic Issues in Ecotourism Management. In Lindberg, K. and D. Hawkins, eds. *Ecotourism: A*

Guide for Planners and Managers. Bennington, VT: Ecotourism Society, pp. 82–115.

Lindberg, K., C. Goulding, J. Mo, Z. Huang, P. Wei, and G. Kong. 1996. *Ecotourism at the Dinghushan Biosphere Reserve*. Johnstone Centre of Parks, Recreation and Heritage Report No. 81.

Lindberg, K., J. Enriquez, and K. Sproule. 1996. Ecotourism questioned: Case studies from Belize. *Annals of Tourism Research* 23(3):543–562.

Lindberg, K., S. McCool and G. Stankey. 1996. Rethinking Carrying Capacity. *Annals of Tourism Research* 24(2): 461–465.

Lobo, U. 1988. "Environmental Aspects of Silica Sand Mining from Coastal Sand Dunes." *Earth Resources for Goa's Development*, pp. 521–523.

Lohman, L. 1993. Thailand: land, power and forest colonization. In M. Colchester and L. Lohmann (eds.) *The Struggle for Land and the Fight for the Forests*. London: Zed.

MacKinnon, J., K. MacKinnon, G. Child, and J. Thorsell. 1986. *Managing Protected Areas in the Tropics*. Gland: IUCN.

Madhupratap, M. and A.H. Parulekar. 1993. "Estuarine Biology and Management." *Environmental Impact on Aquatic and Terrestrial Habitats*, pp. 215–226.

Maille, P. & R. Mendelsohn 1993: Valuing Ecotourism in Madagascar; *Journal of Environmental Management*.

Maini, J. and O. Ullsten. 1993. Conservation and Sustainable Development of Forests Globally: Issues and Opportunities. In K. Ramakrishna and G. Woodwell (eds.) *World Forests for the Future: Their Use and Conservation*. New Haven: Yale University Press.

Mak, J., and M.E.T. Moncur. 1995. Sustainable tourism development. Managing Hawaii's "unique" touristic resource — Hanauma Bay. *Journal of Travel Research* 33(4):51–57.

Mallik, A. and Veeramani, A. (2002) Periyar Tiger Reserve: Ecotourism Initiatives Involving Local Communities, Paper presented in VIth training workshop on "Ecotourism Project Development and Marketing" organised by Wildlife Institute of India, Dehra Dun at Spice Village, Thekkady, Kerala, India.

Manam, I. 1996. Desaru Poised to Become Premier Resort. *New Straits Times*. August 17, 1996, p. 14.

Manning, R.E. 1986. *Studies in Outdoor Recreation*. Corvallis, OR: Oregon State University Press.

Mascarenhas, A. 1990. "Why Sand Dunes are Needed." *The Herald*. 21 December, p. 4.

Mascarenhas, A. 1992. "Our Estuaries in Peril." *The Herald*. 20 April, p. 4.

Mascarenhas, A. 1996. "The Fate of Sand Dunes of Goa." *Voices for the Oceans*. International Ocean Institute of India, p. 111.

Mascarenhas, A., K. Sawkar and O.S. Chauhan. 1997. The Coastal Zone of Goa: Then and Now. Abstract 49. Seminar on Coastal Zone Environment and Management. Mangalore University, 12–14 February, pp. 50–52.

Mattson, L. and C. Li. 1994. How Do Different Forest Management Practices Affect the Non–Timber Value of Forests? An Economic Analysis. *Journal of Environmental Management* 41:79–88.

McKercher, B. 1996. Benefits and costs of tourism in Victoria's Alpine National Park: Comparing the attitudes of tour operators, management staff and public interest group leaders. In J. Jenkins, G. Kearsley, and C.M. Hall (eds.) *Tourism Planning and Policy in Australia and New Zealand.*

Mendez, J.P. and M.P. Gunawan. 1994. Emergence of Ecotourism in Indonesia: A National Park Case Study. *Journal Perencanaan Wilayah Dan Kota.* Edisi Khusus.

Menkans, S. & D.J. Lober 1996: International Ecotourism and Valuation of Tropical Rain Forest in Costa Rica, *Journal of Environmental Management.*

Mercer, D. 1994. Native peoples and tourism: Conflict and compromise. In W.F. Theobald (ed.) *Global Tourism: The Next Decade.* Boston: Butterworth Heinemann, pp. 124–145.

Meredith, G. 1993. *Small Business Management in Australia* (4th ed.) Sydney: McGraw–Hill.

Mieczkowski, Z. 1995. *Environmental Issues of Tourism and Recreation.* Lanham, MD: University Press of America.

Ministry of Culture, Arts and Tourism (Malaysia) [MCAT]. 1995. 7994 *Annual Report.* Kuala Lumpur: Ministry of Culture, Arts and Tourism.

Ministry of Tourism Post and Telecommunications (Indonesia) [MTPT]. 1993. *Indonesia Environment and Heritage.* Jakarta: Directorate General of Tourism.

Mohd Nor, S. and S. Wayakone. No date. Ecotourism in Malaysia: A Status Report. Mimeo.

Muqbil, I. 1995. Thailand. *EIU International Tourism Reports* (3):67–81.

Nababan, A. and A. Aliadi. 1993. Nature Tourism Profile: Indonesia. In J. Nenon and P.B. Durst, eds. *Nature Tourism in Asia: Opportunities and Constraints for Conservation and Economic Development.* Forestry Support Programme: Washington, DC, pp. 43–54.

Naik, S. 1997. *The Navhind Times.* March 19.

Nair, M.G. 1996. Building Anew. *Malaysian Industry* (4) 41:8–13.

National Institute of Oceanography of India. 1996. Comments on the Coastal Zone Management Plans of Goa. Report submitted to India, Ministry of Environment and Forests. New Delhi.

Navrud, S. & E.E. Mungatana 1996: Environmental Valuation in Developing Countries: The Recreation Value of Wildlife Viewing; *Ecological Economics.*

Navrud, S. and Mungatana, E.D. (1994), 'Environmental Valuation in Developing Countries: The recreational value of wildlife viewing', *Ecological Economics,* 11: 135–151.

New South Wales National Parks and Wildlife Service [NSW NPWS], 1996. *Nature and Tourism: An Ecotourism Strategy for the Southern Highlands, Illawarra and Shoalhaven Areas of Southern New South Wales.* Draft report by NSW National Parks and Wildlife Service and Tourism New South Wales.

NFPS. 1992. National Forestry Policy Statement. Canberra: Commonwealth of Australia.

Nordstrom, K.F. 1994. "Developed Coasts." Coastal Evolution—Late Quaternary Shoreline Dynamics. R.W.G. Carter and C.D. Woodroffe (Eds.) London: Cambridge University Press, pp. 477–510.

Odell, M. 1996. Posting to Green–Travel listserve.

Office of National Tourism (Australia). 1997. WWW site at: http://www.tourism.gov.au/factsfig.html.

Pacific Asia Travel Association. 1996. Pacific Asia Continues Strong Travel Growth According to Pata 1995 Statistical Report. June 18, 1996 Press Release.

Parker, T. 1993. Nature Tourism in Nepal. In J. Nenon and P.B. Durst, eds. *Nature Tourism in Asia: Opportunities and Constraints for Conservation and Economic Development.* Forestry Support Programme: Washington, DC, pp. 21–30.

Pedersen, A. 1995. *Promotion of Community–Based Ecotourism in the Maya Forest.* Report prepared for Management Systems International, Washington, DC.

Pfister, R. and A. Jubenville. Forthcoming. Community Co–Management. In Lindberg, K., M.E. Wood, and D. Engeldrum, eds. *Ecotourism: A Guide for Planners and Managers,* 2nd ed. Bennington, VT: Ecotourism Society.

Pond, K.L. 1993. *The Professional Guide.* New York: Van Nostrand Reinhold.

Posey, D. 1993. Indigenous Knowledge in the Conservation and Use of World Forests. In K. Ramakrishna and G. Woodwell (eds.) *World Forests for the Future: Their Use and Conservation.* New Haven: Yale University Press.

Powell, R. and L. Chalmers. 1995. *Regional Economic Impact: Gibraltar Range and Dorrigo National Parks.* Report to the NSW National Parks & Wildlife Service.

Raja, R. 1996. Forestry in India: an update. Website at: http://www.erin.gov.au/land/forests/documents/india.txt

Repetto, R. 1993. Government Policy, Economics and the Forest Sector. In K. Ramakrishna and G. Woodwell (eds.) *World Forests for the Future: their Use and Conservation.* New York: Yale University Press.

Reynolds, J. 1995. National parks and protected areas in the United States. Paper given to the North American Regional Meeting of the Commission on National Parks and Protected Areas. Banff National Park, Alberta, Canada.

Reynolds, W., W. Savage, and A. Williams. 1994. *Your Own Business: A Practical Guide to Success.* Melbourne: Thomas Nelson.

Richardson, J. 1996. Strategic Alliances. In H. Richins, A. Crabbe, and J. Richardson (eds.) *Proceedings of the 1995 Ecotourism Association of Australia Conference.*

Roggenbuck, J. 1992. Use of persuasion to reduce resource impacts and visitor conflicts. In M.J. Manfredo (ed.) *Influencing Human Behaviour.* Champaign, Ill.: Sagamore Publishing, pp. 155–161.

Russel, R.S. (2002) *Economics of Natural Resources and the Environment,* Oxford University Press.

Ryan, C. 1995. *Researching Tourist Satisfaction: Issues, Concepts, Problems.* London: Routledge.

Santhakumar, V. and Achin Chakraborty (2003) 'Environmental costs and their impact on the net present value of a hydroelectric project in Kerala, India', *Environment and Development Economics,* 8: 311–330.

Sarin, M. 1993. *From Conflict to Collaboration: Local Institutions in Joint Forest Management.* New Delhi: Ford Foundation.

Sekartjakrarini, S. 1993. The Role of Parks in Indonesian Tourism. *World Leisure and Recreation* 35(2) 27–33.

Shackley, M. 1996. Community impact of the camel safari industry in Jaisalmar, Rajasthan. *Tourism Management* 17(3):213–218.

Shelby, B. and B. Shindler. 1992. Interest group standards for ecological impacts at wilderness campsites. *Leisure Sciences* 14(1):17–27.

Shelby, B. and T.A. Heberlein. 1986. *Carrying Capacity in Recreation Settings.* Corvallis, OR: Oregon State University Press.

Shukla, R.K. Catering to the Special Needs/Requirements of Adventure and Eco–Travellers: The Hotelier's Perspective. *Proceedings of the 8th PATA Adventure Travel and Ecotourism Conference.*

Singapore Tourism Promotion Board [STPB]. 1993. Through Singaporean Eyes, Singapore Tourist Promotion Board Video, Singapore.

Smith, V. 1989. *Hosts and Guests: The Anthropology of Tourism,* 2nd ed. Philadelphia, PA: University of Pennsylvania Press.

Soemodinoto, A., L. Lubis, and N.N. Oktaviany. Ecotourism and State Foreign Exchange. *Business News: Economic Problems,* No. 650/XIII (September), pp. 1B–4B.

Sousson, J., B. Shestra, and L. Uprety. 1995. *The Social Dynamics of Deforestation: A Case Study from Nepal.* Casterton Hill: Parthenon.

Southern J. 1996. Marketing networks for ecotourism operators. In H. Richins, A. Crabbe, and J. Richardson (eds.) *Proceedings of the 1995 Ecotourism Association of Australia Conference.*

Stecker, B. 1996. *Potential for Conservation and Sustainable Use of Tropical Forests.* Report to GTZ. Eschborn, Germany.

Stevens, S. 1993. *Claiming the High Ground. Sherpas, Subsistense and Environmental Change in the Highest Himalaya.* Berkeley: University of California Press.

Tata Economic Consultancy Services, New Delhi – 110008; Volume 1.

Taylor, A. 1994. Bamboo Forests and Panda Conservation in China. *Earth and Mineral Sciences* 63(1):8–11.

Telfer, D.J. and G. Wall. 1996. Linkages between tourism and food production. *Annals of Tourism Research* 23(3): 635–653.

The Navhind Times. 1997. "Goa's Fish Catch Shows Downward Trend." March 20, p. 1.

The Navhind Times. 1997. "Sea Turtles on the Run as Humans Take over Beaches." February 20, p.

Tilden, F. 1977 (revised ed.). *Interpreting Our Heritage.* Chapel Hill: The University of North Carolina Press.

Tisdel, C. (1987) 'Tourism, the environment and profit', *Economics Analysis and Policy,* 17(1) pp. 13–30.

Tisdel, C. (1996) 'Ecotourism, economics and the environment: observations from China', *Journal of Travel Research,* 34 (4), 1996, pp. 992–4.

Tisdell, C. 1996. Ecotourism, economics, and the environment: Observations from China. *Journal of Travel Research* 34(4) 11–19.

Tourism Authority of Thailand. 1997. WWW site at: http://www.tat.or.th/

Tourism Malaysia. 1997. WWW site at: http://tourism.gov.my/netdata/Intro.html

United Nations Food and Agriculture Organization [UN FAO]. 1988. *National Parks Planning: A Manual With Annoted Examples.* Rome: FAO.

United Press International [UPI], 1997. Press Release. Beijing, 24 April 1997.

Upitis, A. 1991. Interpretive Planning and the "Let's hava" Principle. *Notes of Royal Australian Institute of Parks and Recreation Seminar, Interpretation: Community Involvement in Resource Management,* November 1991. Royal Australian Institute of parks and recreation.

US National Park Service [US NPS]. 1993. *Guiding Principles of Sustainable Design*. Washington, DC: US Department of the Interior.

Valentine, P.S. and J. Wylie. 1993. Forest Ecotourism in the Pacific: A Review of Opportunities and Values. Paper presented at the Heads of Forestry Conference, Nadi, Fiji.

Van't Slot, J. 1995. An Introduction to the Business of Ecotourism in the Pacific Islands. Pacific Business Center Programme. Honolulu: University of Hawaii/Manoa.

Van't Slot, J. 1996. Pacific Islands Seek Ecotourism Solutions: Tough Choices Are Ahead. *The Ecotourism Society Newsletter* Second Quarter, pp. 1–3.

VTOA. 1995. Survey of New VTOA Members. Unpublished. Melbourne, Victorian Tourism Operators Association.

Walker, D., F. Sinclair, and B. Thapa. 1995. Incorporation of indigenous knowledge and perspectives in agroforestry development. *Agroforestry Systems* 30:235–248.

Wall, G. 1994. Ecotourism: Old wine in new bottles? *Trends* 31(2): 4–9.

Wells, M.P. 1993. Neglect of biological riches: the economics of nature tourism in Nepal. *Biodiversity and Conservation* 2:445–464.

Wen, J. and C. Tisdell. 1996. Regional Inequality and Decentralisation of China's Tourism Industry. In Prosser, G. (ed.) *Proceedings from the Australian Tourism and Hospitality Research Conference*. Bureau of Tourism Research, Canberra.

Wight, P. 1996a. North American Ecotourists: Market Profile and Trip Characteristics. *Journal of Travel Research* 34(4):2–10.

Wight, P. 1996b. North American Ecotourism Markets: Motivations, Preferences, and Destinations. *Journal of Travel Research* 35(1):3–10.

Wight, P.A. 1993. Sustainable ecotourism: Balancing economic, environmental and social goals within an ethical framework. *Journal of Tourism Studies*, 4(2):54–66.

Wild, C. 1996. The North American ecotourism industry. In H. Richins, A. Crabbe, and J. Richardson (eds.) *Proceedings of the 1995 Ecotourism Association of Australia Conference*.

William, A. 1997. "Burgeoning Construction May Be Epitaph to Queen of Beaches." *The Navhind Times*. 4 March, p. 1.

William, A. 1997. "Garbage, Vendors Turn Idyll into Nightmare." *The Navhind Times*. 3 March, p. 1.

Wilman, E.A. (1988) 'Pricing Policies for Outdoor Recreation', *Land Economics*, 64: 234–41.

Wilson, D. 1997. "Paradoxes of Tourism in Goa." Annals of Tourism Research. 21(1): 52–75.

Wilson, D. 1997. "Strategies for Sustainability: Lessons from Goa and Seychelles." Sustainable Tourism. M. Stabler (ed.) Wallingford: CAB International.

Wood, M.E. 1997. New Directions in the Ecotourism Industry. *The Ecotourism Society–Newsletter,* First Quarter, pp. 1–3.

Woodwell, G. 1993. Forests: What in the world are they for? In K. Ramakrishna and G. Woodwell (eds.) *World Forests for the Future: their Use and Conservation.* New York: Yale University Press.

Worboys, G., P. Hall, P. Kennedy, P. Hahn, D.N. Collins, and K. Mills. 1995. Managing Ecotourism: Minnamurra Rainforest, Budderoo National Park. Paper presented to the RAIPIR National Conference, Canberra.

World Bank. 1997. WWW site at: http://www.worldbank.org/html/cgiar/25years/forest.html

World Tourism Organization [WTO]. 1996. WWW site at: http://www.world–tourism.org

World Tourism Organization [WTO]. 1997. *Tourism Market Trends: East Asia and the Pacific.* Madrid: WTO.

World Tourism Organization and United Nations Environment Programme [WTP and UNEP]. 1992. *Guidelines: Development of National Parks and Protected Areas for Tourism.* Madrid: WTO.

World Travel and Tourism Council [WTTC]. 1997. WWW site at http://www.wttc.org

WWF (World Wildlife Fund) (1995), 'Ecotourism Conservation Tool or Threat?', *Conservation Issues,* 2(3), 1–10.

Wylie, J. 1994. Journey Through a Sea of Islands: A Review of Forest Tourism in Micronesia. Honolulu: Institute of Pacific Islands Forestry, USDA Forest Service.

Xing, W. 1993. The Increasing Impact of Tourism on Protected Areas in China. *Contours* 6(3–4):38–43.

Yong, F.S.K. 1996. Operationalising Ecotourism. ISIS *Focus* Issue No. 133 (Institute of Strategic and International Studies, Kuala Lumpur), pp. 14–19.

Yongwei, Z. 1995. An Assessment of China's Tourism Resources. In Lew, A. and L. Yu (eds.) *Tourism in China: Geographic, Political and Economic Perspectives.* Boulder, Colorado: Westview.

Zhang, G 1995. China's Tourism Development Since 1978: Policies, Experiences and Lessons Learned. In Lew, A. and L. Yu (eds.) *Tourism in China: Geographic, Political and Economic Perspectives.* Boulder, Colorado: Westview.

Index